A GERMAN HOME.

AT HOME & ABROAD.

BAYARD TAYLOR.

The Mammoth Cave. Ky.

NEW YORK: G. P. PUTNAM.

LONDON: S. LOW SON & CO.

1860

AT HOME AND ABROAD:

A SKETCH-BOOK

OF

LIFE, SCENERY, AND MEN.

BY

BAYARD TAYLOR.

NEW YORK:
G. P. PUTNAM, 115 NASSAU STREET.
1860.

R. CRAIGHEAD,
Printer, Stereotyper, and Electrotyper,
Carton Building,
81, 83, and 85 Centre Street.

PREFACE.

In this volume I have collected together the various detached sketches of men and things, and the records of short excursions, or episodes of travel, for which there was no appropriate place in the narratives already published. Most of them have appeared, at intervals, during the past eight years—have, perhaps, been long since read and forgotten by many of my readers; yet I trust that there are few, the subjects of which are not in themselves of sufficient interest to justify me in thus reproducing them. At least they have the advantage of variety, and the volume, like the sketch-book of an artist, has figures for those who do not appreciate land-scapes, matter-of-fact for those who dislike sentiment, and a close adherence to Nature as a compensation for any lack of grace in the execution. It is a record of actual experiences, and aims at no higher merit than the utmost fidelity.

BAYARD TAYLOR.

New York, *August* 4, 1859.

CONTENTS.

AT HOME AND ABROAD.

I.

THE FIRST JOURNEY I EVER MADE.

My friend, Ida Pfeiffer, relates, in the preface to one of her volumes, that the desire for travel was with her an inborn propensity. When a little girl, she was accustomed to watch the mail-coach as it whirled daily through her native valley; and when it had crossed the verge of the hill which bounded her childish world, she would frequently weep, because she could not follow it and visit the unknown regions beyond. In looking back to my childhood, I can recall no such instinct of perambulation; but on the conrary, the intensest desire to climb upward—so that without shifting the circle of my horizon, I could yet extend it, and take in a far wider sweep of vision. I envied every bird that sat swinging upon the topmost bough of the great, century-old cherry tree; the weather-cock on our barn seemed to me to whirl in a higher region of the air;

and to rise from the earth in a balloon, was a bliss which I would almost have given my life to enjoy. Perhaps the root of the instinct was the same in both cases; but Madame Pfeiffer's desires shot off in a horizontal direction, while mine went up perpendicularly.

I remember, as distinctly as if it were yesterday, the first time this passion was gratified. Looking out of the garret window, on a bright May morning, I discovered a row of slats which had been nailed over the shingles for the convenience of the carpenters, in roofing the house, and had not been removed. Here was, at last, a chance to reach the comb of the steep roof, and take my first look abroad into the world! Not without some trepidation I ventured out, and was soon seated astride of the sharp ridge. Unknown forests, new fields and houses appeared to my triumphant view. The prospect, though it did not extend more than four miles in any direction, was boundless. Away in the northwest, glimmering through the trees, was a white object—probably the front of a distant barn; but I shouted to the astonished servant-girl, who had just discovered me from the garden below: "I see the Falls of Niagara!"

With increase of knowledge, this instinct took the definite form of a longing to see and to climb a mountain. My nurse was an old Swiss woman, in the background of whose stories stood the eternal Alps; some few of the neighbors had seen the Blue Ridge (the members of our community, generally, were as thoroughly attached to the soil as the Russian serfs) and in our native region of softly-rounded hills and small intervening valleys—a lovely reproduction of English Warwickshire—the description of a mountain, mantled with pine, faced with sheer precipices, and streaked with summer snow, seemed to be a fable, a miracle, an impossibility. So I determined—since it was difficult to ascend much above the top of the house at home—that my first journey should be in the direction of a mountain.

It was not so easy, however, to carry this plan into execution. A farmer's boy—tempted on the one hand by books, knives, and breastpins, and on the other, by circuses, menageries, phrenological lectures, pea-nuts, and ice-cream—can rarely save enough from the sale of his rabbit-skins, walnuts, and sumac leaves, or even from his own cherished pig—the "runt" of the litter—to commence any serious undertaking. My private means were chiefly derived from these sources, and every succeeding spring I found myself in the condition of the United States Post-Office Department, in the year 1859. But when my seventeenth May came around, and I was formally apprenticed to the printing business, one stipulation in the paper of indenture opened an unexpected way for me. It was arranged that I should receive forty dollars a year for the purchase of my clothing, and as I entered on my apprenticeship with a tolerable supply, I at once saw the possibility of saving enough out of my first year's allowance to enable me to reach the nearest mountain.

The plan succeeded well. At the termination of the year, I found myself in possession of the enormous sum of fifteen dollars. But my ideas and desires had in the meantime expanded, and the amount of capital secured appeared sufficient to warrant me in undertaking a much more extensive journey than I had originally intended. New York, the Highlands, the Catskills, Berkshire, and the Connecticut Valley! Of course, the tour must be accomplished mostly on foot; and I confess I counted a little upon the hospitality of the country-people for a meal or a bed, if my purse should get very low. A fellow-apprentice, of ample means (I believe he had twenty-seven dollars), agreed to bear me company; and about the middle of May, 1843, the necessary holiday was obtained from our employer. My scanty baggage was contained in a soldier's knapsack, borrowed from a private of the "National Grays"—the sole militia company in the place—and the gilded letters "N. G." upon the back proved afterwards to be a source of curiosity to the public—many persons, supposing me to be an itinerant peddler, taking them to mean "New Goods." My money was entirely in quarter-dollars, as the United States Bank was no more; and such things as drafts, exchange brokers, etc., were unknown to me.

My companion, on account of his extensive means, determined to travel by railroad to New York, while I, who was obliged to foot it across the sands of New Jersey, started a day in advance, the rendezvous being a small soda water shop in John street, kept by a mutual acquaintance. The steamboat from Philadelphia deposited me at Bordentown, on the forenoon of a warm, clear day. I buckled on my knapsack, inquired the road to Amboy, and struck off, resolutely, with the feelings of an explorer on the threshold of great discoveries. The sun shone brightly, the woods were green, and the meadows were gay with phlox and buttercups. Walking was the natural impulse of the muscles; and the glorious visions which the next few days would unfold to me, drew me onward with a powerful fascination. Thus, mile after mile went by; and early in the afternoon I reached Hightstown, very hot and hungry, and a little footsore. Twenty-five cents only had been expended, thus far—and was I now to dine for half a dollar? The thought was banished as rapidly as it came, and six cakes, of remarkable toughness and heaviness, put an effectual stop to any further promptings of appetite that day.

The miles now became longer, and the rosy color of my anticipations faded a little. The sandy level of the country fatigued my eyes; the only novel objects I had yet discovered were the sweep-poles of the wells; and though I nodded to everybody I met, my greetings were not always cordially returned. I had been informed, you must know, that in the land of Jersey the inhabitants were inclined to be offended if you did not give them the short, silent nod, which is the ordinary form of country salutation in America. (People say "I nodded to him"—not "spoke" or "bowed.") The hot afternoon was drawing to a close, and I was wearily looking out for Spotswood, when a little incident occurred, the memory of which has ever since been as refreshing to me as the act in itself was at that time.

I stopped to get a drink from a well in front of a neat little farm-house. While I was awkwardly preparing to let down the bucket, a kind, sweet voice suddenly said: "Let me do it for you." I looked up, and saw before me a girl of sixteen, with blue eyes, wavy auburn hair, and slender form—not strikingly handsome, but with a shy, pretty face, which blushed the least bit in the world, as she met my gaze. Without waiting for my answer, she seized the pole, and soon drew up the dripping bucket, which she placed upon the curb. "I will get you a glass," she then said, and darted into the house—reappearing presently with a tumbler in one hand and a plate of crisp tea-cakes in the other. She stood beside me while I drank, and then extended the plate with a gesture more inviting than any words would have been. I had had enough of cakes for one day; but I took one, nevertheless, and put a second in my pocket, at her kind persuasion. This was the first of many kindnesses which I have received from strangers all over the wide world; and there are few, if any, which I shall remember longer.

At sunset I had walked twenty-two miles, and had taken to the railroad track by way of a change, when I came upon a freight train, which had stopped on account of some slight accident. "Where are you going?" inquired the engineer. "To Amboy." "Take you there for a quarter!" It was too tempting: so I climbed upon the tender, and rested my weary legs, while the pines and drifted sands flew by us for an hour or more—and I had crossed New Jersey!

There was the ocean! At least I thought so, for I heard the dash of waves on the beach, and the Neversink was invisible in the faint mist and moonlight. Instead of supper, I took a bath—tasted the water, and found it bitter-salt. There was no doubt of it: I was swimming in the Atlantic. A deep sleep in some tavern followed; but, hearing at daybreak the sad sea-waves again, I was up, and down to the beach, hunting for shells. I expected to find all the pearly and rosy marvels which I had seen in our County Cabinet of Natural Sciences, profusely scattered along the sand, and was greatly disappointed to see only a few clams. This did not prevent me from writing a poem entitled: "The First Sight of the Ocean," which I thought a very fine production. It never appeared in *Graham's Magazine* however (to which I sent it), and is now totally lost to the world.

The trip from Amboy to New York made a great impression upon me. The beauty of the shores, the breadth of the bay, the movement of the thronging vessels, gave me new and grand ideas of the life of Man, and for the first time I saw the place of my nativity, not as a world around which all other interests revolved, but as an insignificant speck, the existence of which was as unimportant as it was unnoticed. The magic of that first impression has never been weakened. Our stately harbor is to me now, as it was then, a type of the activity of the age, and after years of wandering I never return to it without the old thrill of admiration—the old instinct that here, of all other places in the world, isthe great arena of labor.

I readily found the soda-water establishment, and was joined in the afternoon by my companion. We went out for a stroll up and down Broadway. The first thing we noticed was a red flag, and the voice of an auctioneer selling watches. "Oh," said my friend, "here is one of those places where you can get gold watches so cheap. Let us go in!"—and in we went. Two or three fellows, with heavy chains at their vests, were bidding upon a silver watch. "Only two dollars—going!" cried the auctioneer.

"Two and a half!" eagerly shouted my companion. Evidently the Peter Funks wished to lead him on gently, for they allowed him to get the watch for four dollars. The earnestness and volubility of the auctioneer amused me, and I could with difficulty restrain my laughter. He, however, put a different interpretation on my merriment, and looked quickly away whenever he caught my eye. Innocent as I was, he must have supposed that I understood the whole business. "Let me see that watch—I'm a watchmaker myself," said one of the heavy gentlemen. He opened it, examined the works, and said: "It's worn out; it won't go, but the silver is worth something. I'll allow you two dollars for it, and sell you this, which I carry myself, for five." My companion was taken in a second time, and made the exchange. The watch, however, though it was not silver, kept pretty good time for a few weeks.

At night, the question was, Where shall we go? It occurred to us, finally, that there was a hotel called the Howard House, not far from John street. The size of the building imposed upon us a little, but we had never heard of more than twenty-five cents being paid for lodging, and went cheerfully to bed. But in the morning our eyes were opened. "Six shillings!" said the clerk, in anwer to our inquiry. "SIX SHILLINGS!" we both mechanically repeated, in breathless astonishment. "Yes, that is the regular charge," he replied. We paid the money, in dumb bewilderment, and went around to Gosling's, in Ann street, for our breakfasts. The next day, our names appeared in the published list of arrivals at the Howard House, and *that*, my companion declared, was worth at least four shillings.

At that time, there were several lines of steamboats on the Hudson, and their competition had reduced the fare to Catskill to twenty-five cents—which was greatly to our advantage. We enjoyed to the fullest extent, the scenery of the glorious river—still, to my eyes, after seeing the Danube, the Rhine, the Rhone, the Nile, and the Ganges, the most beautiful river in the world. Insensible to the cold wind and occasional showers of rain, we walked the hurricane deck while the splendid panorama of the Palisades, Tappan Zee, and the Highlands unfolded on either side. While I was trying to pick out Sunnyside among the villas around Tarrytown, I was accosted by a sharp, keen-looking man, with "Ah, here you are! How are you?" I replied, in some little embarrassment. "Is your father well?" he continued. "Quite well, sir." "Is he on board? I'd like to see him." "No, I am alone." "Well, I want to hear something about business. I have my eye on a new speculation. It'll pay mighty well—a sure thing. I think we could manage it very well together." I gave an evasive answer—not knowing whether the man had mistaken me for some one else, or whether it was another form of the ubiquitous Peter Funk. As soon as possible, I got away from him, and carefully avoided him during the rest of the passage.

We landed at Catskill early in the afternoon, shouldered our knapsacks, and set off for the Mountain House. The day had become warm and clear, and the grand masses of the mountains rose before us, clothed in the softest mantle of light and shadow, as if covered with deep-blue velvet. They have never since appeared to me so high, so vast, and so beautiful. The green pasture-land, over which our road lay, with its forests of pine and hemlock, singing in the joy of the spring-time, charmed us scarcely less, and we walked onward in a wild intoxication of delight. After we had travelled about six miles, a country wagon came rattling along behind us. In it sat a short, thick-set farmer, with a wife of still ampler proportions. As the wagon approached us, he reined in his horses and shouted to us: "Get in! get in! there's plenty of room, and we're going the same way." We cheerfully obeyed, and were soon on the most intimate terms with the jolly people. "I said to myself, the minute I saw you!" exclaimed the farmer, with a laugh of intense satisfaction: "Here's a couple of farmer's boys, who have just got their corn planted, and are taking a little lark before hay-harvest. I'll help 'em along, that I will!' and you see I wasn't wrong, Sarah?"—turning to his wife. "No, John," said she, "you're always in the right;" and then whispered to me, who sat on the back seat with her, "I do think my husband's the best man in the world. We've been married now goin' on thirty-six years, and we've never fell out, as other married folks do. No, indeed!" Her broad, happy face, no less than her determined voice, proclaimed the utter impossibility of such a thing.

"I've got a son, John," she continued "and he's lately married, and gone to keepin' house. She's the nicest little daughter-in-law I ever seen. Why, you wouldn't know but she was our own born child!" The old lady was fairly eloquent in praise of her son's wife. She explained to me minutely how she kept her house in order, how many cows she milked, how neat she was, how active, how saving, how cheerful, and how beautiful. While these confidential disclosures were going on, we had reached a little village at the foot of the mountains. "Law!" she suddenly exclaimed, "there's my son John!—John! John! Here's two strangers we picked up on the road. I've been tellin' 'em about you and Hannah Jane!" John, however, who was engaged in the difficult task of dragging along a refractory pig, by a rope fastened to one of its hind legs, and who looked very warm and vexed, was not so cordial towards us. He nodded (here the pig made a bolt.) "Darn that pig! Are you coming our way, mother? (Another bolt across the road, followed by John.) I want to speak about that (back again, and off the other side) calf!"

Here we judged it best to leave our good friends, and commence the ascent of the mountain. With a hearty shake of the hand, the farmer, who had learned our plans, said: "You won't be far from our house, as you go across to Aithyens (Athens), and you must stop and get dinner with us. Don't forget John ——, whenever you come to these parts again!"

We climbed lustily, and just as sunset was fading from the Berkshire Hills, stood on the rocky platform before the Mountain House. Outside of Switzerland, there are few landscapes in Europe of equal beauty; and this first triumphant realization of mountain-scenery was all that my boyish imagination had painted, and more. The nights were moon-lighted; and the view of the vast, mysterious deep, traversed by the faint silver gleam of the Hudson, as I saw it from my pillow, kept me from sleep for hours. The next day was one of unmixed enjoyment. We climbed the north and south peaks, visited the Cauterskill Falls, lay on the grass inhaling the odor of blossoming strawberries and the resinous breath of the pines, and indulged in the delicious intoxication of the hour, without a thought beyond. We were the first visitors that season, and possessed the mountains alone. While sitting on the rocks, I wrote some lines of diluted poetry on a bit of drawing paper, which fell out of my pocket afterwards—as I subsequently discovered, to my great regret. Fortune, however, is kinder towards bad poetry than good. The lines were found by a lady, some weeks later, and restored to me through the columns of the *New York Tribune.* I have lost better poems since, and nobody picks them out of the dust.

On the second morning, we came down to the level of common earth again, and a walk of twenty miles or more brought us to Athens, opposite Hudson, in the evening. Here we slept, and then set off at daybreak, intending to reach Stockbridge that day. But one shower after another delayed us on the road; we got bewildered among the Claverack Hills, and were fain to stop at a farm-house early in the afternoon, to solicit rest and a dinner. The residents were a young couple, still overcome with the pride and happiness of their first child. A judicious nursing of the latter, while the mother prepared dinner, no doubt procured for us the best the house could afford. We had ham and eggs, potatoes, mince pie and coffee (Don't I remember every thing, even to the pattern of the plates?), and were dismissed with good wishes—the honest young fellow refusing to take payment for the meal. This hospitality was well-timed, as our resources (*mine*, at least) were fast dwindling away.

I became suddenly conscious that it would be impossible to carry out my plan in all its original grandeur. What was to be done? We sat down on a bank of damp violets, and held a serious consultation, the result of which was, that we turned about, rather crest-fallen, and marched back to Hudson, where we arrived after dark.

The rain the next day justified our decision, and we therefore took the twenty-five-cent steamer to New York. Here I parted from my companion, slept (not at the Howard House, though!), and then set out for Philadelphia. By taking the cars to New Brunswick, and walking thence to Trenton, in time to catch the evening boat to Philadelphia, I managed to make the journey for one dollar, and thereby cheat our Danish State out of her passenger toll. The day was hot, the road dusty, and my spirits much less buoyant than when on the outward tramp, but by hard walking I got over the twenty-eight miles in seven hours. One more day, mostly on foot, and I was at home, triumphant, with nine cents in my pocket, and a colossal cold in my head.

Humboldt once told me: "Travelling certainly increases a man's vitality, if it does not kill him at the start." This was my first moderate essay, at the age of eighteen. And I advise all callow youths who think it an easy matter to tramp over the whole world, to make a similar trial trip, and get their engines into good working-order, before fairly putting out to sea.

II.

A NIGHT WALK.

Before asking my readers to accompany me across the ocean, in order that we may explore together those out-of-the-way nooks of travel and life, which, because they do not form an integral part of the tourist's scheme, are generally omitted or overlooked (like the closets in a house). Let me recall one more preliminary experience—of trifling import, perhaps, yet it clings to my memory with wonderful tenacity.

A year after my trip to the Catskills, I was occupied with the preparations for a far more extensive and ambitious journey. I found myself at last free, and though the field before me was untried and difficult, I looked forward to it with as light a heart as had carried me across New Jersey and up the Hudson. My preparations were simple enough—French and German grammars, a portfolio, and a few shirts. By the beginning of June (1844) I was ready to set out. My cousin—whose intention of visiting Europe had been the cause of precipitating my own plans—was also ready, when another very important need suddenly occurred to us. We had no passports.

In the country, where no one lived who had ever been outside of his native land, we were quite unacquainted with any means by which our passports could be procured, except by going to Washington. For *my* part, I supposed that when a gentleman wished to travel, he was obliged to report himself at our national capital and probably undergo a strict examination. There was no help for it—we must make the journey. The distance was more than a hundred miles, and we calculated that, by taking a steamboat from the mouth of the Susquehanna River to Baltimore, we could walk the remainder of the distance in two days. So, on a fine June morning, we started.

The first fifteen miles led through a lovely region of farms and villages—a country of richer and more garden-like beauty than any which can be seen this side of England. The semi-tropical summer of Southern Pennsylvania and Virginia had just fairly opened in its prodigal splendor. Hedge-rows of black and white thorn lined the road; fields were covered, as with a purple mist, by the blossoms of the clover; and the tall tulip-trees sparkled with meteoric showers of golden stars. June, in this latitude, is as gorgeous as the Indian Isles. As the hills, however, begin to subside towards Chesapeake Bay, the scenery changes. The soil becomes more thin and sandy; the pine and the rough-barked persimmons supplant the oak and elm; thickets of paw-paw—our northern banana—and *chin-*

capin (a shrub variety of the chestnut) appear in the warm hollows, and barren tracts covered with a kind of shrub-oak, called "black-jack," along the Eastern Shore, thrust themselves between the cultivated farms. Mason and Dixon's line seems here to mark the boundary between different zones of vegetation. The last northern elm waves its arms to the first southern cypress.

As we were plodding along in the heat and dust, having still five miles of our day's work of thirty to perform, we met a curious old man, on foot like ourselves. He was tall and strongly made—an iron frame, whose original vigor was still visible under all the rust and batter of seventy years—with long, grizzly hair hanging over his weather-beaten face, and a pair of sharp, gray eyes. He was, evidently, one of the last of those men in whom the lawless trapper-blood of a portion of the first colonists has been transmitted, by inheritance, long after the occupation of the class has passed away. I remember such a one, whose favorite dish was opossum; who always made his own hat of rabbit-skins; and whose habit of carrying live black snakes in his bosom, made him at once the terror and the admiration of us boys. The old man stopped before us, fixed us with his eye, like Coleridge's "Ancient Mariner," and said, after a moment of keen inspection: "So, boys, you're starting into the world?" We assented. "Well, go on; you'll get through," he continued; "but let me give you one bit of advice. I never saw you before, and I'll never see you again; but if you'll mind my words, you won't be the worse for't. You'll get knocked about a good deal, that's sure; but—*fear no devils but yourselves*, and you'll come out all right." With that, he shook hands with us, smiled in a grim yet not unkindly way, and went on. Doubtless he spoke from bitter experience: he had been his own tempting and tormenting devil.

We reached Port Deposit, on the Susquehanna River, in season to take the evening steamer for Baltimore. There were no other passengers, but we had a dozen or more canal-boats in tow. The sweetness and splendor of that evening will never fade from my mind. It is laid away in the same portfolio with marvellous sunsets on the becalmed Pacific; with twilights on the Venetian lagunes; and with the silence and mystery of the star-lit Desert. The glassy water, reduplicating the sunset, was as transparent as air, and the gentle breeze, created by the motion of the boat, was vital with that sweetest of all odors—the smell of blossoming grasses on the low and distant shores. Standing on the hurricane-deck, we seemed to be plowing through the crystal firmament, steering forth from the fading earth towards some unknown planet. So fair and beautiful seemed to me then the world into which I was embarking—so far behind me the shores of the boyish life I had left.

But towards midnight the winds blew and the waves rose. Two of the canal-boats we had in tow broke adrift, and floated away; and a man, in securing another, had his finger caught in a noose of the hawser and instantly taken off. We ran into shallow water and anchored, where we lay tossing until morning. So new was all this to me, that I imagined we had gone through a terrible storm, and was rather surprised to find the captain so cool and unconcerned. In consequence of this delay, we did not reach

Baltimore until the evening of the next day, and as the steamer's larder was not provided for such an emergency, our fare consisted of salt meat and black coffee. The captain, however, apologised for his bad luck (the fact of our being bound for Washington seemed to inspire him with great respect), and made no charge for our hard fare.

"Let us," said my cousin, as we stepped ashore at Baltimore, "walk on to Ellicott's Mills, which is only eight or nine miles further, and sleep there to-night. We can then easily go to Washington to-morrow." This was a prudent proposal, and we started without delay. The sun set, the short twilight faded away, and it was about nine o'clock, although not yet wholly dark, when we reached the little village below the railroad viaduct. Tired and very hungry —for we had not supped—we halted at the tavern, rejoicing that our day's journey was at an end. To our surprise, the house was dark, and the doors locked. After knocking vigorously for some time, an upper window was raised, and a man's head appeared: "What do you want?" he asked in a surly tone. "We want lodgings. This is a tavern, isn't it?" said we. "Yes, it's a tavern; but it's too late now. The law don't oblige me to keep it open after nine o'clock." "Well," we mildly suggested, "it's not so late but you can come down and let us in." "I tell you," he roared, "the law don't oblige me, and *I won't*,"—whereupon he slammed down the window, remaining obstinately deaf to our further knocks.

This was rather discouraging, especially as everybody in the village seemed to be already in bed. There was nothing to be done but to go on to the next tavern, which—as we learned from a most dissipated man whom we met on the road (actually out at half-past nine in the evening!) was about three miles further. In spite of the balmy coolness of the summer night, and the cheerful twinkling of constellations of fire-flies over the meadows, we were thoroughly wearied out on reaching our second haven of refuge. But our luck was still worse than at the first. All our knocking and shouting failed to provoke a single response. Once or twice we heard a footstep, as if some one were making a stealthy observation, and then deep and persistent silence.

Thoroughly disheartened, we resumed our painful march. We had proceeded a mile or two further, and the time was verging towards midnight, when a blaze of light suddenly streamed across the road, and the sound of music reached our ears. On the right hand, in a grove of trees, stood the mansion of a country gentleman, lighted up as for a brilliant festival. "Here, at least, the people are awake," said I. "Let us inquire whether there is any tavern near, where we can get lodgings." We entered the gate and walked up the lawn, towards the house. The windows were open, each one inclosing in its frame of darkness a picture of perfect light and beauty. Young girls, in white ball dresses and with wreaths of roses in their hair, were moving to and fro in the dance, as if swaying lightly on the delicious waves of the music. I had never before seen anything so lovely. It must be a wedding, or some other joyous occasion, I thought; they will certainly give us a shelter. By this time we reached the portico, which was occupied by a group of gentlemen. My cousin, addressing himself to the central personage, who was evidently the master of the house, said: "Can you tell us, sir, where we can find lodgings for the night?" If a barrel of powder had been fired and the whole house blown into the air, we could not have been more astonished than at the result of this question. The person addressed (I will not repeat the word "gentleman") turned suddenly and fiercely upon us. "Begone!" he shouted: "Leave the place, instantly! Do you hear me? Off!" We were struck dumb an instant; then my cousin, with as much dignity as his indignation would permit, stated that we were strangers, benighted and seeking an inn, and required nothing of him except the few words of information which he could give, and we had a right to expect. A fresh volley of abuse followed, which we cut short by turning and walking away—the other persons having been silent spectators of this singular interview.

We marched rapidly onward into the night, burning with indignation. If joy gives wings to the feet, anger has an effect no less potent. For two hours, the feeling was strong enough to overcome our sense of exhaustion, but Nature yielded at last. We were tormented by raging thirst, and finding no running streams, were forced to drink from ditches and standing pools, closing our teeth to keep out the tadpoles and water-beetles. The draught created a nausea which added to our faintness. The fire-flies still danced over the meadows; the whip-poor-wills cried from the fences, sometimes so near that I could almost have touched them with my hand, and the air was filled with the silvery film of the falling dew. We sat down on a bank, utterly spiritless and desperate. I proposed sleeping under a tree, but we feared the dampness of the earth, and after starting and rejecting various propositions, finally decided to try the fences. These were of the zig-zag kind called "worm fences," with stakes at the corners, held down by heavy riders. Selecting the broadest rails, we lay down; but the first approach of sleep betrayed to us the danger of rolling off such a lofty and narrow perch. To sit on a sharp rail fence is not agreeable; but to sleep, even on a broad one, is still less so. Since that night, I have acquired such a distaste to being "on the fence," that I always take one side of a question at once, at whatever risk of inconsistency.

For another hour we dragged ourselves onward, rather than walked. Every minute I caught myself in the act of falling, and once fell before I could recover the balance. About three in the morning we passed a farm-house, in the cattle-yard adjoining which stood two carts. Here was at last a place of repose, as welcome as a couch of eider-down! We crept in among the startled oxen, who sniffed and snorted their suspicions of such an unusual proceeding, and lay down in the bottom of the cart-bed. I suppose we slept about an hour, when, finding ourselves stiff and sore, though a little recruited, we resumed our journey. The morning twilight now came to our assistance, so that we got at least clean water to drink. At sunrise, we were in Bladensburg, and broke our long fast at a hospitable inn. Two hours more, and we were crossing Capitol Hill, having walked forty miles since sunset.

Dusty, footsore and faint, we trudged along Pennsylvania Avenue, seeking the boarding-house where the Member of

Congress from our district lodged. On applying for a room, the hostess looked at us with suspicion, naturally hesitating, until some references which we gave restored a certain degree of confidence. We lay down and instantly fell asleep. The servant roused us for dinner, after which we slept until called to tea. We then went to bed, and slept until the next morning. In the whole course of my subsequent travels, I have never suffered from fatigue, hunger, and thirst to such an extent as on that night. I have gone without food a day and a half; without sleep four nights; have walked two hundred miles in six days, and ridden three hundred and seventy-eight miles in a cart, without pause or rest, but all these experiences, trying as they were, shook my powers of endurance less than the first trial. I remember them with a certain amount of pleasure; but I never recall my night-walk from Baltimore to Washington without a strange reflected sense of pain.

The member from our district (Hon. A. R. McIlvaine) kindly accompanied us to the Department of State, and presented us to Mr. Calhoun, whose frankness, simplicity, and courtesy made a profound impression upon me. Our passports were immediately prepared, and given to us. In the Hall of Representatives I felt honored in taking the hand of John Quincy Adams, and hearing a few words of encouragement from his lips. Our member was so inconsiderately generous as to purchase five copies of a juvenile volume which I had published, by which means my funds were increased sufficiently to warrant me in returning to Baltimore by railroad. I had had quite enough of the old highway.

We took the same steamer back to the mouth of the Susquehanna, and walked the remaining thirty miles. I reached home after midnight, and entering a bed-chamber through the window, according to my usual custom, threw some guests, who had arrived the day before, into a horrible state of alarm.

III.

FIRST DIFFICULTIES WITH FOREIGN TONGUES.

I am frequently asked whether travel in a country, with the language of which you are unacquainted, is not attended with great difficulty and embarrassment. All difficulties, like all dangers, appear far more formidable at a distance than when one is brought face to face with them; yet a certain amount of experience is always necessary to enable one to encounter perplexities of this kind with that courage and self-possession which take away half their terror at the onset. If all mankind were suddenly deprived of the power of speech, the embarrassment and confusion would be very great for a few days; but a fortnight would not elapse before government, business, and society would move on in their accustomed courses. On entering a foreign country, however, you are only deprived of the faculty of comprehension. The aids of tone and expression are added to those of signs and gestures, and that unused power of interpretation which appears to us marvellously developed in the deaf and dumb, is at once called into action. Thus an imperfect knowledge of a language—especially of the niceties of its pronunciation—is very often a hindrance rather than a help, because it prevents us from using those simple aids which are of universal significance. I once asked Ida Pfeiffer how she managed to communicate with the people in Tahiti, in Persia, Circassia, and other countries where she was unacquainted with the language. "Entirely by signs," she answered, "until I have acquired the few words which are necessary to express my wants; and I have never experienced any difficulty in making myself understood."

In Europe the facilities of travel have multiplied so greatly within the last twenty years, that the veriest Cockney may travel from London to Vienna and find his own language spoken in every hotel he enters—provided he is able to pay for the luxury. Railroads have not only brought about the abolition of all the real annoyances of the passport system, but they have increased travel to such an extent as to make it, in some countries, the chief source of revenue to the people—who are thus obliged to accommodate themselves in every possible way to the wants of their customers. But at the time of my first journey abroad, in 1844, this was still far from being the case, and a more minute account of my initiatory experiences than I have yet given, may be of some interest to the *monoglot* reader.

On an August evening, we looked across the British Channel from the summit of Shakspeare's Cliff. The misty outline of the French coast rose beyond the water, like the shore of an unknown world. England can never seem a foreign country to the American; and hence he cannot thoroughly appreciate and enjoy it until *after* he has visited the Continent—until his home habits and prejudices have been so far obliterated that he can receive impressions without constantly drawing comparisons. I would advise every one who wishes to derive the greatest advantage from a European tour, to visit England last of all.

We were even more excited with the thought of crossing the Channel than we had been, a month previous, with the first sight of the Old World. The Ostend steamer, which left only three times a week, was to start at four o'clock in the morning, and we took early lodgings at one of the famous (or rather infamous) Dover taverns. There were no "through lines" and "through tickets," as now, when one may pass without detention from Liverpool to the railroad stations nearest Asia. The landlord promised to call us in season for the boat, but his looks did not inspire us with confidence; and our sleep, tormented with the fear of being too late, was fortunately very broken and disturbed. At three o'clock we rose and dressed by moonlight. No one was stirring in the house. We waited a quarter of an hour, and then groped our way down-stairs to the coffee-room. Feeling around in the dark, we at last reached the bell-rope and sounded a peal. The echoes rang through the house, but no voice answered. The outer door was double-locked and the key taken away. Just then, we heard the first bell rung on board the steamer, and knew that we had but twenty minutes more. The case demanded desperate means, so we distributed our forces and commenced a simultaneous attack. One rang the bell incessantly; one thumped up and down the staircase with the handle of an umbrella; and the third pounded upon the door of a bedroom which we supposed to be the landlord's. Even this produced no effect: we were caged, to be kept two days longer. At last, the second bell rang—only five minutes more! Our voices were added to the tumult, and our rage and anxiety found vent in a series of the most dreadful yells. Flesh and blood could not stand this, and presently the landlord made his appearance, in his shirt, rubbing his eyes, and pretending to be just aroused from sleep. I believe nothing but the fear of personal violence induced him to unlock the door. We snatched our knapsacks and rushed down the quay at full speed, reaching the steamer just as the plank was being hauled ashore.

The Channel was smooth as glass, and the mild splendor of the summer morning, painting the chalky ramparts of England with a pencil of pink flame, gradually restored our equanimity. At ten o'clock, we ran into the harbor of Ostend. I had learned to read a little French at school, but had never spoken the language, nor was my ear at all familiar with the sound of it. However, there were some other travellers on board, and by carefully watching and following their movements, we complied with the necessary regulations regarding passports and baggage. The train for Bruges did not leave for two or three hours, and we spent the intermediate time in wandering about the city, inspecting its ugly, yellow houses, listening to the queer Flemish dialect, wondering at the clatter of wooden shoes—in short, in a general condition of astonishment and open-mouthed observation.

At the station, the word "Bruges" was sufficient to procure us tickets; the exhibition of the tickets got our baggage checked; and we set out from Ostend, in high glee at our success. In an hour we were at Bruges, feeling a little less confident as we walked away from the station. Here, however, we were accosted by a sort of shabby valet-de-place, who spoke a few words of English, and offered to guide us through the city for a franc. I have not a very distinct recollection of our walk, except of the dim, imposing cathedral (the first mediæval church I ever entered), and some beautiful altar-pieces, from the pencil of Hans Hemling. I remember, however, that the evening was dark and rainy, and that I began, presently, to feel miserably strange and lonely. The guide informed us that a *trekshuyt* was to start that evening, on the canal, for Ghent, and we could get passage, including a bed, for three francs. He accordingly conducted us to the dark old barge, and gave us into the captain's care. We left our knapsacks in the cabin; I went back to the town, in the rain and twilight, to hear the chimes of the belfry in the market-square, while my companions tried their luck in purchasing material for a supper. They could point at the articles displayed in the windows and on the shelves, and offer pieces of money; but their choice was necessarily restricted to what they saw, for they were unable to ask for anything. When we met again, in the low cabin of the *trekshuyt*, they produced a loaf, a piece of powerful cheese, and some raisins and almonds, which constituted our supper.

To youth and hunger, however, nothing comes amiss, and our meal was a cheerful and satisfactory one. The cabin, whose black timbers made it appear a century old, was dimly lighted by a single candle. We were alone in the boat; for, although the hour fixed for our departure was past, neither the captain nor the sailors had made their appearance. Afterwards, we retired to rest, in wide, ponderous berths, containing delicious beds, of the cleanest lavendered linen (of all luxuries on earth, the greatest), and quickly fell asleep. No sound disturbed our slumbers. Only once in the night, opening my eyes as I lay, I saw the dark branches of trees gliding spectrally past the window. In the morning, the shock of the boat striking the pier at Ghent aroused us. By repeating the words "*chemin de fer*," accompanied by an uncertain gesture, the captain comprehended that we wished to know where the railroad station was, and sent a boy to pilot us. There the name of "Aix-la-Chapelle" was again sufficient for our tickets and baggage.

Our journey that day was not so agreeable. For economy's sake, we took third-class places, in open cars, which only furnished standing-room. Soon after passing Mechlin, the rain began to fall and a driving storm set in, the violence of which was doubled by the motion of the train. We huddled together under one umbrella, all three wrapped in a Mackinaw blanket, and endeavored to enjoy the beautiful scenery between Liege and Verviers. But, at last, thoroughly chilled and soaked, the romantic element disappeared, and we thought only of reaching fire and shelter. It was nearly night when we arrived at Aix-la-Chapelle. As soon as the light and easy regulations prescribed on crossing the Prussian frontier had been complied with, we took an omnibus to the Rhine Hotel. (I believe we pointed out the name in the guide-book to the driver.) Here it was necessary to make an effort; we were wet as drowned rats, and wanted to dry ourselves. I accordingly said to the head waiter: "*Un chambre de feu! Nous sommes*——" wet, I would have added, if I had known what the Frenchmen say when they are wet. "*Vous etes*——*?*" repeated the waiter, pausing for the key-word. "*Oui, nous sommes*——" there I stuck again, hesitated, and then, growing desperate, seized his hand, and placed it on my coat. "Oh! you mean you are wet," said he, in very good English. We had no further difficulty during the remainder of our stay in Aix-la-Chapelle.

The next day we took passage for Cologne. We had now entered the German region, and what little French I knew was almost useless. The train was detained for some time at one of the country stations, and we began to feel the want of dinner. Noticing one of the passengers eating a piece of bread and cheese, I said to him, "What is that?" at the same time pointing to the articles. The words were so much like the German that he understood me, and answered, "*Brod und Käse.*" By repeating this, we were soon supplied with bread and cheese. At Cologne, the word "Bonn" was sufficient to guide us to the Bonn railway station, where we gave our baggage in charge to a porter—pointing out to him on the time-table, the train by which we intended to leave. This left us free to spend the afternoon in wandering about Cologne.

At Bonn, that evening, we acquired some new experiences. Murray's Handbook recommends the "Golden Star" Hotel as the cheapest on the Rhine; and thither we accordingly went. It turned out, nevertheless, to be the most stylish establishment of the kind we had ever patronized. The reader must bear in mind that, up to this time, I had been accustomed only to the simplest country-life, and was utterly ignorant of the ways of the world, even at home. When, therefore, I entered the brilliantly-lighted dining-hall, in order to take some supper, and saw three or four officers seated at a table—all the other tables being vacant—I supposed that *theirs*, of course, was the table where supper was served, and, without more ado, seated myself beside them. They must have been utterly astounded at this proceeding; for I still remember the odd, amazed expression of their faces. Really the Germans are a very ill-mannered people, thought I; and sat there, complacently enough, until a servant invited me to take a seat elsewhere.

We had all been infected by the temperance revival, which, set on foot by the Baltimore Washingtonians, had swept over the United States. We might have tasted wine as small children, but its flavor had been wholly forgotten, and we looked upon the beverage as a milder sort of poison. When, therefore, we saw every man with his bottle of Rhenish, we were inexpressibly shocked; still more so, when the servant asked us (in English) what wine we should take. The favorite beverage at home then was—and still is, in the West—coffee, even at dinner; and accordingly we ordered coffee. The man hesitated, as if he had not rightly understood; but, on the order being repeated, brought us coffee, as if for breakfast, with French rolls. He could scarcely believe his eyes, when he saw us place the cups beside our beefsteaks and potatoes. We tried the same experiment once or twice afterwards, but were finally driven to taste the dreaded poison of the Rhine. Finding, after a fair trial, that our health did not suffer, nor our understandings become confused, we came to the conclusion that we had been a little hasty in pronouncing upon the nature of wine, from the representations of those who had been ruined by whisky.

Our next day on the Rhine was a golden one. All these little embarrassments were forgotten, when we saw the Seven Mountains rising, fair and green, in a flood of sunshine—when we passed under the ramparts of Ehrenbreitstein, and heard the bugle-notes flung back from the rocks of the Loreley. To me it was a wonderful, a glorious dream. I have tried, since then, to recall the magic of that day; but in vain. I miss the purple tint breathed upon the hills—the mystic repose of the sky—the sweetness of the air—the marvellous splendor of the sunshine; or, perhaps, the missing note, which alone could have restored the harmony of the first impression, has been lost by me—the ardent inspiration of youth, the light that *is* once, on sea and land—once, and never again!

I left my companions at Mayence, intending to visit Frankfort, before proceeding to Heidelberg, where we designed remaining until we had mastered the German language. My object was to visit Mr. Richard Willis, who was then pursuing his musical studies in Germany. I reached Frankfort in an hour, and at once started in search of the American Consul. After inquiring at a great many shops in the principal streets, I at last found a man who spoke a little French, and who informed me that the Consul resided in the *Bellevue.* (In reality, it was the *Schöne Aussicht*, which means the same thing.) I think I must have walked all over the city, and its suburb of Sachsenhausen, three times, without finding a *Bellevue* street. The thought then occurred to me, to select the streets which really commanded fine views, and confine my search to them. Proceeding on this plan, I presently discovered the Consul's house. I had bought some biscuits, at a baker's, for my breakfast; and, not knowing how else to dispose of them, had put them into my hat. When I was ushered into the consular office, I placed my hat carefully on a table in the ante-room, hoping no one would notice its contents. The old gentleman who then represented the United States, however, persisted in accompanying me to the door —a courtesy I would willingly have dispensed with—and, guided by my own nervous consciousness, made directly for the hat, and looked into it. 'Tis ever thus, from childhood's hour; whatever you particularly wish to conceal, is sure to be detected. I was somewhat consoled by the reflection that Dr. Franklin walked through the streets with a sheet of gingerbread under his arm, which was even worse than if he had hidden it in his shovel-brim.

With this experience, my special embarrassments ended.

Mr. Willis deposited me safely in the *eilwagen* for Heidelberg, where I remained quietly until I knew enough German to travel with ease and comfort. Having mastered one language, a second is acquired with half the difficulty; and I have, since then, had no particular trouble in picking up enough of a strange tongue to express simple and necessary wants. The smallest stock upon which you can conveniently travel, is *fifty words;* which a man of ordinary memory can learn in two or three hours. Let me advise others, however, not to fall into the common mistake of imagining that a man is deaf, because he cannot understand you; neither clip your words, and speak a sort of broken or inverted English, in the hope that it will be more easily comprehended. I have heard of an American, who was looked upon as an impostor in Europe, because he declared he came from "'Mecca," which he thought would be better understood than if he had spoken out, like a sensible man, syllable by syllable, the word—"A-MER-I-CA."

IV.

A YOUNG AUTHOR'S LIFE IN LONDON.

I REACHED London for the second time about the middle of March, 1846, after a dismal walk through Normandy, and a stormy passage across the Channel. I stood upon London Bridge, in the raw mist and the falling twilight, with a franc and a half in my pocket, and deliberated what I should do. Weak from sea-sickness, hungry, chilled, and without a single acquaintance in the great city, my situation was about as hopeless as it is possible to conceive. Successful authors in their libraries, seated in cushioned chairs and dipping their pens into silver inkstands, may write about money with a beautiful scorn, and chant the praise of Poverty—the "good goddess of Poverty," as George Sand, making 50,000 francs a year, enthusiastically terms her—but there is no condition in which the Real is so utterly at variance with the Ideal, as to be actually out of money, and hungry, with nothing to pawn and no friend to borrow from.

Have you ever known it, my friend? If not, I could wish that you might have the experience for twenty-four hours, only once in your life.

I remembered, at last, that during my first visit to London, eighteen months previous, I had lodged a few nights at a chop-house opposite the Aldgate Church-yard. The price of a bed was one shilling, which was within the compass of my franc and a half—and rest was even more to me than food. As I passed through the crowd towards Cheapside and thence eastward to Aldgate, the lamps were lighted and the twilight settled into a drear, rainy night. In the lighted shops I saw joints of the dark crimson beef of Old England, hams, fish, heads of lettuce—everything fresh, succulent, and suggestive of bountiful boards. Men—the very porters and street-sweepers, even—were going home with their little packages of tea, shrimps, and penny rolls. They all had homes to go to, and no care for the morrow: how I envied them!

At last I reached the end of Aldgate, turned up the alley beside the old church-yard, and entered the chop-house. The landlord was a broad, pursy, puffy fellow, and his wife a tall, keen, aquiline, and determined woman, who deserved a better fate. She was intended by nature for the presidency of a Charitable Association. The place had changed proprietors, so that they could not recognise me, as I had hoped. However, as there was a vacant bed, and they did not manifest any special mistrust, I determined to abide with them, and, professing great fatigue, was conducted to my room at once. It was a bare apartment on the second story, containing a miserable bed, an old spinnet, with every key broken or out of tune, a cracked looking-glass, and two chairs. The window commanded a cheerful view of the church-yard.

In the morning, I took a sixpenny breakfast, and offered a franc-piece in payment. The landlord refused to take it, whereupon I informed him that my funds were all in French coin and I had as yet had no opportunity of procuring English. This seemed to satisfy him; so I went forth with the hope of procuring employment as a printer. But all my efforts were in vain, and I returned at night, with only two-pence in my pocket, after I had paid for my breakfast. That night I did not sleep much. The crisis had arrived, and if relief did not come the next day, I saw nothing but starvation or downright vagrancy (the idea of which was even worse) in store for me. I rose early, so as to get away from the house, before I could be called upon to pay for my bed. After trying various printing-offices, always with the same result, I bought some bread with my two-pence, and, by a singular revulsion of feeling, became perfectly happy and careless. I was young and full of life, and had been disheartened as long as my temperament would permit. Nature resumed her rights, and I could not have been more cheerful had my pockets been filled with gold.

This buoyancy of spirits was like a presentiment of coming good-luck. In the course of the afternoon, I found an American publisher, who gave me instant relief, in the loan of a sovereign; and afterwards, sufficient employment to defray the three shillings a day, which I was obliged to expend. When I returned to the chop-house that night, I paid for my lodgings with an air, I fancy, unnecessarily ostentatious; but not without reason—I had seventeen shillings in my pocket! Of course, I was obliged to remain there—for at no better place could I procure a bed at the same price. The chop-house was the resort of actors from some low theatre in Whitechapel, hackmen, sailors occasionally, and pawnbrokers' clerks. I kept aloof from them, taking my chop in a solitary stall, and reading old numbers of the *Times* or a greasy copy of the *Family Herald*, when it was too cold to remain in my room.

The people never interfered with me in any way. They respected my silence and reserve; so I fared better than might have been expected. During the whole six weeks of my stay, I was never asked a personal question. Could the same thing happen in the United States? Sometimes, in the evenings, the company became boisterous and disagreeable, and I would be awakened, late at night, by angry cries and the sound of overthrown chairs and tables. The landlord's eyes, next morning, would then be bigger than usual—frequently the landlady's, also. The little servant-girl, at such times, would whisper to me, as she brought my boots: "O goody! but didn't master and missus fight last night!" All the criminal trials, even those of a nature not to be mentioned in mixed society, were freely discussed there. In a word, my associations were not of the most respectable character—I was reluctantly forced to this conclusion. But how could it be helped? When a man has but three shillings a day, he cannot keep four-shilling society, without cheating somebody. I lodged in a vulgar hole, it is true; but then, I paid my reckoning.

My only riches, at this time, consisted of a number of manuscript poems, written at Florence, during the previous autumn. They possessed great merit, in my eyes, and I did not see how they could fail to make the same impression upon others. One of the first things I did, therefore, was to send three or four to each of the popular magazines —*Ainsworth's*, *Bentley's*, and *Fraser's*—expecting to receive a guinea apiece, at least, for them. But day after day passed away, and the only answer which came, was from the quarter where I had least expected—from Mr. Harrison Ainsworth, the author of "Jack Sheppard," and "Old St. Paul's." The following is his letter, in reply to one which I had written in the hour of my greatest need:

"KENSAL MANOR HOUSE, HARROW ROAD,
"March 27, 1846.

"SIR: I return your poems with reluctance, for I think very highly of them. They exhibit great freshness and vigour, and are certainly above the average of magazine poetry. But, as you conjecture, I am overstocked with both prose and verse—and have more of the latter on hand than I can use in any reasonable time.

"I should be glad to be of service to you; and I may, perhaps, be able to help you to some employment, through my printer, Mr. Charles Whiting, Beaufort House, Strand. You can call upon his overseer, Mr. Gusyn, and show him this note; and if they have any vacancy, and you can offer sufficient credentials of your respectability and fitness, I am pretty sure my recommendation will avail. Under any circumstances, when you have seen Mr. Gusyn, and I hear from him, I would send you some trifling assistance.

"W. HARRISON AINSWORTH."

This note, friendly, yet guarded (as was proper under the circumstances), reached me after I had succeeded in obtaining employment with Mr. Putnam, and I never made use of it. I may add that the assistance Mr. Ainsworth offered had not been solicited in my letter, and therefore, while it illustrated his kindness, was not humiliating to myself. A polite notice of rejection, from *Fraser's Magazine*, reached me after my return to America. I never offered the same poems to any other periodical afterwards, and have every reason to be satisfied with my forbearance.

This, however, was not the only attempt I made to achieve some literary success in London. I had a letter to Mr. Murray, the publisher, from Mrs. Trollope, whose acquaintance I had made in Florence. That lady—whose famous book on America is no gauge of her cordiality towards Americans—received and encouraged me, in a manner which must always command my gratitude. It must be remembered that her speculations in Cincinnati were unsuccessful, and that she left the United States chagrined and embittered at her heavy losses. Her book—which, spiteful and caricaturesque as it certainly was, did us no real harm—was written under the first sting of her failure, and she regretted it sincerely, in later years. We can now afford to be friendly again towards a witty, cheerful, and really warm-hearted woman—who having forgotten what she lost, remembers only what she admired among us.

I had in my knapsack a manuscript poem of some twelve hundred lines, called "The Liberated Titan"—the idea of which I fancied to be something entirely new in literature. Perhaps it was. I did not doubt, for a moment, that any London publisher would gladly accept it, and I imagined that its appearance would create not a little sensation. Mr. Murray gave the poem to his literary adviser, who kept it about a month, and then returned it, with a polite message. I was advised to try Moxon; but, by this time, I had sobered down considerably, and did not wish to risk a second rejection. I therefore solaced myself by reading the immortal poem at night, in my bare chamber, looking occasionally down into the graveyard, and thinking of mute, inglorious Miltons. The curious reader may ask how I escaped the catastrophe of publishing the poem, at last. That is a piece of good fortune for which I am indebted to the Rev. Dr. Bushnell, of Hartford. We were fellow-passengers on board the same ship to America, a few weeks later, and I had sufficient confidence in his taste to show him the poem. His verdict was charitable; but he asserted that no poem of that length should be given to the world before it had received the most thorough study and finish—and exacted from me a promise not to publish it within a year. At the end of that time, I renewed the promise to myself for a thousand years.

Mr. Murray received me with great kindness, and I more than once left my den at Aldgate to dine at his storied residence in Albemarle street. At this time, I wore broad collars, turned down—such as I had been accustomed to wear at home—with flowing, unEnglish locks, and I suspect the flunkeys were puzzled what to make of me. I remember distinctly having purchased a pair of Berlin gloves, which were the cheapest. They were exactly of the kind worn by footmen—but I was entirely innocent of that fact. Walking one day in Hyde Park, with a gentleman to whom I had been introduced, I put them on; and it never occurred to me, until years afterwards, why he looked at them so curiously, and made such haste to get into a less-frequented thoroughfare.

Mr. Murray showed to Lockhart, who was then editor of the *Quarterly Review*, a poem which I had written on Powers' statue of "Eve," and that distinguished gentleman sent me an invitation to breakfast with him a few days afterwards. I called for Murray and walked with him to Lockhart's residence, on Regent's Park. We found there Bernard Barton, the old Quaker poet, and a gentleman from Edinburgh. Lockhart received me with great cordiality, mingled with a stately condescension. He was then not more than fifty years old, and struck me as being the handsomest Englishman I had ever seen. He was tall and well-proportioned, with a graceful, lordly deliberateness in his movements; a large, symmetrical head; broad brow; deep, mellow eyes; splendidly cut nose, and a mouth disproportionately small. His voice was remarkably rich and full. I was a little overawed by his presence, and he no doubt remarked it and was not displeased thereat.

Bernard Barton, however, was a man towards whom I felt instantly attracted. He had a little, round, gray head, merry gray eyes, and cheeks as ruddy as a winter apple. He was dressed in a very plain black suit, with knee-breeches and stockings, and a white cravat. Lamb, Hazlitt, and his other friends had passed away, and he had almost outlived his reputation—yet was as happy and satisfied as if he had just been made poet-laureate. I afterwards became one of his correspondents, and received several delightful letters from the good little man. Lockhart's daughter—the daughter of Sophia Scott—presided at the breakfast-table. She was a lovely girl of seventeen, just entering society, and bore a strong resemblance to her mother, whose portrait I saw in the library. She was rather tall and slender, exquisitely fair, yet with dark Highland hair and eyes—a frail, delicate character of beauty, which even then foretold her early death. Two years afterwards she married Mr. Hope, and one of her children is now the only descendant of Sir Walter Scott.

The principal topic of conversation at breakfast was the battle of Ferozeshah, the news of which had just arrived. Lockhart seemed quite excited by it, and related several incidents with great animation. We afterwards spent an hour in the library, where I saw the fifty volumes of Scott's correspondence, with all the great authors of the world, of his time. Lockhart read with a ringing, trumpet-like voice, from the original manuscript, the first draft of Campbell's "Battle of the Baltic." He also related to us many particulars of the last days of Southey. I felt aroused and inspired by the sight of such relics and the company of such men, and when I returned to the chop-house that night, to pore over my own despised poems, it was with a savage bitterness of spirit which I had never before felt. My day's walk had been from Olympus to Hades and the banks of Lethe's river.

Lockhart's kindness emboldened me to make one more trial. I had still another poem—a story in four cantos, entitled "The Troubadour of Provence"—written in a peculiar stanza which I had invented. I copied a few pages and sent it to him, desiring his opinion of the form of versification—not without a secret hope that he might be sufficiently impressed with the poem, to assist me in finding a publisher. His answer was as follows:

"Dear Sir: No form of stanza can interfere seriously with the effect of good poetry; but I do not think the labor implied in great complication of stanza is ever likely to be repaid. As, however, your poem is done, I can only bid you God-speed; and I am sure if it be, as a whole, as good as the *Eve*, it will have a most encouraging reception here as well as in America. Bernard Barton lives at Woodbridge, in Suffolk; and I have no doubt he will be gratified in hearing from you.

"Yours, very truly,
J. G. Lockhart."

"Regent's Park, April 7, 1846.

This letter, although kind and considerate, was nevertheless a sufficient hint to me. "The Troubadour of Provence" was finally laid away on the same shelf with "The Liberated Titan," and various other aspiring productions of youth. O, the dreams we dream! O, the poems we write! Kind are the hands which hold us back from rushing into print—tender the words which pronounce such harsh judgment on our works! For a year, we proudly curse the stupidity of our advisers—for ever afterwards we bless them as our benefactors. Reader, that knowest, peradventure, how many bad poems I have published, little dreamest thou how many more worse ones a kind fate has saved me from offering thee! I keep them still, as a wholesome humiliation; but they serve a double purpose. They humiliate when exalted, but they encourage when depressed. Therefore they have not been written in vain: but, thank Heaven, they have *only* been written!

These visits, together with occasional excursions to Chelsea—where, at the house of a brother of Mrs. Trollope, I met with authors and artists—introduced a new element into my London life. The chop-house, by force of contrast, became insufferable, yet I could not afford more expensive lodgings. The people were accustomed to my reserve, and respected it: at another place they might be more curious. And so I remained, to hear the cases of *crim. con.* racily discussed, to see continual black eyes and swollen noses, and be greeted with the little servant's whispered information: "Goody! but didn't they go it!" Besides, among my acquaintances, I boldly avowed where my nightly quarters were, and was gratified to find that it made no difference in their demeanor towards me. In London, a man's character is not so strictly measured by his place of residence as it is in New York.

For six weeks I continued to earn, through Mr. Putnam's kindness, sufficient to defray the expenses of living. By this time April was well advanced, a remittance arrived to pay my passage home, and my companions came on from Paris to join me. One by one, all my hopes of literary success had disappeared, and I speedily forgot them in the joy of returning to America. Yet I doubt whether any fragment of my life, of equal length, has done me equal service. I have seen London several times since then, have found publishers kinder, and have associated with authors, without blushing for my place of abode: yet I never visit the great city without strolling down Aldgate, to look upon the windows of the chop-house and the graveyard below, in which lie buried the ambitious dreams of my youth.

V.

THE ATLANTIC.

As far as the novelty of the thing is concerned, one might as well write an account of a trip from Canal street to Coney Island, as of a voyage across the Atlantic. The log-books of all manner of tourists have made everybody familiar with the course of incidents from pier to pier: the disappearance of one's native shore and the coming-on of sea-sickness—touching emotion and deadly nausea—porpoises and the Gulf Stream—fogs on the Newfoundland Banks—perhaps a whale or a vessel within hail, and then a great blank of blue water, over which the voyager's pen glides with scarce a word of record, till old Mizen Head or Cape Clear comes out of the mist and inspires him with a fresh gush of romantic sentiment. It is not so common, however, for travellers to enjoy the trip, unless in anticipation or remembrance. For my part, after considerable experience of the Atlantic and Pacific Oceans, the Mediterranean, Caribbean, and Gulf of Mexico, I never fully knew the pleasures of sea-life, nor appreciated the endless variety and beauty of sea-scenery, until I left home, worn in body and overworked in brain, to seek rest and refreshment in travel.

The spirit of Work infects our atmosphere: we cannot escape the malady. Our souls are pitted and scarred with it, and there is no vaccination whereby we can avoid the disease. If you once plunge into the stream, you must strike out with the boldest, while breath and nerve remain. There is no such thing as rest inside of Sandy Hook, and I felt no relaxation of the unnatural tension, until the Gulf Stream rolled its tropical opiate between me and the maternal shores. Our country gives us everything, but she exacts everything from us in return. What if we play truant now and then? what if we fly from the never-ending task, to dream a Summer day in the quiet air of Europe, or the lazy languor of the East? We leave our household gods to await our return, and we pray that the urn which is to hold our ashes may be placed beside them.

It was near the close of August when I sailed. There was not a ripple on the glassy water, nor a cloud in the sky, and the Atlantic's sentinels slept at the gates of the bay, as we passed them at night-fall. For three or four days we sailed on a tropic sea. The sun came up flaming over the sharp rim of the horizon, wheeled around his course, and sank broad and clear in our wake. Our great ship rocked gently to the lazy pulsations of the ocean's heart—a lulling, not a disturbing motion—and we journeyed in a serene and perfect repose. "Oh, Rest to weary hearts thou are most dear," sang a spirit shut out from

Paradise; but there can be no deeper rest than that which descends alike on heart, brain, and limbs. One must have whirled for a year or two in the very vortex of our American life, to taste the repose of the ocean in its refreshing fulness:

"Duty and Care fade far away;
What Toil may be we cannot guess:
As a ship anchored in a bay,
As a cloud at summer noon astray,
As water-blooms on a breezeless day—
So the heart sleeps,
In thy calm deeps,
And dreams, Forgetfulness!"

With all the monotony of its calm, the tranquil expanse of the Ocean is infinitely suggestive. When the land has disappeared, your vessel is a planet wheeling its way through blue ether. But it is a planet of which you are the creator, and at your will its orbit may touch the shores of many distant regions, passing through zones of heat and cold, of light and darkness. During those Summer days, in the Gulf Stream, it seemed to need but a swerve of the prow to bring all the lands of the Old and New Continents with our reach. Cross the distant ridge of the horizon, glide down the watery slope beyond, and you touch the Pillars of Hercules; yonder lies Teneriffe and there the jungles of Senegambia; here on our right, under the noonday sun, are the palms of Hayti, the perpetual verdure of the Antilles. When the fogs of Newfoundland lift like an arch, and a keen northwester comes straight down from Labrador, look to the north, and you will hear in fancy the hollow booming of the surf in Icelandic fjords and caverns. At least, the sound came to my ear as I was pacing the deck with Mungo Park, and listening to his descriptions of life in the high Arctic region, under the savage shores of Boothia, and among the ice-fields of Prince Regent's Inlet. It was not the ghost of the African traveller that told me these things, but his near relative, the worthy Surgeon of the steamship.

One must cross the Atlantic more than once, before his mind can take in a satisfactory idea of its immensity. On my first voyage I could not by any possibility imagine myself more than fifty miles from shore. The ship went on from day to day, but for all that, there was land just behind the horizon. Even when the sight of the Irish Coast gave me a vivid sense of distance from home, the impression was one of time, not of space. All the Atlantic was embraced in one horizon, sometimes calm, sometimes agitated, but always the same sphere of sky and water. Now it is a grand and beautiful expanse, over which I cannot leap in thought so readily. I must pass great tracts of smooth and gently undulating water; dark, wintry wastes flecked with wreaths of snow; fogs that take away all sense of place and time; and myriads of rolling hills, that flash and foam and sparkle as they lift the vessel, as on the boss of a vast shield, till I can look over the blue convex to its outer edge. Then the alternations of light and darkness, each heightened by the sea, which, spouse of the sky, copies its lightest change; the sunsets, transmuting both water and air; the bright paths trodden by the moon—paths which do not cease at the horizon, but project forward beyond the earth, into the mysterious depths of the heavens. Whither do they lead?

At sea, you look on the life from which you have emerged, as one looks from a mountain top on his native town. It is astonishing how fast your prejudices relax after the land has sunk—how the great insignificances in which you have been involved, disappear, as if they had never been, and every interest of real value starts into sudden distinctness. If the brain could work in such a whirl as it must bear during a heavy sea, there would be no such place on shore for the historian and the philosopher. But the stomach, unfortunately, is your petted organ; you must give it your first care. Your mental enjoyment must be almost entirely of a sensuous stamp. You take in, without stint, the glory of the sea, lose yourself in delicious reverie, start a thousand tracks of thought which might lead to better and grander truths than you have yet attained; but you cannot follow them. The spirit is willing, but the flesh is too weak.

With such enjoyments as these, and that sense of rest, which was the sedative I most needed, two weeks passed by like two days. There was scarce an apology for sea sickness on board, and not a word of complaint on account of head-winds and rolling seas. Finally, as we were sailing on a cloudless afternoon, some keen eyes among us discerned round mountain-heads and rocky islands in the air, above the horizon. I half expected to see them melt back again into the vapor, but they stood fast and grew clear in outline, and point came out behind point as we advanced, till we ran under Fastnet Rock in the moonlight, and turned the corner of Cape Clear.

VI.

RAMBLES IN WARWICKSHIRE.

[SEPTEMBER, 1851.]

Few Americans leave Liverpool without visiting Chester. As the only walled city in England, dating its foundation from the Roman invasion, it is certainly a place of interest, but neither so venerable nor so peculiar in its appearance as I had imagined. I must own, however, that the old towns of the Continent were constantly in my memory during the two or three hours I devoted to its steep streets and winding walls. The only things on which I looked with real interest were the church founded by Ethelred the Saxon, and the crumbling watch-tower from whose top Charles I. watched the fortunes of the battle on Rowton Moor. The walk around the ramparts was charming. The warm, silvery haze of an English autumn filled the air, veiling the more distant of the Welsh mountains, but softening the graceful outlines of the nearer hills and touching with the gentlest play of light and shadow the Valley of the Dee, over whose waters we hung, while turning the sharp angles of the bastions on the southern side.

I took the afternoon train to Shrewsbury. The road passes into Wales soon after leaving Chester, and for many miles follows the hills which inclose the Allen, a tributary of the Dee. The country is hilly, but so varied in its features, so picturesque in the disposition of height and valley, stream and wood, so trim by nature and so luxuriant by culture, that I was ready to regard it as a specimen of landscape gardening on a magnificent scale. Not a dead bough encumbered the trees; not a patch of bare soil showed the earth's leanness. The meadows were smooth enough for a fairy's foot; the streams as tranquil and pellucid, as if only fit

"to roll ashore
The beryl and the golden ore;"

and the horses and cows in the pasture-fields were apparently newly washed and curried. To keep up the impression, at the Wrexham station we found a crowd of Welsh youths and maidens in their holiday dresses, as the great fair had just commenced. At the next station beyond, we passed an excursion train from Shrewsbury, a mile of cars, mostly open, and crammed with delighted children, to whom we all waved our handkerchiefs in return for their shouts.

The sun dipped his crimson disc behind the mountains, as we looked into the renowned Vale of Llangollen, in passing—a stately valley, broad at first and rich with woods, but narrowing in the distance and lost between the interlocking bases of the hills. Then twilight came on; the chimney of a furnace flashed here and there; white mist gathered along the streams, growing thicker as we reached the Severn, till the chimes of "Shrewsbury clock" rang from some invisible station in the air. I had a foggy and ghostly sort of ramble in the streets, getting lost in all kinds of dark windings up and down the hill on which the town is built; so, thinking it a pity to spoil such an appropriate impression of the old place, I left for Birmingham in the morning. Had it not been for a German pedestrian, who arrived at the "George Fox" just before I left, I might have visited the town, so far as my recollection of it is concerned, in the time of Richard III.

The face of the country became more monotonous and the soil poorer, as we approached Birmingham. From Wolverhampton, a large manufacturing town, to the latter place, a distance of ten or twelve miles, we passed an unbroken range of furnaces, forges and other establishments for the manufacture of iron. Scores of tall chimneys belched forth volumes of red flame and black smoke, like so many flues piercing down to the central fires. Whether from this cause or not, I will not venture to say, but the sky, which was mild and clear, after leaving the fogs of the Severn, became dark and lowering, and drops of rain fell at times on passing through this district. Beyond Birmingham, where Agriculture gets the upper hand, we found the sunshine again.

The appearance of Birmingham from the railroad viaduct is most uninviting. The only relief to the view of numberless blocks of dull red houses, roofed with red tiles, is afforded by two or three spires and a multitude of furnace-chimneys in the distance. I left the Shropshire train at the station, took another for Kenilworth, and in less than an hour saw the "three tall spires" of Coventry, that ancient and beautiful city, where, as Leigh Hunt says, "the boldest naked deed was clothed with saintliest beauty." I saw two pictures as I passed: one, the noble Godiva, trembling with shame, yet upborne by her holy purpose, as her palfrey clattered through the hushed streets: the other, an idle poet, lounging with grooms and porters on the bridge, and weaving in his brain the fit consecration of that deed.

The branch road for Leamington here left the great highway to London. It is a kind of railway-lane—a single track, winding by country ways, between quiet hedges, and with the grass growing up to the edges of the rails. Every spare shred and corner of ground clipped from the fields, is a little garden-plot, gay with flowers, and so, with less regret than the sentimental reader would suppose, I first saw the heavy pile of ruined Kenilworth from the windows of a railroad car. The castle is more than a mile distant from the station, but an omnibus was in waiting, for passengers. My companion and I, however, preferred a foot-path across the fields, leading to a gate in a wall which formed the outer defence of the place. As it happened we struck on the tilting-ground, the green level of which we followed to Mortimer's Tower, entering the Castle by the gate selected for the reception of Queen Elizabeth. Passing the ancient stables, which now shelter the stock of the farmer who takes care of the property for the Lord-Lieutenant of Ireland, its present owner, we reached the porter's lodge, a castle in itself, and still in admirable preservation. A superannuated door-keeper admitted us into the grounds and then went to call the guide, who was working in the garden. The latter personage, a little man who had grown old in the business, changed his smock-frock for a rusty blue coat, and took us in charge.

He was a proper guide, and so familiar with his points, that I doubt whether he would have piloted the Lord-Lieutenant (whom he never named without touching his hat), in any but the regular way. Taking us to the centre of the lawn, where the shattered, ivy-grown front of the Castle rose grandly before us, he pointed out the different groups of buildings and gave us the date of their erection. Then he bid us note the thickness of the walls in the Cæsar's Tower (the oldest part, built in a remote and uncertain period), after which he led us by a rough path into the dungeon where Edward II. was prisoner, and then by a well-worn staircase to the top of the tower, whence we looked down on a broad stretch of the loveliest meadow land, dotted with flocks of sheep. "There," said he, "in the Earl of Leicester's time, was a lake two miles long, and all the land you see to the right, sirs, thirty miles from the Castle, was the chase; and down there, where the hawthorns and crabs is, was the pleasure-garden." "Who owns all the land now?" I asked. "The Earl of Clarendon, Lord-Lieutenant of Ireland" (touching his hat), "and he gets £110,000 a year from it; but he never comes anigh it."

Kenilworth has been described so often, that I shall spare you an account of what was once the banqueting hall, and

Queen Elizabeth's dressing-room, looking down on the lake, and the Leicester buildings, the most ruined of all though the latest built. All parts of the Castle are mantled with the most superb ivy, thrusting its heavy arms between the shattered mullions, climbing the towers and topping them with mounds and overhanging cornices of dark, brilliant green. I noticed one trunk three feet in diameter. Our guide did not permit us to lose a single feature of the ruin. After finishing the building, he took us the round of the moat wall, and pointed out the most picturesque effects. He knew the positions to a hair's breadth, and it was in vain that I attempted to disregard them. I must stand with my back to the wall, and my feet in just such a spot. "Now," said he, "look between John o' Gaunt's building and the Leicester building, and you'll catch a nice bit of Cæsar's Tower." He could not go wrong, for the ruins are beautiful and imposing from every direction; they are the crowning charm and glory of one of the most delicious pastoral landscapes in the world.

Warwick Castle, only six miles distant, offers a remarkable contrast to Kenilworth. Like the latter, the date of its foundation is unknown, and its most ancient part bears the name of Cæsar's Tower; but while Kenilworth is fast tumbling to pieces, it remains entire, and is still inhabited in every part. The father of the present Earl expended immense sums in restoring and improving it. The grounds have been so laid out and planted, that the Castle is not seen from any part of the town, but by walking to the bridge over the Avon, one may obtain a grand view of its embattled front. The presentation of a card at the porter's lodge was sufficient to procure us admission. A carriage-road cut through the solid rock, with a fringe of fern and an arch of elms high overhead, leads to a narrow lawn in front of the Castle. The only perceptible change in the exterior, is the substitution of a light stone arch for the drawbridge, and the draining of the moat, which is now a trough of velvety grass, with flowering shrubs leaning over it from the sides. The portcullis still hung in the gateway, snarling at us with its iron teeth.

The inner court-yard, however, has been turfed over, and a new flight of granite steps leads to the entrance hall, in the southern wing of the Castle. The suite of state apartments in this wing is 333 feet in length, and built with so much precision that when the doors are closed one may look straight through all the key-holes to the further end. We were met at the door by the steward, Mr. Williams, who conducted us through the rooms. The old house-keeper died recently, after having amassed £30,000 from the fees of visitors, the whole of which she bequeathed to the Warwick family. I doubt whether Lord Clarendon will ever receive as a legacy the fees taken at Kenilworth. The state apartments are all that is generally shown, but as a friend of mine, a native of Warwick, accompanied me, the steward took us into the breakfast-room, though the table was already set for the Earl, and showed us the celebrated Lions of Rubens, several fine Vandykes, and an original portrait of Sir Philip Sidney, a pale and beautiful face, expressing true nobility of soul in every feature.

We also saw the armory, which is usually closed to visitors. It is rich in ancient armor and rare and curious objects, among which I may mention the crystal hilted dagger of Queen Elizabeth, her shirt of chain-mail, her saddle and the trappings of her horse; but I was most struck with two things: a *revolving musket*, more than two hundred years old, and a mask, taken from the face of Oliver Cromwell, after death. The revolver (of the antiquity of which there cannot be the slightest doubt) is almost precisely similar to Colt's, having a single barrel, to which is attached a revolving cylinder, containing six chambers. There is a flint lock and pan to each chamber, and the firing of one discharge brings the succeeding chamber to the barrel. I had been aware of the existence of this curious weapon, but was not prepared to find the idea of a revolver so perfectly developed.

The mask of Cromwell was found a short time since in clearing out one of the old chambers of the Castle, where the rubbish had been accumulating for a hundred and fifty years. There can be no doubt of its authenticity. The face is that of Cromwell, too hard and rugged, too terribly inflexible to be mistaken, while the prominence of the large eye-balls in their sunken cavities, the slight sharpening of the features, and the set rigidity of the grim mouth, show clearly that the mould was never taken from living flesh. Yet there seemed a kind of hard satisfaction in the expression of the face, as if he had remembered Dunbar at his death-hour. Less interesting than this memorable relic, yet more pleasant to behold, is Vandyke's portrait of Charles I. on horseback, filling up the end of a long gallery. The forward action of the figure and the foreshortening of the horse are so admirable that you stand ready to return the salute of the handsome Cavalier King, when he shall have ridden a few paces further.

After we had taken a too hasty glance at the superb paintings on the walls, and the exquisite views of the Avon from the windows, we returned to the porter's lodge, where some other antiquities, not quite so well verified, were exhibited. The portress, a withered-looking little woman, took her stand in the centre of the room, and went through her part after this wise:—"This here, gentlemen, is the famous porridge-pot of Guy, Earl of Warwick, as takes forty gallons of rum, forty gallons of brandy, and five hundred pounds of sugar to fill it with punch, and was filled when the present Earl was married, likewise three times and a half when Lord Brooke came of age; and this is Guy's sword" (I seized and shook it, but forget whether it weighed nine or twenty-one pounds), "and these is the Spanish lady's shoes, as was worn by Fair Phyllis, Guy's wife, and this is the horn of the dun cow Guy killed" (it was a whale's rib!); "and these is the boar's tusks he killed and was knighted for; and this is an Indian shield made of buffalo hide, and this is Guy's flesh fork, as he dipped out the pieces of meat with—hrrrr-r-r-r———."

Here she stirred up the porridge-pot, ringing such a peal as shook the lodge, and then, fleshfork in hand, stood waiting for her shilling. Before leaving, we took a shady path, under larches and Lebanon cedars, to the garden-house in which stands the renowned Warwick vase. I have seen no vase comparable to this in the blending of perfect grace with the majesty of colossal proportions. The wreathed vine-stalks at its sides, the full vine-bunches and heads of the laughing fauns are none the less graceful that they are magnified beyond nature.

But I cannot linger in the beautiful groves of Warwick, while further down the Avon, girdled by green meadows and embosomed in heavy-foliaged elms and limes, lies happy Stratford, blessed beyond all other villages in all the lands of the Saxon race. On the following morning I clomb to the top of a country coach and was whirled down Warwick Hill, under the gateway of Leicester's Hospital, across a level tract of garden ground, and up a swelling ridge—the summit of which, as we drove along it for several miles, commanded wide views into the heart of Warwickshire—the most charming agricultural region in all England. To the left, beyond the Avon, I saw in the distance the trees of Charlecote Park, the seat of the Lucy family, and the spire of the church where Sir Thomas, of Shakspeare-punishing memory, lies buried. Through alternate groves of elm, oak, and beech, and fields of smooth, fresh mould or smoother turf, dotted with clumps of hawthorn, we descended to Stratford. The coach drew up at the inn of the Red Horse (well known to Geoffrey Crayon), and I set out to visit the haunts of Shakspeare.

As I knocked at the door of the low, dingy cottage, where even princes must stoop to enter, a curious Englishman, who had just arrived, asked the old woman as she bustled out: "Do you allow anybody to cut a piece off this board?" at the same time laying his hand on a rude counter which projected into the street from the open shop window. "Bless you," said she, "Shakspeare had nothing to do with that. The butcher who had the house long after him, put that up." In answer to my inquiry whether the house had ever been damaged by hunters of relics, she said that the worst instance was that of a party of boarding-school girls, who asked to be left alone in the room where Shakspeare was born, in order that nothing might disturb their impression of the spot. After they left, a large square block was found to be cut from the mantelpiece. I entered, mounted the crazy stairs, and saw the sacred room.

I had a note of introduction from my Warwick friend to the teacher of the Stratford Grammar School, which is the same institution where the boy Shakspeare was taught, and is still held in the same rooms. I found the teacher surrounded by a pack of bright-looking boys, from eight to fourteen years of age. I involuntarily looked in their faces to find something of Shakspeare. It seemed impossible that they should not differ from other children; but assuredly they did not. They had frank, healthy English faces, but the calm, deep, magnificent eyes that looked down every vista of the marvellous human heart, were not there. The teacher enjoined quiet on them, and stepped out to show us the old desk, in a room on the ground floor. This desk is as old as the time of Shakspeare, and is supposed to have belonged to the master of the school. It is a heavy affair of rough wood, such as I have seen in the log schoolhouses of our own country. The top is carved with the initials of the scholars, and they show you a "W. S." which I have not the least doubt was cut by—William Smith.

But, notwithstanding, Shakspeare did once stand beside

this desk, making painful conquests of "the rudiments," and perhaps the worn lid I now lift, was once lifted by a merciless "master," to take out the ruler destined to crack the knuckles of William himself. The thing is absurd! Think of rapping the knuckles of Jupiter! We can only imagine the babyhood of Shakspeare as Lowell has described that of Jove:

> "Who in his soft hand crushed a violet,
> Godlike foremusing the rough thunder's gripe."

The teacher kindly obtained us admission into the house and gardens of Mr. Rice, a surgeon, who lives on the site of a house built by Shakspeare, after his retirement from London. The foundations and a single corner wall remain the same, but the house is modern, the garden is changed, and the great mulberry-tree planted by Shakspeare's hand (under which he took so much pleasure in the sweet summer afternoons), is now only represented by a grandchild—the scion of a scion. Mr. Rice has been offered £100 for the privilege of digging in the cellar of his house, in the hope of finding relics.

My last visit was to Trinity Church, on the Avon. The meadows along the river were flecked with soft light and shadow from passing clouds, and the grave-stones in the church-yard were buried warm and deep in thick turf. The gardens beyond, hid from my view the road to Shottery, where Anne Hathaway's cottage is still standing. I approached the church under a beautiful avenue of limes; the door was open, and a dapper young showman had four Englishmen in tow. I went at once to the chancel, where the bust of Shakspeare looked down upon me from the eastern wall. This bust is supposed to have been copied from a mask taken after death; Chantrey unhesitatingly declared this to be his opinion. One of the eyes seems a little more sunken than the other, and there are additional indications of death about the neck. The face is large, serene, and majestic—not so thin and young as in the Chandos picture, nor with that fine melancholy in the eyes, which suggests to you his Hamlet. In contemplating it, Prospero at once recurred to me. Thus might the sage have looked after he had broken his wand and renounced his art. And Prospero, one of Shakspeare's grandest creations, was at the same time his last.

While I was looking on that wonderful forehead, the showman rolled up a piece of coarse matting spread upon the pavement, and, stepping off to allow it to pass, I found these lines under my feet:

"Good friend, for Jesus' sake forbear
To dig the dust inclosèd here;
Blest be the man that spares these stones,
And curst be he that moves my bones."

This was the simple and touching inscription dictated by himself. None have incurred the poet's malediction by disturbing his rest. There is nothing but dust under the stone now, but that dust was once animated by Shakspeare's soul. Thank God that in this irreverent age there are still some spots too holy to profane, some memories too grand and glorious to neglect! I could have knelt and kissed the dusty slab, had I been alone. The profound sadness with which the spot oppressed me, was one of those emotions against which the world soon hardens us. Too subtle and precious to be called up at will, they surprise us at times with the freshness of a feeling we had thought exhausted.

We walked back to Warwick over the same breezy ridge, and in the evening, with our friends, sauntered over the fields to Guy's Cliff. The family were absent, but a housekeeper, flaunting in purple satin, refused to admit us; so, after watching the sunset build a crimson and golden oriel, at the end of a long chancel of arching elms, facing the west, we descended to the Avon, climbed into Guy's Cave, explored the damp cloisters cut in the cliff, by the brief light of lucifer matches, and closed the evening by a walk to Leamington, which we saw to great advantage by mingled gas and moonlight.

Warwick will always be endeared to me by the recollection of the kind English hospitality I received within its walls. I was indebted to Frederick Enoch, a young Warwickshire poet, whose volume I had read in America, for two of the most pleasant and memorable days of my travels.

Before leaving, we went to see another house, scarcely less interesting than Warwick Castle. Few Americans, I presume, have heard of Charles Redfern, yet there are not many of the English nobility to whom his name and person are not familiar. If any sale of rare and curious furniture, old heirlooms, jewelry, or other objects of *virtu*, takes place anywhere between the Alps and John o'Groat's house, Redfern is sure to be there. Does any Lord want to make a rare and costly present to his betrothed, any Dowager wish to surpass some other Dowager, in the attractions of her boudoir, it is to Redfern he or she applies. Redfern, who began life with scarce a penny, was Mayor of Warwick, and had a house crammed from top to bottom with the rarest, most unique and superb articles. There is barely room to get up and down stairs, and to pass in and out of the rooms. Your nerves are in a tingle from the time you enter till the time you leave. Stumble in the entry, and you will knock down an antique bust; open the door too wide, and you smash a vase of gilded porcelain; lean too far to the right, and you shatter some urns of agate and amethyst; to the left, and you break the dressing-case of Charles I. Here is Cromwell's mother, taken from life; there a Holbein or a Salvator Rosa; here jewels that belonged to Marie Antoinette; there the spoils of twenty palaces. The whole collection must be worth at least $75,000.

Our friend declared that after seeing Redfern's house, we ought to visit its owner, who was then holding Court in the Town Hall. So we entered the Court-room, where a case of some kind was being tried, in the presence of forty or fifty spectators. Our friend led the way; the Mayor, on the bench, made a sign to the attendant policemen. "Make way! make way!" cried the officials. The people fell back; the case was suspended, and we walked up to the bench amid the most solemn silence. Mayor Redfern, however, who has a frank, ruddy face, which no one could help liking, was exceedingly affable, and put us quite at our ease with his first words. We did not suspend justice long; the policemen kept the way clear, and we made our exit in state. As we left Warwick an hour afterwards, the spectators had no chance of being undeceived as to our rank.

VII.

A WALK FROM HEIDELBERG TO NUREMBERG

[OCTOBER, 1851.]

PART I.—THE VALLEY OF THE NECKAR AND KOCHER.

ON leaving Frankfort, I decided to take Nuremberg in my route to Vienna. The usual track, via Stuttgard, Ulm, and Munich, was already familiar to me, from having literally measured the whole of it, step by step. There remained, however, for more than three-fourths of the distance, a new route, part of which I had never seen described, and which the guide-books but barely hinted at —that wild, hilly region, lying between Heidelberg and Nuremberg, and watered by the tributaries of the Neckar and the Main. This, I imagined, would amply repay the fatigue of a foot-journey and the additional time required to explore it. With two companions, I made the necessary outlay for knapsacks, forwarded my heavy luggage by the post to Ratisbon, and left Heidelberg at sunrise, by the little Neckar steamer. The first four miles of our way were familiar to me, and in the fresh, cool beauty of the morning, I amused myself by tracing the road on which I travelled in 1845, weary and foot-sore, and with only two kreutzers in my pocket. Beyond Neckargemünd, the bold, wooded mountains (now touched with their first autumnal tints) embrace the river more closely, leaving but a narrow strip of greenest turf next the water's edge. The steamer bent and shook as she worked her way slowly up the rapids. Three tall cranes flew before us from point to point, at times alighting on the grass to wait our approach.

Opposite Neckarsteinach, which, with its four ruined castles, sits in the centre of a semicircle of hills, we saw the old fortress of Dilsberg, crowning the summit of an isolated peak. This place was formerly used as a sort of State Prison for the fractious students of Heidelberg. The penitentiary system in those days, however, must have been much more lenient than at present; for it is related that when a foreigner of distinction once visited Dilsberg and asked permission to see the fortress, the Superintendent answered that it was impossible to gratify his request, the State prisoners being then on a tour of pleasure through the Odenwald, with the keys in their pockets! The Neckar, beyond this place, presents a succession of charming landscapes. Folded lovingly in the heart of the mountains, its waters now mirror the rich foliage of the beech, ash, and maple, now the dark monotony of the fir, and the open and smiling beauty of the fields of corn and vine.

Though not so rich in historic interest as the Rhine, nor so bold in its features, its landscapes present the same enchanting variety, touched with a mellower grace and a tenderer human sentiment. Here there is little to remind one of battle and bloodshed. The quiet villages, nestled at the entrances of yet virgin valleys winding into the hills, are dropping to pieces only by age, and the sombre coloring of the Middle Ages, which they still wear, does no violence to the peaceful repose of the cultivated slopes behind them.

Among the passengers on our little craft was a stout French gentleman, whose musical voice and exquisite pronunciation of his native tongue attracted me to him. In the course of our conversation he confided to me the fact that he had travelled from Liege to Heidelberg with Lola Montes, and had arrived at the latter place on the previous evening. My Frenchman was extravagant in his admiration of that wonderful woman; he could speak of nothing else. "*Elle est une femme extraordinaire—vraiment extraordinaire!*" And he went on to relate to me several curious incidents whereof he was witness. He then pulled out his cigar-case and showed me, carefully laid away in the safest corner, two delicate white cigaritos which the astonishing Lola had made with her own hands and given to him.

We passed Eberbach, a fine old town, situated in the lap of a beautiful amphitheatre of hills and overlooked by the lofty *Katzenbuckel* (Cat's-Back), the highest peak of the Odenwald. Beyond this feline hump, which is arched in a state of perpetual indignation, the mountains are lower and the wild woods stand back to give place to the vine. At Neckarelz, our little steamer ran her nose against the bank and we jumped ashore on the green turf. Following a road which led up the valley of the Elz, we passed through the stately town of Mosbach and took a by-way leading over the hills to Mökmühl, in the valley of the Jaxt. Just as we gained the height, the sun, which had been obscured all day, broke through the clouds and poured over the landscape such long, golden sunset-lights, that in their splendor the ploughed fields, the acres of turnips and beets, and even the stones piled by the wayside, were glorified and imbued with celestial beauty. But soon the shadows grew longer and cooler, and night came on as we reached a little village called Billigheim, sunk in a deep valley.

We found beds at a country *wirthshaus* called the "Golden Stag," and took our places in the guests' room, between two tables full of Baden soldiery. The landlord, who brought us our supper, entered into conversation, and I asked him, among other things, whether the castle of old Goetz von Berlichingen was not still standing, near Jaxthausen. "Ah, you know him, then!" said he, and his eyes sparkled so suddenly that I was delighted to find so much enthusiasm for the name of Goetz, among his native hills. "Of course I know him," I replied; "who does not?" "Then you are going to visit him," he rejoined; "but is it true that he is about to enter the Austrian service?" I made no answer, quite taken aback at being so misunderstood; but very soon the landlord returned, and lifting his cap, asked; "Perhaps the gentlemen would prefer wine of an old vintage?" Of course nothing could be too good for the friends of Berlichingen. Our supper, which was nearly ready, was delayed in order to be served up in such state as the inn afforded, and the landlady, who had rather neglected us, came up with a smiling face and sat down to talk about our distinguished acquaintance. "And so you are going to visit the Herr von Berlichingen?" "Your husband has misunderstood me," I said; "it is not the young Herr that I know, but the old knight, Goetz—the one with the iron hand."—"Ah," said she, "I never saw *him*." However, we were indebted to the grand old Goetz for a good supper, and fresh sheets on our beds: wherefore we blessed his memory.

At daybreak next morning, we resumed our knapsacks. It had rained in the night, and the by-road was very slippery, but after crossing the border into Würtemburg, we found a better path, leading down through forests of beech and oak into the green meadows of the Jaxt. At Möckmühl, where we stopped for breakfast in a queer old inn, the landlord, finding we were Americans, instantly ran out, and after a few minutes' absence, brought with him a strong, intelligent young man, who was to leave for New York next day, with his wife. He was accompanied by a soldier and an old *bauer*, and all three plied me with questions respecting our country, its laws, and institutions. What most troubled the old bauer, was the news which he had somehow received, that nobody was allowed to sit down in an American inn, but each one must drink his beer standing, and immediately walk out. I gave the young emigrant all the information which I thought would be of service to him. Not only here, but at every place where we stopped, many persons had left or were about leaving. The landlord at Möckmühl said that things were much worse since the Revolution. "There is no more confidence," said he; "those who have money hoard it up, through fear of more troubles. Money is therefore very scarce, and the poor people suffer. Besides this, the laws are harder upon us than they were; everything goes badly, and nobody is satisfied."

After striking the Jaxt, a bold, rapid stream, coursing round abrupt points and through wide amphitheatres of vine-hills, we followed its banks for several miles, passing a succession of emerald meadows, starred with the blossoms of the colchicum. The views up and down the stream were remarkably lovely. In one place we passed along the sides of a natural amphitheatre, half a mile in diameter. The stone terraces built for the vines might have served for regular rows of seats, from which five hundred thousand spectators could look on the tilling-ground of the beautiful plain below. At Jaxthausen, an ancient and picturesque village on the right bank, we halted to see the Castle of Berlichingen, in which Goetz was born, and where he spent most of his days. It is a plain, square structure, still retaining its moat and drawbridge, though the buildings are beginning to show the wear of five centuries. The village magistrate, who was a student at Heidelburg in '45, and knew some friends of mine, gave us admission into the chapel and *rittersaal*. In the former place—a dark, dusty chamber—he showed us a flag borne in the battle of Lutzen, the wooden forks and spoons of some of the Crusaders, the sword, stirrups, bridle, battle-axe, and lastly, the Iron Hand of Goetz von Berlichingen. This remarkable relic has just been restored to the Castle, the family having taken it with them to Ludwigsburg, whither they fled during the Revolution of 1848. It is a steel hand, of beautiful workmanship, with a gauntlet of the same metal reaching nearly to the elbow, by which it was fitted to the stump of the right arm. The fingers opened and closed by springs in the wrist, which are now useless; the thumb is still perfect, and bends its iron joints with the greatest readiness. With the hand is preserved a portrait on glass of its owner—a heavy Saxon face, but firm, true, and resolute enough in its expression for him who was called "The Last of the Knights."

After leaving Jaxthausen, we crossed a high and narrow plateau of grazing land, and descended by a wild glen into the valley of the Kocher. For the rest of the day, our road led up the stream, through the most enchanting scenery. For rich pastoral beauty, I know of no valley in Germany surpassing the Kocherthal. Sunk deep between mountains which are covered with vine-terraces to their very tops, the river has yet no bold and abrupt banks, but wanders with a devious will through long reaches of level meadow-land, green and flowery as in mid-May. Every turn of the hills opened to us a new valley, each with a little town in its centre. These towns, which occur at intervals of half a league, preserve entire the walls and towers of the Middle Ages, and, to all appearance, no new building has been erected in them for centuries. The Kocherthal lies in the heart of a region which is touched by no modern route of travel, and preserves, with scarce a change, a faithful picture of Ancient Germany.

Towards sunset, we climbed the side of a long hill, whence we could overlook the valley for many a league before and behind us. At our feet lay the town of Künzelsau, half embosomed in forests which descended from the rugged heights in its rear. The massive white front of a castle belonging to the Prince of Ehringen, rose above the banks of the Kocher, domineering over the dark, pointed gables and mossy roofs of the old place. A mountain stream, leaping from the forests, passes into the streets, roars through an arch under the Rathhaus at the head of the public square, where two flights of stone steps lead down to its bed, and then disappears under the pavement. We saw but little of the town, for it was dark, and we were somewhat stiff from a walk of twenty-five miles. At the "Bell" (to which inn I would recommend all tourists visiting Künzelsau) we found rest and refreshment.

We left the Kocher at dawn, and crossed a stretch of cold upland to Langenburg, on the upper waters of the Jaxt, where we breakfasted. The Prince of Langenburg, whose castle crowned a bluff, high above the stream, is a brother-in-law of Prince Albert. This was told me by the landlord, who also showed me a stag's head, with a superb pair of seven-branched antlers. The stag, he said, was the last of all those with which the forests around had formerly been filled. Once it was a common sight to see groups of eight or ten on the hills; but that was before the Revolution of 1848. When the noblemen fled to the fortresses, the deer had no keepers, and were all chased and slaughtered. This stag alone was left, and for two seasons the hunters had been on his track. Only two weeks before they had brought him to bay for the first time, and slain him. Some of his meat was in the house, and I might have a steak served up in princely style if I liked.

The rest of the day's journey, for more than twenty miles, lay across a high and somewhat barren table-land, dividing the waters of the Neckar from those of the Main. The land is devoted principally to grazing and the more hardy kinds of grain and vegetables, but here and there the road skirts fine forests of fir. The villages, which are rare, are small, and have an aspect of poverty. We learned, too late to take advantage of the information, that the great Fair of Roth-am-See was being held in the meadows of Musbach, not more than a league out of our way. This Fair, which has been held on the same meadow for several centuries, is probably the most peculiar in Germany, as it is frequented principally by the peasants of Suabia and Franconia, and exhibits many curious usages, which elsewhere have passed away.

Late in the afternoon, after enduring two or three showers, we saw, under a dark and gusty sky, the towers of the venerable City of Rothenburg. It was apparently built on a rise in the plain, but on approaching nearer, we found that its walls overhang the brink of a deep gorge, at the bottom of which flows the Tauber, a tributary of the Main. Even from the little I saw of it on approaching,

I felt sure it would richly repay a longer tramp than we had made. Everything about it is fresh and unhackneyed. The landlord said we were the first native Americans he ever saw, and requested us to write our names in his book, at the top of a new leaf.

VIII.

A WALK FROM HEIDELBERG TO NUREMBERG.

[OCTOBER, 1851.]

Part II.—Rothenburg and Nuremberg.

Rothenburg—the name of which is scarcely mentioned in guide-books—is one of the oldest and most remarkable places in all Germany. Founded before the year 800, and till the twelfth century under the dominion of the Counts of Rothenburg, it was for seven hundred years a Free City of the German Empire, having under its jurisdiction one hundred and forty-three villages, and was only incorporated with Bavaria in the beginning of the present century. As the chief city in the old province of Mittel-Franken (Mid-Franconia), it has always been an important place, and through its present isolated position (being at some distance from any travelled route), still preserves much of its ancient appearance and character. These facts I learned from Herr Wolf, the landlord of the "Golden Stag," as we leaned out of the rear window of his house, on the evening of our arrival. The inn is built against the city wall, and our window looked down into the deep and rugged gorge of the Tauber. The old fortress of Rothenburg formerly crowned the very point of the headland, around which the river winds, almost insulating the city, and making it, except on the side towards the table-land, next to impregnable.

Herr Wolf first directed our attention to an old house on the headland, which was built in the eighth century. He then informed us that when the Rothenburg knights returned from the Crusades, they were struck with the singular resemblance between the position of the city and that of Jerusalem—a resemblance to which many later travellers have testified. The Tauber, far below us, was the Brook Kedron; opposite rose Mount Olivet; further down the gorge was the Pool of Siloam, and directly under us a little chapel marked the site of Gethsemane. Near it stands an old church, now disused, to which, in former times, multitudes made their pilgrimage. The localities were carefully compared with Jerusalem, and a new *Via Dolorosa* was made along the sides of the hill, with twelve shrines representing the twelve places where Christ rested under the weight of the cross. I could still trace the path, though the shrines are gone, and the pilgrims come no longer. The ghostly old church is now called the *Koboldskeller* (Cellar of the Gnomes).

The landlord related to me a curious incident connected with the later history of Rothenburg. "The city," said he, "was once besieged by Tilly and Wallenstein, but the Senate and citizens made such a stubborn resistance that it was taken with great difficulty. Tilly was so incensed against the Burgomasters on this account that he ordered them all to be beheaded and the city razed to the ground. Nevertheless, they received him and Wallenstein in the great hall of the *Rathhaus*, and had the finest old Tauber wine brought up from the cellar. The Emperor's goblet was on the table, and Tilly drank, and Wallenstein drank, till the liquor softened their iron mood. 'You have good liquor,' said Tilly, 'and no doubt good drinkers, too. If any of you will drain this cup (lifting the Emperor's goblet, which held about seven quarts) he and his comrades shall be pardoned, and I will spare the city.' The chief Burgomaster was already on his way to execution, and there was no time to lose. Thereupon, Herr Nusch, one of the Senate, filled the mighty bowl, and lifting it to his mouth with both hands, drank it dry, without stopping to take breath. Tilly was as good as his word. A messenger was at once dispatched to stay the execution; and the street where he met the Chief Burgomaster on his way to death, is called the *Freudengasse* (Street of Joy) to this very day."

We tried the Tauber wine with our supper, and found it light, pure, and pleasant. Still, I should rather let the headsman be summoned than perform Burgomaster Nusch's feat. During the evening, a number of persons called at the inn, apparently to drink beer and smoke, but in reality to see and question the Americans. I did my best, talking in an atmosphere of bad tobacco till near midnight, but my endurance was not equal to their curiosity. The fact of my having seen California was almost incredible to them. "Really," said a fat Rothenburger merchant, "this is the most interesting thing that ever happened to me."

Early next morning, one of the teachers in the City School called to accompany us through the city. The weather was dull and rainy, and we had only time to visit the principal places. We went first to the Rathhaus, passing on our way a quaint building with a richly ornamented gable, in which Sultan Bajazet lodged when on his visit to the German Emperor. The Rathhaus has a stately front in the Italian style, a curious winding staircase, and the dark old hall in which Tilly drank with the Senate. Our conductor led us through many dusty chambers to a steep wooden stairway mounting into the tower. After a long journey, we came into a little hot room, nearly half of which was occupied by a German stove. The only inhabitants were an old man and a clock. The former placed a ladder against the ceiling, opened a trap-door, and disappeared through it. I squeezed through after him, felt the rain dash in my face, and then turned away, faint with the giddy view. The slight parapet around the top of the tower overhung its base, and in the wind and driving mist I seemed swinging, not only over the city, but over the chasm far below it. Beyond this, and across its rugged walls, I looked out on the wide sweep of the plain, bounded on the east by a misty range of hills. Savage and strange as the landscape was, I had scarcely nerve enough to bear the sight.

The Church, which we visited, dates from the fourteenth

century, and its interior is a beautiful specimen of the pure Gothic style. It is in complete preservation, and still contains the altar-piece by Wohlgemuth, master of Albert Durer, and fine carvings in wood by the old sculptor, Herlen. Our conductor was acquainted with a physician of the city, who possesses the famous goblet of which I spoke, and was kind enough to take us to see it. The Doctor's sister received us cordially, and brought the precious relic from its place of safety. It is an immense glass tankard, about fourteen inches high and six in diameter, with paintings of the Emperor, Kings, Electors, and Bishops of Germany. I asked the lady what was the effect of such a draught on Burgomaster Nusch, from whom she was descended. She said that, according to the account preserved in the family, he slept two days and two nights, after which he awoke in good health, and lived seven years afterwards to enjoy the gratitude of his fellow Burgomasters.

As the rain continued, we hired a carriage for 5 florins (about $2), to convey us to Anspach, a distance of twenty-five miles. The road lies through a barren upland, crossed by two or three ranges of hills, covered with forests of fir. The driver informed me that the land was costly in spite of its indifferent quality, and that this year nearly every crop was bad. Wheat is already double the usual price, and the poor people begin to feel the effects of it. Here, too, many were leaving for America, and he (the driver) would go if he had money.

Anspach, formerly the residence of the Margraves of Anspach and Baireuth, is a dull town of about ten thousand inhabitants, but has a magnificent *Residenz* and gardens. While our carriage was getting ready for Nuremberg, we took a walk in the superb avenues of lindens, now gleaming golden in their autumnal leaves. This park has a singular and melancholy interest from the fact that Caspar Hauser was stabbed here on the 14th of December, 1833. In a lonely corner, hidden by thickets which always keep the place in shadow, we found the monument, a plain shaft with these words, and no more: "*Hic occultis occulto occisus est.*" The name—which you always pronounce in an undertone in Germany—is not mentioned. And yet, but for the deed here commemorated, Caspar Hauser (according to the secret popular belief) would have been Grand Duke of Baden at this day. We may well shrink from lifting the veil which covers the mystery of his life, when it conceals a strange and terrible tale of crime. A few paces distant is the monument of the poet Uz, a pillar crowned with his bust. When a child, I read an account of the murder of Caspar Hauser, at the time of its occurrence, and while standing on the spot, every word of the story came back to my memory.

"If one the German land would know,
And love with all his heart,
Then let him go to Nuremberg,
The home of noblest art."

So says an old song by Schenkendorf, and so say I, charmed with the little I have seen of Nuremberg. No one knows Germany, who has not visited this place. In other cities you see the ruins of German Art and German life in the Middle Ages; here you see that Art still pre served, that life still vital in all its quaint forms and expressions. You are not reminded of the Past, for you live in it. It requires as great an effort to recall the Present, as it does elsewhere to forget it. And the age into which you step, on leaving the Nineteenth Century which has steamed you hither (for the railroad brushes the walls, but dares not pierce them), is not stern or harsh in its aspect. Its ruder outlines are softened, its shadowy places glorified, by the Divine light of Art. With its crooked streets, grotesque, pointed gables, and peaked roofs, wandering into a bewildering variety of outlines, Nuremberg still ministers to that passion whereof it was once the chosen seat—the love of the Beautiful. Painting, Poetry, and Sculpture once dwelt here, and their sign-manual is Beauty—Beauty in one of her wayward moods, it is true, but none the less dear to those who love her under all her forms.

The only objects in Nuremberg that appear old are the tombstones. Albert Durer's house, on the hill, under the walls of the Castle, keeps its rich, red coloring, its steep gable mounting up into a picturesque, overhanging balcony, and its windows of stained glass, as if he were still within, ready to welcome his friend Willibald. As you walk the streets, you think of him as a living man; but his slab in the church-yard of St. John is covered with the moss of three hundred years. "'Tis Death is dead, not he." Over the door of Hans Sachs's dwelling hangs his portrait, with the flowing white beard so well befitting the *meister-sänger*;

and if you go there at mid-day, you may partake of a dish of *bratwurst* which would have furnished Hans with inspiration for at least six odes. In the court-yard of the Castle there is a mighty linden-tree, green and full of lusty leaves, which the frost seems to spare. Seven hundred years ago that tree was planted there by the hand of the Empress Kunigunde. In the church of St. Lorenz, they show you the renowned pyx by Adam Kraft and his two apprentices; you would think the dust of their chiselling fresh upon it. Contemplate its glorious workmanship; and if your eyes do not fill with tears—spontaneous tribute to that Beauty which is a perpetual joy, and of pity for its creator, who perished in obscurity and want—its stony leaves and blossoms are softer than your nature.

The situation of the city is peculiar, and in the highest degree picturesque. It is divided by the river Regnitz into two nearly equal parts, called, from the two grand churches they contain, the Lorenz side, and the Sebald side. The river washes the walls of the houses, and is spanned by a number of bridges, one of which, from its form, is named the Rialto. There is also a Bridge of Sighs, leading to the prison. A number of mill-wheels turn in the stream, which makes its entrance into and exit from the city through arches in the walls. The Sebald side ascends towards the north, and you climb steep streets lined with the houses of the old patricians, to the Castle, which is built on a massive sandstone crag, overhanging the city. The battlements command wide and beautiful views on every side. On the morning of my visit, the sky was clear and soft, and I could see the broad meadows stretching away till they met the blue Franconian mountains in the north-east. Below me yawned the great moat, fifty feet deep and one hundred feet wide, still surrounding the city walls. From the opposite battlement, the city sloped to the river, but rose again from the other side—a mass of quaint notched gables, sharp roofs, broken with windows of every fashion, turrets and Gothic pinnacles, shooting up so thickly that the spires of St. Sebald and St. Lorenz seemed but older plants which had been allowed to run to seed. They blossomed naturally from a bed of such architecture. The four round towers of Albert Durer, in their models the perfection of simple strength, mark the four points of the compass. Beyond them, and over the wall and moat, and scattered buildings outside, spreads the fruitful plain of Franconia.

I will not attempt to describe in detail the sights of Nuremberg. My time was too short to do them justice, yet long enough to receive some impressions which I shall never forget. Of course I visited the Rathhaus, and the Picture Gallery, where I was most struck with Albert Durer's "St. Peter;" and Rauch's bronze statue of Durer himself; and the Beautiful Fountain, a specimen of the purest Gothic, which furnished the idea for Sir Walter Scott's Monument in Edinburgh; and the Little Goose-herd, a cunning fountain, representing a mannikin with two geese under his arm; and the Castle Well, cut three hundred feet through the solid rock; and the Gymnasium founded by Melancthon, with many other noteworthy buildings and monuments. The church-yard of St. John, outside of the city walls, is one of the most remarkable cemeteries in Europe. The graves are ranged in rows, and each is covered with a ponderous slab of sandstone, raised on a foundation, and regularly numbered from 1 to about 2,000. They nearly all date beyond the last century, and some are so old as to have lost every trace of their original inscriptions. The moss has eaten into their crevices, the sharp corners are rounded and broken, and they lie as shapeless as so many boulders left by the Deluge. Among them I found the resting-place of Dürer, which has been carefully restored; of Hans Sachs, with a poor specimen of his poetry upon it; of Peter Vischer, whereon a crown of oak-leaves, cast there many days before, was rotting in the rain; of Veit Stoss; and lastly, of the good Willibald Pirkheimer, ever to be remembered as Dürer's friend. A few flowers were growing rankly about the corners of the stones, but so desolated and ruined is the aspect of the place, that even without the prohibition posted up at the entrance of the gate, no one would venture to pluck them.

The last visit I made was to the Church of St. Lorenz—the crown of all that Nuremberg has to show. It is one of the largest Gothic churches in Europe, and more impressive than any I have seen, except St. Ouen in Rouen, and the unfinished cathedral of Cologne. The nave is 320 feet in length and 86 in height, and finished in a style so rich and harmonious as to produce the finest possible effect. Unlike the minsters of Ulm and Strasbourg, whose imposing exteriors promise too much, St. Lorenz startles you with a grandeur you had not anticipated, and you measure with breathless delight the perfect symmetry of the columns, the single arch spanning the nave, and the beautiful intricacy of the laced and intertwined ribs of the chancel-roof. You follow the guide from pillar to pillar, halting to contemplate the works of Wohlgemuth, of Dürer, of Vischer, Veit Stoss, and the other cunning artists of that day; but when you reach the pyx (house containing the sacramental vessels) of Adam Kraft, there you will stop, and thenceforth the church will contain little else worth your seeing.

This pyx stands beside one of the pillars of the chancel, and spires upwards like a fountain, under the arch, to the height of more than sixty feet. It is of pure white sandstone, and of the most rare and wonderful workmanship. The house containing the vessels is imbedded in an arbor of vines, forming leafy grottoes, with niches in which stand statues of the Apostles. The Gothic pinnacles which shoot up through this canopy of foliage bud into leafy ornaments at their tops, and bend over and wave downwards like vines swinging in the air. Upwards, still diminishing, rises the airy tracery of the spire, with spray-like needles leaping from every angle, till at the summit, where you expect the crowning lightness of the cross, behold! the frail stem of stone curves like a flower-stalk, and hangs in the air a last tendril over the wondrous arbor out of which it grew. Grand Adam Kraft! glorious old master! God grant that this beautiful creation sometimes consoled the bitterness of thy destitute and neglected old age, and that the sacrament of that Beauty, of which this was but a faint symbol, hallowed thy dying hour!

Our conductor through the church was a girl of fifteen, whose flushed cheek and frequent cough gave a painful effect to the sad, slow monotone of her voice, while telling us of Adam Kraft, as we stood by his pyx: how he, with his apprentice and journeyman, made it in five years, and received therefor only 770 florins (not $300); how the people had no faith in his work, but believed he had a secret method of softening the stone and casting it into moulds; and how it was examined from top to bottom and proved to be really chiselled. She pointed to the pedestal, in confirmation of the story, and there, sculptured with their own hands, the figures of the master and his two associates, kneeling, upbore the weight of the structure. A quaint fancy, but how significant! Adam's eyes are closed, as if with the exertion, and his face expresses that serene patience which only comes from the enthusiasm of the Artist. Here the apprentice and the journeyman, who wrought with an equally devoted purpose, have their share of the glory. The master of that day was too pure and single-minded in his devotion to Art, not to be just. There was then no monopoly of Fame in a great name. What would Kraft and Dürer have thought of the romances of Dumas and the battle-pieces of Vernet?

IX.

PANORAMA OF THE UPPER DANUBE.

[OCTOBER, 1851.]

While plodding along the highway from Vienna to Linz, in the summer of 1845, I frequently saw the Danube gleaming to the northward in the lap of its magnificent valley. I crossed it afterwards at Ulm, where it comes fresh from its fountains, and parted from it with my love for its name and associations strengthened by the slight acquaintance. But within the last five days I have sailed four hundred miles on its breast, and felt its might and majesty as never before. It has completely displaced the Rhine, which I had held to be without peer among European rivers; and as this preference is contrary to the general opinion (probably because one person visits the Danube where ten visit the Rhine), a rapid sketch of the scenery from Donauwörth to Vienna may help to justify it.

The Danube is a lordly river. It does not drip from the edges of the glaciers, like the Rhine, the Rhone, and the Po, but gushes at once to life, a lusty stream, in the garden of a Prince. Nor does the flood, in its waxing course, sully the nobility of its birth. One race and one language alone cannot measure its extent, but from its cradle in the Black Forest till it mingles with the Euxine, it draws its waters from Suabia and Bavaria and Franconia; from the meadows of the Engaddin, in the Upper Alps; from the hills of Bohemia; from Tyrol and Illyria; from Hungary and Servia; and from the lands of the Turk and the Wallachian. Its youth is crystal-clear, rapid, and bears the aroma of the Northern fir; its old age stagnates in the lazy languor of the Orient. It is like one of those Vikings of the eighth century, who went with the frost and fire of Iceland to wallow in the luxury of the Byzantine Court. It hears the hymns of Luther sung in the places where Luther dwelt, and it hears the muezzin call from his minaret the name of Mohammed.

But its historical interest!—What grander associations than Attila and his Huns, or the Dacians before them! And is not Belgrave's stirring name, and John Sobieski's victory before the walls of Vienna, something to remember? Cœur de Lion's prison looked on the river; and its waves are still lighted with the splendor of the Niebelungen Lay. What has the Rhine to surpass these? It has much, to be sure: a tower on every headland, and a legend to every tower. It sings a legend throughout the length of its Highlands—a powerful melody, like that of the Lorely, but no grander strain. The Rhine is legendary; the

Danube is epic. Its associations have a broad and majestic character; they are connected with historical movements more vast, and lead us back to more remote and obscure periods. The stream itself, as it flows with a full current, now losing its way on interminable plains, now plunging into mountain defiles, where there seems no hope of outlet, has something vague and undefinable in its expression. The ruins which crown its banks are grim and silent; they have lost their histories, or refuse to give them up. The wild woods of the Middle Ages still keep possession of valleys that come down from the mysterious Böhmer-Wald, and as you look up their silent depths, home of the stag and wild bear, you think of the wehr-wolves with a slight shiver in your blood.

But I am giving you the effect of the Danube, before I have shown you its landscapes. Take, with me, an affectionate leave of Nuremberg. It rains dismally, and the high and barren watershed of Middle Europe, over which the Railroad passes, is fast becoming a quagmire. The plains are drowned with six months of incessant moisture, and the low hills of ragged fir-trees seem slowly sinking into them. We pass numerous dull villages and two or three tolerable towns, and after more than fifty miles of such travel, strike an affluent of the Danube, and descend with it through the hills to Donauwörth. This town is of no note, except as being the head of navigation on the river. We did not even enter it, but took lodgings in "The Crab," which stands by the water-side, and which gave us, without lifting our heads from the pillows, a night-view of the plain towards Ulm, and the swollen flood flashing in fitful gleams of moonlight. In the morning we took the steamer for Regensburg.

The arrowy river swung our bow around with its course, and carried us rapidly onwards, through vast, marshy flats, thickly set with willows, where, at times, we were in as complete a solitude as the untenanted banks of our Western rivers exhibit. The current is exceedingly tortuous, and we frequently faced all points of the compass, in going a single league. On the northern side, a chain of rolling hills, the first terraces of the central table-land, sometimes approach the river, but do not add to the amenity of its landscapes. They are covered with a scattering growth of beech and oak, cleared away in places for grain, or planted with lean-looking vineyards; still, there is something fine and bold in their outlines, especially when, on turning a corner, we see the next headland before us, stretching far into the blue distance. On our right appears the *Donau-moos*, a morass which fills all our southern horizon. It is drained by 132 canals, but the river is now so high that the current in these sluices flows backwards and fills them.

We pass Ingolstadt, a town surrounded by a massive wall, a deep moat, and outworks of most ponderous character—all as new and shining as the helmets of the Bavarian soldiers on guard. Why this fortification is wanted now, and why it should be built in the centre of a plain, where it commands nothing and protects nothing, is about as clear to me as to the aforesaid soldiers. But before I have fairly settled the question, we are among the mountains again. Here they are, steep and abrupt; woods of autumnal brown and purple, relieved by the dark-green of the fir, wave from their precipices of white limestone rock, and soften their outlines against the clear sky. A large white Benedictine cloister, under the shadow of the cliffs, now comes into view: but what is this? The Danube is at an end, and we are drifting with the furious flood full against a crag two hundred feet in height. A rough image of the Madonna looks out from a niche scooped in the rock, and the crew take off their hats as we shoot past. Lo! a miracle has been wrought; the terrible wall has been cleft at right angles, and our boat turns so sharply into the narrow strait, that the giddy summit overhangs our deck.

Crash! goes a report like the peal of a thousand cannon, but it is only one, which the captain has ordered to be fired for our astonishment. Thc sound rolls down the chasm, striking heavily on the perpendicular walls, as if the Indian's Bird of Thunder were caught here, and flapping his wings in a vain effort to escape. He reaches the top at last, and sullenly soars off into silence. Still downwards we speed with the foaming river, almost grazing the sides of our passage-way as we clear its sudden windings, till at length a wider reach in the mountains opens before us, and we take a long breath of relief. All through these cañons of the Danube, the rocks are pierced with bolts near the water, from which hang iron rings, used by the boatmen in their slow and difficult ascent.

The great plain of Bavaria, extending beyond Munich to the Alps, was evidently at one time the bed of an inland sea, whose waters at last tore this passage through the mountains. The rocks exhibit the same appearances as those of the Rhine at Bingen, and the Potomac at Harper's

Ferry, but the pass is much more narrow, rugged, and peculiar than either. Beyond it, the mountains give the Danube room, and his vexed current takes a broader sweep, and rolls with a more majestic motion. As we approach Ratisbon (Regensburg) they disappear from the southern bank, and leave the city seated on the plain.

At Ratisbon, which we reached at four o'clock in the afternoon, we remained the following day, in order to visit the Walhalla. This celebrated edifice, built by the Ex-King Louis of Bavaria, stands on the summit of a hill overlooking the river, about six miles to the eastward of the city. The morning brought with it a dense fog, through which we felt our way to the village of Donaustauf. The Walhalla was not visible, but some peasant women showed us a footpath leading up to a church on the hill. There were shrines on the way, and we were obliged to step carefully past several persons who were ascending on their knees. Behind the church, the path plunged into a wood of young oaks, redolent of moist autumnal fragrance. After half a mile of gradual ascent, we issued from the trees upon a space of level ground, on which stood the Walhalla, looming grandly through the up-rolling mists. I deem it fortunate that my first view was from the summit of the hill, on a level with the base of the building. Seen thus, it will be accepted, without hesitation, as among the most admirable architectural works of modern times. It is closely modelled after the Parthenon, and therefore has not the merit of originality—at least, externally. Its material is white Alpine marble, brought from the Untersberg, where, according to the old legend, Charlemagne sits with his Paladins awaiting the deliverance of Germany. Schwanthaler's colossal group of the victory of Herman over the Romans, fills the pediment of the northern front, which overlooks a lovely green valley. An allegorical group by the same artist, from designs by Rauch, occupies the southern front, which is raised on vast foundation terraces of masonry, 120 feet in height.

The Walhalla stands in the centre of an arc of hills washed by the Danube, and looks beyond his waters and over the plains of Bavaria, to the snowy lines of the Noric Alps. Its position is finely chosen, but the effect of the superb building is painfully marred by the clumsy mass of foundation work on which it stands. The introduction of oblique lines of stairway, which as you descend rise beyond the terraces against which they are built, disturbs the imposing contrast of the simple uprights and horizontals. The temple itself is dwarfed, and the eye is drawn away from its airy grace and symmetry to rest on the blank, glaring, dead-walls which uphold it. The interior is finished in the chromatic style so lavishly employed by the ancient Greeks, and dazzles one with its gilded roof, its mosaic floor, and its walls of precious marbles. It forms a single hall, between two and three hundred feet in length and nearly sixty in height. The walls are broken by two heavy pilaster-like projections, on each side, upon which stand statues of the Northern Valkyrie or Fates, holding on their heads the bases of the arches supporting the iron roof. The general impression produced is one of great richness and splendor, with a dash of barbaric extravagance. The fourteen statues of the Fates, upholding the roof, are painted and gilded, and remind one rather too strongly of Dresden china.

Around the sides of the hall the busts of ninety-eight distinguished Germans, executed in Carrara marble, are placed on separate brackets, while a frieze of the same material above them, typifies the history of German civilization.

The fine harmony of the coloring, the soft gleam of the polished marbles, and the imposing dimensions of the hall, give it an effect which at first bewilders the judgment, but cannot keep it captive. The Parthenon is not adapted to a German Walhalla. The pure and perfect simplicity of Grecian Art does not represent the exuberant German mind, so rich in its fancy, so subtle in its imagination, so profound and far-thoughted, yet always serious in its expression, always removed from the grace, the poise, the wondrous balance and symmetry of the Greek Apollo. Nor are the natural adjuncts of the temple more fitting. The sombre fir, or even the oak, is too stern to grow in its shadow; the clouds and storms, the pale sky of the North, are too cold to be its background. It should stand high on a headland, above a sparkling sea, with the blue of a summer noon behind it; where the spiry cypress might mock its shafts, and the palm lift beside them a more graceful capital.

As a great work, the Walhalla is a failure; as a great copy, we shall accept it, and accord all honor to the patriotic spirit which consecrates it. The busts are generally well executed, but the six statues of Rauch—different embodiments of Victory, or Triumph—belong to the finest specimens of modern art. Half the busts are those of Dukes or Electors, whose names are not familiarly known outside of Germany; poets, artists, scholars, and composers make up the other half. Schiller is there (and *his* head would not be out of place in the true Parthenon) between Haydn and the dry, contracted, almost idiotic little head of Kant. Goethe, Herder, Lessing, and even Bürger, have a place. But I looked with the most lively satisfaction at the head of Luther, which was at first omitted (Bavaria being Catholic), but which the universal outcry of all Germany forced the King to restore. And not only Luther, but that fiery reformer, Ulrich von Hutten, whose motto, "*Ich hab's gewagt*" (I have dared it), accompanies his bust. Melancthon is still wanting, though Erasmus finds a place.

Ratisbon is a quiet city, with a beautiful old Cathedral and pleasant promenades. I had no curiosity to see the Chamber of Torture under the Rathhaus, in spite of the solicitations of four valets-de-place, who wished to earn a fee by accompanying me. With German caution the porter roused us at four o'clock in order that we might leave by half-past five. We wandered to the boat shivering in the mist, and sat there four mortal hours before the Captain ventured to start. The hills were shrouded, and the Walhalla was invisible as we passed, but soon the Danube wandered out upon a plain, which his current, brimmed to the top of the banks, threatened to overflow. Towards noon the spires of Straubing were close at hand, but so remarkably crooked is the river, that we chasséed backwards and forwards before the town for nearly an hour, before dancing up to it. As we passed under the bridge I thought of the beautiful Agnes Bernauer, the wife of Duke Albert of Bavaria, who was thrown from it into the Danube during her husband's absence, by his savage father's order.

Now the blue mountains of the *Böhmer-Wald* or Bohemian Forest, rose on our left, but the high, wooded summits leaned to each other and shut us out from a look into their wild recesses. In one place only they touched the river. Elsewhere a chain of lower but not less picturesque hills kept them in the rear. Soon after leaving the plain we reach Passau, the last Bavarian town, built on a bold height at the junction of the Danube and the Inn. Here we touch for a few minutes, and then start for Linz, as the passengers suppose, although it is late in the afternoon. The scenery is strikingly bold and beautiful. The only dwellings we see are the wooden cottages of the woodmen and the herdsmen: here and there a slope of pasture-ground breaks the monotony of the unpruned forests. A rosy sunset colors the distant peaks of the Böhmer-Wald, and the gorges through which we pass are growing dark with twilight. A rude village appears, in a nook of the mountains ; the steamer's gun is fired, and we swing around to the bank and make fast, for the Captain is afraid of whirlpools and other terrors.

As we step ashore we are met by beggars and Austrian Custom-House officers. While the latter are politely explaining to us that we must leave all our baggage on board, the church-bell chimes vespers. Officers and beggars take off their hats and stand silent, repeating their prayers. There is a *wirthshaus* on the bank with a landlady as thick as a barrel, who gives us each a double bed (the upper bed much larger than the under) and half a pint of water, to wash our faces in the morning. Our room secured, we go down to the guests' room and order supper. The village magistrate and two priests and a number of Austrian soldiers, take their places at our table, and drink large draughts of "nasty porter," as I heard it called by a cockney in Nuremberg. The smoke soon becomes so thick, and the tobacco is of such rank Austrian growth, that we retire to our smothering beds. The steamer's cannon rouses us at four o'clock; we are off at daylight, sweeping down between the cold, dark mountains, and in spite of two hours' delay on account of fogs, succeed in reaching Linz by ten o'clock.

Nothing could be more gentle and agreeable than the Custom-House and passport examination, soothed as it was by the extreme politeness of the officials. Austria received us as tenderly as a mother would receive her returning children; and so far as concerns her people, we profited by the change. The Southern warmth, the grace and suavity of the Austrian character, impress one very pleasantly after leaving the muddy-headed Bavarians. We were obliged to remain till next morning in Linz; but the soft, warm air, the gay Italian aspect of the streets, and the beauty of the surrounding scenery reconciled us to the delay. Besides, from the parapet of the Schlossberg, did we not hail the airy ranges of the Noric and Styrian Alps?

At last, however, after losing three hours in waiting for the fog to disperse, we are off for Vienna. The sun comes out bright and warm over the thousand islands in the channel of the Danube. We are a motley crew: three Russians; an American, fresh from Moscow, and on his way to Poland; a Scotch physician; an Austrian, whom I take to be a secret spy, because he has a sneaking face, and talks in whispers about Hungary; and a Carmelite monk, who is the very picture of jolly humor and good living. The brisk air and rapid motion give us an appetite, and we are not sorry that dinner is ready at twelve o'clock. Before we have finished three of the ten courses, we notice through the cabin windows that we have passed the rich meadow-lands and are among the forests and hills. The monk, whose capacious girdle is getting tight, is anxious we should not lose the best points of the scenery; and, as we shoot under the Castle of Grein, says hastily: "I think the gentlemen ought now to go on deck." We rush up stairs bareheaded, the monk rolls after us, and the rest of the company follow. The Danube is shut in among the hills; a precipitous crag, crowned with a ruin, rises in front, and the monk says we shall pass behind it, but we do not believe him. Nevertheless, the current carries us onward like the wind and we shoot into a gateway scarcely wider than our boat, down a roaring rapid. The crag and the ruin are now behind us, but there are two others in front. Between them the river turns sharply round a ledge of rocks, and boils in a foaming whirlpool. This is the celebrated *Wirbel*, the Charybdis of the Upper Danube. Our strong steamer walks straight through its centre, but slightly shaken by the agitated waters, and, satisfied that we have done justice to the exciting passage, we go below to finish our dinner.

For nearly fifty miles further, our course lies among the mountains. From the summit to the water's edge they are mantled with forests, broken here and there by cliffs and jagged walls of granite. Somtimes a little village finds place at the entrance of a side-valley, or a grim ruin is held against the sky by a peak which challenges access, but the general aspect is wild, sublime, and lonely. Here, again, I found the

Danube grander than the Rhine. The mountains are infinitely finer in their native clothing of forests, rough though it be, than in their Rhenish veneering of vine-terraces, through which their crags of sterile rock show with the effect of a garment out at the knees and elbows. The hills of the Danube wear their forests of pine and larch and oak as Attila might have worn his lion's hide.

As we pass the magnificent monastery of Mölk, our Carmelite talks juicily of the glorious wines in the cellar, and the good dinners which the Benedictines enjoy within its walls. He tells of the hills in Hungary and Moravia where the best wines grow, and his eyes are still sparkling with the remembrance of them as we reach the shattered crags of Dürrenstein. We look up at the crumbling tower in which Richard of the Lion Heart was imprisoned, and wonder on which side of it stood Blondel, when he sang the lay which discovered the royal captive. We feel our blood grow warm and our hearts beat faster, as we think of that story of faithful love. But the boat speeds on and brings us to Stein, where we leave the mountains, and leave, alas! our ruddy Carmelite. The best of wines be poured out to him, wherever he goes!

The sun is just sinking into a bed of molten crimson and yellow and amber-green, as we reach Tuln. Vienna is but an hour distant, and the twilight is long and clear, but the captain says stop, and we stop, heartily wishing ourselves in an American boat, with an American captain, "bound to put her through by daylight." We are indebted to the influence of a young officer, in getting a bad supper from an uncivil landlady on shore, and go back to the boat, where

we lie all night in the cabin with aching bones, and a child's wooden stool for a pillow.

In the morning an hour's steaming brought us to Nussdorf, a village about three miles from the city, where we were landed and left to shift for ourselves. Four of us hired a fiacre and started with our baggage. A certificate given us at Linz saved us the trouble of examination, and we were not asked for our passports.

X.

THE ROAD FROM VIENNA TO TRIESTE.

[1851 AND 1857.]

STARTING from Vienna alone, on my way to the Orient, I took my place in the afternoon train for Gloggnitz, at the foot of the Semmering Alp. The level basin of the Danube, at first barren, but afterwards covered with vineyards and maize-fields, extended wide on the left; on the right, veiled in clouds, ran the ranges of the Styrian Alps. After passing Neustadt, forty miles from Vienna, one of my neighbors directed my attention to a spire which marked the position of a village about two miles to the eastward. That village, he said, was in Hungary, and so also was a bold wooded ridge—one of the last spurs of the great Alpine chain—which rose behind it. This ridge gradually approached us on the left, and the plain by degrees narrowed into a valley. The beautiful vineyards which covered the slopes of the mountains now gave place to woods of fir and cliffs of naked rock, and finally, as twilight came on to deepen their sombre hue, we reached Gloggnitz, at that time the terminus of the railroad.

[The road was completed throughout from Vienna to Trieste in 1857, and the transit from the Danube to the Adriatic, a distance of about 350 miles, is now made by the express trains in sixteen hours and a half. Many years have been employed in surmounting the two chief difficulties on this route—the passage of the Semmering Alp and of the high Carinthian table-land, both of which are great triumphs of engineering. The first is a bold spur of the Styrian Alps, dividing the waters of the Danube from those of the Drave. After ascending a long, sloping valley, the road boldly takes the mountain side, which it climbs by a series of zigzag grades, the heaviest of which are upwards of 140 feet to the mile. Near the summit, 3,000 feet above the sea, the road skirts a terrific gorge, through galleries hewn in the solid rock, and by bridges thrown across the lateral ravines. The descent on the southern side into the valley of the Mur, a tributary of the Drave, is much more gradual. The distance from Gloggnitz to Mürzzuschlag, by the road, is thirty miles, but less than fifteen in a straight line. The cost of the work is said to have been upwards of $10,000,000. The passage of the Semmering, however, is not a more remarkable undertaking than that of the Alleghanies, on the Baltimore and Ohio Road, or some of the sections on the Pennsylvania Central, and New York and Erie lines. The heaviest grades on these roads are, I believe, respectively

120, 103, and 98 feet to the mile, though there are a few rods on the Baltimore and Ohio which reach 140 feet. The engineers who built the track over the Semmering first visited the latter road, to which belongs the credit of inaugurating mountain grades.]

At Gloggnitz I was obliged to wait until midnight for the stage over the mountains to Mürzzuschlag. A handsome Slave, whose acquaintance I had made in the car, accompanied me to a café, where he took supper with me, before going to his home, a few miles further. In the warmth of his heart, he wanted me to go with him, and spend the night under his roof. He had the most amiable wife in the world, and a darling little boy, the very pearl of all infants, only four months old. Before he was married, he was very fond of dogs, but now they disgusted him: one child was worth a million dogs. And then followed the whole history of his love and courtship, so naive, so simple, and told with such delightful frankness, that my heart overflowed towards the good Slave. At parting, I gave him my hand and a silent blessing on his honest and confiding nature.

When one is obliged to wait at night in the barren room of an inn, the hours are dreary enough. They had an end, however, and I crept into a small stage, with three Germans, who instantly insisted on closing all the windows and lighting their pipes. I like the Germans most heartily in many respects, and I love their land next to my own. I can sleep under their big feather-beds, and eat their heterogeneous dinners, and bear with patience their everlasting delays: but I cannot tolerate their inveterate dread of fresh water and fresh air. Except Vienna, the German cities are shockingly deficient in baths, and even in the best hotels, a small decanter of water is thought to be amply sufficient for one's ablutions. My companions in the stage had each an overcoat and cloak, and yet they persisted in keeping the windows fast during four suffocating hours. Of the Pass of the Semmering I can only say that we went very slowly up-hill one-half of the way, and very fast down-hill the other half. I rubbed off the moist coating of the panes, and looked out occasionally. The moon gave a straggling light, and I saw some black, ghostly mountains near at hand, but not with sufficient distinctness to separate their forms.

We left Mürzzuschlag at dawn, and sped down the valley of the Mur, the right arm of the Drave. We were now deep in the rough, picturesque old province of Steyermark. In the early dusk the blue and red flames flickered from the chimneys of furnaces in the valleys, but as it grew light, quaint cottages of home-like aspect appeared on the slopes, and the black woods of fir higher up were broken with brilliant patches of pasture-ground. Following the windings of the river, we enjoyed a rapid diorama of very rugged mountain scenery, which was only dark and melancholy because the clouds lowered heavily upon it. The mountains on either hand were from three to five thousand feet in height, and so sterile and abrupt as to defy all attempt at cultivation. In some places they terminated in sheer walls of rock, dropping almost from the summit to the base. The valley, which widened to a plain as we approached Gratz, is well cultivated; grain and vegetables seem to thrive, but the vine is poor and scanty. Gratz is finely situated, on level ground, at the foot of an isolated hill which is crowned by a citadel. The place is much visited in summer, on account of the excursions which may be made from it into the wilder parts of the Styrian Alps.

About noon we crossed the Drave, already a broad and full stream. The road then left the mountains, and ascended to a tract of barren and rolling upland, with frequent swamps and thickets of rank growth. Part of it was adapted for grazing, but cultivation was scarce, and the inhabitants few and scattered. After some twenty miles of this travel, the mountains again began to appear, and we descended to a wild stream of transparent emerald color, which was our guide to the Save, in whose milky blue waters its own crystal was lost. Among our passengers were a company of peasants from Krain, or Karniola, returning home from their work on the Semmering. They were dressed in coarse white woollen garments of their own manufacture, and spoke a Slavonic dialect which no one could understand. They had low, narrow foreheads, high cheek bones, black and snaky eyes, and sharp, hanging moustaches, while their complexion was a reddish olive. The expression of their faces was even more villanous than that of the Croat regiments in the Austrian service.

The last fifty miles of our road followed the course of the Save, enchanting us with a succession of the grandest mountain landscapes. For the whole distance, the gorge through which the river passes is little less than a cañon, in the most Californian sense of the term. The water roared at our feet in a continuous rapid. The road has been cut through the rock or built up with much labor from below, while, owing to the windings of the river, its curves are abrupt and frequent. The barren peaks, so closely ranged together that scarcely a side glen finds its way to the river, towered thousands of feet above us, and the only road at their base, besides our own, was a little path that hung like a thread on the opposite side, now notched carefully along the edge of a precipice, now dropping to the water, and now climbing wearily around some impassable corner. At first, the mountains were covered nearly to their summits with forests which the frost had stained with a deep, dark crimson hue, changing to purple as they stood more distant. The effect of this royal drapery—these broad and grand tints, contrasted with the dusky blue of the water and the light grey of the granite rock—was indescribably gorgeous. But the mountains, as we advanced, grew more barren, broken, and lofty. Cloudy fleeces were piled high on their summits, and the invisible Oreads spun them into glittering threads which slipped through their fingers and dropped from cliff to cliff into the lap of the glen. In one place I found a natural copy of the Fountain of Vaucluse. A large stream burst up full and strong from the foot of a precipice, and after driving a rude mill that stood below, tumbled foaming into the Save.

Towards sunset, we issued from the mountains, and in a few minutes afterwards reached Laybach, then the termination of the road. This town, the capital of Carinthia, is a meagre-looking place, and contains nothing of interest Most of the passengers for Trieste took the diligence on arriving and travelled all night, but I preferred remaining till morning, in order to make the journey by daylight. At the principal hotel I found an English Colonel, on his way to India, who had made the same choice. We went to bed early, and were called up before daylight to take our coffee and make ready to start. The Colonel was very anxious to have a comfortable place, with not too many fellow-passengers, and gave the *kellner* no rest on the subject. Finally, as the diligence was ready to start, the latter came up, saying that he had found the very place—a sort of coupé, in which there was no one but a lady. "Is she young and handsome, and does she speak French?" asked the Colonel, who was innocent of German. "She is very young and beautiful, and of course she speaks French," replied the kellner. Hereupon the officer took up his cloak and went down, rejoicing over his agreeable companion; but what was his horror, when the day broke, to find a Styrian Baroness, old, fat, frightfully plain, and ignorant of French! I was more lucky, in finding a separate vehicle, in which there was a young Bavarian officer. I gave him a cigar, he spread half of his camp-cloak over my knees, and thenceforth we fraternized perfectly.

It was a damp, dark morning, but the horns of the postilions blew a merry peal as we rolled out of Laybach. The roads were in a miserable condition from recent rains, and the wet plain over which we drove seemed interminable. During the forenoon we passed over many ranges of hills, running parallel with the coast, and inclosing valleys of green and pleasant aspect, but the country grew more bleak and cold as we approached the Adriatic. The woods, which were just touched with the frost when I left Vienna, were here bare of leaves. Cultivation was confined almost entirely to the valleys, where the young wheat was beginning to look green. I saw a few herdsmen on the hill-tops, tending their sheep and goats among the stones, but most of the inhabitants were employed in keeping the roads in order or begging of the passengers. They are a starved-looking race, kin to the Croats. I have no doubt that Goldsmith's record of the inhospitality of the "rude Carinthian boor" is perfectly correct. The American Bloomers will be surprised to learn that the Carinthian women are before them in the movement. Their skirts just reach to the knee, but they have not yet got as far as the Turkish trowsers. They either go bare-legged or wear hussar boots.

If anything had been wanting to convince me of the poverty of this region, it was supplied by the dinner they gave us at Adelsberg. The force of leanness and of meanness could no further go. The necessity of reaching Trieste a day before the departure of the steamer, prevented me from visiting the celebrated Grotto of Adelsberg, near the village, and the quicksilver mines of Idria, which are not more than twenty miles distant. The geological character of the country between Adelsberg and Trieste is very remarkable. It is called the *Karst*, and consists of ranges of stony hills, almost destitute of vegetation. The sides of these hills and the valleys between them, are pierced with cup-like hollows, from which the rains are evidently carried off by subterranean drains. They are in some places quite deep and precipitous, and the road winds along on the narrow partition walls between them.

[That portion of the railroad which crosses the Karst is a work of immense labor. The descent to Trieste is so steep that the track is carried many miles to the westward, whence it returns in a sharp angle. The wind called the Bora, which blows over the southern edge of the table-land, is at times strong enough to stop the trains, which are often detained several hours from this cause. On the old post-road there are special officials, chosen for their familiarity with the wind and its accompanying signs, whose duty it is to inform travellers whether they can pass with safety. When the wind is at its height, it is strong enough to overturn the heaviest wagons, and the officials have then authority to prevent every one from passing. During the Italian Revolution of 1849, a company of dragoons, on their way to Lombardy, were stopped for this reason. The officer, a young fellow with more brag than brains, said, "We are going to beat the rebels, and it is foolish to think the wind can stop us," marched on in defiance of the official warning, and was presently, horse and all, blown off the precipice. Out of the whole company, but sixteen men escaped.]

We were very anxious to reach Trieste before dark, but after twelve hours of tedious driving the sun went down and we were still distant. We had heard much of the magnificent view from the crest of the mountains behind the town—a view, which, it is said, takes in the entire curve of the Adriatic, from Venice to the mountain headland of Pola. This was nothing, however, to the lazy Carinthian postilion, who scarcely allowed his three horses to stretch their rope traces. The last light of sunset showed us the mountains of Friuli, far to the right, and then we leaned spitefully back in the carriage and dropped the subject. We were deep in criticisms on Jenny Lind's voice, when a sudden exclamation from both of us put a stop to the conversation. A dark gulf yawned far below us, half girdling a dusky plain, and just in the centre of the curve sparkled a glittering crescent of lights, branching into long lines or breaking into showers of fiery dots. This was Trieste, gleaming like a tiara on the forehead of the Adriatic. Beyond it and far to the south, the hills of Istria loomed darkly along the horizon. All else was vague and indistinct in the starlight. The air grew milder as we descended, and when I walked along the quay on my way to the hotel, hearing the sweet Italian tongue on all sides, I could scarcely believe that the sun was not still shining.

Trieste is comparatively a new town, and owes its rise entirely to its commerce. Therefore, though it is clean, bright, and pleasant, the traveller dismisses its edifices with a glance, and finds much more interesting material in the crowds that throng its streets. The Orient is much nearer than at Vienna. The Greek meets you at every turn. The Turk grows familiar, and you make acquaintance with the Egyptian, the Albanian, and the fur-capped Dalmatian. The mole is crowded with copper-colored sailors in dirty turbans and baggy trowsers. Chibouques are smoked in Lloyd's Café, and newspapers in Hellenic text cover the tables of the reading room. The Frank and Mussulman are seen cheek by jowl in the arcades of the Exchange, and if you go there at two o'clock your ears will be stunned with the clatter of a dozen different languages.

XI.

SMYRNA, AND THE GRECIAN ARCHIPELAGO.

[OCTOBER, 1851.]

THE fare from Trieste to Alexandria, by way of Smyrna—a voyage of twelve days—is about $40. This does not include provisions, which cost about 75 cents a day additional. There is a third place for "the scum of the earth," so that the second cabin is considered quite respectable, though not aristocratic. It is very neat, tolerably ventilated, and furnished with berths which are perfectly clean and flealess, though rather hard. As I had already been seasoned to planks, I found them very good. We rose at daybreak and were immediately served with small cups of rich black coffee. At ten o'clock there was a substantial breakfast, and at four a dinner of six courses, both of which meals were accompanied with wine *ad libitum*— a light, pure Italian vintage, which Father Mathew might quaff without endangering the sanctity of his pledge. There was a barrel of the coarser sort on deck, which served the mongrel Greek and Dalmatian sailors instead of a water-butt. Our day wound up with a cup of tea, made in good English style. If one cannot endure such hardships as these, while skirting the mountain-shores of Greece and Albania, let him stick to his easy chair.

Our passengers were brought together from all parts of the earth, and from some odd corners of Society. In the after cabin there was a Greek, of the noble family of Mavrocordato; the English wife of a Turkish Bey, and a German missionary with an English wife, bound for Beyrout. In the fore cabin, there were three Italian singers, going to the Constantinopolitan opera; an Ionian; a most ignorant Prussian, bound for Athens, and a Swiss. The deck was occupied by a Jew and his family, on their way to Jerusalem. The man wore a greasy gown of black serge, with a beard reaching to his waist, and the whole family represented to the life Thackeray's

> "filthy Jews to larboard,
> Uncombed, unwashed, unbarbered."

They had a young child, which squalled twice as loud as any uncircumcised infant I ever heard. I recollect once hearing a camp-meeting hymn which commenced "What's became of the Hebrew children?" I think I could have given information as to the locality of one of the aforesaid children.

We pass unnoticed, the distant view of the Dalmatian

coast, which I have since then visited and described. At Corfu, we first touch classic earth. Here Homer has been before us, and here we may still behold the Phæacian galley which bore Ulysses to his home, transformed into a rock by the vengeance of Neptune, in sight of its destined haven. Thence by Leucadia, Ithaca, and the shores of Elis and Arcadia, our keel ploughs illustrious waters. Beyond the shallow bay of Arcadia, however, our thoughts are recalled to later times: we are in the Gulf of Navarino. The harbor where the great maritime battle took place is almost excluded from view of the sea by the long island of Sphagia (the scene of Byron's "Corsair"), which lies across its mouth. A short distance further, in passing between the island of Sapienza and the mainland, we run close to the town of Modon, whose massive walls, the memorial of Venetian sway, project into the sea. Another headland brings us to the Gulf of Coron, and to the sight of the sublime mountain peninsula which divides this, the ancient Messenian, from the Laconian Gulf beyond. Towards its extremity the Taygetus suddenly terminates, but the narrow strip of Cape Matapan is thrust in advance, like the paw of a sleeping lion, driving its rocky talons into the sea. The aspect of this promontory, which is the most southern point of Europe, is remarkably grand. The perpendicular walls of dark-red rock which form the cape are several hundred feet in height, and the wild ridges of the Taygetus rise gradually behind them to an elevation of 7,000 feet.

When I went on deck the next morning, we were in the Grecian Archipelago. The islands of Serphos and Siphantos were already behind us; Anti-Paros, Paros, and Naxos retreated beyond each other, far to the East; the low shores of Delos rose in front, with Mykonos still further off, and the hills of Tinos blushed in the sunrise over the nearer coast of Syra. We doubled a rocky cape and entered the harbor, just as the sunshine reached the top of the mountain-cone on which the old city is built. The brilliant white of the flat Oriental houses, which rise tier above tier up the craggy steep, contrasted finely with the soft morning sky and the perfect ultramarine of the water. It was something more than a sunrise to me; it was the dawn of the Orient.

During a day and a half that we lay at anchor there, I became quite as well acquainted with the city as I desired. Its Oriental character holds good in every respect—all fairness without and all filth within. There is but one respectable street, which you enter on landing—a sort of bazaar, covered with ragged awning, and occupied by the principal merchants. The rest is a wilderness of dirty lanes, barely wide enough for two persons to pass each other, and spread for more than a mile along the mountain-side. You ascend and descend between walls, just too high to prevent your seeing anything, and after much labor, come to a halt in a vile little court, breathing anything but balm, or perhaps on the flat house-top of some astonished Greek. Then you return, picking your steps with much trouble, and try another course, but the twists and turns, the steps here and there and the culs-de-sac so bewilder you, that you finish by finding yourself just where you did not wish to go. I tried the experiment twice, and after looking in on the domestic arrangements of half the families in Syra, gave up the attempt.

The new town, which contains upwards of 20,000 inhabitants, has grown up entirely within the last thirty years. The refugees from other islands, during the Revolution, first built their huts on the shore; afterwards the harbor, on account of its central position in the Archipelago, was made the stopping-place of the French and Austrian steamers. It is now a Grecian naval and quarantine station, and has an extensive and increasing commerce with the other ports of the Levant. The town at present exhibits every sign of prosperity except cleanliness. The quay is crowded with sailors, wearing the semi-Turkish dress of the islands, and the traffic in fruit, wood, fish, grain, spices and tobacco, is carried on with great briskness. The shopkeepers are busy, the little markets are thronged, and the mechanics who ply their several avocations in their rough way look too cheerfully industrious to lack work. In the ship-yard I counted ten vessels (two of 300 tons) on the stocks, besides a number of small craft. Several large and handsome edifices were going up, in addition to the many one-story boxes which the common people inhabit.

I accompanied the baritone of our Italian company on a visit to a Greek family of his acquaintance. We found at home an old lady and her daughter, who received us very cordially, and immediately brought us Turkish coffee, with a little jar of quince jelly. They spoke no language but Greek, the rich, whispering flow of which is not less sweet to the ear, though less crystalline in accent, than Italian. Both ladies had regular and agreeable features, and their manners possessed a native grace which I hardly expected to find in such a locality.

I rose before sunrise and went on shore, to make the ascent of the lofty peak which rises behind the town. Escaping from the tortuous lanes of New Syra, I crossed a narrow plain to the foot of the old town, which rises like an immense sugar-loaf, at the opening of a deep and rocky glen. Here there are not even lanes, but only steps from the bottom of the town to the top, up which the asses, laden with water-jars, toiled painfully. The houses are very old, and raised on arches in many places, where there is not soil enough to hold them. For a while I climbed the fatiguing steps without losing the way, but finally went astray on the house-tops, and surprised the inhabitants. A bare-legged boy, looking down from the next house above me, shouted "San Giorgios?" I nodded my head, and with a spring he was beside me, and went capering up the steps as a guide. Three or four other urchins followed, and when we reached the Church of St. George, which crowns the sharp top of the cone, I had six attendants. The glen below me was filled with a long array of women, with water-jars on their heads, and boys driving laden asses, going to and from the fountain behind the town. I pointed to the fountain and then to the peak, which lifted its marble crags high above us, and made signs to the boys that they should accompany me. Their wild black eyes sparkled assent, and the tassels of the red caps fluttered in the wind as they leaped down the rocks. We went at a breakneck rate into the bottom of the glen, the shelvy sides of which were laboriously formed into terraces, planted with figs, oranges, and vines.

My six guides took a path which led up the bed of a winter torrent, till it opened on the bare sides of the mountain. The sharp masses of rock, of which it was composed, were scantily covered with wild sage and other plants, which gave an aromatic and stimulating taste to the air, as they were broken under our feet. The nimble lizards scampered into their holes, but they were not more nimble than my little Greeks, whose caps bobbed up and down as they bounded with hands and feet up the rocks. They chattered incessantly to one another and to me, and I talked to them in English and Italian, both parties enjoying the conversation, though neither understood it. At last, when we had reached a rocky shoulder, not far from the summit, I dismissed them and ascended alone. I gave each of them a piece of 10 lepta (the largest Greek copper coin); they laid their hands gravely across their breasts and bowed, after which their capers of delight were most amusing. They shouted and danced on the rocks, and then, clutching the coins tightly in their hands, went out of sight with the fleetness of young goats.

A few moments more of breathless climbing brought me to the top of the peak, which cannot be less than two thousand feet in height. Some friendly hand had piled a tottering tower of stones, up which I mounted, and then sat down to breathe the delicious air and contemplate the magnificent view. The horizon was so extended as to take in nearly the entire group of the Cyclades, with a few of the Sporades. I counted twenty-five islands, besides Syra—some rising into cloudy summits, some low and barren, some lying in dark purple shadow, some gleaming bright and yellow in the sun, and all girdled by the same glorious blue of the sea. Here, almost at my feet, was Delos, where Latona gave birth to Apollo and Diana; yonder Paros, the birth-place of the Medicean Venus and the Dying Gladiator; behind it Naxos, sacred to Bacchus and Ariadne; and faint and far to the south, Nio, where Homer died. To the west lay Thermia, Zea, and Andros, and away beyond Andros the shadowy hills of Negropont, the ancient Eubœa. Zea concealed the promontory of Cape Colonna, but between the island and Negropont, dim as a dream, stretched the mainland of Attica, the tops of Hymettus. In the northeast I distinguished Icaros and Samos, and in the south the topmost summit of Milo. The feeling with which I gazed on that panorama can scarcely be expressed in words; or if in words, only in that speech taught by him who was born on Delos.

On my return, I descended to the fountain, which gushes from the solid rock, in the ravine behind the old town. It is the same to which the pilgrims of old resorted for purification, before visiting the shrine of Apollo at Delos. Without the supply of soft and pure water which it affords, the island would not be habitable. I found a number of women grouped around it, waiting to fill their heavy jars, which they then bore off on their shoulders. The water is sold in the town and even retailed by the glass to the sailors along the quay. I came on board like one of the messengers from Eshkol, bearing a cluster of transparent pink grapes, which weighed more than four pounds.

We left Syra towards evening, our deck crowded with Greeks, Turks, and Jews. On passing the strait between

Tinos and Mykonos, we entered the open sea, and made for Scio, about fifty miles distant. As the night was dark, and we only touched at the island for half an hour, some time past midnight, I kept my berth, but rose at dawn to see a sunrise in Asia, for the first time. We were just entering the bay of Smyrna—a magnificent sheet of water, between thirty and forty miles long, and varying from five to ten in breadth. Its shores are mountains, whose green and wooded slopes present an agreeable contrast to the bare hills of Greece. The narrow plains at their feet are covered with gardens and grain-fields, and dotted with white villages and country-houses.

After passing the "Castle of the Sea," a large white-washed fortress commanding the channel, we first see the minarets of Smyrna. Mount Pagus, on the southern side, crowned by its ruined citadel, keeps the city in shadow, but as we approached, the mass of houses—flat, dome-like roofs, gay mosques and light minarets, stretching for nearly two miles along the shore and climbing to the dark cypress-groves of the burial grounds, high on the hill—grows distinct in all its novel and fantastic features. Our boat passes slowly to the Frank quarter, in the northern part of the city, and drops anchor within a hundred yards of the shore.

Smyrna is sometimes called, in the flowery tongue of the East, the "Ornament of Asia." No one, who first beholds the city from the sea, or from the slopes of Mount Pagus, will hesitate to accord it so graceful a title. The grand and harmonious features of the landscape, of which it is the central point, give it an air of dignity and importance,

6

which neither its streets and public edifices, nor the indications of foreign traffic in its harbour, would convey. It lies at the head of the gulf, and at the mouth of a broad and beautiful valley, watered by the River Hermes, its southern end resting on the mountain, as an oriental beauty, reclining after the bath, lifts her head on the pillows of her divan. Its aspect is that of majestic repose; the simple and compact array of its tiled roofs and white walls, broken here and there by the light shaft of a minaret, a slender cypress, or the plumy top of a palm, presents no point sufficiently striking to call one's attention to the details of the view. The city, the sparkling gulf, the Mediterranean on the horizon, the garden-valley, compassed on all sides by the cloud-capped off-shoots of the Taurus range—all are blended in one superb panorama, and colored by the blue and violet pencils of the Ionian air. Here Asia—grand, though fallen Asia—has most solemnly, most sublimely impressed the seal of her destiny.

The city, after you have entered it, loses this impressive effect, but gives you an endless variety of bizarre and picturesque forms. I landed alone, within an hour after my arrival, and selected one from the crowd of shabby dragomen on the quay, to be my guide through the city. The subject of my choice turned out to be a Spanish Jew, whom I ignominiously dismissed, when he attempted to palm off an old synagogue as the chief mosque of Smyrna. The main street of the Frank quarter, which lies next the water, is narrow, crooked, ill paved, and very dirty. There is no house in the city more than two stories in height, and none of any pretensions to architectural beauty, though the

Franks boast several cool court-yards with fountains. The Frank signs are principally in Greek and Italian, but the porters, donkey-drivers, and boatmen, who beset you on landing, are full of English and Spanish phrases.

Nearly every man one meets here is a study. The very boatmen who came to take us ashore, with their red bags for pantaloons, brawny brown arms, and weather-beaten tarbooshes, were picturesque. Then, as I first touched Asian soil, I jostled against a group of shawl-girt mountaineers, armed with heavy sabres, and turning down the first street, I met a string of camels, laden with water-skins. In the crowd that followed them I recognised Arabs, Greeks, Armenians, and Egyptians, besides the different varieties of Turks and Franks. Tall Mussulmans stood in the entrances of the courtyards, beside baskets of transparent pink, green, and purple grapes; porters, with small board-yards and brick-kilns strapped on their backs, steered their blind way through the crooked alleys; a company of Turkish women, masked and muffled in loose robes, stared in the faces of the Franks, and the long-drawn "*guard-a-a!*" (take care!) of the donkeymen, sounding every instant behind me-obliged me to take the wall and suspend my observations. The streets are so narrow that the projecting eaves of the houses touch in many places, and a laden donkey almost blocks the passage.

My Jewish guide set off on a quick trot and soon brought me to the entrance of the bazaars. The Smyrniote bazaars, I should here state, are merely streets of one story shops, covered with a loose roofing of boards, which makes them very cool and agreeable during the hot mid-day hours.

They are open thoroughfares, and the cry of "*guarda!*" is never out of one's ears. Some skill is required to avoid being run over by a camel, knocked down by a donkey, or punched in the head by a perambulating board-pile. The first bazaar I entered is mostly occupied by the Franks, who have a large display of printed cotton goods. I wasted no time on the red-capped Italian and Greek shopkeepers, but hastened on to the Turkish quarter, where the calm impassive merchants, reclining on their carpets, scarcely put aside the amber mouth-pieces of their chibouks, to reply to a customer. Here the plash of water from the public fountains sounds cool and grateful, and the air is impregnated with the subtle and delicate aroma of spices. At the corners stand the venders of sherbet, and near them the smoke ascends from pans of simmering kabobs and various other Turkish dishes, which I was content with beholding. The rich gleam of the silks of Brousa, the Persian scarfs, and the golden fringes and embroidered work displayed in the shops of the Turkish and Persian merchants, was a much less gorgeous sight to me than that of the lazy owners, with their large black eyes, half closed in beatific dreams, over the bubbling narghileh. In the Persian quarter, I saw several beautiful children, but one boy whose face was that of an angel. Raphael's cherubs, in his Madonna di San Sisto, are less divine in their loveliness. If the children of the Moslem Paradise are thus beautiful, I know no artist who would not willingly go there.

I also visited the slave bazaar, which is in the Turkish part of the city. The keepers at first objected to my entrance, but a small backsheesh removed their scruples. I was ushered into a court-yard, around which about twenty Nubians lay grouped in the sun—small, thick-lipped, flat-headed creatures, whose faces exhibited a sort of passive good-humor, but not the slightest sign of intelligence. They are the lowest and cheapest kind of slaves, bringing from $50 to $150 each, and are purchased by the Turks for house-servants. The keeper assured me that he would buy provisions for them with the backsheesh, but I have no idea that he kept his word.

After dismissing my guide, I took my bearings as accurately as possible and plunged into the Turkish quarter, seeking a way to the burial-ground. The further I went from the bazaars, the more quiet grew the streets, and very soon I saw no more Frank dresses. A masked Turkish lady who passed, looked at me steadily with two of the most superb eyes I ever saw, but the next that came drew her mantle over her head and crouched close to the opposite wall, so that the unclean Frank might not even brush her garments. As the streets began to ascend the hill, I was at a loss which to take, but climbed the stones at random, till I reached a fountain. A number of children who were gathered around it, made signs that I should return, and cried out "*chkatch! chkatch!*"—which I took to be the Turkish for "dogs!" since I had not gone a dozen steps further before a whole pack of those animals set upon me and forced me to beat a hasty retreat. I reached the grove of cypresses without further adventure, and sat down to rest on a broken pillar, taken from the ruins of Ancient Smyrna to be the headstone of a Turk. The Turks, unlike the Christians, never bury one generation in the ashes of another, and consequently the burial-ground is always enlarging its limits. The tombstones, with their turbaned tops, are innumerable, and the pride of some families, whose names are emblazoned in golden Arabic letters on pillars painted scarlet or sky-blue, is doubly vain and ridiculous amid the neglect and decay which the hoary cypresses have looked upon for many centuries.

I climbed the breezy sides of Mount Pagus to the ruins of the ancient citadel, passing on my way many fragments of cut stone, traces of walls and gateways, which, with some cisterns and foundations, are all that remain of the old city. The hill was covered with droves of camels, who lifted their solemn heads from the dry shrubs upon which they were browsing, and looked at me with the same passive faces as their masters. From the crest of Mount Pagus I looked down into the valley of the Meles, on its southern side, and beyond, over the rolling plains that stretched far inland. But the view of Smyrna and its gardens, the mountains and the sea, attracted me still more. I sat for hours on a rock, under the battered wall of the castle, without being able to take my eyes from the sublime landscape. I was afterwards told that I ran the risk of being robbed, as the Franks of Smyrna are rather shy of wandering alone among the ruins. I then descended the eastern side to the Caravan Bridge, a favorite resort of the Smyrniotes. The banks of the Meles are crowded with coffee-houses, and one may there inhale the perfume of genuine Latakia under the shade of plane-trees and acacias.

The night of our departure from Smyrna we saw Mitylene, the ancient Lesbos, and Scio, by moonlight. I saw little except the illuminated outline of Scio, but that alone was beautiful. When I arose at sunrise, the rock of Patmos was just vanishing in the rear, and the blue cliffs of Cos appeared in front. The home of Apelles is rocky and barren, and I could distinguish little sign of habitation on its western coast. But this island, like the other Sporades between which we sailed, presents such an unfailing harmony in their forms, the sunshine lies so warm and rosy along their sides, the shadows of their peaks are so deeply violet in their hue, and the sea and sky which hold them in their embrace, are so pure and brilliant, that we forget their past glory and their present desolation. Rhodes and Karpathos were the last we saw; they formed the portal of our highway to Egypt, and they lingered for hours on the horizon, as if to call us back to the Grecian Isles.

XII.

A WALK THROUGH THE THURINGIAN FOREST.

HAD it not been for the Prussian Consul in Constantinople —a gentleman whom I never saw, and of whose name I am ignorant—I should probably never have visited the Thüringian Forest. The chain of causes, events, and sequences, which is interwoven with a very important portion of my life, reaches back to him and there stops. He is consequently responsible for more than he knows, or has ever dreamed of. Trace back any event of your life until you find the starting-point whence you set out upon the track of it—the *switch*, in railroad parlance, which throws the car of your destiny upon quite another line of rail than you had chosen for it—and how unnoticed, how trifling, how absurd, frequently, is the beginning! The merest accident (yet who shall dare to say that such things are accidental?) frequently leads a man into his true career, which he might not otherwise have found. I remember to have seen an ingenious genealogy of the American Revolution, which was traced back, step by step, to a quarrel about a pig. Zschokke has written a curious double story based upon this singular succession of causes, in which a poor boy, by throwing down a dough-trough, attains wealth and rank; while a nobleman of talent and character is reduced to disgrace and beggary, by spilling a bottle of ink.

But you ask, how is the Prussian Consul at Constantinople responsible for my visit to the Thüringian Forest? In this way. A German traveller reached Constantinople in October, 1851, on his way to Greece and Palestine. Having made the acquaintance of the Prussian Consul there, the latter prevailed upon him, at the last moment, to change his plans, and visit Egypt instead. So urgent was he, that he gave the traveller letters to the Consul in Smyrna, who seconded his advice—and it was not until after he had reached the latter place, that the traveller decided to embark for Alexandria instead of the Piræus. The Lloyd steamer for Egypt was ready to start, and among the last arrivals on board was the German. One of the passengers already on board was an American, bound for the White Nile. A chance remark led to an acquaintance, the two travelled together to the Nubian frontier, and parted under the palm-trees at Assouan, as friends for life.

The rest of the chain is easily followed. I promised to visit my friend in his Thüringian home. In August of the following year I returned from the Orient by way of Italy and the Tyrol, and reached Gotha towards the end of September. The ten days to which I had limited my stay, previous to leaving for China and Japan, extended to twenty or more under the influence of true German hos pitality. A part of the entertainment, with anticipatory descriptions of which my friend had often beguiled the sweet Egyptian twilights, was a journey through the Thüringian Forest. The season had been cold, and the autumn was fast waning at the time of my arrival, so we started in a day or two afterwards.

Taking the road to Eisenach, we climbed the hill of the Wartburg, on a sunny morning. The famous old castle, which has since been restored to its ancient condition, as near as can be ascertained, was at that time very dilapidated, although still habitable. It is known to us principally from the fact that Luther was sheltered within its walls for a year, and there completed his translation of the Bible; but to the German it is rich in historical associations. Here lived Elizabeth of Hungary, wife of the Landgrave Ludwig (read Charles Kingsley's "Saint's Tragedy"), whose holy charity not only justified her in the utterance of a lie, but procured a miracle to confirm it. Sausages and cold chickens turned to roses in her apron, that her lord might not see and censure her lavish gifts to the poor. Here, also, in 1207, occurred the famous *Sängerkrieg*, or Battle of the Troubadours, in which the renowned Minnesingers, Heinrich von Ofterdingen, Walter von der Vogelweide, and Wolfram von Eschenbach, took part. Few other spots in Germany shine so brightly in knightly and ecclesiastical story.

Luther's room is still preserved in its original bareness and simplicity. A single window looks westward over the wooded hills· a huge stove of earthen tiles, a table, and some chairs of rough oak, are the only furniture. The famous ink-blotch on the wall is conscientiously renewed every time the room is whitewashed. An original portrait of Luther, his autograph, and the plain suit of armor which he wore, as "Squire George," are also preserved here. The visitors' book lay open upon the table where he was wont to write. As I approached it for the purpose of inscribing my name, the last entry on the page (written only the day before) was: "*Thomas Carlyle, in Luther's room, full of reverence.*" On visiting the same room, two years ago, I was confronted by a stout, full-bearded, handsome gentleman, who appeared to be very much at home there. Supposing him to be an artist, I brushed past him into the room. He looked very fixedly at me; but artists have a way of examining faces, so I paid no attention to it. He was the reigning Duke of Saxe-Weimar.

In the armory there is a small but very curious collection of weapons and coats of mail. Among them is that of Kunz von Kaufungen, who carried off the two young princes, progenitors of the Ernestine and Albertine lines of the House of Saxony. The old walls have been replastered and adorned with frescoes representing the history of Elizabeth of Hungary, and famous incidents in the Lives of the Landgraves of Thüringia. There is Hermann with his hunters, on the site of the castle, charmed with the view, and exclaiming: "Wait, mountain, and I'll build a fortress upon you!" (whence the name Wartburg); there Ludwig walks unarmed against the escaped lion, and drives him back to his den; and there another Landgrave, whose name I have forgotten, proudly exhibits his means of defence to the German Emperor. When the latter, who was visiting him, remarked that his castle was without walls, the Landgrave replied: "I will show your Majesty my walls to-morrow." The next morning, the Emperor was aroused by the sound of trumpets. The Landgrave conducted him to a balcony, whence he beheld the castle surrounded by a triple circle of armed men. "There, your Majesty!" said he; "a *living wall* is the best."

Leaving the Wartburg, we wandered down into the deep Marienthal, or Glenmary, a picturesque valley, formed by the junction of two or three narrow dells. A pile of rocks on our left is called the Maiden's Den, from an old tradition that a princess, for some misdeed, was shut up within them, only to be released when some one should say "God bless you!" twelve times in succession, in answer to her sneezing. As she can only try the experiment at midnight, it is needless to say that she is still confined there. Once, indeed, a belated knight made the proper response to eleven sneezes, but when the twelfth came, his patience gave way, and he uncourteously exclaimed: "Oh! the devil take you!"

At the end of the valley we entered the Annathal, which is a curious natural split, extending for more than a mile through the mountains. Formerly it was the bed of an impetuous little stream, now bridged over for nearly the whole distance, so that the roar of waters is constantly beneath your feet as you walk between the twisted walls of rock. The foliage of the forest on the summit of the cliffs completely intercepts the sky; brilliant mosses cover the moist walls, and fringes of giant fern spring from every crevice. Deep, cool, dark, and redolent of woodland aroma, it resembles a dell in fairyland, and the ferns and harebells were yet vibrating from the feet of the retreating elves, as we passed along. Fresh from the blazing Orient, where the three delights of life are shade, moisture, and verdure, I was enchanted with the successive beauties which our semi-subterranean path unfolded.

Emerging, at last, upon an open height, we found an inn, with the ambitious name of the Lofty Sun, where we ate fresh mountain-trout in an arbor of clipped lindens. Thence a path of some miles over the hills brought us to the village of Ruhla, famous through all Germany for its meerschaum pipes and beautiful girls. At the inn where we stopped, it was the eve of a wedding-day. The landlord's daughter, in whom I found the reputation of the village justified, was to be married on the morrow, and the kitchen was full of rosy damsels, baking and brewing with might and main. The bride—not without a pretty blush—brought us each a glass of wine and a piece of cake, and we, of course, drank to her wedded happiness. But our quarters for the night lay beyond another and higher mountain, and the dusk was gathering in the deep valley.

Had we not taken a guide, we should have lost our way in the forest. Finally, a sparkle appeared ahead—then a broad flame, gilding the white trunks of the beech-trees, and brightening the gold of their autumnal leaves. The forester was at his post, awaiting our coming, at the ducal hunting lodge on the mountain. The costly timber crackled on the bonfire he had made, and the torch of our encampment was seen by many a distant village. There was a supply of beer, potatoes, black bread, and sausage—true hunter's fare—and our jovial supper was made by the firelight. We talked of Egypt, and the forester listened, only repeating now and then, with hearty emphasis: "To think that it should happen so! That you two should meet, away in that savage country, and here you are by my fire!" This was my first acquaintance with the forester, who was the last friend to bid me farewell at Hamburg, on my last return from Europe.

We slept on a bed of hay in the lodge, washed our faces in the cold mountain spring, and ate our breakfast by a new fire. During the forenoon our route lay westward over the mountains to Altenstein, a summer residence of the Duke of Meiningen. As we approached the castle, the duke himself—a remarkably handsome man, plainly dressed in a green frock-coat and black felt hat—passed us on the lawn. He answered our salutations with a friendly bow. We lingered awhile on the terrace, which commands a lovely view, stretching away over leagues of valley-land to the mountains of the Rhön. In fact, the castle and park of Altenstein occupy the whole of a natural mountain-terrace, lifted high above the subject lands. The declivity, leading down to the mineral springs of Liebenstein, is interrupted by bold and picturesque formations of rock. We visited the Altar, the Basket of Flowers, the Pulpit, and various curious basaltic piles, and finally reaching the Giant's Harp, threw ourselves down on the warm grass to rest. Here, in a narrow, perpendicular cleft, between two rocky pillars, thirty feet high, wires have been inserted, after the manner of an Æolian harp. The cleft is closed by a shutter, the opening of which, when there is any breeze, creates a draft sufficient to awake the weird, oracular music.

The mountains around loomed softly through golden vapor, as we lay upon the lonely hill-side, gazing on the vanishing blue of the landscape, with lazy, receptive minds, which nothing, it seemed, could either have especially disgusted or inspired. Presently a sweet, timorous, penetrating tone grew upon the air, falling and swelling in appealing pulsations—then a chorus of many notes, so blended in one delicate breath of harmony that you knew not whether they were sad or jubilant; and finally, gathering courage, the full volume of wandering sound wrapped us in its powerful embrace. Tones that traversed all space, that bridged the profoundest chasms of time, met our ears. We heard the timbrel of Miriam, the shawms and dulcimers of David, the wail of Jephthah, and the honeyed madrigals of Solomon—Delphic strains from the hollows of Grecian hills, and the sea-born songs of Calypso and the Sirens. But under, or above all, recurred at intervals a sobbing string—a note of despairing longing, of unutterable, unsatisfied passion, which struck along every shuddering nerve until it reached the deepest cell of the heart. "No, this is not to be borne any longer," said my friend, echoing my own feeling. "Away!" said Jean Paul to Music; "thou speakest of that which I cannot have, yet the desire of which consumes my life!"

At Liebenstein we saw the little grotto, drank the disagreeable water, and then continued our journey through the valleys on the southern slope of the Thüringian Mountains. At dusk we reached the inn on the Inselsberg, one of the highest summits, 3,000 feet above the sea. There, on a clear day, you stand "ringed with the azure world." The view reaches from the Brocken, seventy miles in the North, to the tops of the Franconian mountains. Friends from Gotha had come to meet us, and we passed the evening comfortably beside a cheerful fire. In the morning we walked down the sunny side of the mountain to Friedrichsroda, a charming village, which in summer is a favorite resort of the Berliners. In the street I caught a glimpse of Wilhelm, one of the Brothers Grimm, the great lexicographers of Germany.

In the afternoon, we continued our journey in a more luxurious style, in my friend's carriage. Following the green Alpine dell behind Friedrichsroda, we mounted to the summit ridge of the mountains, along which runs an ancient road, called the Rennstieg, traversing their whole extent, from Eisenach down to the borders of Franconia. At the top, on the edge of the fir forest, stands a beer-tavern, with this enticing sign:

"I am the landlord of the Wolf;
  Ye travellers, come to me;
For you, the landlord is no wolf—
  A little lamb is he!"

"Ho! thou lambkin! thou wolf in sheep's clothing! bring us two *seidls* of beer!" cried out my friend. "Here, you lions in asses' hides, or asses in lions' hides—which is it?"—answered the landlord, as he brought the foaming glasses. I warrant the Berlin cockneys, who manage to climb hither in summer (with many exclamations of "Ach, Jott!") get as good wit as they give, and a little better.

Rain was brewing, and the raw clouds now and then tore their skirts in the tops of the firs as we drove along the Rennstieg. Meadows that widened as they descended, shone with a gleam that counterfeited sunshine, between the dark shores of the forest. This is the characteristic charm of the Thüringian Mountains—the rare and incomparable beauty which distinguishes this region above all other portions of Germany—its meadows of perfect emerald, never barren of blossoms, framed in dark, magnificent woods, or overhung with sheer walls of rock. It is a character of landscape which only the German language can properly describe. We have no such superb words in English as *Waldlust* and *Waldeinsamkeit.*

Our destination for the night was the *Schmücke*, a little inn kept by an original character named Father Joel, and the highest inhabited dwelling in the Thüringian Forest. Far and wide through Saxe-Coburg and the neighboring Duchies every one knew Father Joel, and many of his witty sayings will remain in circulation for a generation to come. We found the old man rather ill and broken: he died in the following year. "How goes it, Father Joel?" asked my friend. "Ah," he replied, "badly, badly; I have no appetite. I can eat nothing but partridges, and not more than three of them." No one could prepare venison, trout, pheasants, hares, or coffee, like Joel's wife, and the wine-cellar had its treasures, not to be enjoyed by every chance visitor. My friend was the bearer of a message from some of the members of the Ministerial Cabinet, that they would dine at the *Schmücke* on the morrow; but he was wise enough not to mention it until our own supper had been secured. We certainly should otherwise have lost that marvellous haunch of venison, which still lingers in my memory as the realization of an ideal to be enjoyed only once in a lifetime.

Father Joel's album was a curiosity. Poets had written impromptus for him, artists sketched himself and his bountiful table, composers scored down hunting-songs or pathetic farewells, and philosophers and lawgivers perpetrated stiff puns in his praise. I added after my name, as I had done at the Inselsberg, "*on the way from Central Africa to Japan*," which was literally true, and gave my autograph an especial value in the eyes of the old man. "Father Joel," said my friend, "have you said any funny things lately?" "Ah! that is past," said he, sadly; "I am done with my fun, and nothing to show for it. You remember what I said to the old Duke?" "What was that?" I asked. "Well, the old Highness was here once—a good-humored man he was—and, during dinner, he pestered me with: 'Joel, say a funny thing—say a funny thing!' At last, I stopped in the door, as I was going out, and said: 'Excuse me, Highness; I'm afraid to do it.' 'Why afraid?' he asked. 'For fear your Highness would give me the cross of the Ernestine Order!' said I, shutting the door behind me." The Duke had been so lavish in bestowing the order, that it had come to be a cheap honor; and Father Joel's remark was a home-thrust. It is said that his Highness took the hint, and profited by it. Other sovereigns might do the same thing. It is a common saying, in Middle Germany: "In Prussia there are two things you cannot escape —death and the Order of the Red Eagle."

Bidding farewell to Father Joel—a last one for me—in the morning, we spent the day in visiting Elgersburg and Ilmenau, with their water-cure and pine-needle-bathing establishments, and, late in the afternoon, reached Schwarzburg, on the Saale—one of the seats of the princely line of Schwarzburg-Rudolstadt. The town is built on a low cape of the mountains, projecting into a deep, romantic valley. Hundreds of deer were feeding on the castle meadows, and from the forests rising beyond sounded the trumpet-call of the stag. A short distance further up the valley is Rudolstadt—classic with the memories of Goethe, Herder, Schiller, and Jean Paul.

We had now reached the termination of the range known as the Thüringian Forest, but our return journey to Gotha, the next day, embraced landscapes of equal beauty to those we had enjoyed. We descended the Saale to an open valley, called, on account of its richness and loveliness, the Chrysoprase, thence crossed the base of the mountains westward to Paulinzelle, where there is a ruined cloister of the eleventh century in admirable preservation, and sped rapidly through rain and darkness over the rolling plain to Gotha, which we reached late at night. This was my first but not my last trip over and among those dear and glorious hills.

XIII.

MY SUPERNATURAL EXPERIENCES.

Let sceptical, hard, matter-of-fact men talk as they may, there is a lingering belief in the possibility of occasional communication between the natural and the supernatural—the visible and the invisible world—inherent in human nature. There are not many persons whose lives do not contain at least some few occurrences, which are incapable of being satisfactorily explained by any known laws—remarkable presentiments, coincidences, and sometimes apparitions, even, which seem to be beyond the reach of accident or chance, and overcome us with a special wonder. The error, however, is generally on the side of credulity. Men are reluctant to accept any rational interpretation of such things, since the veil which they believe to have been agitated, if not lifted, is thereby rendered as still and impenetrable as before. The remarkable prevalence of "Spiritualism," in spite of its disgusting puerilities, can only be accounted for in this way. A sort of mental epilepsy —infectious, as well as congenital—receives the powerful aid of personal egotism; and the result is a tendency to reject all explanations which discredit the supernatural theory. When the nature of Mind, and the laws which govern it, are as well understood as those of Matter, much that is now wrapped in mystery will be clear and plain.

I propose, simply, to narrate a few incidents which lie outside the range of ordinary experience, attaching to each one my own interpretation. Were facts of this character more generally noted, we might the more readily proceed to the deduction of some general law; but if the proportion of men who really think for themselves is small, how much smaller is the number who are capable of studying, with introverted vision, the operations of their own minds! I have found but one man, as yet, who ascertained, by self-experiment, that the ecstatic condition of the so-called "spiritual mediums" may be gradually developed and produced at will. That lazy state of dreamy reverie, which is the favorite dissipation of certain minds, is but a milder form of the same disease.

The first instance I shall relate cannot strictly be called supernatural, since—even if true—it is, at the best, but a romantic adventure. But, I think, it illustrates the possibility of two simultaneous conditions of the mind—one awake, through the medium of the senses; the other still wandering among the phantasms of sleep. (Would a momentary difference in the action of the two lobes of the brain explain this?) But to the story:

In December, 1845, I was travelling on foot from Florence to Rome. Chill rain-storms swept the Apennines. I plodded wearily along, wet to the skin, and occasionally stopping for shelter at the rude inns frequented by the peasants. I think it was the fourth day of my journey, when I was obliged, by the violence of the storm, to take shelter in a lonely little tavern, somewhere between Arezzo and the Lake of Thrasymene. We (I had one companion) were kindly received, and placed in opposite corners of the great, open fire-place, to dry our clothes by a bright blaze of brushwood. The family consisted of an old woman, a beautiful girl of twenty, and three children. There were also two men, of middle age; but it was evident, from the conversation, that they had come down from the neighboring mountains. As the evening closed in, and a dreary rain beat against the windows, they drew nearer the fire; and the conversation became so animated that I could, with difficulty, catch the meaning of their words. While we were taking our scanty supper of eggs, maccaroni, and wine, at a table in the farther corner of the kitchen, I remarked that their conversation was carried on in whispers, of which I could only detect the words "robbers" and "to-night" frequently repeated.

I paid no particular attention to this circumstance, but conversed with the family for an hour or two, as far as my limited Italian would go. The girl had one of those sweet Madonna faces—only with an expression of more passion and less purity—which are not unusual in Italy. Her manner towards us was marked by a cheerful friendliness; but the men were silent and uncommunicative. We went early to bed, being sorely fatigued. There was but one bed-room—a large loft over the kitchen—in which were two or three coarse couches. One of these was given to us twain —the old woman occupying another, and the men a third. Ours stood alone in one end of the loft, opposite the landing—which was covered by a hatch—and I took the outer side of the bed, with my face towards the staircase. Over the landing was a single window, in the gable end of the hut, admitting a little light from the sky.

I soon fell into a sound sleep, which was not broken when the old woman and the two men crept to their beds. My companion, with his face to the wall, was as insensible as a log. Towards midnight, however, I suddenly awoke. The clouds were thinner, and the moon, behind them, shed light enough to enable me to distinguish, though dimly, the objects in the room. The sleepers all breathed heavily and regularly; and I was about giving myself up to slumber again, when I heard voices in the kitchen below. Presently the door leading to the staircase was opened, and cautious feet commenced ascending the steps. As the hatch was lifted, and the forms appeared, drawn in black outline against the window, I recognised the young girl, accompanied by a man whom I had not seen before. There was a moment's pause, while the latter appeared to be looking around the loft, and then I heard the words: "Which are they?" "There!" said the girl, in a low tone; "but are they really coming?" A whispered consultation ensued, of which I could only distinguish that her tones had a character of persuasion or entreaty. At last the man said: "They will be here soon; but I will leave the sign," or something to the same effect—for I cannot remember his precise words. He then approached our bed on tip-toe. I closed my eyes, and counterfeited sleep; but I felt the light movement of a hand about the head of the bed—and once the tips of fingers touched my neck. The two then withdrew noiselessly to the kitchen.

I felt no fear—but an intense curiosity to know the meaning of this. It was too dark to discover what was the sign referred to; and in half an hour I had forgotten all about it, for I was sound asleep. After two hours, as it seemed to me, I was a second time awakened by footsteps on the stairs. The first mysterious visit immediately recurred to my mind, and I waited, in great anxiety, for further developments. The hatch was raised, as before; but this time there were two men, neither of whom appeared to be the former visitor. One of them carried a small lantern, wrapped in a handkerchief, so as almost completely to muffle the light. When they turned towards the bed, I closed my eyes, and imitated the respiration of sleep, lest I should be caught watching. I believe, however, that my heart beat a little faster than usual. I heard stealthy footsteps, inaudible whispers, and then a low exclamation: "*Here is the sign!*" The two came to the head of my bed, and apparently made a cautious examination; a few more whispers followed, and they retreated down stairs. After they were gone, I opened my eyes, and asked myself: —"Is all this real?" A few muffled sounds came up from the kitchen, and then all was still. There was the window, with its square of dim, stormy sky; there were the beds, barely visible in the gloom; and my companion still snored, with his face to the wall. I cogitated long upon this singular adventure; but the knowledge that if there had really been any danger to our lives or scanty property, it was now over, quieted my apprehensions—and I finally slept again.

When we arose at daybreak, according to our custom, I naturally examined the bed for some trace of the visit; but in the indistinct light, I detected nothing. The girl was as calm and cheerful as ever; and though I watched her sharply, I found in her manner no justification of my suspicions. We paid our light bill, and took to the road again, accompanied by friendly "*buon viaggios*" from all. Not till then did I relate to my companion the incidents of the night. He had travelled on the "through train" of Sleep, without change of cars, and, of course, had seen and heard nothing. The circumstances were so curious and inexplicable, as to shake a little my own faith in their reality. The impression was that of actual fact—every feature distinct and tangible. The figures, the voices, the conversation in Italian—which I then knew but imperfectly—were real; and yet the whole occurrence was as improbable as the wildest adventure of a dream.

I am now inclined to believe that the whole thing was one of those rare pranks which the mind sometimes plays on that border realm between sleeping and waking, when a second of time frequently contains the impressions of years: in other words, that I was really awake with the eyes, and saw the loft in which I lay; while the mind, excited by the fragmentary words we had heard at supper, created the rest. In this case, the only thing remarkable about the story would be the coherence between the two visits; but this coherence, again, would be less singular in the intermediate state referred to, than in the dreams of a perfect sleep. It is *possible* that the incident was real: many persons would have accepted it as being so; but I did not feel sure enough of its reality to include it in my narrative of travel. It is certainly more valuable as an illustration of the singular force and vividness which mental impressions attain, when the senses are in conscious operation, than as a piece of actual experience.

An undoubted instance of the same kind happened to me, while in California, in November, 1849. Starting from Sacramento, on horseback, for a journey to the Mokelumne and the American Fork, I was detained three days at a lonely ranche near the Cosumne River, by a violent storm of rain. On the fourth morning, the clouds broke away. I saddled, swam the river, and took a faint trail leading over the plains, intending to make Hick's Ranche, twenty-four miles distant, among the foot-hills of the Sierra Nevada. Very soon, however, I lost the trail, which had been completely washed out by the rain. Riding at hazard towards the mountains, a sudden blind instinct—which I never felt before, and cannot intelligibly describe—told me to strike a bee-line in a certain direction. I thereupon took my bearings by the distant snowy peaks, and rode slowly on, my mare sinking to her knees at every step in the loose, saturated soil. It was during this ride that I came upon four grizzly bears, eating acorns in a little grove of oaks. Our interview was like that of two Englishmen in the desert: a momentary pause—a long stare—and each hurries to get out of sight of the other. To be candid, I did not desire an introduction.

I made such slow progress, that night came on as I was entering the foot-hills. I had kept my bee-line faithfully all day, and when I halted at dusk, in a little wooded dell, blazed two trees, so that I might resume the same direction in the morning. Giving my mare the length of her lasso, that she might crop the shrubs—as there was no grass to be had—I built up a large bonfire of dead limbs, and sat down beside it on a fallen tree. There was no moon, but the stars twinkled clearly through the bare branches overhead. I had depended on reaching the ranche, and was therefore without provisions. My supper consisted of a cigar and some rain-water, which had gathered in a hollow. What a comfort there is in a fire! I might give a thrilling picture of my sensations—lost, alone, and famishing—which my pecunious reader would shudder at, behind his lobster-salad. But it would not be true. I felt as cozy and comfortable as if before my own wide fire-place in the oaken chamber, and the starry silence of the night filled my heart with a soothing sense of happiness and peace.

Taking the saddle for a pillow, I wrapped myself in my blanket, and lay down, with my back to the field and my feet to the fire. But my slumbers were short and fitful. The neighborhood was famous for bears, and I was apprehensive that my mare would take fright, get loose, and forsake me. So I lay awake half an hour at a time, watching the culmination of the stars on the meridian line of a slender twig over my head. It was, perhaps, an hour past midnight, when, as I thus lay with open eyes, gazing into the eternal beauty of Night, I became conscious of a deep, murmuring sound, like that of a rising wind. I looked at the trees; every branch was unmoved—yet the sound increased, until the air of the lonely dell seemed to vibrate with its burden. A strange feeling of awe and expectancy took possession of me. Not a dead leaf stirred on the boughs; while the mighty sound—a solemn choral, sung by ten thousand voices—swept down from the hills, and rolled away like retreating thunder over the plain. It was no longer the roar of the wind. As in the wandering prelude of an organ melody, note trod upon note with slow, majestic footsteps, until they gathered to a theme, and then came the words, simultaneously chanted by an immeasurable host:—"*Vivant terrestriæ!*" The air was filled with the tremendous sound, which seemed to sweep near the surface of the earth, in powerful waves, without echo or reverberation.

Suddenly, far overhead, in the depths of the sky, rang a single, clear, piercing voice, of unnatural sweetness. Beyond the reach of human organs, or any earthly instrument, its keen *alto* pierced the firmament like a straight white line of electric fire. As it shot downwards, gathering in force, the vast terrestrial chorus gradually dispersed into silence, and only that one unearthly sound remained. It vibrated slowly into the fragment of a melody, unlike any which had ever reached my ears—a long, undulating cry of victory and of joy; while the words "*Vivat cœlum!*" were repeated more and more faintly, as the voice slowly withdrew, like a fading beam of sunset, into the abysses of the stars. Then all was silent in the dell, as before.

It is impossible to describe the impression produced by this wonderful visitation. I slept no more that night; and for days afterwards, the piercing sweetness of that skyey voice rang through my brain. Walking in Broadway, years later, the memory of it has flashed across my mind, as sharp and sudden as a streak of lightning; and if it now returns more faintly and less frequently than before, its weird and supernatural character remains the same. Yet, to my mind, the explanation is very simple. I was undeniably awake at the time, and could recall neither fact, reflection, nor fancy of a nature to suggest the sounds; but I was fatigued, famished, alone in the wilderness, awed by the solemnity and silence of the night—perhaps even more than I suspected—and my excited imagination, acting involuntarily and unconsciously to myself, produced the illusion. I have often observed that complete repose of the body, after great fatigue, is accompanied—when continued to a certain time—with a corresponding repose of volition, a passive condition of the mind, highly favorable to the independent action of the imagination. Then, if ever, are we in a fit state to hear

> "The airy tongues that syllable men's names
> On sands, and shores, and desert wildernesses."

The dream is none the less a wonder. How does one faculty of the brain act, so far beyond our conscious knowledge, as to astound us with the most unexpected images? Why should it speak in the Latin tongue? How did it compose music—which would be as impossible for me as to write a Sanscrit poem?

There is another interesting fact connected with this adventure. When daybreak came, I saddled my mare;

and, with the aid of the blazed trees, resumed the bee-line of the previous day. It was no easy matter to follow it, up and down the precipitous hills; but I had not proceeded an hour before my course was blocked by the very ranche to which I was bound! A blind animal instinct had guided me for twenty miles, over hill and plain, and hit the target exactly in the centre.

One more incident, of a more decided character, closes the list of my experiences. During my last visit to London, I accepted an invitation to pass two or three days with a banker, who occupies a fine estate on the Thames, near Windsor. The house—which was a palace in its extent and the character of its appointments—was built by a former Earl of T———, who ruined himself in erecting it. Gardens, graperies, and a noble park, stretching along the bank of the Thames, completed the attractions of one of the loveliest places in England. When the hour for rest arrived, I was conducted to a chamber looking towards the towered entrance, and a group of magnificent cedars of Lebanon, on the lawn. The night was misty and moonless—so that, after I had extinguished the candle, the room remained in almost complete darkness.

It was midnight when I went to bed; and I had slept, I suppose, until somewhere between two and three, when I suddenly awoke, and to my surprise, found that my candle was still burning. My first idea was, that I had forgotten to extinguish it. Closing my eyes, while revolving this question in my mind, I opened them again upon a room darkened as before. Through the uncurtained window, I saw the dim tops of the cedars rising against the misty

November sky. At the same instant, I detected a slight noise at the door—as if some one was cautiously trying to enter. But as the key was turned, the attempt was in vain; and I presently heard the same noise at the door of the adjoining dressing-room. Listening intently, I became aware of a slight creak at the door of communication between the two rooms. This was followed, not by a footstep, but by the hushed, rustling sound of a long dress trailing upon the floor. The sound marched slowly across the room, and approached the bedside, where it stopped. Then the gentlest touch—as, indeed, of airy fingers—drew the bed-clothes straight, and tucked the ends of the coverlids and sheets into the space between the mattress and bedstead. Meanwhile, I lay perfectly still, in a passive state of surprise and wonder.

When, however, the gentle ministry ceased, and I again caught the rustle of the trailing dress on the carpet, I sprang bolt upright in bed, and peered into the gloom, in hope of seeing the figure. But the room was a gulf of darkness, except the bit of window not covered by the cedars; and by this time the rustle had reached the dressing-room door. In a few seconds more, it had passed away completely; and, after exhausting myself in speculations as to the character of the visit, I slept. On mentioning the incident at breakfast, I found that none of the guests had been disturbed; nor could I learn that anything of the kind had previously happened in the house, although one gentleman affirmed that the old mansion, which was pulled down by Lord T——— before building the present one, had the reputation of being haunted.

Two different explanations occurred to me. Either the imaginative part of the brain was dreaming, while the senses were awake—as in the former cases—or the incident was real, and the mysterious visitor was a somnambulist—possibly a housekeeper or a chambermaid, unconsciously repeating her rounds to see that everything was in order. The vision of the lighted candle must have been an illusion—an instantaneous dream—suggested by that electric spark of light which is sometimes struck from the eyes on opening them suddenly.

In all these experiences, notwithstanding the liveliness and permanence of the impression produced on my mind, I am fully satisfied that there was nothing whatever of a supernatural character. So long as the visible world, and the constitution of our *mortal* nature, furnishes us with a sufficient explanation of such phenomena, why should we lay hold upon the invisible and the immortal?

XIV.

MORE OF THE SUPERNATURAL.

There is a class of mental phenomena, to which I have not yet alluded, of a character much more nearly allied to the supernatural than those described in the last chapter. In certain conditions of the body, the mind seems to become possessed of a new and unsuspected power, independent of volition—elusive and unmanageable as the plot of a dream to which we fain would give an agreeable solution, yet are helplessly carried on through a series of accumulated difficulties. Perhaps the term "natural clairvoyance" will best describe this power; since the eye of the mind looks straight through all material hindrances, and not only perceives that which is beyond the horizon of the bodily eye, but foresees what has not yet come to pass.

The credulous will, no doubt, reject the rational interpretation I have given to the experiences already described; and the sceptical, I presume, will be as ready to deny the existence of any such faculty as I now assume. Yet this faculty exists—abnormal, perhaps, yet not supernatural—I am fully convinced. Many persons live out their allotted term of years, without ever experiencing its operation; others are so rarely and so dimly conscious of it, that they class it among the ordinary delusions produced by fear, anxiety, or excitement of any kind; while a few receive such distinct and palpable evidences, that they are forced to admit the insufficiency of all other explanations. I see no difficulty in recognising this half-acknowledged faculty. When we understand the awful capacity of the mind to receive impressions—every word of the thousands we hear during the day, every form of the million objects we behold, though forgotten as soon as heard and seen, being indelibly stamped upon tablets which are stored away in some chamber of the brain, whereto we have no key—when we ponder upon this fact, with its infinite suggestions, we find it easy to believe that those operations of the mind of which we are *conscious*, are far from being the full measure of its powers.

But an ounce of illustration is better than a pound of theory. Let me relate a few instances, taken from my own personal experience, and that of some of my friends. The bee-like instinct of direction, referred to in the previous chapter, is not unusual among men accustomed to the wild life of the woods and mountains. More than one of my Rocky-Mountain acquaintances possess it in an eminent degree. A noted explorer, whose blanket I have often shared as we slept under the stars, assured me that frequently, while threading the interlocking folds of a mountain-pass, he has had a sudden vision of the landscape beyond, even to its minutest details. The same thing once occurred to me in Mexico, between Tepic and Guadalajara. He has, also, after searching all day for grass and water for his animals, in an unexplored wilderness, been seized with a blind instinct, which led him, against all reason, to the only spot where they were to be found.

During a visit to Boston, four or five years ago, I accepted an invitation to take tea with a distinguished author. A gentleman who had often visited him, offered to accompany me, as his residence was in a part of the city with which I was then unacquainted. We were walking along the street, conversing very earnestly upon some subject of mutual interest, when all at once I was seized with the idea that we were passing the author's house. "Stop!" I said; "Mr. —— lives here." My friend halted, surprised, and surveyed the house. "No," said he, "that is not his residence; it is in the next block. But I thought you had never visited him." "Nor have I," I replied; "I never was in this street before, but I am positive he lives there." "And I am positive he does not," my friend rejoined; "there is a large brass plate upon his door, with the name upon it; and, you see, here is no name whatever. Besides, it is not in this block." "I will go further with you," was my stubborn answer; "but we shall have to return again." The presumption of his certain knowledge did not in the least shake my confidence. We searched the next block, but did not find the author's name on any door. With some difficulty, I persuaded my friend to return, and try the house I had pointed out: it was the right one! I can explain this curious incident in no other way, than by assuming the existence of a natural clairvoyant faculty in the mind.

Of course, such experiences are very rare; and, as they generally occur at the most unexpected moments, it is next to impossible to go back, and ascertain how the impression first makes itself felt. Once, only, have I been conscious of the operation of the faculty. This took place in Racine, Wisconsin, on the morning of the 1st of March, 1855. My bed-room at the hotel was an inner chamber, lighted only by a door opening into a private parlor. Consequently when I awoke in the morning, it was difficult to tell, from the imperfect light received through the outer room, whether the hour was early or late. A lecturer, especially after his hundredth performance, is not inclined to get up at daylight; and yet, if you sleep too long, in many of the western towns, you run the risk of losing your breakfast. I was lying upon my back, *with closed eyes*, lazily trying to solve the question, when, all at once, my vision seemed to be reversed—or rather, a clearer spiritual vision awoke, independent of the physical sense. My head, the pillow on which it rested, and the hunting-case of my watch, became transparent as air; and I saw, distinctly, the hands on the dial pointing to eleven minutes before six. I can only compare the sensation to a flash of lightning on a dark night, which, for the thousandth part of a second, shows you a landscape as bright as day. I sprang up instantly, jerked forth my watch, opened it; and there were the hands, pointing to *eleven minutes before six*—lacking only the few seconds which had elapsed between the vision and its proof

Is this, after all, any more singular than the fact that a man can awaken at any hour that he chooses? What is the spiritual alarm-clock which calls us at four, though we usually sleep until six? How is it that the web of dreams is broken, the helpless slumber of the senses overcome, at the desired moment, by the simple passage of a thought through the mind hours before? I was once, of necessity, obliged to cultivate this power, and brought it, finally, to such perfection, that the profoundest sleep ceased as suddenly, at the appointed minute, as if I had been struck on the head with a mallet. Let any one tell me, clearly and satisfactorily, how this is done, before asking me to account for the other marvel.

But, in certain conditions, the mind also *foresees*. This may either take place in dreams, or in those more vague and uncertain impressions which are termed presentiments. I will only relate a single instance, since it is useless to adduce anything which is not beyond the range of accident or coincidence. I spent the winter of 1844–5 at Frankfort-on-the-Main, living with Mr. Richard Storrs Willis, in the family of a German merchant there. At that time there was only a mail once a month between Europe and America, and if we failed to receive letters by one steamer, we were obliged to wait four weeks for the next chance. One day the letters came as usual for Mr. Willis, but none for me. I gave up all hope for that month, and went to bed in a state of great disappointment and dejection; but in the night I dreamed that it was morning, and I was dressing myself, when Mr. Willis burst into the room saying: "The postman is below—perhaps he has letters for you. Come up into the dining-room, and you can see him from the window." We thereupon went up to the dining-room on the third story, looked down into the street, and there stood the postman—who, as soon as he saw us, held up a letter at arm's length, holding it by the lower right-hand corner. Though he was in the street, and I in the third story, I read my name upon it.

I arose in the morning with my head full of the dream. When I was about half dressed, Mr. Willis came into my room, repeating the very words I had heard in my sleep. We went into the dining-room together, looked down, and there stood the postman, holding up a letter by the lower right-hand corner! Of course I could not read the address at that distance; but my name *was* upon it. In this case, the circumstances were altogether beyond my control; and the literal manner in which the dream was fulfilled, in every minute particular, is its most astonishing feature. Nothing was added or omitted: the reality was a daguerreotype of the vision. Never before had my friend entered my room at so early an hour—never before had the postman held up a letter in that manner. If a coincidence only, the occurrence is therefore all the more marvellous.

When I was last in Florence, the sculptor Powers related to me a still more remarkable story, which had come to pass only a few days before my arrival. A young English lady of his acquaintance, who was living with her brother in the city, was on terms of great intimacy and affection with a lady of her own age, who was spending the summer with her father in a villa among the Apennines, near Pistoja. This friend had invited her to visit her during the summer:

she had accepted the invitation; and the middle of August was fixed upon as the time. Three weeks before, however, the young lady had a remarkable dream. It seemed to her that the day of her departure for the villa near Pistoja had arrived. Her trunk was packed; and early in the morning, a very curious old carriage drove to the door to receive her. The vetturino slung her trunk to the axletree with ropes—a disposition of baggage which she had never before seen. She took her seat, and for several hours journeyed down the vale of the Arno, noticing the scenery, which was entirely new to her. Several trifling incidents occurred on the way, and there was a delay occasioned by the giving way of the harness; but towards evening she reached the Apennine villa.

As the carriage approached the building, she perceived the father of her friend standing in the door, with a very troubled countenance. He came forward, as she was preparing to alight, laid his hand on the carriage door, and said: "My daughter is very ill, and no one is allowed to see her. To-night is the crisis of her fever, which will decide whether she will recover. I have made arrangements for you to spend the night in the villa of Mr. Smith yonder; and pray heaven that my daughter's condition will permit you to return to us to-morrow!" Thereupon he gave directions to the vetturino, who drove to Mr. Smith's villa. The host received her kindly, ushered her into a broad entrance-hall, and said: "I will endeavor to make you comfortable for the night. *That* will be your room," pointing to a glass door, with green curtains, at the end of the hall. Here her dream suddenly stopped.

The next morning she related the whole story to her brother. For a few days afterwards, they occasionally referred to it; but as she received information that her friend was in excellent health, she gradually banished from her mind the anxiety it had caused her. The day fixed upon for her journey at length arrived. What was her astonishment, when the identical queer old carriage of her dream drove up to the door, and her trunk was slung by ropes to the axletree! This was the commencement; and during the whole day everything occurred precisely as she had already seen it. Towards evening, she arrived at the villa near Pistoja; and the father of her friend stood in the door, with a troubled countenance. He came forward, repeating the intelligence of his daughter's illness in the same words, and ordered the vetturino to drive to the villa of Mr. Smith. The excitement and alarm of the young lady had been continually on the increase; so that, when she finally reached the broad entrance-hall, and Mr. Smith said, "I will endeavor to make you comfortable for the night. *That* will be your room" (pointing to the glass door with green curtains), her nerves, strung to their utmost tension, gave way, and she fell upon the floor in a swoon. Fortunately, there was no ground for superstitious forebodings. The crisis passed over happily, and the very next day she was permitted to nurse her convalescent friend.

Here the dream, in all its details, was narrated three weeks before its verification—thus setting aside any question of the imagination having assisted in the latter. It is one of the most satisfactory examples of second-sight I have ever heard of, and this must be my justification for giving it to the world.

I cannot close this chapter, without giving one more authentic ghost story—to which, in my opinion, the same explanation will apply as to those I have related in the preceding article. A gentleman (permit me to withhold his name, station, and the date of the occurrence) was once travelling in the interior of Sweden. On a raw evening, in October, he arrived at a large country-town, where a fair was being held. All the inns were full, and he found it no easy matter to obtain lodgings for the night. He was weary, from a long day's journey, and after applying at the third or fourth inn without success, announced to the landlord his determination to remain there, with or without a bed. He procured some supper, smoked his pipe in the guests' room, and finally, feeling inclined to sleep, demanded to be shown some place where he could lie down. "Have you no sofa, or bench, or bundle of hay vacant?" he asked the landlord. "No," said the latter—"not one; but—" here he hesitated—"there is a room with a bed in it, in a small house at the back of the court, only"—dropping his voice to a whisper—"the place is haunted; and nobody dares to spend the night there." "Oh! if that is all," laughed the traveller, "give me the room at once. I don't believe in ghost or demon; and, besides, I'm far too tired to be troubled with anything of the sort."

The landlord still hesitated, as if doubtful whether he should expose his stubborn guest to such dangers; but, finally, gave orders to have a fire made in the ill-omened room, and fresh sheets put upon the unused bed. Taking his saddle-bags on his arm, and his sword in his hand, the traveller followed the servant across the court-yard, and entered the building. The room was low and bare, the windows closed by shutters, whose rusty bolts showed that it was long since they had been opened. A ruddy fire of pine wood was blazing on the raised hearth, in one corner, but there was no furniture, except a narrow bed and two chairs. The servant, having placed the candle on one of the chairs, made haste to leave; but the traveller detained him a moment, saying; "You see my sword—and here are two pistols, loaded and capped. If anything disturbs me in the night, man or ghost, I shall immediately fire upon it. Unless you hear a shot, leave me alone." He did this, from a suspicion that the ghost might be some person connected with the inn, who, for purposes of his own, was concerned in banishing all nightly visitors from the house.

After the servant left, the traveller heaped more wood on the fire, carefully examined the windows and door, and after locking the latter, suspended the heavy key upon the latch, in such a manner that the least movement would cause it to fall. He then undressed, with the exception of his trowsers, placed the chair with the candle at the head of the bed, the pistols under the pillow, and lay down, with his sword beside him on the bed-clothes, within reach of his hand. He then blew out the candle, and composed himself to rest. As he did not feel the slightest fear or trepidation, he soon fell into a sound sleep.

About midnight, he was suddenly awakened by a feeling like that of a rush of cold wind over his face. Opening his eyes, he found the room quiet as before; but the candle by his bedside was burning. He distinctly recollected having extinguished it, but nevertheless persuaded himself that he must have been mistaken—got up, threw more wood on the fire, examined the doors and windows, and, after having returned to bed, snuffed the candle short, that there might be no mistake this time. Half an hour afterwards he was again awakened by the same rush of cold wind. The candle was burning once more! This inexplicable circumstance made him feel excited and uneasy. He extinguished the candle, and resolved to lie awake, and see whether it would be lighted a third time.

Another half hour had elapsed, and his heavy eyelids had closed, in spite of all his struggles to keep them open, when the rush of wind returned, more violent than before. The candle was not only relighted, but a tall figure, clothed in a long, heavy gown, with a hood falling forward so as to conceal the face, stood in the centre of the room. An icy chill ran through the traveller's frame. He attempted to seize his sword and pistols, but his frame seemed paralysed, and his arms refused to obey the direction of his will. Step by step the figure advanced towards the bed. It reached the bedside; it slowly lifted its arms, enveloped in the wide sleeves of the gown—and, with an awful deliberateness, bent down towards the traveller's body. In the frenzy of terror, he burst the spell which seemed to confine his limbs, seized the snuffers which lay nearest his right hand, and stabbed, again and again, at the breast of the figure. This was the last thing he remembered.

He was recalled to consciousness by a loud knocking at the door, followed by the fall of the key from the latch, and heard the servant's voice calling: "Open the door, if you please, sir; I have come to make the fire." He was lying, not in bed, but upon the floor, in the middle of the room. The snuffers were still in his hand; but the long steel points were bent double. The morning light already shone through the crack of the door. By the time he was fully aroused, he had recovered his self-possession, and at once admitted the servant. "Holy cross!" exclaimed the man—"how pale you are! What has happened?" "Nothing whatever," answered the traveller, "except that the fire has gone out, and I am almost dead of cold." He protested to the landlord that he passed a very pleasant night, and ridiculed the notion of the house being haunted; but took good care, nevertheless, to leave the town in the course of the day.

My readers can themselves apply to this story the explanation I have suggested. And so, let us now bid farewell to the border-land of dreams!

XV.

A NOVEMBER TRIP NORTHWARDS.

[1854.]

IF there is any form of dissipation which I detest and abjure, it is, getting up at half-past four in the morning. The unfortunates who indulge in this vicious habit show the same infatuation, in other forms, as the devotees of opium or alcohol. They foresee the misery which the indulgence will occasion them, but no persuasion can induce them to abstain from it. The man who gets up at half-past four, in order to leave by the early train, is always tormented by a horrible fear that he will not be called in time. It needs the solemn assurances of the hotel-clerk, and of each of the attending servants, to give him a little composure; but his trepidation is still so great, that, after he is snugly stowed away in bed, and has fallen into an unquiet doze, he starts up, half a dozen times, thinking that the fateful hour is at hand. By-and-bye he drops off into a deep sleep, from which he awakens with a sudden shock, after having slept, as he supposes, for the space of twenty-four hours. He gropes for his watch with a trembling hand, and looks at the dial. There is just light enough to bewilder his vision, but he dimly sees a hand pointing to VI! A cold sweat breaks out over him, but he finally secures a match, ignites it, and finds the hour to be *half-past twelve.* Again he falls asleep; but this time he is aroused by a sound like the storming of the Malakoff—it is the waiter knocking at his door. He gets up, dresses with a haste which does not allow him to wash the gossamers of sleep fairly out of his eyes, and then wanders down endless stairs and passages of the dark, unfriendly edifice, with a vague doubt in his mind, as to whether it is yesterday or to-morrow. Breakfast is not ready until the last moment, and nothing but the knowledge that he shall get nothing else until 5 P.M. induces him to swallow the leathery beefsteak, and the brown, earthy beverage, supposed to be coffee. Mastication is impossible, and as for digestion, it must take care of itself. Then the porter seizes him, and, after many worries, he finally steps aboard the cars, just as the conductor cries "Go ahead!" and secures the half of a small seat behind the door.

Such was your correspondent's experience on the morning of Oct. 31, 1854; and his pleasure was further enhanced by the raw, thick fog, through which the gas-lamps of Chambers Street glimmered with a weak yellow glare. For an hour and a half we ran through the same know-nothing atmosphere, until the peaks of the Highlands tore and scattered the vapors, battling against their onsets. Cro'-nest and Butter Hill stood out clear and unconquered, and when we passed the pines of Idlewild, on the breezy terrace across the river, there was an opening of blue sky beyond Snake Hill. I never saw more gorgeous autumnal tints than those of the sumacs, sassafras, and beech along the banks of the Hudson. But as we whirled northwards, the day became raw and gloomy, and the colors of the forests more dull and monotonous. In Vermont the trees were robed in dull brown, and as we drew near Lake Champlain, even this last sad garment was stripped off, and the landscapes were naked and bleak as winter.

Beyond Rutland the road was new to me, and my imagination, clothing the country with summer, restored its lost beauty. The view of Champlain, at Vergennes, with the misty lines of the Adirondac in the background, reminded me of Lake Thrasymene, which I saw on just such an afternoon of an Italian December. At Burlington we were obliged to wait two or three hours for the Whitehall boat. It rained dismally, and we northern travellers were huddled together on the cold, windy pier, comforted by the assurance that the train would not leave Rouse's Point until we arrived. When we finally reached the latter place, about half-past nine, we were coolly informed that the train *never waited* for the evening boat, and had left nearly two hours before. There is a hotel in the station-house (or a station-house in the hotel, for I hardly know which predominates), and I secured a long cell, with a window higher than my head. By getting on a chair I saw a bridge in the moonlight, which I took to be the famous bridge of Rouse's Point.

The next morning, while waiting for the cars, I was familiarly addressed by a gentleman, as "Mr. Joseph Whipples." Until I meet the real Whipples, I cannot tell which of us is complimented by the resemblance. There was a polite Canadian Custom-er in attendance, who took my simple word as evidence that I was no smuggler, and marked a double cross on all my baggage, which admitted it unopened into Canada. The words "*Traverse de chemin de fer*" (Look out for the locomotive when the bell rings!), at the crossings, first told me that I had crossed the frontier. The country was flat as a pancake, wet and dreary; log huts, painted red, stood here and there, alternating with stunted woods and fields full of charred pine-stumps. At the stopping-places, I saw men with round fur caps, and broad, hardy faces, who spoke French with a savage accent, which made it sound like another language. In some places they were ploughing in the fields with *real* Canadian ponies. We followed the course of the St. Johns River, which gleamed brightly on our right, and in something over an hour came to the flourishing town of St. Johns, near which there is a very picturesque, isolated hill. Here the road swerved to the north-west, and made direct for St. Lambert, opposite Montreal.

When we got out of the cars, on the long pier, and saw the stately city rising behind its massive quays, I could have believed myself—but for the breadth and swiftness of the St. Lawrence—on the banks of the Seine. The sun suddenly shone out, gilding the lofty towers of the cathedral, the tall spires of churches, the domes and tinned roofs that stretched along the river for more than a mile and a half, to which the bold, wooded mountain in the rear formed a majestic background. I was at once reminded of Auxerre, Montreuil, and other old provincial cities of France. A mile of the clear, cold, green St. Lawrence, running at the rate of eight or ten miles an hour, lay between me and the city—a type of the vigor and impetuosity of the New World, encircling the repose and solidity of a scene which seemed to have been borrowed from the Old.

In spite of its massive and solid aspect, few towns have suffered more from fires than Montreal. The northern and eastern portions still abound with the melancholy ruins left by recent conflagrations. In spite of this, however, and in spite of narrow and dirty streets, the city has a *finished* air, which distinguishes it from all towns of equal size in the States. The principal material used in building is a dark-gray limestone, which is very easily worked in the quarry, but becomes quite hard by exposure to the air. The water of Montreal has a flavor of this stone, which is by no means agreeable, nor always wholesome to strangers. The principal street, the Grande Rue St. Jacques, is a bright, cheerful thoroughfare, but more English than French in its character. I was more interested in the old streets nearer the river, which still have a certain Gallic quaintness about them.

The weather, after my arrival, was delicious. The next morning dawned without a cloud, and with a pure, sweet, bracing air, such as I have rarely breathed on the Atlantic

8

side of our Continent. Its inhalation was a violation of the Maine Law, which prohibits the use of all intoxicating beverages. It contained a stimulus as keen and active, if not so poisonous, as alcohol. I went out after breakfast, and became so inebriated that I found it difficult to return to my hotel. I got quite high—in fact, I did not stop until I had reached the summit of the mountain behind the city. On the way, I passed a large reservoir of masonry, which the city authorities are building on the slope at the foot of the mountain. The water will be forced up by a wheel at Lachine, above the rapids, and will furnish a supply, which, it is hoped, will prevent Montreal from being again laid waste by fires. The thought of so much water, all with the same limestone flavor, and the same horrid intestinal qualities, filled me with repugnance. Give me the iced champagne of this glorious air in my lungs, and let those drink water who will!

Montreal has shown great taste and good sense in preserving the mountain, with its clothing of primitive forest, within fifteen minutes' reach of her 70,000 inhabitants. Behind the reservoir, we jumped over a stone wall, and were in the wild woods. There was a rugged, zigzag path up the steep slant of the hill, but it was almost hidden under the fallen leaves. Although a good climber, my knees became weak and my breath short, before reaching the crest. The groves of pine and silver birch obstructed the view, except at one point, where we found an Irish boy, lying in the sun, pointing out "Mr. Smith's house" to another Irish boy. Here I was greeted with the sight, not only of Mr. Smith's house, but of all Montreal, of many leagues of the St. Lawrence, flashing splendidly in the sun, of the broad plains beyond, sprinkled with the white cottages of the *habitans*, and far in the dim south, the outflying spurs of the Vermont and Adírondac Mountains. It was a grand and inspiring panorama, embraced by the cold, bright blue of the Canadian sky. Well did the followers of Jacques Cartier call this the Royal Mountain.

We found another faint trail leading northwards through the pines and birch, and having followed it up for a short distance, reached the opposite brink of the mountain, whence we looked away beyond the Island of Jesus, girdled by the blue arms of the Ottawa, to a distant horizon of low hills and forests. In the keen northern air, which came to us over the rim of that horizon, there was a whisper of Hudson's Bay and of those snowy lodges by the Great Fish River where lie the corpses of the Arctic explorers. It requires but a slight elevation to make the ends of the earth seem near to us. Along the Ottawa River there are settlements for two hundred miles, and many hundred leagues further to the North-West Passage, yet to my fancy the site of that useless problem was just beyond the range of vision. There are bears and deer in some of the forests I saw, and the "ravages" of the moose may be reached in a few days' journey.

In the afternoon I had the pleasure of inspecting the works of the Victoria Bridge, which is to span the St. Lawrence at this place. I was indebted to the courtesy of Mr. Holmes and Mr. Grant, of the Grand Trunk Railroad Company, for the opportunity of seeing in detail the beginnings of this colossal undertaking. The bridge, which is to be of iron, and tubular, like that over the Menai Strait, will be *two miles* in length, and its central arch will have a span of 333 feet. The material used is black limestone, and the Titanic piers, which compete with the grand masonry of Egypt, are based upon the solid natural rock which here forms the bed of the St. Lawrence. Immense strength is required in the piers, in order to resist the pressure of the ice. The huge blocks of stone are laid in hydraulic cement of the firmest character, and melted lead, and strongly clamped together with iron. In the middle of the river the current runs at the rate of nine or ten miles an hour, and the force of the immense masses of ice, carried down at the breaking up of winter, is so great that the old residents of Montreal shake their heads and predict that the bridge will be a failure. But I cannot conceive how these piers can be shaken any more than so many masses of natural rock. Certainly, human genius never better counterfeited the strength of nature. It is refreshing to see on this continent, where the most that is done is temporary and transitory, a work which rivals the Pyramids. The cost of the bridge, when completed, is estimated at £1,500,000, but will probably be nearer £2,000,000.

On leaving Montreal, your correspondent was guilty of the same dissipation as on leaving New York: he got up at half-past four. There is some difference, however, between a Montreal hotel and a New York hotel before daylight. We had been promised our breakfasts, but on descending to the office at a quarter past five, found only two Irish girls washing the floor. They were "know-nothings" in the fullest sense, and snubbed all my endeavors to obtain information. Finally, "the Superintendent," as he styled himself—a dark gentleman who had probably once been white property, and now retaliated by looking upon all whites as *his* property—made his appearance. His assumption of superiority was so sublime that I was amused rather than annoyed by it. He majestically disdained all explanations, declining all conversation by a wave of his hand, and the oracular remark that "everything was right." It happened, in the end, that we reached the ferry-boat before she pushed off, but the rapidity with which we underwent breakfast would have astonished a weaker stomach than your correspondent's. On landing from the omnibus on the quay, we found the ticket-master in waiting, with a lantern and a pocketful of tickets. I held the lantern for him, while he counted out my change. Of course there could be no crowding at the window with such an arrangement.

The sky was a dull gray blanket, with a strip of fiery red binding, in the north-east, over St. Helen's Island. As the wind blew it threw upwards a hidden fringe of the same crimson hue, and the dark, cheerless landscape faded into the colors of dawn. Before we were half-way across the St. Lawrence, a snow-squall came down upon the river, almost hiding from view the stately city we were leaving. The air was searchingly raw and cold, and I took but a hasty farewell glance, with the wish that I may one day see the same shores in the glory of summer. As we sped over the wet plains, on our way to Rouse's Point, the snow continued, and the country was soon whitened, far and near. The atmosphere had lost all its purity and elasticity, and I felt glad that my course was southwards.

At Rouse's Point, we found the train for Ogdensburg in waiting. The Canadian plains appear to cease at the frontier, for the country through which we passed was moderately undulating, with occasional hills in the distance. It was a dreary alternation of pine woods, stumpy clearings, barren-looking fields, and meagre villages. The raw, gusty day, with frequent flurries of snow, undoubtedly added to its bleak and forbidding aspect, but I do not believe that even June could make it inviting. The road passes through the northern edge of Clinton, Franklin, and St. Lawrence counties, crossing many of the tributaries of the St. Lawrence, among which I noted the Chateauguay, Salmon, St. Regis, Hatchet, and Grass Rivers. The country is all well watered and timbered. The only town which made any show from the railroad was Malone, which had a flourishing air. At one of the stations, where I got out to warm myself with a cup of coffee, I was much interested in the aspect of a female waiter. She stood with folded arms, gazing into vacancy, and when requested to furnish the coffee obeyed with the least possible expenditure of movement, removed the cup and took the money in the same way, without honoring me with a single glance, and then folded her arms again. The freezing dignity of her countenance repelled all idea of conversation. Were I a sculptor, I should be delighted to find such an excellent model for a statue of Indifference.

The country improved after passing Potsdam, and the road descended to the St. Lawrence. The sun, breaking through the clouds, shone with a cold brilliance on the farms and farm-houses of the Canada shore, as we reached

Ogdensburg, the end of the day's journey. I found comfortable quarters at the St. Lawrence Hotel, and they were truly welcome, for as the sky cleared, the air became intensely cold. The windows of my room were covered with a thick crust of ice the next morning, and the temperature could not have been higher than 15°.

Under the guidance of Judge James, I saw as much of Ogdensburg as the cold permitted. The Judge is well versed in the early history of this region, which he repeated to me while we were seeking a distant view of Chimney Island—so called from the ruins of the old French fort, destroyed by Lord Amherst. The situation of the town is fine, with the exception that it faces the north. The banks of the Oswegatchie, which here empties into the St. Lawrence, are high and bluff, forming a crescent-shaped curve, open to the west. The crest of the right bank is lined with handsome dwelling-houses, and has a charmingly picturesque air when viewed from the bridge below. Conspicuous among the buildings is the Court-House, which still bears the marks of a cannon-ball sent across the river, during the last war. Ogdensburg, like Montreal, has suffered terribly from fires, but in spite of these drawbacks to its growth, it has a population of nine or ten thousand.

I left for Sackett's Harbor the next evening in the steamer Niagara. The night was superbly moonlit, but bitterly cold. We dropped down the river, ran across to Windmill Point, the scene of Schultz's defeat during the Rebellion of '37, and rounded up to Prescott, whence a railroad has been opened to Ottawa, on the Ottawa River. I gave up all hopes of seeing the Thousand Islands, which it was said we should not reach before midnight, but did not seek my state-room until we had touched at Morristown and Brockville, the former on the American, the latter on the Canadian shore. They are both thriving places, but Brockville bore away the palm of appearance, in the moonlight.

Speaking of palms reminds me how I longed to be back again inside the Tropics that night. When I went to my state-room, the pitcher contained a solid lump of ice instead of water. The loose window rattled in the wind, and as the bedding was cut according to the width of the berth, I leave the reader to imagine whether a man could tuck himself in or not. The long night passed away in a weary battle, wherein Cold did not lose a single intrenchment, but Sleep was utterly routed, and fled. I diversified my misery by looking out on the wintry shores, which were coldly lighted by the moon. I have an idea that I saw some of the Thousand Islands, but I was in such a numb, torpid, half-awake state, that I cannot to this day tell whether it was a dream or a reality. I certainly have in my mind the images of three or four natural piers of rock, surmounted with dark clumps of pine, but they are of such a singularly weird aspect that I half-suspect they belong to the realm of dreams.

The lurid glare of the dawn upon a black sky at last called me from my freezing berth. We were in the harbor of Kingston, trying to make fast to the wharf, for it blew a gale. The wind was so violent that the captain at once gave up all idea of proceeding further. I saw a boat, manned by six oarsmen, put off in the endeavor to reach a brig which lay about a hundred yards out, but it could not make the least headway, and finally was driven back again. The sea was not very high, but terribly rough and chopping. As there was no chance of reaching Sackett's Harbor that day by the Niagara, I decided to try my luck in the ferry-boat which runs across to Cape Vincent, connecting with the Rome and Watertown Railroad, and in the meantime took a stroll through Kingston.

The place is very much like an English seaport town—solid, quiet, sober in its hue, and yet with a rakish air which is not easily described. The same black limestone is used as in Montreal, and I noticed two or three fine Gothic churches—minus the towers—built of it. The Market Hall is really a noble edifice, and presents an imposing front to the harbor. Kingston has the reputation of being a very immoral town; whether deservedly so or not I cannot say. My survey of it was very limited, for the air was intensely keen and strong, and the dust, at times, blinding. I noticed in the port a vessel of 1,000 or 1,200 tons, built for an English house, and was informed that shipbuilding is getting to be quite an important business in the place, on account of the cheapness of timber and the facilities for procuring it.

At half-past eleven the little steamer Star dashed out into the gale, hoping to reach Cape Vincent in time for the 3 P.M. train. She was obliged to go below Grand Island, in order to avoid the force of the wind, which increased the distance to thirty-two miles. She was a staunch little craft, and made good time after we got under the lee of the island, so that by three o'clock we were in sight of the Cape, and had the satisfaction of seeing the train start.

Luckily, we had the engineer on board, and the conductor waited for us at the freight dépôt, which we reached fifteen minutes after the time. Grand Island, which is twenty-seven miles in length, is a wild, bleak tract, belonging to Canada.

The country between Cape Vincent and Watertown has a poor, unfertile appearance, but seems well adapted for grazing. It is undulating and rather monotonous for the greater part of the way. Chaumont Bay, an estuary of Lake Ontario, recalls the name of Le Ray de Chaumont, who is concerned in the history of the Rev. Eleazer Bourbon. As we approached Watertown there was a visible improvement both in soil and scenery, and the picturesque banks of the Black River were all the more agreeable after the monotonous country through which we had passed.

I was very pleasantly impressed with the appearance of Watertown. It is, without doubt, the stateliest town of its size in the country. At the Woodruff House I found accommodations not inferior to any first-class hotel in New York, and the view of the public square from its windows needs only a crowd to be metropolitan in its character. In the centre of this square is a fountain, which, unlike our City fountains, *plays.* The main street is a boulevard, with a double row of trees between the sidewalk and the central highway. On either side thereof are neat residences, each embowered in its own private trees and flowers. The Black River skirts the town, foaming down a gorge of dark limestone rock. Here and there it plunges into cataracts, which fringe its dark-brown translucence with streaks of snow. Its color is that of a *shaded* river—

a son of the forests and the mountains, steeped in the flavor of hemlock and fir. But, wild mountaineer as it is, it must labor like the rest of us, and keeps many a mill-wheel going.

From Watertown I came southwards, and succeeded in enjoying the last days of the Indian Summer, before the winter from which I had fled overtook me again.

XVI.

THE MAMMOTH CAVE.

[MAY, 1855.]

PART I.—THE JOURNEY THITHER.

WE were a family party of six, and ourselves and our baggage, including a bucket for the horses, just filled two carriages. It was our intention to have left New Albany, Ind. (where we had been sojourning a day or two), in the morning, in order to reach Elizabethtown the same evening; but the heavy rains of the previous night prevented us from starting before noon. Crossing the Ohio River to Portland we struck the Nashville turnpike on the outskirts of Louisville, and took up our journey towards Salt River, twenty-two miles distant. The country through which we passed is low, slightly undulating, and very fertile. Now and then appeared an old family mansion surrounded by its orchards and gardens, and presenting much the same aspect of comfort and repose as the country homesteads of Pennsylvania and Virginia. There were the same avenues of locusts, now in snowy and fragrant bloom; the same heavy brick dwelling with its portly front door, rarely opened but on state occasions; the same bowers of honeysuckle, trellises of grapes, beds of peonies and crown-imperials, and the same scattered clusters of out-houses, backed by the rounded tops of the orchard trees. The season is nearly a month in advance of the valley of the Hudson; all forest trees—even the latest—are in their young foliage, the apple and pear blossoms are gone, and the corn is ready for its first harrowing.

The afternoon was intensely hot and sultry. Heavy thunder-clouds were piled up on the northern and southern horizon, but they gradually rolled away without crossing our path. The latter part of our journey was through forests of beech, oak, and elm. The former tree, which greatly predominated, attains a size and beauty rarely seen east of the Alleghanies. Its foliage is the purest and most brilliant green, charmingly relieved by the smooth, white trunk, and the long, slender, feathery curve of the drooping boughs. We were delighted with the alternation of woodland and farm-scenery which the road afforded us. Towards evening we came again upon the Ohio—the Beautiful River, here as elsewhere—and followed its bank to the mouth of Salt River, on the opposite bank of which is West-Point, our resting-place for the night.

Where it debouches into the Ohio, Salt River is not more than fifty or sixty yards in breadth, but very deep. It is never fordable even in the dryest seasons; and, being navigable for fourteen miles above its mouth, has not been bridged at this point. We descended its steep and difficult banks, embarked our carriage upon a flat ferry-boat, and were conveyed across. The view, looking up the river, was very beautiful. Tall elms and sycamores clothed the banks, dropping their boughs almost to the water, and forming a vista of foliage through which the stream curved out of sight between wooded hills. I longed to be rowed up it. While on the spot, I took occasion to inquire the derivation of the slang political phrase, "Rowed up Salt River," and succeeded in discovering it. Formerly there were extensive salt-works on the river, a short distance from its mouth. The laborers employed in them were a set of athletic, belligerent fellows, who soon became noted far and wide for their achievements in the pugilistic line. Hence it became a common thing among the boatmen on the Ohio, when one of their number was refractory, to say to him: "We'll row you up Salt River"—where, of course, the bully salt-men would have the handling of him. By a natural figure of speech the expression was applied to political candidates, first, I believe, in the Presidential campaign of 1840, and is now extensively used wherever the Native-American language is spoken.

About nine o'clock the next day the clouds broke a little, the rain of the night ceased, and we started for Elizabethtown. After passing two or three miles of fertile bottoms, studded with noble beech woods, the road entered a glen in the Muldraugh Hills—a long, lateral branch of the Cumberland Range, which stretches quite through the centre of Kentucky. The road we were travelling is one of the finest in the United States—broad, smooth, and thoroughly macadamized. It follows the windings of the glen for three or four miles, so well graded that the ascent is barely perceptible. A brook swollen by the rains formed below us, now on this side, now on that, while numbers of tiny streams spouted from openings in the limestone rocks on either hand. The elms and beeches in the bed of the glen almost met above our heads, yet did not hide the slopes of splendid foliage of which they were the hem. In one of the wildest spots the mouth of a cavern opened on the right hand, pouring out a smooth cascade of silvery water. The scarlet aquilegia, the phlox, the white purslane, the violet, and other Spring flowers, grew in the crevices of the rocks, and brightened the fairy solitude.

After reaching the summit of the glen, we entered a rolling upland region, heavily wooded with forests of oak, hickory, and maple. The soil was thin and stony, and the country had rather a poor and unfertile aspect compared with that along the Ohio River. The farm-houses were mostly built of logs, and many of them had what might be termed an inclosed portico—a square opening of the height of the first story—passing entirely through them. All, even the poorest, had their negro hut or huts adjoining, though some of the latter appeared to be tenantless. The impression these establishments made upon me was that of moderate activity, intelligence ditto, and content with things as they are. We met many men on horseback, dressed in what appeared to be homespun cloth—tall, large-limbed, robust individuals, and fine specimens of animal health and vigor. Occasionally we passed large, canvas-covered wagons, drawn by three or four horses. The farmers saluted us with the stiff, silent nod peculiar to Anglo-Saxons, but the negro teamster frequently raised his hat to the ladies. We saw but a single carriage, driven by a gentleman who politely gave us the best side of the road, notwithstanding he was entitled to it. The same thing would not have happened north of the Ohio River.

We stopped for dinner at the Cool Spring tavern. The landlord, who had very much the air of a parson, received us with much ceremony, and then blew dolorously upon a conch-shell until "the boys," who were at work in a distant field, heard the summons and hurried home to take charge of our horses. We were regaled with Kentucky ham, eggs, excellent coffee, and corn-bread of that peculiar sweetness and excellence which only a Southern cook can give it. Indeed, the excellence of the country taverns in Kentucky was a matter of constant surprise to me. Without a single exception we were treated with a cordiality, and even kindness, which gave them all a friendly and home-like air, quite different from the dreary aspect of similar institutions north of the Ohio. The fare also was as notably good as it is notably bad in the more progressive States of the West. Kentucky may be called *slow* in comparison with Ohio and Illinois, but there is more genuine comfort and more genial social feeling within her borders than in either of the latter States.

Beyond Elizabethtown, we journeyed for ten miles through a rich, well-wooded rolling country to the village of Nolin, on the creek of the same name, and halted for the night at the tavern of Mr. Gehagan. We found a wood fire in the wide chimney very agreeable, for the evening air was unexpectedly cool. I am told that fires are frequently kindled in the evenings as late as the beginning of June. With this custom, however, is connected that of leaving the doors open, which insures ventilation. It belongs perhaps to the out-door life of the Kentuckians, for I found few doors that would shut closely. We were greatly amused by the impossibility of keeping our doors closed. In almost all cases every one who enters, master or servant, leaves them wide behind him. I rather like the habit, but it takes a little time to get used to it.

We started early the next morning, for the macadamized road ceased at Nolin, and we had eighteen miles of "dirt road" before us. Weary miles they were, for the rain had softened the sticky red clay soil, and our horses, though willing enough, were rather too light for such work. The country was similar to that we had passed, but richer, more open, and better cultivated. With the wide, undulating landscape blooming and breathing of Spring, and a pale-blue sky of the utmost clearness overhead, I found the journey delightful. After passing a long wooded ridge, we saw the blue wavy line of the Green River Hills before us, but we approached them very slowly until we struck the turnpike again, four miles from Munfordsville. In the woods through which our road lay we frequently saw fat rabbits leaping among the bushes, and once a large wild turkey darted across the path before us. Wood-robins and cat-birds sang among the trees, and in the evening long, rustling lines of pigeons flew over our heads on their way to the north-west.

The wooded hills assumed more broken and picturesque forms as we approached Munfordsville, and Summerseat Knob, beyond Green River, made a prominent feature of the landscape. The road followed the windings of a shallow glen, clothed with small oaks, for two or three miles; after which we came upon Munfordsville, the county town of Hart County. We drew up at Judge Kerr's, near the Court-House, and while our dinner was preparing had an opportunity of inspecting the natives, who were gathered together to vote at a county election. No important offices were at stake, and the occasion seemed to be passing off without much excitement of any kind. There were nearly as many horses present as men, and a few, but not many, good specimens of horse-flesh. A grocery opposite appeared to be doing a good business in the corn-whiskey line —a business which appears to be confined to groceries, for we saw but one tavern on the road where liquors were sold. The tall, sun-burned voters were collected into groups, discussing K. N. and S. N. matters, but in rather a quiet, listless way, as if they did not consider the welfare of their country wholly at stake.

We were furnished with a dinner admirable in all respects, and after consulting with the Judge concerning the roads to the Mammoth Cave, decided to go on to Ritter's Tavern, at Woodlands, and there rest for the night. The Cave was but fifteen miles distant by the nearest road, but it was a very rough way among the hills, and there was not enough daylight left to accomplish it with our jaded horses. We descended a steep bank to the bottom of the glen in which flows Green River, crossed the stream in a ferry-boat, and ascended the opposite bank to Woodsonville. The two towns seem not more than a stone's throw apart, but are separated by a hollow even more wild and beautiful than that of Salt River. The river is a clear green hue, fringed by noble elms, beeches, sycamores, and sweet gum-trees, which rise in walls of foliage from its translucent floor. I thought of Bryant's "Green River," to which his lines are not more applicable than to its Kentucky brother:

> "Yet fair as thou art, thou shunnest to glide,
> Beautiful stream! by the village side;
> But windest away from haunts of men,
> To silent valley and shaded glen."

Five miles beyond Woodsonville we came to a cluster of houses on a hill, which constituted an election precinct. There was the usual congregation of men and horses. Some ten or twelve of the former—full-grown, voting citizens—were playing marbles in the middle of the road, with as much interest as any group of school-boys I ever saw. They paid not the least regard to our approach, and we were obliged to drive around them to avoid a collision. A gaunt individual, mounted on a lean sorrel horse, rode up to me with the question: "How are the Know-Nothin's gittin' along whar you come from, stranger?" I replied: "They are pretty well split up: I come from New York," and asked him, in turn, what they were doing in the present election. "Oh," said he, "they can't do nothin' this year, no how, but next year they'll make a good show: I sort o' *lean* that way, *myself*"—and suiting the action to the word he leaned over his horse's neck until the saddle, which was ungirthed, began to turn, and his head being none of the steadiest, he had some difficulty in regaining his equilibrium.

The turnpike here ceased, and we came upon a heavy dirt-road leading through woodlands and pleasant green valleys between the abrupt "knobs" with which this part of the country is studded. Many returning voters on horseback kept us company. There was one who passed us in a state of unconsciousness mounted on a mare, behind which ran a little black mule. He reeled in the saddle at such a rate that I expected every moment to see him tumble into the road, but he always regained his balance miraculously at the last moment. Towards sunset we found him again, doubled up in a corner of the fence dead asleep, but still holding on to the bridle of his mare, who was grazing around his feet. At dusk we reached Woodlands, a capacious tavern, seated behind a lawn covered with ornamental shrubbery—a very cheerful, home-like place. Everything in and about the house gave tokens of neatness and comfort. The negro quarters were clean and commodious, and the spruce servants seconded our genial host, Mr. Ritter, in his endeavors to make our stay pleasant.

Woodlands is eleven miles from the Cave, by a wild road over the hills. Mr. Ritter gave me minute directions for finding the way, as the country is almost uninhabited. After travelling two miles through the woods we passed a log cabin and clearing, beyond which our way was blocked up by a tree which had been blown down by the winds. Two of us took rails from the fence to serve as levers, and as the ladies joined in the work with good will, the log was gradually heaved aside sufficiently to allow the carriages to pass. After our labors were over three men (inmates of the log-cabin) arrived for the purpose of assisting us. Crossing a deep valley, we climbed an opposite ridge, by a very steep and difficult road, and seeing the long, wooded crest of the hill extending far before us, supposed that the worst part of the journey was over. But exactly at this juncture the tongue of my carriage snapped in twain in consequence of a sudden wrench, and we were left stranded. We had neither ropes, knives, nor implements of any kind, and, after holding a council of war, decided that the only thing to be done was to leave the wreck in the woods. We succeeded in detaching the broken parts, lashing them to the remaining carriage, and mounting three persons upon the two horses, using the carriage cushions as saddles. One of the natives of this region, who had ridden up immediately after the accident, stood watching us during these proceedings, and at their close observed: "Well, I guess you're the right stripe: you can get along"—after which he left us.

We made slow but merry travel through the seven miles of forest intervening between us and the Cave Hotel, where we arrived in season for dinner, without further accident.

XVII.

THE MAMMOTH CAVE.

[MAY, 1855.]

PART II.—THE FIRST JOURNEY UNDER GROUND.

NOTWITHSTANDING the irregular order of our arrival, after our mishap in the woods, we were cordially welcomed by Mr. Miller, the host. The hotel is a long, straggling pile of wooden buildings, with stone chimneys attached to the exterior at the gable ends. A wing of furnished apartments joins its northern end, fronting upon a lawn where tall forest trees have been allowed to stand in their natural attitudes and groupings. The main body of the hotel, with this wing, furnishes at least six hundred feet of portico, forming one of the most delightful promenades imaginable for Summer weather. Around the place intervenes a narrow girdle of cleared land, beyond which stand the primitive woods, wherein the deer and wild turkey still make their habitation. We heard the call of the latter as we sat in the shaded portico. The rooms are sufficiently large and comfortable, though their doors have the same inability to be closed which I have already noticed as a characteristic of Kentucky architecture.

The season for travel had hardly commenced, and we found but seven visitors on our arrival. Two of these had just returned from a trip beyond the rivers, under the charge of "Stephen," the famous cave guide, and their clothes, bespattered with mud, gave us some indication of the character of the trip. As our stay was limited to two days, we decided to visit the cis-fluvial avenues the same afternoon, reserving the grand journey over the water for the next day. The rivers had been gradually rising for four days, and were then of precisely the most inconvenient stage, though not yet impassable. Mr. Miller informed me that they rarely rose more than four days in succession, and there was no likelihood at present that we should not be able to cross them. I engaged Stephen for the next day, and took Alfred, one of the other guides, for our initiatory excursion.

After dining off a noble haunch of venison, Alfred made his appearance with a bundle of lamps, and announced that everything was in readiness. Turning around the hotel to the northward, we entered a rocky ravine in the forest, and in a few minutes were made aware by a gust of cold wind that we had reached the entrance to the underground world. The scene was wild and picturesque in the extreme, yet the first involuntary sensation was something akin to terror. The falling in of the roof of the main avenue of the cave as it approached the surface of the earth has formed a gap, or pit, about fifty feet in depth, terminating in a dark, yawning portal, out of which a steady current of cold air was breathed in our faces. Trees grew around the edges of the pit, almost roofing it with shade; ferns and tangled vines fringed its sides; and a slender stream of water falling from the rocks which arched above the entrance, dropped like a silver veil before the mysterious gloom. The temperature of the cave is 59° throughout the year, and that of the upper air being about 75°, the colder stratum was ebbing out. When the inside and outside temperatures are equal, as they frequently are, there is no perceptible current.

Taking each a lighted lamp, we descended some rocky steps to the floor of the cavern, passed behind the tinkling cascade, and plunged into the darkness. The avenue rapidly contracts, and is closed by an artificial wall, with a door, which is sometimes locked to exclude pilferers. Having passed this, the daylight disappeared behind us. Our eyes, blinded by the sudden transition to complete darkness, could barely see a roof of solid rock not far above our heads, and masses of loose stones piled on either side. This part of the avenue is called "The Narrows." The space gradually expanded; the arch of the ceiling became more dim and lofty, and the walls only showed themselves by a faint and uncertain glimmer. The floor under our feet was firm and well-beaten, the air we breathed pure and refreshing, and a feeling of perfect confidence and security replaced the shrinking sensation which I think nearly every one must feel on first entering.

As the pupils of our eyes expanded, and we began to discern more clearly by the light of our lamps the dimensions of the grand avenue, we reached a spacious hall called The Vestibule, which is said to be directly under the Cave Hotel. It is seventy or eighty feet in height, branching off on one side into a spacious cave called Audubon's Avenue. Near it is the Great Bat-room, which hundreds of bats have chosen as a place of hibernation. We were now in the Main Cave, which extended for three or four miles before us with an average height of about fifty, and an average breadth of at least eighty feet, in some places expanding to one hundred and fifty feet. What are the galleries of the Vatican, the Louvre, Versailles, and the Crystal Palaces of London and Paris to this gigantic vault hewn in the living rock? Previous to the crossing of the Bottomless Pit in 1838, and subsequently of the Rivers in 1840, all the published accounts of the Mammoth Cave described only this avenue and its branches. The sides are perpendicular walls with a distinct and sometimes bold cornice, and a slightly-arched ceiling which often resembles a groined vault. The limestone lies in horizontal strata with scarcely a fault, and all the wonderful forms which it assumes are clearly traceable to the action of water.

Immediately on entering, you see the remains of the saltpetre works, which were carried on here from 1808 to 1814. The old hoppers or leaching vats, the sluices for carrying off the water, and many other appliances, are still almost as perfect as if the manufacture had just been relinquished. The wood-work remains perfectly sound and uncorrupted, and even the ruts made by cart-wheels, and the prints of the oxen's hoofs in the then moist soil, have not been effaced. It is said that saltpetre to the value of $20,000 was washed from the earth in one year, and that in the course of three years the same earth became as richly impregnated as before. This property is also communicated to the air, but probably in a less degree. I am not aware that it has ever been analysed; but whether from the absence of vegetable exhalations and the consequent purity of its constituent elements, or from the presence of some exhilarating property, it is certainly more bracing and invigorating than the air of the upper world. After we had become accustomed to its diminished temperature, its inhalation was a luxury. I can only compare it to a very mild nitrous oxide. The oxen which were taken into the cave to haul earth to the saltpetre vats became fat and plump in the course of two or three months without any extra feed. As a sanitarium for consumptive patients, the cave does not seem to answer; but the experiment has not yet been fairly tried—most of the invalids who came here having been in the advanced stages of the disease. Besides, the absence of sunlight—which seems to exercise a subtle influence upon human as upon vegetable vitality—might counterbalance in many cases the advantages of an equable and stimulating air.

Nearly a quarter of a mile beyond The Vestibule, we came to a second dome inserted like a transept in the main avenue or nave, and called The Church. The roof, which is about eighty feet high, is almost Gothic; and on the left hand is a gallery or choir with a projecting pulpit at one of the angles. Here service is often performed on Sundays during the summer. We took our seats on some timbers taken from the saltpetre vats, while the guide ascended to the gallery and finally took his station in the pulpit. Here he kindled a Bengal light, which hissed and sputtered like a sacrificial flame, throwing a strong pale-blue lustre upon the vast, rude arches, and bringing out the jagged walls in vivid relief against the profound darkness on either hand. In spite of the semi-sanctity given to the place this illumination seemed to me nothing less than an offering to the Kentucky gnomes and kobolds—the underground fairies who have hollowed for themselves this marvellous palace under her green hills.

Continuing our walk, with eyes that now saw clearly not only the grand dimensions of the avenue, but its rude suggestions of pilasters, friezes, and cornices, and the dark cloud-patterns that mottled its gray ceiling, we passed in succession the Kentucky Cliffs (so called from their resemblance to the rocks on Kentucky River), Willie's Spring, a tiny thread of water which has channelled itself a fantastic fluted niche from the top to the base of the wall, and the Second Hoppers, where the operations of the old miners seem to have been prosecuted on a very extensive scale. Above these hoppers, on the right hand, is the mouth of the Gothic Avenue, branching off at right angles to the main cave. It is reached by a flight of steps. The subterranean scenery became more and more striking as we advanced. The roof is coated with a thin incrustation of gypsum, which is colored in patches with black oxide of manganese, giving it a rude resemblance to a gray sky flecked with dark clouds. In the waving and uncertain light of the lamps, these clouds seem to move as you walk, and to assume capricious and fantastic forms. Now you see an oval lake surrounded with shrubbery, now a couchant beast, or a sitting figure like the colossal deity of a Theban tomb. In one place there is a huge ant-eater, very perfect; in another an Indian chief wrapped in his blanket; then a giant, with his wife and child; and finally, a charcoal sketch, in which the imaginative can see Napoleon crossing the Alps.

Under the last of these pictures Alfred stopped, and after stating that we were just one mile from the entrance, threw the light of his lamp upon a large white rock which lay upon our right hand, and asked us what it resembled. "Why," said one of us, "it is very much like a coffin." "You are right," said he; "it is the Giant's Coffin, 57 feet in length." He then informed us that he should leave the main cave and take the road to the River Styx, in order to show us some of the most remarkable objects on this side of that stream. We followed him, one by one, into a crevice behind the coffin, at the bottom whereof yawned a narrow hole. Half-stooping, half-crawling, we descended through an irregular, contracted passage, to a series of basement halls, called the Deserted Chambers. The first of these is the Wooden Bowl, a room about 100 feet in diameter, with a low, slightly concave ceiling. The name may have been suggested by this circumstance, although there is a story of an ancient wooden bowl having been found in it by the first persons who entered. A staircase called the Steps of Time—for what reason it is impossible to say—leads to still lower chambers, two of which are connected by a passage called the Arched Way, from the smooth and regular curve of its white ceiling. In the furthest one is "Richardson's Spring," a little bowl of crystal water, which we found very cool and refreshing, despite the flavor of the limestone rock.

The roof presently shot up into a pointed, irregular vault, and we heard the sound of dropping water. Alfred, who was in advance, cautioned us to remain still while he leaned forward and held out his lamp, which disclosed the mouth of a pit. The sides were as smooth as if hewn by a stone-cutter, and worn into deep grooves and furrows by the waters of ages. A log is placed along one side to protect visitors, and we leaned upon it while he kindled a sheet of oiled paper and suffered it to whirl slowly down into the gulf, glimmering on the wet walls and the dark pools of water in its mysterious womb.

Leaving the deserted chambers, we descended a steep staircase into the Labyrinth—a winding way thirty or forty feet high, and barely wide enough for two persons to pass. This brought us to another pit, along the brink of which we walked, clambered up a ledge, and at last reached a window-like opening, where Alfred bade us pause. Leaning over the thin partition wall, the light of our united lamps disclosed a vast glimmering hall, the top of which vanished in darkness and the bottom of which we could only conjecture by the loud, hollow splash of water-drops that came up out of the terrible gloom. Directly in front of us hung a gigantic mass of rock, which in its folds and masses presented a wonderful resemblance to a curtain. It had a regular fringe of stalactites, and there was a short outer curtain overlapping it at the top. The length of this piece of limestone drapery could not have been less than one hundred feet. In a few moments, Alfred, who had left us, re-appeared at another window on the right hand, where he first dropped some burning papers into the gulf, and then kindled a Bengal light. It needed this illumination to enable us to take in the grand dimensions of the dome. We could see the oval arch of the roof a hundred feet above our heads; the floor studded with the stalagmitic pedestals as far below; while directly in front the huge curtain that hung from the centre of the dome—the veil of some subterranean mystery—shone rosy-white, and seemed to wave and swing, pendulous in the awful space. We were thoroughly thrilled and penetrated with the exceeding sublimity of the picture, and turned away reluctantly as the fires burned out, feeling that if the cave had nothing else to show its wonders had not been exaggerated.

Leaving Goran's Dome—the name which has been given to this hall—we retraced our way through the Labyrinth, and following the main passage a short distance further, came to the Bottomless Pit, formerly the limit of excursions in this direction. It was finally crossed by means of a ladder, and is now securely bridged, and the path along its brink protected by an iron railing. The bridge is renewed every four years, even though the timbers remain sound, in order to guard against all possibility of an accident. The Pit is 175 feet deep, and is covered by a pointed dome forty or fifty feet high. It is a horrid gulf—dark, yawning, and awful as the mouth of Tartarus. Pieces of burning paper dropped from the bridge slowly fell into the depth, eddying backwards and forwards and showing the black, furrowed walls on either side. The vault above our heads, in its grooves and niches and projecting points, reminded me very vividly of the Moorish domes in the Alhambra. There is a *stalactitic* element in Saracenic architecture which must have had its suggestion in Nature.

The avenue beyond the pit leads to the River Styx, but as we had reserved that portion of the cave for the next day's trip, we returned through the Deserted Chambers to the Main Cave. A short distance beyond the Giant's Coffin we reached the Great Bend, where the avenue changes its direction at a very acute angle. It is still upwards of one hundred feet wide, and sixty or seventy in height, with the same rough friezes and cornices, and the forms of clouds and phantom figures on its ceiling. We passed several stone and frame houses, some of which were partly in ruin. The guide pointed them out as the residence of a number of consumptive patients who came in here in September, 1843, and remained until January. "I was one of the waiters who attended upon them," said Alfred. "I used to stand on that rock and blow the horn to call them to dinner. There were fifteen of them, and they looked more like a company of skeletons than anything else." One of the number died here. His case was hopeless when he entered, and even when conscious that his end was near he refused to leave. I can conceive of *one* man being benefited by a residence in the cave, but the idea of a company of lank, cadaverous invalids wandering about in the awful gloom and silence, broken only by their hollow coughs—doubly hollow and sepulchral there—is terrible. On a mound of earth near the Dining Room I saw some cedar trees which had been planted there as an experiment. They were entirely dead, but the experiment can hardly be considered final, as the cedar is of all trees the most easily injured by being transplanted.

I now noticed that the ceiling became darker, and that the gray cornice of the walls stood out from it in strong relief. Presently it became a sheet of unvarying blackness, which reflected no light, like a cloudy night-sky. All at once a few stars glimmered through the void, then more and more, and a firmament as far off and vast, apparently, as that which arches over the outer world, hung above our heads. We were in the celebrated Star Chamber. Leaning against a rock which lay upon the right side of the avenue, we looked upwards, lost in wonder at the marvellous illusion. It is impossible to describe the effect of this mock sky. Your reason vainly tells you that it is but a crust of black oxyd of manganese, sprinkled with crystals of gypsum, seventy-five feet above your head. You *see* that it is a fathomless heaven, with its constellations twinkling in the illimitable space. You are no longer upon this earth. You are in a thunder-riven gorge of the mountains of Jupiter, looking up at the strange firmament of that darker planet. You see other constellations rising, far up in the abyss of midnight, and witness the occultation of remoter stars.

The fascination of that scene would have held us there for the remainder of the day if the guide had permitted it. After indulging us for what he considered a sufficient length of time, he took our lamps, and descending into a branch cavern that opened from the floor, treated us to some fine effects of light and shade. By a skilful management of his lights he produced the appearance of a thunder-cloud rising and gradually spreading over the sky. The stars are lost; the comet, gleaming portentous on the horizon, disappears; and the gorge is wrapped in shadow. Then the clouds break and clear away, and the stars seem to twinkle with a more bright and frosty lustre after their obscuration. "Take care of yourselves!" cries the guide, and we hear his footsteps passing under the floor. He has all our lamps, and we can now see but a faint glimmer through the opening he entered. Now it is but the ghost of a glimmer; and now, as his footsteps are more indistinct, it ceases altogether. Yes, this is darkness—solid, palpable darkness. Stretch out your hand and you can grasp it; open your mouth and it will choke you. Such must have been the primal chaos before Space was, or Form was, or "Let there be light!" had been spoken. In the intense stillness I could hear the beating of my heart, and the humming sound made by the blood in its circulation.

After a while a golden nebulous glow stole upon the darkness, seemingly brighter than the sunrise radiance of the East, and increased until our guide and lamps rose above the horizon. We now returned to the Second Hoppers, and mounted to the Gothic Avenue. For more than a quarter of a mile this avenue has a ceiling perfectly flat, with every appearance of having received a coat of plaster. It is smoked over in all parts with the names of vulgar visitors, from which circumstance it is called the Register Room. Persons formerly carried candles in their trips through the cave, and by tying them to poles, succeeded in not only smoking their names upon the ceiling, but in many instances their portraits—for there were frequently rude attempts of drawing the figures of sheep and pigs. The lamps used at present prevent all such desecration, but there are still (and probably always will be) touching applications for candles.

The roof gradually became broken and rugged, studded here and there with unfinished stalactites, and we now entered the Gothic Chapel, where those stony icicles become large enough to form ribbed pillars and fair Gothic arches. The ceiling is not more than thirty feet high, so that this hall has nothing of the grandeur of Goran's Dome, but it is very curious and beautiful. Beyond this the specimens of stalactitic formation are very numerous, and I have not time to describe them minutely. We passed Napoleon's Breastworks, Vulcan's Shop, the Elephant's Head, and the Pillars of Hercules, hard by which is the Lover's Leap, where the journey ceased. Here the floor of the avenue suddenly falls away, leaving a gulf about fifty feet deep, over which projects a long, pointed rock. By descending into the gulf you can enter a lower gallery leading to other wonders, among which the guide mentioned "The Devil's Cooling Tub," but we had scarcely sufficient time to explore it.

We retraced our steps to the Second Hoppers, and then returned to the mouth of the cave, having been four hours underground, and travelled about five miles. When we reached the entrance and looked out from behind the falling skein of water the trees seemed to be illuminated with an unnatural fire. The daylight had a warm yellow hue, intensely bright, and the sky was paler but more luminous than usual. The air, by contrast with the exhilarating nitrous atmosphere below, felt close, unpleasantly warm, and oppressive—like that of an ill-ventilated greenhouse in Winter. There was too much perfume in it—too many varieties of vegetable smells—for I found that the short absence had made my scent unusually keen and intelligent. This first sensation soon wore off, and left us with no other unpleasant effect from our trip than that of great hunger, of which Mr. Miller speedily relieved us.

XVIII.

THE MAMMOTH CAVE.

[MAY, 1855.]

PART III.—A DAY BEYOND THE STYX.

THE next morning we made preparations for an early start, as we had a long day's journey before us. Our party was increased to eleven by the addition of a bridal pair, a young Tennessean, and two silent Boston gentlemen. We had two guides: Stephen, whom I had specially engaged, and Mat. The ladies, with one exception, were attired in Bloomer costume, greatly to the merriment of the party, but much to their own convenience. Dresses are kept at the hotel for the use of lady visitors, and I would advise all such to make use of them. In addition to the supply of lamps the guides carried canteens of oil and baskets of provisions for the dinner we were to make in the regions beyond the Styx. Thus equipped and provided for, we set out immediately after breakfast.

Stephen, who has had a share in all the principal explorations and discoveries, is almost as widely known as the Cave itself. He is a slight, graceful, and very handsome mulatto of about thirty-five years of age, with perfectly regular and clearly chiselled features, a keen, dark eye, and glossy hair and moustache. He is the model of a guide—quick, daring, enthusiastic, persevering, with a lively appreciation of the wonders he shows, and a degree of intelligence unusual in one of his class. He has a smattering of Greek mythology, a good idea of geography, history, and a limited range of literature, and a familiarity with geological technology which astonished me. He will discourse upon the various formations in the Cave as fluently as Professor Silliman himself. His memory is wonderfully retentive, and he never hears a telling expression without treasuring it up for later use. In this way his mind has become the repository of a great variety of opinions and comparisons, which he has sagacity enough to collate and arrange, and he rarely confuses or misplaces his material. I think no one can travel under his guidance without being interested in the man, and associating him in memory with the realm over which he is chief ruler.

Mat, who ranks next to Stephen among the guides, is also a mulatto, of about the same age—a careful, patient, intelligent, and amiable man, but with less geological knowledge than the latter. He does not belong to the cave property, but is hired out by his master. Stephen and Alfred belonged to Dr. Croghan, the late owner of the cave, and are to be manumitted in another year, with a number of other slaves. They are now receiving wages, in order to enable them to begin freedom with a little capital, in Liberia, their destined home. Stephen, I hear, has commenced the perusal of Blackstone, with a view to practise law there, but from his questions concerning the geography of the country, I foresee that his tastes will lead him to become one of its explorers. He will find room and verge enough in the Kong mountains and about the sources of the Niger, and if I desired to undertake an exploration of those regions, I know of few aids whom I would sooner choose.*

There was no outbreathing from the regions below as we stood at the entrance to the Cave, the upper atmosphere having precisely the same temperature. We advanced in single file down the Main Avenue, which, from the increased number of lamps, showed with greater distinctness than on our first trip. Without pausing at any of the objects of interest on the road, we marched to the Giant's Coffin, crawled through the hole behind it, passed the Deserted Chambers, and reached the Bottomless Pit, the limit of our journey in this direction the previous day.

Beyond the Pit we entered upon new ground. After passing from under its Moorish dome the ceiling became low and the path sinuous and rough. I could only walk by stooping considerably, and it is necessary to keep a sharp look-out to avoid striking your head against the transverse jambs of rock. This passage is aptly called the Valley of Humiliation. It branches off to the right into

* Stephen, however, remained at the cave until manumitted by Death. He died in 1858.

another passage called Pensico Avenue, which contains some curious stalactitic formations, similar to the Gothic Gallery. We did not explore it, but turned to the left and entered an extremely narrow, winding passage, which meanders through the solid rock. It is called Fat Man's Misery, and any one whose body is more than eighteen inches in breadth will have trouble to get through. The largest man who ever passed it weighed two hundred and sixty pounds, and any gentleman weighing more than that must leave the best part of the cave unexplored. None of us came within the scope of prohibition (Nature, it seems, is opposed to corpulence), and after five minutes' twisting we emerged into a spacious hall called the Great Relief. Its continuation forms an avenue which leads to Bandits' Hall—a wild, rugged vault, the bottom of which is heaped with huge rocks that have fallen from above. All this part of the Cave is rich in striking and picturesque effects, and presents a more rude and irregular character than anything we had yet seen.

At the end of Bandits' Hall is the Meat-Room, where a fine collection of limestone hams and shoulders are suspended from the ceiling, as in a smoke-house. The resemblance, which is really curious, is entirely owing to the action of water. The air now grew perceptibly damp, and a few more steps brought us to the entrance of River Hall. Here the ceiling not only becomes loftier, but the floor gradually slopes away before you, and you look down into the vast depths and uncertain darkness, and question yourself if the Grecian fable be not indeed true. While I paused on the brink of these fresh mysteries the others of the party had gone ahead under the charge of Mat; Stephen, who remained with me, proposed that we should descend to the banks of the Styx and see them crossing the river upon the Natural Bridge. We soon stood upon the brink of the black, silent water; the arch of the portal was scarcely visible in the obscurity far above us. Now, as far below, I saw the twinkle of a distant lamp, then another and another. "Is it possible," I asked, "that they have descended so much further?" "You forget," said Stephen, "that you are looking into the river and see their reflected images. Stoop a little and you will find that they are high above the water." I stooped, looked under an arch, and saw the slow procession of golden points of light passing over the gulf under the eaves of a great cliff; but another procession quite as distinct passed on below until the last lamp disappeared and all was darkness again.

We then resumed the regular trail, which led us along the edge of a cliff about thirty feet above the waters of the Dead Sea, a gloomy pool, which is evidently connected with the Styx. An iron railing has been placed along the edge to protect those whose nerves are weak. At the end of the cliff we descended a long ladder, clambered over masses of rocks made slippery by the water, and gained the Natural Bridge, which is a narrow path or ledge around a projecting rock, bridging the river. The path is only about eighteen inches wide, and a false step would precipitate the explorer thirty feet below into the Styx. Such is the caution of the guides, however, and the sense of security which even the most timid feel, that no accident has ever happened. Five minutes more and the roughest and most slippery scrambling brought us to the banks of the Lethe River, where we found the rest of the party.

The river had risen since the previous day, and was at the most inconvenient stage possible. A part of the River Walk was overflowed, yet not deep enough to float the boats. Mat waded out and turned the craft, which was moored to a projecting rock, as near to us as the water would allow, after which he and Stephen carried us one by one upon their shoulders and deposited us in it. It was a rude, square scow, well plastered with river mud. Boards were laid across for the ladies, the rest of us took our seats on the muddy gunwales, the guides plied their paddles, and we were afloat on Lethe. One hundred feet above our heads hung the vaulted rock; half-way down there ran a regular cornice, arched on the under side, and with jagged edge, showing that there had formerly been two grand corridors, placed vertically, which some convulsion had broken into one. Either end of this mighty hall was lost in the darkness, but the sound of our voices rose to the roof and reverberated along it until they seemed like the voices of unseen beings speaking back to us out of the distance. The water has a steady temperature of 54°; it is clear, apparently of a pale green color, and pleasant to the taste. It had a very perceptible current, and flowed in a diagonal course across the line of our march, or, as nearly as I could estimate, in the direction of Green River.

After a ferriage of about one hundred yards, we landed on a bank of soft mud beside a small arm of the river, which had overflowed the usual path. We sank to our ancles in the moist, tenacious soil, floundering laboriously along until we were brought to a halt by Echo River, the third and last stream. This again is divided into three or four arms, which, meandering away under low arches, finally unite. At present, owing to the high water, there is but one arch open, so that instead of the usual single voyage of three quarters of a mile, we were obliged to make several short ferriages. Twice again were the guides obliged to carry us on their shoulders through the shallows, and once we succeeded in passing along a narrow ledge of rock overhanging a deep pool, only by using Stephen's foot as a stepping-stone. After crossing the second branch of Echo River we found ourselves at the foot of a steep hill of loose sand, beyond which we could see masses of rock piled up almost to the ceiling of the lofty hall. This was the commencement of Purgatory, a portion of which domain we were obliged to traverse on account of the difficulty of getting through what is called the Second Arch.

Stephen here entered the boat alone, lay down on his back in the bottom, shot under a low projecting rock, and was soon lost to our sight. Under the guidance of Mat we climbed the sand-hills, mounted the loosely-piled rocks, and after a short purgatorial experience, descended again to a low arch opening on the last branch of Echo River. As we stood on the wet rocks, peering down into the black translucence of the silent, mysterious water, sounds—first distant, then near, then distant again—stole to us from under the groined vaults of rock. First, the dip of many oars; then a dull, muffled peal, rumbling away like the echoes of thunder; then a voice marvellously sweet, but presently joined by others sweeter still, taking up the dying notes ere they faded into silence, and prolonging them through remoter chambers. The full, mellow strains rose until they seemed sung at our very ears, then relapsed like ebbing waves, to wander off into solitary halls, then approached again, and receded, like lost spirits seeking here and there for an outlet from the world of darkness. Or was it a chorus of angels come on some errand of pity and mercy to visit the Stygian shores? As the heavenly harmonies thickened, we saw a gleam on the water, and presently a clear light, floating above its mirrored counterfeit, swept into sight. It was no angel, but Stephen, whose single voice had been multiplied into that enchanting chorus.

The whole party embarked in two small boats, and after a last voyage of about two hundred yards, were landed beyond the waters, and free to explore the wonderful avenues of that new world of which Stephen is the Columbus. The River Hall here terminates, and the passages are broken and irregular for a short distance. A few minutes of rough travel brought us to a large circular hall with a vaulted ceiling, from the centre of which poured a cascade of crystal water, striking upon the slant side of a large reclining boulder, and finally disappearing through a funnel-shaped pit in the floor. It sparkled like a shower of pearls in the light of our lamps, as we clustered around the brink of the pit to drink from the stores gathered in those natural bowls which seem to have been hollowed out for the uses of the invisible gnomes.

Beyond Cascade Hall commences Silliman's Avenue, a

passage about twenty feet wide, forty or fifty in height, and a mile and a half in length. The floor is in some places smooth and firm, in others broken and rough, with deep dips which often communicate with smaller passages or "side cuts" that, after winding through the rock for some distance, find their way back to the main avenue. The walls on either side have bold, projecting cornices, above which springs a well-arched ceiling. There are few objects of special interest in this avenue, but I was never tired of watching the procession of lamps as they wound up and down its rocky floor, and the picturesque play of light and shade on the gray walls and cornices, the niches and hollow vaults.

After a steady walk of a mile and a half—the distance is not exaggerated, for I timed it—we reached a gigantic bluff, which, facing us, divided the avenue into two parts. That to the left retains the name of Silliman, and continues for nearly a mile further without leading to any result. The other was called "The Pass of El Ghor" by some traveller who had been in Arabia Petræa—but the name is a pleonasm, as *el ghor* signifies a narrow, difficult pass between rocks. While we rested a few minutes on some broad stones at the base of the cliff Stephen climbed up to the platform behind the broad cornice of the wall, and brought us down a handful of fibrous gypsum as white as snow. The ladies eagerly appropriated pieces of it as specimens, but he observed depreciatingly, "You will throw that away before long."

Our lamps were replenished and we entered El Ghor, which is by far the most picturesque avenue in the cave. It is a narrow, lofty passage meandering through the heart of a mass of horizontal strata of limestone, the broken edges of which assume the most remarkable forms. Now there are rows of broad, flat shelves overhanging your head; now you sweep around the stern of some mighty vessel with its rudder set hard to starboard; now you enter a little vestibule with friezes and mouldings of almost Doric symmetry and simplicity; and now you wind away into a Cretan labyrinth most uncouth and fantastic, whereof the Minotaur would be a proper inhabitant. It is a continual succession of surprises, and, to the appreciative visitor, of raptures. The pass is somewhat more than *a mile and a half* in length, and terminates in a curious knot or entanglement of passages leading to two or more tiers of avenues.

We were now, according to Stephen's promises, on the threshold of wonders. Before proceeding further we stopped to drink from a fine sulphur spring which fills a natural basin in the bottom of a niche made on purpose to contain it. We then climbed a perpendicular ladder, passing through a hole in the ceiling barely large enough to admit our bodies, and found ourselves at the entrance of a narrow, lofty passage leading upwards. When all had made the ascent the guides exultingly lifted their lamps and directed our eyes to the rocks overhanging the aperture. There was the first wonder, truly! Clusters of grapes gleaming with blue and violet tints through the water which trickled over them, hung from the cliffs, while a stout vine, springing from the base and climbing nearly to the top, seemed to support them. Hundreds on hundreds of bunches clustering so thickly as to conceal tl.e leaves, hang for ever ripe and for ever unplucked in that marvellous vintage of the subterranean world. For whose hand shall squeeze the black, infernal wine from the grapes that grow beyond Lethe?

Mounting for a short distance, this new avenue suddenly turned to the left, widened, and became level; the ceiling is low, but beautifully vaulted, and Washington's Hall, which we soon reached, is circular, and upwards of a hundred feet in diameter. This is the usual dining-room of parties who go beyond the rivers. Nearly five hours had now elapsed since we entered the cave, and five hours spent in that bracing, stimulating atmosphere might well justify the longing glances which we cast upon the baskets carried by the guides. Mr. Miller had foreseen our appetites, and there were stores of venison, biscuit, ham, and pastry, more than sufficient for all. We made our mid-day or rather midnight meal sitting, like the nymph who wrought Excalibar,

"Upon the hidden bases of the hills,"

buried far below the green Kentucky forests, far below the forgotten sunshine. For in the cave you forget that there is an outer world somewhere above you. The hours have no meaning: Time ceases to be: no thought of labor, no sense of responsibility, no twinge of conscience, intrudes to suggest the existence you have left. You walk in some limbo beyond the confines of actual life, yet no nearer the world of spirits. For my part I could not shake off the impression that I was wandering on the *outside* of Uranus or Neptune, or some planet still more deeply buried in the frontier darkness of our solar system.

Washington Hall marks the commencement of Elindo Avenue, a straight hall about sixty feet wide, twenty in height, and *two miles* long. It is completely incrusted from end to end with crystallizations of gypsum, white as snow. This is the crowning marvel of the cave, the pride and the boast of the guides. Their satisfaction is no less than yours, as they lead you through the diamond grottoes, the gardens of sparry efflorescence, and the gleaming vaults of this magical avenue. We first entered the "Snow-ball Room," where the gnome-children in their sports have peppered the gray walls and ceiling with thousands of snow-white projecting discs, so perfect in their fragile beauty, that they seem ready to melt away under the blaze of your lamp. Then commences Cleveland's Cabinet, a gallery of crystals, the richness and variety of which bewilder you. It is a subterranean conservatory, filled with the flowers of all the zones; for there are few blossoms expanding on the upper earth but are mimicked in these gardens of Darkness. I cannot lead you from niche to niche, and from room to room, examining in detail the enchanted growths; they are all so rich and so wonderful that the memory does not attempt to retain them. Sometimes the hard limestone rock is changed into a parterre of white roses; sometimes it is starred with opening daisies; the sunflowers spread their flat discs and rayed leaves; the feathery chalices of the cactus hang from the clefts; the night-blooming cereus opens securely her snowy cup, for the morning never comes to close it;

the tulip is here a virgin, and knows not that her sisters above are clothed in the scarlet of shame.

In many places the ceiling is covered with a mammary crystallization, as if a myriad bubbles were rising beneath its glittering surface. Even on this jewelled soil which sparkles all around you, grow the lilies and roses, singly overhead, but clustering together towards the base of the vault, where they give place to long, snowy, pendulous cactus-flowers, which droop like a fringe around diamonded niches. Here you see the passion-flower, with its curiously curved pistils; there an iris with its lanceolate leaves; and again, bunches of celery with stalks white and tender enough for a fairy's dinner. There are occasional patches of gypsum, tinged of a deep amber color by the presence of iron. Through the whole length of the avenue there is no cessation of the wondrous work. The pale rock-blooms burst forth everywhere, crowding on each other until the brittle sprays cannot bear their weight, and they fall to the floor. The slow, silent efflorescence still goes on, as it has done for ages in that buried tropic.

What mostly struck me in my underground travels was the evidence of *design* which I found everywhere. Why should the forms of the Earth's outer crust, her flowers and fruits, the very heaven itself which spans her, be so wonderfully reproduced? What laws shape the blossoms and the foliage of that vast crystalline garden? There seemed to be something more than the accidental combinations of a blind Chance in what I saw—some evidence of an informing and directing Will. In the secret caverns, the agencies which produced their wonders have been at work for thousands of years, perhaps thousands of ages, fashioning the sparry splendors in the womb of darkness with as exquisite a grace, as true an instinct of beauty as in the palm or the lily, which are moulded by the hands of the sun. What power is it which lies behind the mere chemistry of Nature, impregnating her atoms with such subtle laws of symmetry? What but Divine Will, which first gave her being, and which is never weary of multiplying for Man the lessons of His infinite wisdom?

At the end of Elindo Avenue the floor sinks, then ascends, and is at last blocked up by a huge pile of large, loose rocks. When we had reached the foot, the roof of the avenue suddenly lifted and expanded, and the summit of the Rocky Mountains, as they are called, leaned against a void waste of darkness. We climbed to the summit, about a hundred feet above, whence we looked down into an awful gulf, spanned far above our heads by a hollow dome of rock. The form of this gigantic hall was nearly elliptical. It was probably 150 feet in height by 500 in length, the ends terminating near the roof in the cavernous mouths of other avenues. The guides partly descended the hill and there kindled a brilliant Bengal light, which disclosed more clearly the form of the hall, but I thought it more impressive as its stupendous proportions were first dimly revealed by the light of our lamps. Stephen, who discovered this place, gave it the name of the "Dismal Hollow."

Scrambling along the ridge of the Rocky Mountains, we gained the entrance to the cavern opening on the left, which we followed for about two hundred yards, when it terminated in a lofty circular dome, called Croghan's Hall. The floor on one side dropped suddenly into a deep pit, around which were several cushions of stalagmite, answering to short stalactites, hanging from the ceiling far above. At the extremity of the hall was a sort of recess, formed by stalactitic pillars. The wall behind it was a mass of veined alabaster. "Here," said Stephen, "is your Ultima Thule. This is the end of the Mammoth Cave, nine miles from daylight." But I doubt whether there is really an end of the cave any more than an end of the earth. Notwithstanding the ground we had traversed, we had left many vast avenues unexplored, and a careful search would no doubt lead to further discoveries.

We retraced our steps slowly along Elindo Avenue, stopping every few minutes to take a last look at the bowers of fairy blossoms. After reaching Washington's Hall we noticed that the air was no longer still, but was blowing fresh and cool in our faces. Stephen observed it also, and said: "There has been a heavy rain outside." Entering the pass of El Ghor again at Martha's Vineyard, we walked rapidly forward, without making a halt, to its termination at Silliman's Avenue. The distance is reckoned by the guides at a little more than a mile and a half, and we were just forty minutes in walking it. We several times felt fatigue, especially when passing the rougher parts of the cave, but the sensation always passed away in some unaccountable manner, leaving us fresh and buoyant. The crossing of the rivers was accomplished with some labor, but without accident. I accompanied Stephen on his return through the second arch of Echo River. As I sat alone in the prow, gliding under the low vaults of rock and over the silent, transparent darkness of the mysterious stream, I could hear the tones of my boatman's voice gliding down the caverns like a wave, flowing more and more faintly until its vibrations were too weak to move the ear. Thus, as he sang, there were frequently three or four notes, each distinctly audible, floating away at different degrees of remoteness. At the last arch there was only a space of eighteen inches between the water and the rock. We lay down on our backs in the muddy bottom of the boat, and squeezed through to the middle branch of Echo River, where we found the rest of the party, who had gone round through Purgatory.

After again threading Fat Man's Misery, passing the Bottomless Pit and the Deserted Chambers, we at last emerged into the Main Avenue at the Giant's Coffin. It was six o'clock, and we had been ten hours in the Cave, but as my party proposed leaving on the morrow, I determined to push my journey a little further, and to visit the Chief City at the end of the Main Avenue. This was the principal object of curiosity before the discovery of the rivers, but is now rarely visited. I took leave of the party, and with Stephen for a guide started off alone. We passed the Star Chamber, beyond which no path has been cleared in this direction. The floor is covered with loose rocks which have fallen from above, and walking becomes a very rough and laborious process. A portion of the avenue is called the Salt Room, from the crystals of pure glauber salts which fall from the ceiling in flakes, and cover the floor like a light snow.

Just one mile from the Star Chamber a rough stone

cross has been erected, to denote that the distance has been carefully measured. The floor here rises considerably, which contracts the dimensions of the avenue, although they are still on a grand scale. About half a mile further we came to the Great Crossings, where five avenues meet. In the dim light it resembled the interior of a great cathedral, whose arched roof is a hundred feet above its pavement. Turning to the left, at right angles to our former direction, we walked (still following the Main Avenue) some ten minutes further, when the passage debouched into a spacious hall, with a cascade pouring from the very summit of its lofty dome. Beyond and adjoining it was a second hall, of nearly equal dimensions, with another cascade falling from its roof. We turned again to the right, finding the avenue still more irregular and contracted than before, but had not advanced far before its ceiling began to rise, showing a long slope of loosely-piled rocks, lying in strong relief against a background of unfathomable darkness.

I climbed the rocks and sat down on the highest pinnacle, while Stephen descended the opposite side of the slope and kindled two or three Bengal lights which he had saved for the occasion. It needed a stronger illumination than our two lamps could afford to enable me to comprehend the stupendous dimensions of this grandest of underground chambers. I will give the figures, but they convey only a faint idea of its colossal character: length, 800 feet; breadth, 300 feet; height, 120 feet; area, between four and five acres. Martin's picture of Satan's Council-Hall in Pandemonium would hardly seem exaggerated if offered as a representation of the Chief City, so far and vanishing is the perspective of its extremities, so tremendous the span of its gigantic dome.

I sat upon the summit of the hill until the last fires had burned out, and the hall became even more vast and awful in the waning light of our lamps. Then taking a last look backwards through the arch of the avenue—to my mind the most impressive view—we returned to the halls of the cascades. Stephen proposed showing me the Fairy Grotto, which was not far off, and to accomplish that end I performed a grievous amount of stooping and crawling in the solitary cave. The grotto, which is a delicate stalactitic chamber resembling a Gothic oratory, was very picturesque and elegant, and I did not regret the trouble I had taken to reach it. Both of us were somewhat fatigued by this time, however; we were trenching upon the night hours, and beginning to feel symptoms of hunger, so we here turned about, and resumed the most direct way to the mouth of the cave.

When we heard the tinkling drops of the little cascade over the entrance, I looked up and saw a patch of deep, tender blue set in the darkness. In the midst of it twinkled a white star—whiter and more dazzling than any star I ever saw before. I paused and drank at the trough under the waterfall, for, like the Fountain of Trevi at Rome, it may be that those who drink there shall return again. When we ascended to the level of the upper world we found that a fierce tornado had passed along during the day; trees had been torn up by the roots and hurled down in all directions; stunning thunders had jarred the air, and the wet earth was fairly paved with leaves cut off by the heavy hail—vet we, buried in the heart of the hills, had heard no sound, nor felt the slightest tremor in the air.

The stars were all in their places as I walked back to the hotel. I had been twelve hours under ground, in which time I had walked about twenty-four miles. I had lost a day—a day with its joyous morning, its fervid noon, its tempest, and its angry sunset of crimson and gold; but I had gained an age in a strange and hitherto unknown world—an age of wonderful experience, and an exhaustless store of sublime and lovely memories.

Before retiring to rest I engaged one of the servants to give me a grooming after the manner of the Orientals, finishing with an external application of Kentucky whiskey, in consequence whereof I arose the next morning at sunrise without the least soreness or fatigue. Stephen, notwithstanding his labors, and the prospect of their repetition the same day, was up and in readiness to accompany me to White's Cave, which is about three-quarters of a mile from the Hotel in a south-western direction. It was discovered in 1805 by one of the saltpetre miners, after whom it was named. The entrance is a narrow opening in the side of a knoll studded with gray limestone rocks.

We crawled into the hole, which might have been a panther's lair in former times. The floor speedily drops, so that we were able to stand upright. Two stout pillars of stalactite upheld the roof, and the light of our lamps showed us a row of similar pillars stretching away into the darkness. This is the striking feature of the Cave, which is not more than six or seven hundred feet in length by fifty to eighty in breadth. There is a dyke in the limestone rock which forms the ceiling, crossing the cave obliquely from one end to the other. The water, oozing through, has gradually built a row of reeded Gothic pillars, singly or in clusters, with pedestals of stalagmite between; and sometimes broad curtains of semi-translucent stone hang from one to the other. The work is still going on, and apparently with great rapidity, for new points were already formed on stalactites which had been broken off some years ago. The water which dripped into the hollow basins in the floor was so wonderfully transparent as to be almost invisible, and it needed measurement to convince me that some of the pools which appeared to be only three inches in depth were actually as many feet.

Beyond this colonnade we found another and a shorter one, striking it obliquely, at one end of which is the most remarkable stalactite formation I ever beheld. It was a perfect tent, about eight feet in diameter at the base, with a height of twenty feet. The interior is hollow, and the smooth incrustations hanging from the top fall around you in folds like those of loose canvas, with a broad fringe sweeping the floor. Stephen gave it no name, but it might appropriately be called the Tent of the Gnomes. Near the end of the main line of pillars is a mass of fluted and channelled stalactite eight feet in breadth, which he called the Temple of Diana. It has a faint resemblance to a Grecian façade. Near this the floor suddenly terminates, leaving a yawning pit whose opposite side ascends steeply to the fretted ceiling, closing up the cave. The place is well worthy of a visit on account of the variety and beauty of its stalactitic formations, which far surpass those of the Mammoth Cave.

During our stay at the hotel the carriage had been brought in and repaired, our horses were thoroughly recruited, and we now prepared to leave, regretting the necessity which did not allow us to spend a few days longer under its pleasant roof. Mr. Miller, the kindest and most genial of landlords, was about setting out for Louisville, and offered to be our guide by a near way over the hills to Munfordsville. Before taking a final leave of the Mammoth Cave, however, let me assure those who have followed me through it, that no description can do justice to its sublimity, or present a fair picture of its manifold wonders. It is the greatest natural curiosity I have ever visited, Niagara not excepted, and he whose expectations are not satisfied by its marvellous avenues, domes, and sparry grottoes, must be either a fool or a demigod. Yet very few comparatively of those who travel in the West ever find their way to it. The number of visitors averages about two thousand a year, the greater part of whom are Kentuckians, Tennesseans, and foreigners.

An erroneous impression has gone abroad with regard to the facilities for crossing the subterranean rivers. The timid are scared by stories of parties being imprisoned beyond the Styx by a sudden rise of the water, and kept in peril of a lingering death. There is no possibility of any such accident occurring. The rivers rise slowly, and do not reach a height sufficient to make the arches impassable more than twice or thrice in a year. At such times visitors are not allowed to proceed beyond them; but even at their highest point there is always an opening through Purgatory, communicating with the transfluvial avenues which the water never fills. It may add to the interest of a narrative to depict the risk of being cut off by the waters and left to starve, but in other respects it is simply ridiculous. From the discovery of the Cave to the present time no fatal accident has ever occurred.

Owing to the rise in the rivers, we did not succeed in procuring any eyeless fish, which are only found at low water. Mat caught a few crawfish, which, like their finny companions, have neither eyes nor rudimentary hints of eyes. In other particulars they did not appear to differ much from the ordinary crawfish of our country streams. In the Solitary Cave I found crickets of large size, with very diminutive eyes, which, however, did not appear to possess the faculty of vision. I menaced them repeatedly with my finger without disturbing them in the least, but if I touched one of their long antennæ ever so lightly, they scampered off in great alarm. There are rats in some of the chambers, but they are probably vagrants, attracted by the dinners of visiting parties, and not permanent inhabitants.

XIX.

MACKINAW, AND THE LAKES.

[1855.]

By some coincidence or fatality I never visit St. Louis, or Springfield, Ill., without taking rain with me. When I left the former city, on the morning of the 17th of May, the streets were full of mud and the sky dark and leaky. As we reached Alton the rain began to fall vigorously, brightening the green of the prairies over which we sped, it is true, but shutting in their horizon, so that we had all of their monotony with none of their glorious expansion. Springfield, which we reached in due time, was in a state that recalled my Winter's experiences—including loss of overshoes. I made no allusion to the fact, however; for I have already discovered that you cannot touch up a Western town or railroad, even in a jocular way, without exciting some rampant local prejudice and superfluous indignation. In the West all the traits of our national character are intensified—its energy, its impulsiveness, its independence, its aggressiveness, its ambition, and its sensitiveness. I remember hearing Sir Henry Bulwer once say that no man was more skilful in turning a penny than a Yankee, and none more splendid in squandering a guinea. This is still more true of the Western man than of the New-Englander; but the former—to his credit be it spoken—has much less of the chaffering and huckstering spirit than the latter. The taint of selfishness which characterizes all money-making operations is less apparent: his ventures are bolder, his habits more free and liberal. It is a milder form of the same business-life which I found in California in 1849; and this is probably one reason of the charm which Western life exercises upon nearly all who come within its influence.

I must do Springfield the justice to say that it has its sunshiny side, when the mud dries up with magical rapidity and its level streets become fair to look upon. The clouds cleared away on the morning after my arrival, and when my friend, Captain Diller, took me to the cupola of the State-House and showed me the wide ring of cultivated prairie, dotted with groves of hickory, sugar-maple, and oak, which inspheres the capital of Suckerdom, I confessed that it was a sight to be proud of. The young green of the woods and the promising wheat-fields melted away gradually into blue, until the fronts of distant farm-houses shone in the morning sun like the sails of vessels in the offing. The wet soil of the cornfields resembled patches of black velvet—recalling to my mind the dark, prolific loam of the Nile Valley.

I left in the midnight train for Chicago. At Bloomington, which we reached at 2 A.M., our conductor left us; but his substitute did not make his appearance. The train waited, the passengers grew impatient, but nobody knew where the gentleman lodged; there was no one in the office who cared to look after the matter; the engineer said it was not his business, and so the train still waited. After a strong remonstrance from some passengers who were bound east and feared to lose the morning trains from Chicago, a man was sent to search for the conductor, but he returned unsuccessful. Finally, at daybreak, after a delay of two hours and a quarter, the missing man appeared—having overslept his time. He remarked, jocosely, "You've been waiting, I guess," and started the train. But, owing to the delay, we met the down train in the centre of a wide prairie, backed ten or twelve miles to switch off, waited for a Rock Island train at Joliet, and came into Chicago about noon—losing the morning trains and obliging the Eastern travellers to spend their Sunday in Cleveland instead of New York.

The difference of season between St. Louis and Chicago is very apparent. We left the trees in summer foliage at the former place, and watched the green gradually grow paler and paler, until, on the shore of Lake Michigan, only the buds of the earliest trees were open, and their leaves half-grown. The great prairie between Bloomington and Vermilion River was spread out flat to the horizon like a green ocean, sprinkled with flakes of pink and blue and golden and crimson foam. It was a great contrast to the dreary, brown expanse I had looked upon during the winter. But a prairie cannot be properly appreciated from the window of a railroad car. I longed for the little black Arab of Newark, Ohio, or the gray Morgan of Dixon, to career across its flowery solitude, chasing the flying horizon. Give me a prairie for a race-course or a hunting-ground; but not—though it yield me 150 bushels of corn per acre—for a habitation!

Having already tried every railroad leading out of Chicago, I determined to return home by the Lakes. The steamers on the new route to Collingwood and Toronto had just commenced running, and offered the greatest inducements in the way of scenery; so we took passage on the "Queen City," and left Chicago at a late hour on Sunday evening, the 20th. The boat, which was a fleet and handsome steamer, newly fitted up for the season, was not crowded, and we secured pleasant state-rooms in the after cabin. We found intelligent and amiable officers, an attentive steward, a good table, and all other requisites to the enjoyment of a lake voyage, and were favored, in addition, with the smoothest water and the clearest skies.

When I awoke next morning, we were in Milwaukee River. Here the boat was detained a day in order to take in freight; and I had the opportunity of revisiting some Wisconsin friends. The stay was made fortunate by an unexpected meeting with two shipmates of the Japan Expedition; and I heard the adventurous youth who climbed with me the precipices of the Bonin Islands relate his more perilous feat of scaling the walls of Nanking and astonishing the Chinese rebels. In the evening it was discovered that the boiler had sprung a leak, and that the necessary repairs would detain us another day—a delay which none of us regretted. Milwaukee is as pleasant a place to visit as it is beautiful to look upon. Seen from the hills in the rear, with its pale yellow houses rising against the blue of the lake, it is a copy, in cooler tints, of some town on the Mediterranean shores.

As I was sauntering down to the boat on the second evening I was overtaken by an African gentleman of peculiar blackness and purity of race. He accosted me—desiring to know where the mailboat from Chicago came in. I pointed out what I supposed to be the place, whereupon he drew near and commenced a more confidential conversation. "I'm gwine down to the boat," said he, "'cause of a lady and gentleman. De gentleman I seed a while ago in de street; de lady—she's coming in de boat. I'se bound to be dar when de lady comes." Supposing he had been dispatched by some gentleman to meet an expected guest, I asked, "Will you know the lady when you see her?" "Gosh!" he answered, with a grin; "I'se ought to know her—she's my wife! She's comin' on, thinkin' she's gwine for to marry de gentleman what I seed; but I tell you she don't marry nobody else in dis here State 'ceptin' myself." He added that he had only been married three months, in which time she had spent all his money, and that he had known her intention of running away from him a week previous. "Well," said I, "if you knew it, why didn't you take measures to prevent her?" "Oh," he answered, chuckling at his own sagacity; "I tought I'd jist wait, and see whether she'd be *elewated* enough to go." The other gentleman, he informed me, was in the whitewashing business, but—with a shake of the head and a display of ivory—he'd "spile dat gentleman's 'spectorations; he'll make no more contracts in dat dere line." I regretted that I could not await the arrival of the boat and witness the meeting, which must have been still more characteristic and diverting.

We left Milwaukee at sunrise on Wednesday morning, running northward along the Wisconsin shore. The country is low and covered with woods except where they are broken in upon by small farms, picketed here and there like the advanced sentries of that besieging civilization which shall soon sweep away the serried ranks of the forest. The pine becomes more frequent, lifting its dark, ragged arms high above the gray of the budding birch and the faint green of the larch. Ozaukee or Port Washington, thirty miles north of Milwaukee, appears to great advantage from the lake, with its clusters of white houses rising gradually from the water's edge to the summit of the low hills. Sheboygan, which we reached about noon, is a considerably larger and more important place. It is one of the outlets of the rich and growing country around and beyond Lake Winnebago, and is connected by a plankroad with Fond du Lac. Judging from the number of buildings in the course of erection, it is no exception to the general law of progress in the West.

In the afternoon we touched at Manitowoc and Two Rivers, both so young that there is barely ground enough cleared for them to stand upon, and the primitive forest still shuts out their sunset view. There are already stores, taverns, German lager-beer saloons, and other signs of growth in abundance. The Michigan shore, although between sixty and seventy miles distant, was lifted into the air by a mirage, and distinctly visible. This effect is continued until after sunset; and I even saw Manitou Island, sixty-five miles off, by moonlight. The air was clear, bracing, and pure, but so cold that I did not venture on deck without a thick overcoat.

In the morning we were opposite Beaver Island, where a branch of the Mormon sect is colonized. So far as I could learn they are not polygamists, and are independent of the Salt Lake organization. The Michigan shores soon afterwards came into sight, and a lighthouse far ahead announced our approach to Mackinaw Straits. The country on both sides is densely covered with woods, which in some places were on fire, sending thick columns of smoke into the air. I noticed several steam saw-mills, and some new frame houses standing in cleared spots, but the greater part of the coast is yet uninvaded by settlers. Passing the promontory of St. Ignace, on the northern shore, we entered Lake Huron, heading for Mackinaw Island, which is about twenty miles distant. The long island of Bois Blanc lay to the southward. The surface of the lake was scarcely ruffled by the sweet western wind; the sky was of a pale, transparent blue, and the shores and islands were as sharply and clearly defined as if carved on a crystal tablet. It was a genuine Northern realm we had entered—no warmth, no depth of color, no undulating grace of outline, but bold, abrupt, positive form, cold, pure brilliancy of atmosphere, and an expression of vigor and reality which would make dreams impossible. If there is any air in which Action is the very charm and flavor of Life, and not its curse, it is the air of Mackinaw.

We ran rapidly up to the town, which is built at the foot of the bluffs, on the southern side. A fort, adapted for times of peace and with a small garrison, overlooks it. The houses are mostly of wood, scattered along the shore, with few trees and fewer gardens interspersed. The appearance of the place is nevertheless very picturesque, with the wooded centre of the island rising in the rear, and the precipitous cliffs of gray rock flanking it on both sides. The associations of two centuries linger about those cliffs, and the names of Hennepin, La Salle, Marquette, and other pioneers of Western civilization make them classic ground to the reader of American history.

We remained five hours in order to take on some coal, which two schooners were discharging at the pier. I made use of the time to stroll over the island and visit its two lions—the Sugar Loaf and the Arched Rock. The road, after we had passed through the fort, led through woods of budding birch, and the fragrant arbor-vitæ (thuya occidentalis), which turned the air into a resinous wine, as grateful to the lungs as Falernian to the palate. We passed around the foot of the central hill, three hundred feet high, whereon are the remains of the old fortifications. On a terrace between it and the eastern cliffs stands the Sugar Loaf—a pointed, isolated rock seventy feet high. The rock, which appeared to be secondary limestone, is honeycombed by the weather, and reminded me very strikingly of "Banner Rock," in the interior of the island of Loo-Choo. The structure is precisely similar, and the height very nearly the same. We now struck across the woods, which abounded with anemones and white trilliums in blossom, to the edge of the cliffs, which we followed for some distance, catching occasional glimpses through the thick clumps of arbor-vitæ of the transparent lake below and the Northern shore, stretching away to Sault St. Marie and Lake Superior. The forests in that direction were burning, and the dense volumes of white smoke, carried southward by the wind, blotted out the Eastern horizon for a space of thirty or forty miles.

The Arched Rock stands a little apart from the line of the cliffs, with which it is connected by a narrow ledge. It is one hundred and fifty feet high, forming a rude natural portal, through which you can look out upon the lake. The arch is ten feet thick, and in the centre not more than eighteen inches wide. I climbed out to the keystone, but the rock was so loose and disintegrated that I did not venture to cross the remaining portion. On our return to the boat I visited some Chippewa families, who were encamped upon the beach, but as they knew neither English nor French, the conversation was limited. The water of the lake is clear as crystal and cold as ice, and I had an opportunity to verify the reports of its marvellous transparency. The bottom is distinctly visible at the depth of from fifty to sixty feet.

We left Mackinaw towards evening, and at sunrise next morning were abreast of the Isle of Coves, at the entrance of the Georgian Bay. The islands which separate the Bay from Lake Huron are rather low, but those beyond, lying nearer the Canada shore, rise abruptly from the water in cliffs of red rock, crowned with forests of larch and pine. Alternately advancing and retreating behind each other as we passed along before them, they presented a shifting diorama of the wildest forms. The sky was cloudless, softened with a slight haze, and the air so cold that the water used in washing the decks made icicles on the guards. Cabot's Head, the north-eastern point of the Canadian promontory, terminates in a range of precipices two hundred feet high, back of which the unbroken forest sweeps away into a wide, rolling, upland region, which is said to be an admirable wheat country wherever it has been cleared. After passing the Head we lost sight of the coast, which trends southward for a time; but our attention was called to the steamer Keystone State of the Collingwood Line, which had passed us at Milwaukee, but which we were now rapidly overhauling. It was not a race, for the Queen City had already proved herself the swiftest, but we were not unwilling to see her prove it again.

As the Keystone State fell into our wake, the shore east of Owen's Sound came into sight on the right hand, and Christian's Sound on our left, showing that we were approaching the head of the Bay. The distance from the Isle of Coves to Collingwood is about 100 miles. The southern coast was still bold and precipitous, resembling the Hudson Palisades, to within ten miles of the latter place, when it gradually sloped down to a low country overgrown with the densest of forests. The smokes of Spring clearings were burning far and wide on the hill-sides, and as we turned in towards Collingwood, the very sunshine was obscured by them. We entered the harbor, or rather roadstead, cautiously, sounding our way along a narrow channel, which has been marked by buoys, between two shoals. The town of Collingwood, which now contains about eighty houses, is only a year old, and most of the lots are still in the primitive forest. The purchaser may build his shanty with the timber he cuts off to make room for it. The streets are full of stumps, the dwellings are of fresh, unpainted clapboards, and there is not yet a hotel in the place. The Ontario, Simcoe, and Huron Railroad Company have built out a pier, with a large storehouse at the extremity, on both sides of which steamers can be moored and tranship their passengers and freight directly into the cars. In this respect the arrangements are as convenient and expeditious as could be desired.

We found a train for Toronto in waiting, and as the Keystone State arrived soon afterwards with her load of passengers, the cars were overcrowded until we reached Barrie. We bade good-bye to Capt. Wilkins, whom we shall long remember as one of the kindest and most genial of commanders, passed through *the future* Collingwood, and in the twinkling of an eye were deep in the heart of the forest. The trunks of the trees in many places almost touched each other, so thick was the growth, and those which had been cut away to make room for the road were piled up on either hand to be burned. The work had already commenced here and there: the huge logs were masses of live coal roaring and crackling with a mighty sound, while sheets of bright-red flame eddied among the smaller limbs, and clouds of smoke swept around us, pouring into the cars in stifling volumes. As we sped on at the rate of thirty miles an hour through these avenues of flame, which the wind occasionally hurled into our very faces, I felt ready to agree with a rough fellow, who said in plain Saxon, "We're going to Hell, sure." The scene was certainly infernal enough to justify the suspicion.

After passing Barrie, a beautiful town on Lake Simcoe, we entered a more advanced region. Clearings became abundant, and substantial farmhouses replaced the primitive shanties. The season changed also; the willows were in full leaf, the elms half-fledged, and the maples cast an entire shadow. The country was rich, undulating, and beautiful, becoming more thickly settled as we advanced, until having finished our ninety-four miles in three hours and a half, we reached Toronto.

XX.

A TELEGRAPHIC TRIP TO NEWFOUNDLAND.

[AUGUST, 1855.]

I.—Halifax and Port-aux-Basques.

The steamer James Adger, chartered by the New York and Newfoundland Telegraph Company for the purpose of laying the submarine cable across the Gulf of St. Lawrence, left New York on the 7th of August. In addition to Peter Cooper, Cyrus W. Field, and Professor Morse—the managers of the enterprise—and their families, a large number of invited guests, several of whom were ladies, accompanied the expedition. A summer voyage to regions then so little known presented strong attractions, and the trip was commenced under the most cheerful and agreeable auspices. The line of telegraph from New York to St. Johns, which was then nearly completed, with the exception of the submarine portion, was the precursor of the Transatlantic Cable, and the prospect of finally carrying out the great undertaking gave an increased interest to this initiatory step.

A voyage of three days, during which we enjoyed both extremes of sea-experience—a calm and a storm—brought us to Halifax. As Capt. Turner designed taking on board a supply of coal, we had three hours' leave of absence to visit the lions of the place. Our appearance created but little sensation. Several gentlemen who were interested in the Company came down to greet Mr. Field, and a few ragged boys in search of employment and reward grouped about the pier-posts; but beyond these there was neither astonishment nor curiosity concerning us. No cry of "Carriage, Sir?" greeted us from the pier; no hotel-runner thrust greasy cards into our hands; no loafing idlers were there to stare at us or openly criticise our appearance; but we landed and walked up into the town without attracting more notice than so many of its own quiet denizens. The general impression was that Halifax is a slow place. For my part I found this Oriental indifference quite refreshing, and was not disposed to complain of it. It is pleasant to find that there are communities on the American side of our globe which are slow to become excited.

The town stretches along the harbor and around the foot of a fortified hill, and consists mainly of two long streets crossed by a number of steep short ones. The houses are dingy wooden structures, interspersed with an occasional stone or brick building, or a plain, dark-colored English church with a tall spire. My companion, who was a Briton, insisted that we had not yet reached the principal part of the town; but after passing the parade ground and the Government buildings—a square pile of semi-Grecian architecture—he was forced to admit that we had seen the best it had to offer. We engaged a one-horse carriage—the Halifax boys called it a "conveyance carriage," whence, I suppose, the keeper of carriages to hire is a conveyancer—and ascended to Fort George, the citadel. Another company of our passengers arrived at the same time and were boldly entering, when they were stopped on the drawbridge by the sentinel, who stated that no one was allowed to pass without an order from the Quartermaster-General.

A soldier off duty went around the shoulder of the hill to point out the office of that functionary to two of us, who undertook to procure the permission. We were fortunate enough to meet the Deputy-Quartermaster at the door. On making known our desire, he at once wrote an order for the admittance of the whole party. We crossed the drawbridge, passed through a heavy stone arch tunnelling the ramparts, and found ourselves in a spacious inclosure, where two companies of raw recruits for the siege of Sebastopol were going through their drill. They were mostly Germans, and seemed anything but easy while they stood at ease, and not a little disordered while they ordered arms. The raw material was good enough, no doubt, but it needed a great amount of discipline to produce from it the solid English files—the bulwarks of battle. One of our company, who was a clergyman, took occasion to make a few remarks on the immorality of war in general, and the Eastern War in particular, to two subalterns who were lounging on the rampart in the shade of a sentry-box. But I fear he was sowing seed on stony ground.

We mounted to the parapet and made the circuit of the fortress, looking over its coping on a beautiful picture of Nova-Scotian scenery. The crescent-shaped town half encircled the hill, its extremities stretching back towards the country in lines of suburban villas. The harbor, with McNab's Island lying across its mouth, extended beyond the town, sending a blue arm several miles further, where it bent out of sight among woody hills. Directly opposite lay Dartmouth, a small town of white wooden houses, with a church or two, and a background of dark green hills, partly clothed with forests, and their lower slopes dotted with cottages and farm-houses. On either side of McNab's Island, over the white line of the ever-foaming breakers, was an azure segment of ocean. Turning to the south and west, we looked inland across a level of farm-land, to ranges of dark wooded hills, with scarps of white rock jutting out here and there along their summits. The wind was strong, with a cool, October tang in it; the dark hills and the pale sky were alike suggestive of the North; yet the people complained of the heat, and imagined themselves in the midst of summer!

After dinner a small party of us went ashore to employ the remaining hour and a half in a gallop into the country, but neither saddle-horse nor carriage was to be had. "It is the first fair day after a rain," said the conveyancers, "and everybody is a riding out." Finally we found a man who offered us the identical carriage in which the Admiral had ridden that very morning, for four dollars; but on learning that we were Yankees, and did not consider the Admiral's seat a peculiar honor, he reduced his demand to three dollars. We had a pair of matched grays and a ruddy, red-whiskered coachman, and whirled out around the foot of the citadel in gallant style. A good macadamized road conducted us out of the town, where we came at once upon hay and grain fields. The grass had just been cut, and the air was full of its fragrance. Wheat and barley were in head, but had not yet begun to ripen. A drive of two miles, partly through thickets and patches of fir and larch trees, brought us to the head of the main arm of the inner harbor, which is completely landlocked. Surrounded by dark green hills, with not a vessel, and but two or three houses in sight, it resembled a lonely inland lake. The sight of the clear, green waters dancing to the shore tempted us to leave the Admiral's carriage and take a hasty bath. The bottom was covered with a growth of brilliant sea-weed, whose branching streamers of purple and emerald reached to my waist, threatening to drag me down, like Hylas, to the Nova-Scotian naiads; but no water could be more deliciously cold and invigorating. By this time it was six o'clock, and the cool shadows of evening were creeping across the landscape. The grays trotted merrily back along the shore-road, and we reached the pier to find the James Adger with steam up, and all on board except the gentleman from Truro.

We waited half an hour longer, but the gentleman from Truro did not come, notwithstanding an express had been sent eighteen miles into the country to meet him. Mr. Field then reluctantly gave the order to leave. As the steamer glided out of the dock, the passengers, gathered on the quarter-deck and paddle-boxes, gave three parting cheers. There were a number of persons on the pier, who received the salute with perfect equanimity. We then gave them three times three, and succeeded in eliciting two in return. An old fisherman of the place profited by our delay in disposing of two baskets of "murr's eggs." These are the eggs of a seafowl on the coast of Labrador. They are about the size of a turkey's egg, pointed at one end, and of a pale-blue color, curiously spotted, and streaked with black. The fisherman informed us that "the gentry eats 'em," and we had some of them boiled, but after testing the odor thereof, none of us had courage to break the shell. I kept one as a curiosity, greatly to my embarrassment. I could not have it boiled, for they crack in boiling; I could not pack it away, for fear of smashing it; I could neither carry it about with me, nor leave it in my state-room without great risk, but was constantly troubled by it until the last day of the voyage, when it was broken.

While in Halifax we obtained a pilot for Newfoundland: a little, brown, wiry, wide-awake fellow, who had gathered coast-knowledge in many a tough north-easter. His own apparent self-reliance inspired confidence in us, and we sailed for the Land of Fogs with a glow of cheerful expectation. It was dusk before we emerged from the harbor, but the long northern twilight lingered on the borders of the sky; and, as night deepened, the stars shone more brightly than they ever shone before, to our eyes. The planet Jupiter cast a long wake upon the sea; the Milky Way burned like a luminous cloud, making pale the lustre of the neighboring stars; while scarcely a minute elapsed but some meteor shot across the heavens, leaving a silvery trail behind it.

There seemed not one vault only, but deeps beyond deeps of glory, overspanning each other until the eye ceased to follow them. The meteors, some far, swift, and faint, some near and dazzling, fell from the inner to the outer circles of the heavens, like telegraphic messages between the several "spiritual spheres." Many of our company remained on deck till nearly midnight, notwithstanding the cold northern wind.

All the next forenoon we ran along the dark Nova Scotian shores; the sea, the sky, and the land were alike cheerless and forbidding, and the air so cold that we felt a chill through overcoats and thick shawls. The coast was low and undulating, covered with fir forests which looked black under the clouds, and faced with rugged ramparts of gray rock. A few fishing craft were hovering outside the breakers, ready to run into any sheltered cove in case the wind should increase to a gale, as it threatened. Towards noon we made the light on Cape Canso, and shortly afterwards crossed the mouth of the Gut of Canso, which divides Nova Scotia from Cape Breton Island. The coast of Cape Breton is from six to eight hundred feet high, and presents a bold front to the sea. Its aspect is peculiarly desolate on an overcast day. In the evening, we passed Cape Pleasant, not more than six miles from the old harbor and town of Louisbourg, so famous in our Colonial history. The ruins of the ancient French fortifications are still to be seen, but the trade of the town has long since been transferred to Halifax and Sydney, and it is now almost deserted. It is the only spot in the north-east which is prominent in our early history, and must still be a very interesting old place.

At midnight we entered the Gulf of St. Lawrence. The sky was cloudless, inconceivably clear and radiant, and an arch of white auroral fire spanned the northern horizon. It was so brilliant as to cast a glow upon the water, and to make the segment of sky inclosed within it appear black by contrast. It steadily brightened until the arch broke, when the fragments gathered into lustrous balls, or nuclei, which sent long streamers and dancing tongues of light almost to the zenith. Then the whole pageant faded away, to be reborn in the air, and brighten as before.

The expected gale did not come, and the next morning was as splendidly clear as an Arctic midsummer. We sailed between two hemispheres of blue, fanned by a wind which was a tonic to both soul and body. The only vapor which blurred the horizon was a white, filmy band, lying over the coast of Newfoundland, dead ahead. I saw the faint blue loom of land early in the morning, when it must have been between thirty and forty miles distant, but the outline of the coast was not very distinct until about nine o'clock. Immediately after breakfast there were religious services in the after cabin—prayers by the Rev. Dr. Spring and Mr. Sherwood, and a sermon by Mr. Field. An hour or more passed in the performance of this duty, and when we ascended to the deck we were rapidly nearing the long line of bold, barren hills. Cape Ray, the extreme southwestern point of the island, was on our left, rising from the sea in a lofty conical peak, which was separated by a broad natural gap from the mountain-wall, 1,200 feet in height, which rose inland, behind the southern coast. The aspect of this shore was sublime in its very bleakness. Not a tree was to be seen, and the gray of its hoary rocks was but partially veiled by the grass and stunted shrubs coaxed into life by the short Summer of this latitude.

Our pilot headed directly for Port-aux-Basques, our destination, but to the eye the coast presented a long line of iron rocks, without any apparent place of shelter. Even after we had made out the straggling huts of the fishermen, along the brow of the cliffs, and seen their tanned sails creeping outside the line of snow-white surf, there was no sign of a harbor, such as our chart indicated. Our little pilot, however, knew the ground, and when he had brought us within half a mile of the gray rocks, we saw the narrow mouth of the harbor on their right. The hue of the water showed deep soundings everywhere, and we ran securely into the port, which was deserted, except by a fishing boat that put out to meet us. The bark Sarah L. Bryant, which sailed from Liverpool on the 3d of July with the submarine cable on board, had not arrived. We were too soon for our errand, and the chiefs of the company immediately decided to leave for St. Johns, after communicating with the shore.

I seized this chance of putting my foot on Newfoundland soil. We jumped into a rough but very serviceable boat, of native manufacture, manned by two oarsmen—stout, lusty fellows, with red cheeks, tanned breasts, and clear, honest, cheerful eyes. Half way to the shore a four-oared boat met us, with Mr. Canning, the engineer of the Mediterranean Submarine Telegraph, on board. He had come from England especially to superintend the laying of the cable to Cape Breton, and had already been two weeks at Port-aux-Basques. He was quite a young man, but active and resolute in appearance.

We passed behind the piles of gray, weather-beaten rocks, which we now saw formed an island, called Channel Head by the boatmen. The water was full of floating kelp of great size, and the oars and rudder frequently became tangled in it. In the narrow strait between the rocks and the mainland the water was shallow, showing a rich and brilliant vegetation. The rocky bottom was covered with sea-mosses of the purest emerald, purple, dark-red, and amber hues, over which dragged the long orange stems, and thin, glutinous ruffles of the kelp. But now we approached the village, whose one-story wooden houses began to stud the bluff, grassy knobs. Further back, on higher mounds, were groups of the inhabitants, principally women, who seemed to be watching us. We sprang ashore on some rocks, climbed the hill, despite the fishy odors which saluted us, and were in the village of Port-aux-Basques.

It was one of the queerest places in the world. Fancy a line of the roughest mounds or knobs, formed of marshy soil sprinkled with boulders of gneiss, or some kindred rock, and flung together in the most confused and irregular manner possible. Drop a square, clapboarded, veteran hut here, and another there, with a studied avoidance of order; stack quantities of dried codfish, after the manner of haycocks, in any convenient place; infuse a smell of salted fish into the air and a smell of cooked fish into the huts; add a few handsome dogs, some stalwart specimens of men, and children each of whom would furnish vitality for four New Yorkers—and you have the prominent features of the place. Where there were no rocks there was swamp, even on the hill-tops; and where the grass and weeds had bridged over the oozy soil, it was as elastic beneath our feet as a floor of India-rubber. The vegetation was that of Spring and Autumn combined; the golden ranunculus was in blossom beside the aster and the golden rod; the delicate blue harebell grew beside the white flowering elder bush; the fragrant, vernal grasses scented the air (in places distant from fish); and the azure iris, or *fleur-de-lis*, rose in thick beds between the rocks.

The village contains between seventy and a hundred houses, which are scattered along the knobs for a distance of three-quarters of a mile. These knobs are separated by ravines, two of which are crossed by wooden bridges. There are footpaths branching in all directions, but I saw nothing like a regular road. Near the centre of the place, at the head of the sheltered cove, there is a large two-story building for the storage of fish. A flagstaff behind it had the English and American ensigns hoisted together. Hereabouts the stacks of dried fish were very plentiful. I was forcibly reminded of the description of the Norwegian fish-market at Lofoden, in Mügge's romance of "Afraja." Some of the houses were painted white or dark-red, but the greater part showed the dingy, leaden hue of the native wood. There was neither tavern, church, nor store to be seen, but we were told that various articles might be bought at the house of a man named Waddell—which house was distinguished by the figure-head of the Prince Charles, lost on this coast, planted beside it.

There is also service on Sundays, occasionally; but the minister, it seems, had charge of several similar parishes, and was preaching somewhere in the wilderness. This fact might have explained the absence of the inhabitants, who had gone forth for a holiday, but I half suspected that they had retreated at our approach, out of shyness or fear. Many of them have never seen any other part of the world. When the Telegraphic Company sent two horses there the year previous, there was a great excitement in the place. Horses had never been seen before, except in pictures. Those which were left to winter there were speedily slaughtered and eaten. The line of telegraph poles, however, which crosses the hills, is a streak of light which will soon illuminate this benighted corner of the world.

I was much struck with the free, vigorous, healthy look of the inhabitants. The men were noble examples of physical vigor. The women—except one old dame—I did not see; but the children showed the soundness of the stock from which they sprang. There was one little girl, with a cloud of auburn curls around her head, whose blue eye and tan-roseate cheek made a very sunshine in the shaded doorway where she sat. The men were not only pre-eminently healthy and vigorous, but they had honest, happy, reliable faces—faces which it strengthens you to look upon. I should be perfectly willing to spend a month or two among them, notwithstanding their rude mode of life, and their complete isolation.

We had but an hour allowed us, and so went springing from rock to rock, or bounding over the elastic marshes, inhaling alternate whiffs of fish and flowers, until we had made a rapid tour of the village. Under that glorious sky, and in the breath of that bracing air, the scenery had a singular charm for me. The sea, blue as the Mediterranean, thrust its shining arms deep among the hills, which, divided by lagoons, resembled an archipelago of green islands. The white rocks along the shore hurled back a whiter wall of snowy breakers; and westward, beyond the peaked headland of Cape Ray, rose the blue mountain-wall, streaked with the gray of its rocky parapet. Not a tree, not even a large shrub was in sight; nothing but grass, flowers, and rocks. The bare forms of the landscape harmonized with its monotony of color; it was sublime in its very bleakness and simplicity. It resembled nothing I have seen on the American Continent, but rather the naked, heathery hills of the western coast of Scotland.

In two hours we resumed our course, standing eastward along the coast, whose beautiful stretch of swelling hills turned to a deep violet in the flush of sunset. The night was cloudless, sparkling with stars, streaked with meteors, and illuminated by a twilight which wheeled slowly from west to east, under the North Star, but never faded away. In the morning we saw the uninhabited islands of Miquelon and Langley, which belong to France, and passed near enough to the fishing-station of St. Pierre to discern the lighthouse at the entrance of the little harbor. The neighboring waters were dotted with the red or tan-colored sails of the French fishing smacks. The town of St. Pierre contains but about 1,500 inhabitants, but I was informed that during the Summer season there are frequently 400 sail in the harbor, and from 30,000 to 40,000 persons in the streets. We should probably have touched there but for the fact that the French government exacts a duty of three francs a ton on all foreign shipping entering the port. St. Pierre is to be made a naval station, and the Government designs sending large numbers of recruits for the marine to be educated in the fishing service. There is no better school in the world to make hardy sailors.

XXI.

A TELEGRAPHIC TRIP TO NEWFOUNDLAND.

[AUGUST, 1855.]

II.—St. Johns, and a Walk to Topsail.

I was lying in my berth, in one of the deck state-rooms, on Monday morning, when a sailor came up to the open window and said: "You'd better get up, Sir; we shall be at St. Johns in an hour." I took his advice at once, hurried on my clothes, and got on deck in time to see us pass Cape Spear, a bare, green headland, crowned with a lighthouse, beyond which the coast trends westward for several miles. The land was lofty, presenting a bold front to the sea, and the entrance to St. Johns Harbor, which our little pilot pointed out to me in front of us, was a narrow gap between two precipitous hills whose bases almost touched. The morning was rainy and overcast, but not foggy, and the approach to the shore was so secure that we made directly for the entrance, which we had almost reached, when a four-oared boat, carrying a pilot, put off to meet us. The town of St. Johns already began to appear through the gap or gorge, and in a few minutes we were sailing between nearly perpendicular walls of dark red sandstone, which rose to the height of 700 feet on the southern, and 520 feet on the northern side. We were hailed from a small lighthouse and battery at the entrance. The passage is not more than three or four hundred yards wide.

Signal Hill, on the north side, is crowned with an old battery and barracks, now converted into a military hospital. There is also a water battery of five guns at its foot, opposite Chain Rock, so called from the fact that in former times a heavy iron chain was stretched from this rock across the channel, to prevent the passage of ships. Beyond this point we entered the harbor, which curved around South-side Hill, extending inland for nearly a mile. It has plenty of water everywhere, with excellent holding ground, and is completely sheltered by the high hills of the coast. The town is built on the western side, facing the entrance. Its old-fashioned houses of brick and weather-beaten wood line the shore for the distance of a mile, climbing the steep side of a hill which is crowned by the Roman Catholic Cathedral, the Colonial Buildings, the Government House and two small fortifications. Beyond it, other hills, partly cultivated, and dotted with small white country-houses, rise inland. A crowd of schooners and small craft lay at the wharves, and fishing boats were moving hither and thither over the harbor. All around the shores, wherever space could be found, were the flakes of the fishermen—light wooden platforms, supported by poles, and covered with salted codfish in all stages of drying. These picturesque flakes, not unlike the grape arbors of Italy, and a powerful fishy smell in the atmosphere, proclaim at once to the stranger the principal business of St. Johns.

We moved slowly up the harbor and came to anchor near its western extremity. The arrival of the James Adger produced a much more decided sensation than at Halifax. Notwithstanding the early hour there was a crowd gathered upon the wharf, and some of us who landed for a stroll before breakfast were stared at by all the men we met and followed by most of the boys. The principal business street in the town is near the water, running along the western side of the harbor. The houses are mostly two-story dwellings of brick or stone, with heavy slate roofs, and more remarkable for solidity than beauty. This part of the town has all been rebuilt since the great conflagration in June, 1846, from the effects of which St. Johns has but recently recovered. At that time a space of 150 acres was burned over, and 2,300 buildings consumed. Twelve thousand people were made homeless, and property to the amount of £1,000,000 destroyed. Those districts which escaped still retain the dingy old wooden houses of which the town was originally built. The population of St. Johns at present is estimated at 20,000.

In the course of the morning I visited all of the principal sights of the place, under the guidance of Mr. Winton, editor of *The Public Ledger*. The most prominent building is the Catholic Cathedral, which had just been completed. It occupies a commanding position on the crest of the hill, and being built of gray stone, with tall square towers, bears some resemblance to the Cathedral of Montreal, which it equals in dimensions. The interior, however, does not bear out its exterior promise. The nave is low, and therefore does not produce the effect which might be expected from its length and breadth; the architectural ornaments are tawdry and inharmonious. The palace of Bishop Mullock stands beside the Cathedral, with a little garden in front. On this part of the hill is an earthwork called Fort Frederick, which contained but a small garrison. In fact, the entire number of troops stationed at St. Johns, including those in Fort William, Chain Rock Battery, and upon Signal Hill, amounts only to about two hundred men, who belong to what is called the Royal Newfoundland Company, and are not transferred to other stations. I never saw a more healthy and vigorous body of men. There are in England no ruddier faces, no clearer eyes, no more sappy and well-conditioned bodies. I looked with great admiration at one of the sentries on duty at Fort William. Tall, straight as a lance, with firmly chiselled, half-Grecian features, a thick, soft mustache and a classical chin, he had a complexion like that of a ripe peach, a mellow, ruddily golden flush, which showed the noblest painting of air and sunshine, and was worthy of the Titianic pencil of Page.

Capt. Bowlin courteously conducted us over Fort Frederick, where the most interesting thing I saw was the library and reading-room of the soldiers—a neat little apartment, containing 1,650 well-selected volumes, and a number of newspapers and periodicals. I am not aware that so profitable an institution as this has ever been attached to any of our own garrisons. The fortifications are all small, and seem to me quite insufficient for the defence of so important a place. The Government House, on the contrary, is built on a scale of needless magnificence, having cost £30,000, on an estimate of £9,000. It is a long, heavy-looking mansion, of dark gray stone, on the ridge of the hill, and surrounded by an inclosure planted with trees, which appear to grow very slowly on the thin soil. In the outskirts of the town, towards the north and west, there are several neat private residences with gardens attached, where the more hardy varieties of fruit ripen, and even apples, with proper protection, are made to bear; but strawberries (which were just disappearing) gooseberries, currants, and cherries, are the only certain fruits.

The Colonial Building, with its Grecian portico, stands near the Government House. The Council Chambers were closed, but I saw the Library, and the nucleus of a museum of the natural history of Newfoundland, which promises to be valuable. There were seals of all sizes and ages, wolves, foxes, partridges, grouse, hawks, owls, the heads and horns of the cariboo or reindeer, beaver, otter, hares, and various other animals, some of which seem to be peculiar to the island. The cariboo is said to be almost identical with the Lapp reindeer, whence some have conjectured that it was first introduced by the Norsemen, who, it is well known, first discovered Newfoundland, which they named *Helluland*, or "The Land of broad, flat stones." In the hall of the building there is a vacant niche, which ought to be filled with a statue of the gallant old Admiral, Sir Humphrey Gilbert, who in the year 1583 founded St. Johns.

The Episcopal Cathedral stands on the slope of the hill, below its Catholic rival. Only the chancel has been erected, which is of dark stone, of a plain but pleasing form of the Gothic style. From its imposing dimensions, the building, when completed, will surpass the Catholic Cathedral in size, as the latter surpasses it in position. The animosity between the two sects is very bitter, and since an independent Colonial Government has been given to Newfoundland, it enters into politics, and is the source of endless bickerings. There are several other Protestant churches, the principal of which is the Congregational Church, but none of them add much to the beauty of the place. In fact, Nature has done nearly everything for St. Johns. Spread along the slope of a long hill, almost every house commands a view of the beautiful harbor, the grand gateway between Signal and South-side Hills, and an arc of blue ocean beyond; while, looking inland, picturesque hills, black fir-woods, yellow hay-fields, cottages, and the white ribands of admirable roads, branching off in various directions, form landscapes of very different character, but equally as attractive. The air is always pure and exhilarating, and though there is much rain during the Winter and Spring months, fogs are quite rare. The thick mist-curtains which enshroud the great fishing-banks roll up, day after day, to within a mile or two of the shore, and there tower, like immense walls, leaving all within them in clear sunshine. The harbor of St. Johns is much less subject to fog than that of Halifax.

In calling Newfoundland the Land of Fogs, we have made the mistake of applying to the island the climate and atmosphere of the Grand Bank, from which it is separated by a belt of deep water from forty to sixty miles in breadth.

The morning of our arrival was rainy, but about noon the wind came out of the south-west, rolling the masses of cloud before it, and leaving spaces of blue sky in their place. As the time of our stay was uncertain, and I was anxious to see something of the country, I acceded to a proposal of Mr. Winton, that we should walk out in the afternoon to a farm belonging to his mother, near Topsail, on Conception Bay, eleven miles distant, and there spend the night. Mr. O'Brien and Mr. Middlebrook joined me, and we started at once. Following the main street in a south-western direction, past the head of the harbor, we soon emerged into a fine macadamized road, which left the valley and gradually ascended over the undulating slopes of the hills. For some distance it was lined with suburban cottages, surrounded with potato-patches, gooseberry-bushes, or clumps of fir and spruce trees, which sometimes attain a height of thirty feet. The largest trunk I saw was about eighteen inches in diameter. To these followed fields of thick grass, sometimes brown and shorn, sometimes striped with fragrant swathes or dotted with rounded haycocks. There were also some fields of oats and barley, which were still quite green, one only coming into head. We met a few rough country carts, driven by hardy, sunburned men or boys, going to St. Johns, but neither horsemen nor pleasure-carriages, nor pedestrians, except unmistakable laborers. It was evidently a land of work.

After travelling four or five miles at a pace which would have been fatiguing but for the constant exhilaration of the south-west breeze that blew in our faces, we reached a wild, rolling upland, where the signs of cultivation became more scarce, and from the character of the wild land I could perceive how much labor and expense are requisite to fit it for cultivation. The timber is short, but exceedingly hard and tough, and after the trees are cut and the stumps grubbed up, the soil is covered with loose stones, which must be picked off over and over again before there is a sufficient foothold for grain or potatoes. In spite of all this, and the fact that the soil is but a thin layer upon a basis of solid rock, which continually crops out through it, the yield of hay is remarkably good, and potatoes, when they escape the rot, produce very well. The price of cleared land varies from £5 to £15 per acre, according to quality and location. Farming, in this part of the island, can scarcely be remunerative, except at a crisis like the present, when all the necessaries of life are very dear.

The scenery through which our road lay reminded me continually of the western coast of Scotland. It certainly bore no resemblance to any part of the American continent which I have visited. High, bald ranges of hills, following the line of the coast, stretched away southwards, where they blended with the rolling inland, covered with dark woods of spruce, fir, and larch. From every ridge we overlooked stern tracts of wilderness, which embosomed lakes of cold, fresh water, bluer than sapphire. Occasionally, streams whose tint of golden brown betrayed the roots and trunks through which they had filtered, brawled over their rocky beds. A few cattle and sheep grazing along the edge of the woods gave a pastoral air to this region, which would otherwise have been desolate in its ruggedness and loneliness.

We stopped a few minutes at a wayside tavern, where, in a room with sanded floor and colored prints on the walls, we were served with spruce beer, bitter with the resinous extract of the tree. We had walked eight miles, and were now upon the dividing ridge between the Atlantic and Conception Bay, a deep sheet of water which reaches to within three miles of Placentia Bay, on the southern side of the island, and almost insulates the promontory on which St. Johns is built. Two hills opened like a gateway, and between them spread the blue waters of the bay, with its dim further shore, and the long, undulating hills of Bell Isle basking in the soft light of the afternoon sun. The road, which was as hard and smooth as an English highway, led downwards to the shore, revealing with every step a wider stretch of bay, over which towered, on the right, the pale red and gray rocks of Topsail Head, rising to a height of seven or eight hundred feet. In a little glen, the bottom of which, by careful clearing and draining, had been turned into a smooth field of thick, mossy turf, we found the neat white cottage which was to be our resting-place for the night. A rapid stream foamed beside it, and hills of fir inclosed it on all sides, except the north, which was open to the bay. The mistress of the house was absent, but we found a man and maid-servant, who conducted the affairs of the household in her stead.

As there were still two or three hours of daylight, we

walked on to the village of Topsail, and followed the road along the shore to a place called Chamberlain's Point. The views across the bay, and south-westward towards its head, were very beautiful. Bell Isle lay stretched out before us in its whole length, with the picturesque little fishing village of Lance Cove opposite to us. Little Bell Isle and Kelly's Isle were further south, and beyond them the shore was no longer bold and bluff, but sank into gentle hills. The road was lined with the wooden huts of the fishermen, with here and there the more ambitious summer cottage of a St. John's merchant, buried in a sheltering grove of fir-trees. The scenery became less bleak and rugged as we advanced, and I regretted that I had not time to follow the road to Holyrood, eighteen miles further, at the head of the bay.

We returned to the cottage under a sunset sky as clear and cold as it is possible for a sky to appear. The fire of dried boughs in the capacious chimney-place was very comfortable in the evening, and in spite of a brilliant white auroral arch and shooting lances of golden flame in the northern sky, we preferred remaining in-doors, lounging on the benches in the chimney corner, smoking, and listening to tales of cod-fishing, and wolf or bear hunting, told by the shrewd, sturdy, serving-man, William of Dorsetshire. William was farmer, hunter, and sailor, all in one, and his originally frank and honest nature had ripened vigorously in the exercise of the three manliest occupations in the world. His blunt, expressive language and rough experiences of the Newfoundland shores and forests had a real charm for me, and the early bedtime of the country came on apace. I enjoyed a sound sleep after the day's tramp, and awoke with the first blush of a morning as frostily cool as our October. We had hired a horse and light wagon from Mr. Daly, who kept a store and tavern for the fishermen at Topsail; Mr. Winton added his own wagon and gray pony, and two hours' drive over the hills, in the cloudless sunshine and elastic air, brought us back to St. Johns.

We found our fellow passengers preparing for an excursion to Portugal Cove, on Conception Bay. The hospitality of St. Johns was already exerting itself to find means for our diversion, and every available private carriage in the town (where there is not a single hack to be hired) had been secured. Before one o'clock all our passengers and twenty or thirty ladies and gentlemen of the place were on the road. We passed the Cathedral and Government House, catching, from the other side of the hill, a glimpse of Quidi Vidi Lake, a picturesque sheet of water which lies behind Signal Hill, and slowly climbed to the rolling, wooded uplands of the interior. To the north extended a shallow basin, containing 1,700 acres of dwarf spruce forest, beyond which arose the blue headlands of the coast, with slips of the ocean horizon between. All this tract might be cleared and cultivated, but much of it would require drainage, and the expense of preparing it for grain would hardly repay the scanty and uncertain yield. All this region is remarkably well watered: in fact, the same remark applies to the whole island, and it is estimated that one-fourth of its surface consists of lakes and ponds. We passed several beautiful lakes, swarming with trout, and gleaming cold and blue in the sunshine. Twenty-mile

Pond, a picturesque sheet of water, is six or seven miles in length, and contains several islands. There were a few cottages and hay-fields along the road, and I saw some stacks of peat, which must have been cut more from custom and tradition than necessity, for wood is abundant.

After skirting the shores of Twenty-mile Pond, the road crossed another ridge, and descended rapidly towards Conception Bay, which, as on the Topsail Road, opened finely between two lofty headlands, with the northern half of Bell Isle before us, and the line of the opposite shore stretching away dimly to its extremity. The bight below us, inclosed by the headlands, was Portugal Cove; and the huts of the fishermen, sprinkled over the rocks, formed a crescent a mile in length, in the middle of which a stream from the lake above fell in sparkling cascades into the bay. Flakes covered with odoriferous codfish arose like terraces from the shore, where the boats of the fishermen were moored, while others, with their lines out, dotted the surface of the water. There was a wild and picturesque beauty in the place, which made us forget its fishy atmosphere. Some of the party strolled around the cove; others climbed rocks for a wider lookout; others read the epitaphs in an ancient graveyard; but after an hour or two all were willing to return to the village tavern, where our hosts had provided an admirable lunch. We returned to St. Johns early in the afternoon on account of the dinner to be given on board the steamer in the evening.

XXII.

A TELEGRAPHIC TRIP TO NEWFOUNDLAND.

[AUGUST, 1855.]

III.—St. Johns—Excursions and Festivities.

I arose on the following morning at five o'clock, and accompanied Mr. Field on a trip to Logie Bay, a cove in the coast about six miles north of St. Johns. We had a light open wagon, an Irish driver, and an old stager of a horse, which took us over the ground in a few minutes less than an hour. The road passed through a portion of the stunted fir-woods which we had skirted on the way to Portugal Cove, and then turned eastward towards the coast, approaching a lofty headland of red sandstone rock, which is a prominent feature in the view northward from St. Johns. The rolling upland gradually sloped into a narrow valley, with a stream at the bottom. Following this, we descended to a cluster of fishing huts at the head of a rocky cove, less than a quarter of a mile in breadth, between the two headlands. The shore was everywhere perpendicular, or nearly so, and the huts were perched upon the brink of cliffs seventy or eighty feet high, at the bottom of which the sea rolled in and broke in volumes of spray. A steep footpath descended between the flakes of the fishermen to a gap or split in the rocks, across which was built the boat-house, a light timber framework high above the water, and provided with falls for hauling up the boats in rough weather.

An old fisherman, who appeared to be the only male at home, the other inhabitants having gone off before daylight to their fishing labors, accompanied us to the boat-house, and pointed out the spot where a part of it had been carried away by the fall of an overhanging mass of rock. We walked along an elastic platform, made by poles fastened together, to the end, whence there was a magnificent view of the cove, with its walls of dark-red sandstone, fringed with moving lines of foam, and its grand buttress of Red Head, as the promontory is called, rising almost perpendicularly to the height of 780 feet. A few fishing craft dotted the gray surface of the sea, over which the mist hung low in the distance.

The fishermen's wives were employed in spreading out upon the flakes the fish which had been stacked together during the night, with the skins uppermost to protect them from moisture. They informed us that the season was unusually good, but as the price of fish was low they would gain but little by their abundance. Last year, they said, fish had sold at fifteen and sixteen shillings the quintal (120 lbs.) but this year the price had gone down to twelve and thirteen shillings. The value, let me here explain, is not so much regulated by the demand in foreign markets as by the will of the merchants of St. Johns, who not only fix the price of the fish they buy but of the goods they sell to the fishermen. They thus gain in both ways, and fatten rapidly on the toils and hardships of the most honest and simple-hearted race in the world. It is their policy to keep the fishermen always in debt to them, and the produce of the fishing season is often mortgaged to them in advance. It is an actual fact that these poor fishermen are obliged to pay for their flour, groceries, and provisions from 50 to 100 per cent more than the rich and independent residents of St. Johns. It is no wonder therefore that the merchants amass large fortunes in the course of eight or ten years, while their virtual serfs remain as poor and as ignorant as their fathers before them. These things were mentioned to me by more than one of the intelligent citizens of St. Johns, and confirmed by all of the fishermen with whom I conversed on the subject. Several of the latter said to me, "Ah, Sir, if your people had the management of things here it would be better for us." This monopolizing spirit of gain is the curse, not only of St. Johns, but of all Newfoundland. It is the spirit which resists all progress, all improvements for the general good which seem to threaten the overthrow of its unjust advantages—which has made Newfoundland at the present day, three hundred and fifty years after its discovery by Sebastian Cabot, an almost unknown wilderness, and which would fain preserve it as a wilderness, in order that no other branch of industry may be developed but that upon which it preys.

The fishermen in some cases deliver their fish to the merchants, cured; in others, the latter purchase the yield as it comes from the boats, and have the drying done upon their own flakes. The livers are usually sold separately to those merchants who carry on the manufacture of oil. The dried cod, after having been assorted, are stored in warehouses, ready to be shipped to foreign markets. The greatest demand is from Spain, Cuba, and the West Indies generally. The whole town is pervaded by the peculiar odor of the fish, which even clings to the garments of those who deal in them. This odor, very unpleasant at first, becomes agreeable by familiarity, and finally the nostrils cease to take cognizance of it. St. Johns is decidedly the most ancient and fish-like town in North America. I saw a man in the street one day whose appearance and expression were precisely that of a dried codfish.

We returned homewards from Logie Bay by way of Virginia Water, the residence of Mr. Emerson, Solicitor-General. This is one of the most charmingly secluded hermitages which it is possible to imagine. We first turned into a stony lane, leading through the midst of a young forest of fir and spruce trees. As the lane descended the trees became taller and more dense, until we arrived at a cottage-lodge, shaded by a willow, on the edge of a beautiful lake, entirely encompassed by the dark woods. Passing this lodge, we found ourselves on a grassy peninsula, twenty yards in width, between what appeared to be two lakes, but were in reality the two ends of one, which curves itself into a nearly perfect circle, three miles in extent. A gate at the end of this isthmus ushered us into the woods again, between trees thirty or forty feet high, and so dense as to be almost impenetrable. Out of the dark avenue we came at last upon an open lawn of about two acres, sloping from Mr. Emerson's cottage to the lake. The cottage had a veranda in front, completely overrun with hop-vines and the fragrant woodbine, and the edges of the wall of fir trees behind it were brilliant with the blossoms of a variety of hardy garden-flowers. The lawn sloped to the south, looking across the lake to the woods beyond, whose dark-green tops hemmed in the sky. The keen north-west wind which rippled the water was unfelt around the cottage, so completely was it sheltered by its fir palisades.

Mr. Emerson and his daughters received us cordially, and offered us some delicious coffee, which our long ride in the cool morning air made very acceptable. I regretted that time would not allow us to explore the wild wood-paths over the island on which his house is built, and that the carriage-road along the borders of the lake was so much out of repair that we could not pass over it. The lake swarms with trout, and as Mr. Emerson is fortunate enough to possess the whole of it, he has at hand an unlimited supply of this prince of fish. The cottage was originally built by a former Governor of the island. Were it in the vicinity of New York or London, the property would be beyond all price; but when I looked up at the cold sky overhead, and remembered the brief, barren Summer of Newfoundland, I felt that I should prefer a simple tent beneath the Oriental palms.

In the afternoon I walked out to Signal Hill, the peak of which I have already spoken, forming the northern side of the gateway to the harbor. It is a mass of old red sandstone, rising 520 feet above the sea. The summit is devoted entirely to military purposes. There was formerly a battery, which, being of little use, has been abandoned ; also a hospital, which has been converted into barracks for the married soldiers, and a station whence approaching vessels are signalled to the town. A steep and rugged foot-path over the rocks led us to the block-house, out of which rises the signal-staff, on the apex of the headland. The door was open, the house untenanted, and I made my way to the look-out gallery, and used the excellent telescope, without hindrance from any one. The panorama from this point is superb, embracing the town and harbor of St. Johns, the country inland, clouded with forests and spangled with blue lakes, as far as the western headlands which rise above Conception Bay. At my feet yawned the throat of the wonderful harbor; Southside Hill, gray and mossy, rose beyond it, with the long, narrow inlet of Freshwater Bay to the left, and the bold green hills of the coast stretching away to Cape Spear. Between me and the latter point the boats of the St. Johns fishermen swarmed over the water, and on a distant horizon arose the wall of white fog which marks the boundaries of the Grand Bank.

I had a strong desire to visit the fishing village of Quidi Vidi, at the foot of the lake of the same name, and on descending Signal Hill took a path which led to the right, along the top of a range of grassy fields. The people of

St. Johns account for the name of the lake by a tradition of an old Portuguese sailor, its discoverer, who at first beholding it, cried out in his native language, "What do I see?" This lake is a favorite resort in summer, and the place where the annual regattas are held. It is about a mile long, lying in a deep valley, the sides of which are covered with hay-fields. A stream from its further end falls in a succession of little cascades down a rocky ledge into the land-locked cove, around which the village of Quidi Vidi is built. We pursued our path over a sloping down covered with dwarf whortle-berries and wild roses of delicious perfume. The *Kalmia latifolia* grew in thick clumps, and its flowering period was not entirely past. After a walk of a mile we reached the village, which contains forty or fifty houses, built at the head and along the sides of an oval sheet of water, completely inclosed by the red rocks, and so silent and glassy that no one would ever suppose it communicated with the turbulent sea without.

Quidi Vidi is entirely a fishing village, and a more picturesque one an artist could not desire. Except the smells of the codfish drying on the lofty flakes, which at once disenchant a romantic visitor, it seems almost Arcadian in its air of neatness and of quiet. The flakes, notwithstanding the uses to which they are dedicated, are really picturesque objects, their light platforms shooting above the grassy knolls around the village, and even above the houses and lanes, so that portions of the place are veritably roofed with cod-fish. The boat-houses, constructed of light poles with the bark on, extend over the water, whose green depths mirror the white cottages, the flakes, and the red rocks towering above them. Three or four fishermen who had just returned from their day's work, saluted us in a friendly manner, and at our request manned a boat and pulled us to the mouth of the cove, where a gut between the rocks, thirty or forty feet in breadth and two hundred feet in length, conducts to the sea. This gut is so shallow, that at some seasons the fishermen are confined within their cove for a week at a time, unable to get their boats outside. A heavy sea also imprisons them, and although there was a very light swell at the time of our visit, our boatmen preferred waiting for the pauses of smooth water. The outside cove, between the headlands of Sugar Loaf and Cuckold's Head, is small but exceedingly beautiful, the nearly vertical strata of red sandstone shooting like walls to the height of several hundred feet above the water. A herring net was set inside of the cove, and two or three youths in a boat with a gun, were endeavoring to shoot a salt-water pigeon. Our fishermen were fine, athletic, honest fellows, and I should desire no better recreation than to live a month among them, sharing their labors so far as I might be able, and drawing strength from their healthy and manly natures.

In the evening the grand ball, given to the officers of the Telegraph Company and their guests, came off at the Colonial Buildings. It had only been determined upon at the dinner on board the James Adger the evening before, and the citizens of St. Johns, who had taken upon themselves the labor of getting up the entertainment, were in a ferment of preparation from morning till night. A large private party which had been appointed for the same evening was postponed until the next week, and all the resources of the place called upon to furnish a display which should be creditable to it and to the occasion. They succeeded admirably, and the festivity no doubt passed off with greater spirit and cordiality on account of its impromptu character. The Colonial Buildings were brilliantly illuminated; libraries and offices were converted into dressing-rooms, the Supreme Court became a ball-room, and the Assembly Chamber contained more good things (in the way of supper) than for a long time before. At the extremity of the ball-room the English and American flags were displayed, and the band of the garrison played loudly for the dancers. At supper we had speeches from Mr. Little, Mr. Cooper, and Mr. Field, with the usual amount of cheers and enthusiasm.

All the belle sof St. Johns were present, and we had an opportunity of verifying the reports of their beauty. There are no fresher and lovelier complexions out of England. They retain the pure red and white—milk and roses, say the Germans—of their transmarine ancestry, with the bright eyes and delicate features of our own continent. I was glad to see, however, that our young American ladies bore the test of comparison without injury, and that it was not merely the courtesy due to strangers which attracted the Newfoundland bachelors towards them.

I have already spoken of the healthy appearance of the people. Statistics show that there is no climate in the world more conducive to health and longevity; but probably the quiet, unexcitable habits of the Newfoundlanders contribute somewhat to this result. There are, I have been informed, no prevalent diseases. I have heard of some cases of consumption among the fishermen, probably occasioned by extreme hardship and exposure; but fevers and diseases of the digestive and nervous systems are rare. No race of people that I have ever seen shows more healthy and vigorous stamina, and the natural morality which accompanies this condition. They are nourished by the pure, vital blood, unmixed with any of those morbid elements which so often poison the life of our physically and spiritually intemperate American people. When shall we learn the all-important truth that vice is oftener pathological than inherent in the heart, and that a sound body is the surest safeguard against those social evils with which we are threatened?

Our passengers invested largely in dogs. The pure Newfoundland breed, however, is about as difficult to be obtained in St. Johns as elsewhere, owing to its being continually crossed with exported curs of all kinds. Now and then you see a specimen, whose beauty, sagacity, and noble animal dignity proclaim him to be of the true blood, but such are held in high estimation and rarely offered for sale. In the out-ports, especially towards Labrador, the genuine breed is more frequently met with. Of the fifteen or twenty on board, three or four were very fine animals. They were all jet-black, long-haired, and web-footed, but of very different degrees of beauty and intelligence. The prices range from two to ten dollars, according to age and quality.

On Friday morning I made the ascent of South-side hill, which is the highest point near St. Johns, rising to an altitude of seven or eight hundred feet above the sea. Crossing the bridge at the head of the harbor, I took a steep, stony path, which presently separated into a number of sheep-tracks, and branched off among the scrubby undergrowth which covered the hill. I therefore made a straight course for the crest of the ridge, which I reached after a rough walk of nearly two miles, over boggy shelves of level soil, up stony declivities, and through tearing thickets of stunted spruce. The top of the hill is covered with a spongy, peat-like carpet, a foot or more in depth, formed from the accumulated deposits of the leaves and boughs of the trees which once covered it. The view is not so picturesque as that from Signal hill, but embraces a much greater extent of country to the south and east—a wild, unsettled chaos of dark, wooded hills rolling away to the Atlantic headlands.

We walked for a mile or more (I had one companion) along the ridge to get a better view of Freshwater harbor, which lies just east of the hill. Rougher travelling could not well be. The summit was cut and gashed both laterally and in the line of its direction by chasms of various depth and breadth, sometimes forming little dells with cold ponds at the bottom, sometimes so concealed by a dense growth of spruce that we slipped down to our waists among the bony branches before we were aware. No ordinary boots or garments could stand more than three days of such work. At last we reached the shoulder of a hill overlooking Freshwater harbor, which we found to be merely a long, narrow cove, the end of which was closed by a sand-bar. There were two or three fishermen's huts on its banks, and a narrow strip of grazing land along the edge of the bleak wilderness in which it was inclosed. The ocean was dotted with fishing craft, sprinkled all over its blue surface. On a favorite bank inside of Cape Spear a crowd of forty or fifty had collected together.

Our labor was repaid by stumbling upon a path which led from Freshwater to St. Johns. On our return I noticed a lonely cabin among the thickets on the northern side of the hill, and left the path to pay it a visit and learn who the people were who lived in such a wild place. We made our way with difficulty through the trees and over the chasms until we reached a little glen where some clearing had been done and two patches of weakly potatoes had been planted, in the black, spongy soil. The cabin stood on a stony knob just above. As we approached, a little girl ran in and closed the door, and a dog set up a fierce clamor. I knocked, and after some delay an Irishwoman with wild eyes, unkempt hair, and a dirty face, made her appearance. I asked her for a drink; whereupon she presently came with a small pitcher, and requested us to wait until she should go to a spring at a little distance, the water of which was superior to that of the stream near the house. When she returned we entered the house, which was the very counterpart of an Irish cabin—the walls of stone and mud, the floor of earth, and the furniture of the rudest and scantiest sort. Three girls were squatting around a pile of smoky brushwood in the chimney-place, and the dog, not yet satisfied in regard to our characters, stood sullenly growling beside them.

The woman, in spite of her appearance, had that natural courtesy which springs from the heart. After giving us some water she produced a slab of oaten bread an inch thick, and strongly resembling a specimen of gritstone. The taste, however, was better than the appearance; and when she added a fragment of salt codfish and insisted on our drinking a pot of coffee, which I have no doubt she had prepared for her own and her children's dinner, we found her hospitality by no means to be despised. The humble fare had an excellent relish after our scramble, and the hearty good will with which it was offered freshened the sapless codfish and smoothed the asperities of the oatmeal slab. A large gray cat came into the cabin while we were thus engaged, and after having regarded us with much gravity for a few moments, marched out again. "Och!" said the woman, "but that is a wonderful cat, sure. There niver was such a cat in the world at all at all. She's not afraid, sir, of the biggest dog that ever barked; she'll fly at his throat, an' if ye didn't take her off she'd kill him mighty quick, I tell ye. She knows everything that's goin' on, and she understands your words as plain as any Christian. One night me husband and meself was sittin' in this blessed room, an' we heard a scratchin' like, at the door. Says my husband, 'Peggy, I think there's a rat comin'.' Well, the cat was up in the loft, and she heard what he said, and she came down that very instant and waited by the door till the rat came in. It was a dirty, big rat, bigger nor the cat herself, and she says nothin' but lets it go down into the cellar in yon corner; thin she heads it off and jumps on it. Oh, Holy Virgin, didn't the rat roar! And it was the king of the rats, so my husband said, and never a rat put his ugly nose into this house since that night, an' its four years ago."

The cat was the object of the woman's boundless enthusiasm; and her stories of its sagacity were so amusing that we were lavish in our expressions of wonder and admiration, for the sake of encouraging her. "She a'most frightens me sometimes," she added,—"she looks into my face like a human craytur, an' I think she'll up an' spake to me. When she sees anything strange she jist sits down on her hinder claws, an' she houlds her fore claws on each side of her head, an' she looks straight forrid till her eyes blaze, and her body stretches right up, gittin' thinner an' thinner, an' longer an' longer, till she's full a yard and a half high." We took our departure after this, giving the woman a small recompense for her stories, her oaten bread, and her kindness, and receiving the invocation of the Virgin's blessing in return.

In the evening there was a social gathering at the house of Mr. Stabb, which was attended by nearly all our guests. A portion of our company were conveyed thither in carriages; but as there were not enough of the latter to accommodate all, the remainder set out on foot. I presume it was a new sight for St. Johns to witness fifteen or twenty gentlemen and ladies in evening dress promenading the streets. We had not gone far before we were aware of a convoy of attendants or admirers rather loud than respectful. The procession increased at every step; couriers were sent in advance to spread the news, and the dark side-streets poured little rills of rowdyism into the great current upon which we were borne. The demonstration was confined to whistles, yells, and other outcries, with occasional remarks on the appearance or dress of some of our party, made in that quaint, picturesque style which is peculiar to the *gamins* of London and New York. We were fearful lest they should carry the joke beyond the limits of endurance; but the crowd was a thoroughly good-humored one, and on our arrival at our destination, the whole convoy, then numbering between two and three hundred, united in giving us three cheers.

The hospitality of St. Johns never flagged up to the last moment. Our party lived almost entirely on shore, in a round of festivities, which were very delightful, because they were spontaneous. We found it impossible to accept half the invitations which we received, from sheer want of time. We all retain the most agreeable recollections of our visit, and not a few of our party cherish the hope of returning at some future day, and renewing the acquaintances so auspiciously commenced.

As we were passing Chain Rock battery, on the afternoon of our departure, we noticed the boats of Mr. Huested anchored over the Merlin rock, lying in the channel, the removal of which had been completed during our visit. Mr. Huested hailed us, saying he would give us a parting salute. Nearly all the passengers were gathered on the hurricane-deck at the time, looking their last on the receding harbor. There was a movement on Mr. Huested's boat; a handling of wires; a touch—and then followed a dumb, heavy explosion which shook our steamer—then not fifty yards from the spot. In a second a circle of water forty or fifty feet in diameter over the rock was violently agitated; a narrower circle was hurled into the air to the height of thirty feet; and from the centre a sheaf of silvery jets sprang seventy or eighty feet above the surface of the sea. The enormous masses of water curved outwards as they ascended, and stood for an instant like colossal plumes waving against the sun, which shone through their tops and blinded our eyes with the diamond lustre. It was a Great Geyser of the sea—a momentary but sublime picture which no volcanic well of the Icelandic valleys can surpass. As it fell, the shower of airy spray drifted down upon us, drenching ourselves and the decks, but creating a sudden rainbow over the paddle-boxes—an arch of promise which spanned our course for an instant, and melted into air with the sound of our parting cheers.

XXIII.

A TELEGRAPHIC TRIP TO NEWFOUNDLAND.

[AUGUST, 1855.]

IV.—A Tramp into the Interior.

After clearing Cape Spear, on Saturday afternoon, we stood down the coast, intending to stop for the night at the Bay of Bulls, about twenty miles distant, in order to put the steamer in proper trim. The hills rose abruptly from the water's edge to the height of seven or eight hundred feet, their ribs and shoulders of dark-red rock but scantily clothed with a covering of gray moss, sheep's laurel, and dwarf fir-trees. There are neither rocks nor shoals on this part of the coast, and the steamer might have sailed to Cape Race within a gunshot of the land. The deep sea-swells, caught in the innumerable clefts and hollows of the rocks, burst upwards in enormous jets of foam, which subsided to rise again after a minute or two of calm. In one point there was a spout or breathing-hole through the rock, opening about fifty feet above the sea. After each swell rolled in, a slender plume of snow-white spray, thirty feet high, shot through the orifice and waved a moment on the brink of the cliff. The picturesque inequalities of the coast and these curious and graceful caprices of the sea made us forget its terrors as a lee shore, and its bleakness and sterility as a place for the dwelling of man.

We had a very strong south-west wind to contend against, with a long, rolling head-swell, which was severely felt by all who had indulged in the late hours and sumptuous suppers of St. Johns. It was a partial relief when we rounded into the Bay of Bulls and ran through a mile of smooth water to its head. The harbor is nearly elliptical in shape. The northern shore rises into a high conical peak, partly covered with stunted spruce and fir-trees, and sloping on its western side into a range of hills which sweep like an amphitheatre around the bay. The village is built around the head of the harbor, and contains about one hundred and fifty houses. The hills behind it have been cleared and turned into fields of barley and grass. The place, with its wooden church, its fish-flakes along the water, its two or three large storehouses, its yellow fields of late hay, and the dark, dwarfish woods behind, reminded me strongly of a view on one of the Norwegian fjords. A large white house was pointed out to me as the residence of a lady who is godmother to thirty-nine children—a fact which shows either that children are very plenty or godmothers very scarce.

As the signs of good weather continued and the ship

proved to be in tolerable trim, we landed a St. Johns pilot whom we had taken aboard for the harbor, and immediately put to sea. As long as it was light we kept near the coast, and at dusk passed the bay or cove of Ferryland, where two of the Arctic's boats came to land, with the few who were saved by that means. The shores are here low and green, but the light was too indistinct for objects to be readily perceived. After night we stood a little further from the coast, still keeping near it, in spite of a fog which was at times so dense that nothing could be seen a ship's length distant. At daylight Cape Pine was in sight; Cape Chapeaurouge, forty miles off, showed itself once or twice during the forenoon; and before sunset we had again passed St. Pierre and Miquelon. The sea subsided a little in the afternoon, and nearly all were on deck at sunset to watch one of the most superb skies of the North fade more beautifully, through its hues of orange, amber-green, and carmine, than all the dolphins that ever died.

Early on Monday morning we saw Cape Ray, and, running westward along the coast, made the rocky point off Port-aux-Basques in an hour or two. Through the glass we saw the little steamer Victoria at anchor in the harbor and the top-masts of a three-masted vessel. All was anxiety on board to know whether she was the long-expected bark Sarah L. Bryant, with the submarine cable on board, when, five or six miles out of port, a boat approached us, and Capt. Sluyter of the Victoria confirmed the welcome news. The James Adger, owing to her length, reached a good anchoring-ground at the head of the harbor with some difficulty. We soon ascertained that the machinery requisite for paying out the cable had not yet been put up, and the work could not be commenced for a day or two. Mr. Cooper, therefore, determined to cross to Cape North, the Cape Breton terminus, and select a proper place to bring the cable ashore.

As soon as this announcement was made, a number of our passengers prepared to go ashore, and spend the intervening time in becoming acquainted with the village and the neighboring country. But short time was given us to fit out, and I barely managed to snatch a shawl, a sketch-book, a few ship's biscuits, and a handful of red herring, before the boat pushed off with us. A party of four—Mr. Sluyter, Mr. O'Brien, Mr. Middlebrook, and myself—determined to make a foray into the hills behind the village, in the hope of shooting a cariboo, or reindeer; and our first care, on landing at the piles of codfish before Mr. Waddell's house, was to procure guns, supplies, and guides. Mr. Waddell—who acted as if his house and all that was in it belonged as much to ourselves as to him—not only gave us a good dinner of bean-soup and duff, but all his fowling-pieces, ammunition, and equipments. He even consented to keep tally of the quintals of dried codfish which his men were carrying on board of a schooner lying below his storehouse, in order that his tally-man, John Butt by name, might act as our pilot over the marshy hills. Butt was a stout St. Johnsman, with a strong, tanned face, clear, light-blue eyes, and a shock-head of curled and grizzly hair. At my suggestion he procured two other men—Genge, a bony fisherman, with prominent nose and enormous sandy whiskers, and his step-son Robert, a bright-eyed youth of twenty-two. We added a loaf of bread and a dried codfish to our slender stock of provisions—trusting to our muskets for a further supply—and turned our backs on the village and our faces towards the misty range of Cape Ray Highlands.

Following a bridle-track beside the telegraph poles, over a black, quaky soil, we soon reached one of the bights of the harbor, where Butt had a boat moored to the rocks. He proposed to cross to the opposite shore in order to avoid a tedious circuit around the head of the harbor; and, as the water was still, we all embarked in his tight little skiff, which sank to within two inches of her gunwale. By careful trimming she carried us safely over, when the men drew her ashore at the head of a narrow inlet, and thrust the oars into a thicket of dwarf fir-trees. We now took up the line of march—climbing a glen embraced by two gray and ragged hills, the sides of which were furrowed with deeply-worn gullies, while pools of dark-brown water filled up every inequality of the soil. The footing was of spongy moss, mixed with a sort of furze, into which our feet sank to a depth of three or four inches at every step. In the innumerable hollows which crossed our path the ground was often completely saturated with water, and occasionally bridged over with some of those hardy plants whose tough fibre in these latitudes rivals that of the human frame. In other places the stubborn, stunted growth of spruce and fir so filled the lateral clefts across the hills that I could walk on their tops, at the risk, it is true, of making a false step and slipping down to my waist among the horny branches. There was no path, nor anything that would serve as a landmark; for each dip or rise of the hills seemed the counterpart of that we had just seen. Gray rock, gray moss, dark spruce thicket, and dark tarn, were mingled and mottled together so bewilderingly, with such endless repetitions of the same forms and hues, that I should have found it difficult to lay down a clue that could be readily taken up again. I noticed that Butt, under whose guidance we had placed ourselves, chose his course rather by the compass than by the appearance of the objects around us.

We had proceeded three or four miles in this way, making frequent detours in order to get around the long, deep ponds of black water, or the deeper ravines whose walls of perpendicular gray rock effectually barred our passage, when a shot from one of our party gave the first signal of game. A covey of grouse had been started, and a short but lively chase over the rough ground resulted in our bagging five of the six birds which arose. Two or three of the more enthusiastic sportsmen followed over the higher ridges in search for more, while the rest of us plodded on towards the highlands, eager for a sight of cariboo, and hurried by Butt's desire to reach a good camping-ground before dark. The deep carpets or cushions of plants and decaying vegetable mould over which we walked were studded with berries of various kinds, all of which the men plucked and ate. There was a small plant with a dark-purple leaf and an orange-colored pulpy fruit about the size of a cherry, which they termed "bake-apples (in reality the *Rabus chœmemorus*, or *multeberry*, of Norway), the flavor of which, containing a mild, pleasant acid, really resembled that of a frozen apple. The whortleberry, which they called "hurts" or "whorts," was not more than two or three inches in height, and the fruit was scanty. The "cranberry," growing on a short, green moss, was about the size and appearance of a juniper berry, with a pungent, bitter, but not unpleasant taste. There was another fruit, called the "stoneberry," a bunch of small, scarlet berries, which are much less insipid to the eye than to the palate.

We were at last so far in advance of the sportsmen that we were obliged to halt while one of the men ascended the nearest hill to look for them. By this time we were five or six miles from the harbor, and the scenery began to assume a very different character. We overlooked a deep valley, the bottom of which consisted of woods of spruce, fir, and larch trees, interspersed with open, grassy bottoms. A range of dark, wooded hills rose opposite, down a gorge, in the midst of which a large stream fell in a succession of sparkling cascades, their noise reaching even to where we sat. Beyond all towered the long blue rampart of the Cape Highlands. I enjoyed this wild and lonely landscape for a time, but the sportsmen did not appear, and Robert, who lay at full length on the moss, rolling over in his search for "hurts," expressed a wish to go down to a pond below us and "strip." I offered to accompany him, and we soon reached the edge of the dark, sepia-colored water. It was shallow, with a deposit of snuffy mould at the bottom, sprinkled with yellow pond-lilies, and so cold as to make my skin shrink, but I plunged in and endured it for five minutes. Robert, who had the real Newfoundland nature, and was, I have no doubt, web-footed, floundered about for three times as long, splashing, blowing, and stirring up the deposits of the pond until his sinewy, well-knit body showed through the water like new bronze.

We met no more game after this except gnats and musketoes, which became both plentiful and venomous as we descended into the valley. The mountain stream we had seen from the height was a tributary to Grand Bay Brook, a rivulet which empties into the sea between Port-aux-Basques and Cape Ray. The ground was boggy where we approached the brook, and there was no convenient fordage; whereupon Butt conducted us about two miles further to the eastward, near an inclosed mountain meadow called the Green Gardens, where we came upon a dense wood of well-grown spruce and fir trees, sloping down to a rapid in the stream. The view from the rocks in its bed was charming. Wild, dark, ragged woods, opening to the sunset, overhung us on either hand; in front, up the stream, rose a cliff of silvery rock; and the summits of the unmolested hills on both sides towered above the trees and shut us out from the world. Trout-lines and hooks were at once produced, and while Butt, Genge, and I went into the woods to make our camp, the others made flies of grouse-feathers and took their stations beside the eddies of the water. We three selected a dry place on the slope, felled some trees, collected fuel, started a gay fire of resinous logs and branches, and trimmed spruce boughs enough to make us an elastic, fragrant bed, six inches deep. The musketoes had been terrible in the bed of the brook, but when the draught of the blazing logs began to toss the branches above our heads, they speedily disappeared. Our caterers came up at dusk, bitten, weary, wet, and hungry, and ready to give a hearty assent to my declaration that there is no completer comfort than a seat by the camp-fire—no sweeter rest than when the boughs of the forest are both our bed and canopy.

The five grouse were skewered and spitted on long sticks stuck into the ground, the twelve small trout laid to broil on a flat stone placed on the coals, the hard pilot bread distributed, and we gradually made a supper all too slender for our needs. But the game had not been so abundant as we anticipated; it was seven miles yet to the "ravage" of the cariboo, with the wind blowing off sea and carrying our scent a league before us; and so we laid the loaf and the codfish aside for breakfast, and turned to the pipe for solace. Wrapped in our shawls, we formed the spokes of a wheel whereof the fire was the blazing centre, while Butt and Genge dragged up log after log of dead fir-wood, and cast them upon the pile until the clouds of snapping sparks rose above the tree-tops. The dense, dusky foliage, lighted from beneath, glowed like a golden fretwork against the jet-black patches of sky above us, and the mossy fir-trunk and silvery birch-boles seemed to grow transparent and luminous as they sprang out of the darkness. Warmed by the magical blaze, spiced by the odor of the crushed boughs, and soothed by the mild influence of the Cuban herb, I lay, for a long time, unable to sleep, looking on the yellow-bearded followers of Biörne and Lief Ericsson as they once clustered around their camp-fires in this their ancient *Helluland.* Eight or nine centuries have passed away since their Norse-dragons anchored in its deep bays and rock-guarded coves; but except the stumps of two or three trees in the woods near us, there was no evidence that our mountain solitude had since that time known the presence of civilized man.

The logs at last fell into heaps of red coal; Butt, who had climbed into the top of a tree, where he sat singing sea-songs, descended and coiled himself around its foot; the other men lay on their backs and slept silently, and I too forgot Biörne and his Norsemen and slept among the fragrant boughs. The night passed away silently, and dawn came gray and misty, threatening rain, over the woods. Our fishers went down to the brook again, and Butt took to the hills with a gun; but after an hour the latter came back empty-handed, and the former with eight small trout. We roasted the codfish, which was wonderfully salt, carefully divided the loaf, distributed the trout (one apiece), and made a rather unsatisfactory breakfast. The fact is, the trip, as a sporting excursion, had failed, although it had amply repaid us in all other respects. Our steamer was expected to return at noon, and the necessity of reaching Port-aux-Basques by that time prevented us from penetrating further into the hills. Besides there were sprinkles of rain, and other tokens of a bad day. We therefore decided while breakfasting to take the homeward trail. Familiarity with salt cod had bred contempt in our men, and one of them threw his share into the bushes, with the exclamation: "It's downright murder to eat *that!*" But Genge wisely remarked that it was the best thing for short allowance, "because," said he, "it makes you so dry that you're always keeping yourself filled up with water."

There had been a heavy dew, and the moss was like a wet sponge. We had rather a soaking return tramp of it, often stopping to drink of the brown rills, or to refresh our palates with the acid "bake-apples," yet never seeing a grouse or a hare. The clouds, after some ominous leakings, lifted, and the wind blew cold from the north-west. While resting on a rock about a mile and a half from the harbor, we were startled by the sound of an engine-whistle and the blowing of steam from an escape-pipe. Supposing it to be the James Adger, we hurried on at a breathless pace, plunging into gullies and tearing through thickets in breakneck style, until an opening in the holes showed us that the sound proceeded from the little steamer Victoria, which was just moving out of the harbor. She was on her way to Cape Ray, ten miles distant, to select the initial point of the submarine cable. Our own transfer across the harbor was safely accomplished—the water being quite smooth—and we reached Mr. Waddell's house in time to partake of the very good dinner which his broad-shouldered and red-whiskered cook had prepared. I here had an opportunity of tasting *calabogus*, the national beverage of Newfoundland. It is a mixture of rum and spruce beer in nearly equal quantities, and has a better flavor than one would suspect from the ingredients. The spruce beer, pure, is made from the young boughs of the tree boiled with molasses, and is just the beverage—sparkling, resinous, sweet, and bitter—to nourish so virile and vigorous a people.

In the afternoon I went off to the bark Sarah L. Bryant, to see the preparations which had been made for paying out the cable. I never saw a vessel in a worse condition.

Nearly all her bulkheads and stanchions had been cut away to make room for the two immense coils of forty and thirty-five miles, into which the iron-corded cable was bent. According to the captain's account there never was a more unmanageable cargo, and he declared he would much rather ship a load of live eels. Its activity was incredible. He was obliged to cut up all his spare spars to shore up and support the slippery bulk; yet, in spite of all his precautions, it once or twice slipped through his fingers and came near capsizing his bark. On one occasion he was obliged to turn completely about and scud before the wind for nearly two days. Under such circumstances it is not remarkable that he was forty-eight days in making the passage, but very lucky that he was able to make it at all.

XXIV.

A TELEGRAPHIC TRIP TO NEWFOUNDLAND.

[AUGUST, 1855.]

V.—CAPE RAY, AND THE NEWFOUNDLAND FISHERMEN.

It was dusk on Tuesday evening before the James Adger made her appearance off Port-aux-Basques, returning from Cape Breton. I had made arrangements to pass the night in one of the houses on shore, and as the fog was beginning to gather, and the Victoria had not yet made her appearance, judged that I should be safe in remaining. Dr. and Mrs. Sayre, who had made a journey to Cape Ray the previous day, and camped all night in a thicket of spruce, had found accommodations with our friend Butt, and Genge offered me similar hospitality. Both of these men offered us every kindness in their power—bringing us their heavy, well-oiled boots and thick woollen socks in exchange for our own, which were thoroughly soaked by our tramp over the hills. Their rough, hearty bluntness assured me that I should be welcome to all they could offer, and when there is warmth within a hut I care not how rude its exterior may be. All our other passengers had gone off on board the steamer, but I greatly preferred remaining ashore.

The Victoria came in about ten o'clock, and the fog soon afterwards became so dense that we were satisfied neither of the vessels would venture out of port. I called at Butt's house, where, in a neat kitchen with an ample fireplace, we found Mrs. Butt nursing a rosy child of fifteen months old, while a son of twelve or thirteen years sat at the table reading the Bible. The sounds of children's voices—and there were many of them—came from a sleeping-room adjoining. Everything about the house was neat and orderly, and there was an appearance of comfort which I had not looked for. Genge lived in a smaller cottage, the inside of which was blackened by the smoke of a wide chimney, and dimly lighted by a swinging oil-lamp. There were broad benches on either side which evidently did duty as beds. The floor was of earth, and the only furniture was a table, two old chairs, some shelves, and a large, dingy cupboard in the corner. Mrs. Genge shook hands with me and bade me welcome, and on my saying that I should be content with a corner to spread my shawl in, her husband turned to me with "Don't talk about corners; we'll try to make you comfortable." I was pleased to see that my presence did not embarrass the good family in the least, and that, while they showed me every kindness, I occasioned no apparent change in the household.

I was ushered into a little side-room, which to my surprise contained a curtained bed, white and perfectly clean, a table upon which lay a number of books, a looking-glass, a wash-bowl and a pitcher of stone-ware, with a fine linen towel, combs, brushes, soap, and all ordinary appliances of the toilet. Everything in the room was scrupulously neat, and arranged with a knowledge and propriety which I should never have expected to find in such a place. Among the books were Mrs. Beecher Stowe's "Sunny Memories," Chambers's "Information for the People," and some novels, besides a large family Bible. I was so tired that I immediately tumbled into bed and slept so soundly that when I awoke at five in the morning I had some difficulty in ascertaining where I was. Genge, who was already stirring, accompanied me to Butt's, where I found Dr. and Mrs. Sayre, whose experience was similar to mine. They had been received with the same kindness, and treated to the same unexpected comforts. Our hosts refused to accept the slightest compensation, and we were only able to repay them indirectly, by engaging them to row us out to the steamer.

The people of Port-aux-Basques are unusual specimens of ripe and healthy physical vigor, and they possess those simple virtues which naturally belong to such an organization. Though their education is very deficient, they are shrewd and quick-witted; open and trustful unless deceived, when they become excessively suspicious; generous, honest, hospitable, and enduring; remarkably free from immorality and crime notwithstanding—perhaps on account of—their distance from efficient legal authorities; and I do not know any other community which surpasses them in sterling manly qualities. They are not only very healthy but very prolific; and the place, like many others on the coast, has grown up almost entirely from the natural increase of the first families who settled there. This accounts for the fact that the population of the fishing villages on the southern and western sides of the island are nearly all related to each other. I heard it stated that in some of the remote settlements which began with a single family, the brothers and sisters formed incestuous marriages; but I was glad to hear this story positively denied afterwards. The intercourse between the fishing-ports is carried on almost entirely by sea, on account of the rugged character of the land-travel. There is a communication in winter between Port-aux-Basques and St. George's bay, over the Cape Ray highlands; but it is very rarely travelled by any except the Indians—a branch of the Micmac tribe, who have emigrated hither from Cape Breton. The distance across is about sixty miles, which they travel occasionally in two days.

The Victoria, which had returned in the night, brought word that a place had been selected just inside of Cape Ray as the starting-point of the submarine cable, the materials for a house landed, and the frame already erected. A deep cove in the harbor of Port-aux-Basques was at first chosen, on account of its sheltered situation, and the circumstance of the cable falling at once into deep water; but as Cape Ray was three or four miles nearer Cape Breton, Mr. Field and Mr. Canning went thither in a boat on Monday, and fixed upon a spot at the head of Cape Ray harbor, where there was a beach of soft sand somewhat guarded from the ice which lodges here in great quantities during the winter and spring, by groups of rocks on both sides. The next day the frame and complete materials for a house were taken up by the Victoria, together with a number of passengers who offered themselves as amateur carpenters. On reaching the bay the timbers were lashed together as a raft and towed near the shore, where, on account of the violence of the surf, it parted, leaving Captain Sluyter and two or three others, who were on it, to float to the beach on the pieces. The boat's load of passengers succeeded in landing, and immediately went to work in company with the fishermen of the place and their dogs to rescue the timbers. Boards, beams, rafters and bundles of shingles were caught and dragged out of the surf; and in the course of two or three hours all the materials of the raft were got ashore. In this work the dogs rendered capital service—plunging boldly into the sea and seizing upon every stick which they could manage. Sometimes two of them would take a plank between them, and, watching the proper moment with a truly human sagacity, bring it to the beach on the top of a breaker and there deliver it into the hands of their masters. It was really wonderful to behold the strength, courage, and industry of these poor beasts, who, when but few fragments were left, fought savagely for the possession of them, and even tried to drown each other.

By night, with the assistance of the people, the frame of the house was raised, and the Victoria returned to Port-aux-Basques. She started again the next day at noon, with Mr. Field and another company of amateur carpenters on board, leaving the James Adger to follow with the bark in tow as soon as the weather would allow. While waiting on board the Victoria I witnessed the performance of some of the Cape Ray dogs, two of which were on board. If a stick was thrown into the water, they would spring over the rail, seize it, swim around the vessel or chase other floating objects, until some one let down the bight of a rope over the side, when the dog would immediately make for it, place both fore-paws over it, thrust his head forward and hold on until he was drawn upon deck. One of these dogs had followed the Victoria's boat the day previous and was taken on board. This little circumstance produced a marked change in the temper of the inhabitants of Cape Ray. They became shy, suspicious, and reserved; and nothing but the explicit declaration of Mr. Field—which was afterwards carried into effect—that the dog should be returned or his full value paid the owner, restored their confidence.

We ran up the coast, passed Grand Bay, the embouchure of the stream on which we had encamped, and in an hour and a half came to in front of the six or eight fishermen's huts which constitute the settlement of Cape Ray. I found that the lofty isolated peak which I had taken to be the Cape itself was four or five miles inland, separated from the point by a low, undulating promontory covered with dense, stunted woods. Two other peaks appeared, retreating along the western coast, and behind them all towered the dark Cape Highlands, twelve hundred feet in height. We were carried ashore in the Victoria's boat, and landed at the head of a little cove where the boats of the fishermen were pulled up in front of their huts, after which the steamer returned to Port-aux-Basques to assist in bringing up the bark.

Following a rough, boggy path along the shore, sometimes on the brink of black cliffs overhanging the breakers, a walk of a mile conducted us to the new telegraph-building on a grassy knoll near the head of the bay. We found all the male population of the place employed in completing it, under the direction of old Tapp, the patriarch of the fishermen, and a Cape Ray carpenter. Some were nailing on clapboards, others shingling the roof, and others digging a trench from the front of the house to the beach, while planks, beams, bundles of shingles, boxes, and carpenters' tools were scattered around on all sides. Our first thought was for dinner, as we had taken the precaution to carry a box of provisions with us. Seated on the shingles, with the fresh sea-breeze blowing over us, and the keen edge of our sea-appetites not in the least blunted, the cold beef-steak, red herring, pilot-bread, and other delicacies rapidly disappeared. But we were soon summoned to work; and the spectacle we presented would have afforded great amusement to some of our New York friends. Mr. Field, spade in hand, led the ditching party; Dr. Spring, with his coat off and a handkerchief tied around his head, was hard at work sawing out spaces for windows; Dr. Sayre, myself, and two or three others, nailed on layer after layer of shingles; and of the rest, some took to flooring, others to clapboarding, and others to making frames for batteries. We had but a single accident—a scaffold fell, and one of the fishermen, in falling within it, barked his shins. All worked with a will, and by night the roof was completed, the sides closed in, the house floored, and a deep ditch dug down to the edge of the breakers. This ditch terminated in the house, in the centre of which a circular pit was dug, and the frame of a hogshead without the headings, planted in it, allowing a clear space about eighteen inches around it. A wooden pillar, buried six feet, was placed inside the hogshead, which was filled with earth rammed hard—the whole forming a sort of capstan or belaying-post for the cable. The battery frame was also stayed against the side of the house, the glass jars fixed in their appropriate places, and nothing was wanting but the proper apparatus to fit the building for immediate use.

Mr. Field, with most of the amateurs, determined to remain all night in the building, and men were dispatched to collect spruce boughs enough to turn the floor into a bed. Dr. Spring and myself, however, preferred trying one of the fishermen's huts, and Mr. Tapp sent one of his grandsons to conduct us to his residence. We retraced our way to the cove, and were guided by little Steve to the largest hut, which was a very small one, just opposite the landing. On entering, a woman of about fifty-five, short, stout, with gray eyes, and queer, frizzled, yellowish hair, rose from her seat by the wide fireplace. "Are you Mrs. Tapp?" I asked. "I'm Tapp's wife," she answered, stretching forth her hand, and when I took it, bobbing nearly to the floor in a respectful but grotesque courtesy. I introduced Dr. Spring, who was received with a still deeper courtesy, and mentioned Mr. Tapp's message and our desire to remain there for the night. "To be sure," said she, "you shall stay; it's a difficult house, but such as it is, you are welcome to it." There was a tea-kettle on the fire, and a pan of bread with a heap of live-coals on the lid, hanging to a hook. Tapp's wife set about preparing tea, giving us, meanwhile, a variety of information about herself and family. Her language was very quaint and peculiar, and she spoke in the short, quick way common to some tribes of Indians. I gathered from her words that she had been born and raised on Codroy river (about thirty miles north of Cape Ray); that she had five cows before she left her mother; that all the cows and sheep in the settlement belonged to her; that she had had nine daughters and two sons, but God Almighty took one of the latter when he was two months old; that she had never been further than Port-aux-Basques, and thought it must be a fine thing to see the world. She added, however, that she had plenty to eat and drink, and was well contented where she was. Two of her daughters—great, shy, sunburnt, blowsy tomboys of fourteen and sixteen—came into the house. "They would be good girls," said she, "if they had their rights"—meaning if they had a chance to go to school. I asked for a drink of water, and received a bowl of a sepia-colored mixture tasting of mud. "It's very difficult water," said the old lady, "and you'd better not drink much."

Presently she spread a piece of painted oil-cloth on the table, set out some plates, cups, bread and butter, took the tea-kettle off the fire, and invited us to sit down, saying, "If I had anything better, you should have it; I can't do no more than that, you know." She apologized for her bread, assuring us that she had very "difficult" flour, but added, as if to console us, "here you have a chaney dish and here you have a chaney tea-cup, only they don't match." With all her oddity nothing could be kinder than her manner; and her difficult bread, and tea sweetened with molasses, had a relish for me beyond what my hunger gave it. We had just finished our meal when old Tapp appeared, accompanied by Dr. Sayre and Mr. Roberts, who were dispatched by the party to procure a supply of bread and tea. They gave such an account of the comfort of the new house with its bedding of spruce boughs, that Dr. Spring and myself were persuaded to return with them. We had not proceeded far, however, when the fishermen saw the lights of a steamer off the bay, and presently a second light appeared, still more distant and indistinct. The first steamer gradually rounded in towards the land, but a light fog was gathering over the water, and we could not make out from her lights whether she was the Adger or the Victoria.

Old Tapp, supposing she was the former vessel, put off towards her in his boat, and after some deliberation Mr. Roberts and myself took two of the fishermen and followed him. The steamer was at anchor by this time, and burning blue lights, which were answered by rockets from the vessel outside. She proved to be the Victoria, which had run up in advance of the Adger, which latter had the bark in tow. It was now nearly nine o'clock, and the fog was at times so thick as entirely to hide the Adger's lights. The captain, finally, worn out with the day's labors, had lain down, and we were thinking of the same thing, when the sound of oars was heard, and one of the Adger's boats drew alongside. She had Mr. Lowber on board, and came for the purpose of taking out Captain Sluyter to assist in piloting the steamer in.

I embarked in the boat with the captain, and about ten o'clock she put off, steering out to sea in the supposed direction of the steamer, whose lights were nowhere to be seen. The water was fortunately smooth, with but a light swell, and the men pulled vigorously for nearly half an hour before the quick eye of our coxswain could detect any sign of light. Even then it was immediately obscured again by the fog; and as we were losing sight of the Victoria's lights by this time, it was decided to burn a Roman candle which we had with us. This was accomplished with some difficulty, for the powder was damp; but it procured us a return signal and showed us our true course. Shortly afterwards a gun was fired on board the Victoria, according to Captain Sluyter's direction. In another half-hour we seemed to be rapidly nearing the Adger, when she stood further out again and almost disappeared from view. We had now lost sight of the shore, and began to fear we should have to pass the whole night on the water. Another long and weary pull followed, but we did not feel entirely safe until within hail of her steamer. The swell was heavy, and it was with the utmost difficulty and danger that we succeeded in getting upon the gangway ladder. Our men had been obliged to pull a distance of eight or nine miles, and it was nearly midnight when we got on deck.

The next day we commenced laying the submarine cable. The end was safely landed and secured, and by sunset we had made about forty miles, when a gale, which had been rising all day, blew so violently that it was found necessary to cut the cable in order to save the bark from foundering. Thus disastrously terminated our expedition, which, however, was repeated with complete success the following summer. The next morning we reached Sydney, on Cape Breton, took on board a fresh supply of coal, and then returned to New York, having been absent a month.

XXV.

HOLIDAYS IN SWITZERLAND AND ITALY.

[1856.]

On leaving Germany for a holiday tour of six weeks, which we proposed extending as far as Rome, we first spent a day in delightful old Nuremburg, and thence hurried on by the Danube and Augsburg to Lindau on the Lake of Constance, which we crossed to Romanshorn, and so entered Switzerland. There was no call for passports, no examination of baggage, and the conductors on the train to Zurich, although each one had the word Snob (the initials of the German words for "Swiss North-Eastern Railway") on his buttons, were nevertheless gentlemen, and handsome as they were courteous.

We left Zurich in a carriage for Goldau, at the foot of the Righi, in order to ascend that fashionable peak before sunset. While dining at Zug, I was accosted by a Swiss guide, who wished me to take him into my service. Now, I had determined to take no guide (none being necessary) until we should reach the Furca Pass; but the minute I saw the man full in the face, and looked into the clear depths of his unwavering dark-blue eyes, he had me completely in his power. I felt that I must take him, before his proposition was half spoken; yet, like a prudent man of the world (a fool, rather), I hesitated, and bargained, and made conditions, all savoring of mistrust, while in reality I would have trusted all my worldly possessions in his hands. Why must we ever distort our features with these conventional masks? Why not say at once: "I know you and believe in you?"—for our natural instincts are a thousand times truer than the judgment of the world.

Joseph being engaged (blushing up to the roots of his hair as he confessed to the knowledge of a few Alpine melodies), we pushed on to Goldau, and commenced the ascent. Our Alpine luggage, consisting of two heavy portmanteaus, probably one hundred and twenty pounds weight, was transferred to the shoulders of a rather lean native, who rejoiced at the prospect of earning five francs by carrying it to the very top of the Righi. It would have broken the back of a New-York porter before the end of the first mile. Our Swiss, however, reached the top in fifteen minutes after us, and we were less than three hours in climbing the eight miles. There was no sunset, and the delicious tones of the Alpine horn awoke us at dawn, to see no sunrise. We shivered on the summit half an hour, to no purpose; many travellers went down in disgust, but there is no use in losing one's temper, and we took coffee.

Then we went up again and took our station in the cloud. Presently appeared Joseph, who said: "I have seen something; look that way," pointing to the west, "and wait a little." Soon there was a glimmer, as of a strip of cloud lighted by the sun, then the vapors parted, and for an instant the whole line of the Bernese Alps, from the Finsteraar-horn to the Jungfrau, stood unveiled in the face of morning. Horns of immaculate snow, golden, clear flushes of topaz on the frosted silver on the glaciers—a moment naked and beautiful as the goddesses on Mount Ida, then veiled in their floating cloudy drapery from eyes that were almost too weak to bear their splendors.

Now came the wind and cleared the peak, and as far as the hills of the Rhine all was mottled light and shadow; gleams of beryl from the lakes and starry flashing of white towns, dots on the distant blue. We had all we came to see, and more than we had hoped for. Yet I met an American, who had stood on the Righi, on as clear a morning, and was much disappointed. "It was just like a painting," said he, "the panoramas you see on exhibition are a great deal finer."

Our way led up the Lake of the Forest Cantons to Fluellen and Altorf. Joseph engaged a good carriage, with a driver who sang; and, as we drove up the valley of the Reuss towards St. Gothard, next day, the rocks echoed with the *jodel lieder*, and the quaint, naïve peasant-songs of Switzerland. Tony had a fine baritone, which harmonized well with the clanging mountaineer tenor of Joseph. The melting, undulating, horn-like cadences of the *jodel* choruses, heard in the deep Alpine valley, with the roar of the Reuss below, and the tinkling of the musical herd-bells on the pasture-slopes, were so many strains of that unwritten poetry, for which there are no words in any language. One of the songs had the following droll refrain:

"What good living is, if you would know,
You must straight unto my Jura go:
Jura is the prettiest girl, you'd say,
If the others all had gone away."

At the inn at Andermatt we found plenty of snobs. The landlord was a physician and prescribed for us, not one having escaped a sprain or a pain. Joseph collected the guides, and towards midnight gave us a serenade, beginning with the *Ranz des Vaches*, accompanied with the most wonderful variations, all performed on the human voice. The performer was a lusty young fellow, who drank too much for his good, but who, as he boasted, could make any note he pleased, high or low. His execution was as marvellous as Jenny Lind's, and as full of mountain echoes.

Our route was over the Furca Pass, by the glacier of the Rhone, the Grimsel, and down the valley of the Aar to Meyringen; then over the Scheideck, by the Rosenlaui glacier to Grindelwald, and over the Wengern Alp to Lauterbrunnen and Interlacken. We had six days among the high Alps, without a cloud in the sky—at most a gauzy scarf of vapor floating around the snowy cones, to soften the sharpness of their profiles on the deep blue of the air. We crept into the ice-caverns of the glaciers, and from under their vaults of translucent sapphire looked on the rose-tinted foam of the cataracts; we saw the splendid Wetterhorn hanging over the dark-green fir forests; we listened to the roar of avalanches from the Jungfrau, and watched their snow-dust tumbling a thousand feet down the precipice, while tranquilly consuming our chamois ragout on the Wengern Alps; we held our heads under the Staubbach which flung its waters upon us from a height of nine hundred feet, and wet our backs through and through; we leaned over the Aar, where it plunges down the gorge of Handeck, and noticed its wonderful resemblance to boiled cauliflower; and finally, at Interlacken, we bade adieu to the Bernese Alps, and to Joseph, from whom we parted with mutual tears.

Switzerland swarmed with travellers this Summer. The mountain passes were alive with brown straw flats, drab skirts, checked coats and wide-awakes. Even at the hospice on the Grimsel, six thousand feet above the sea, you heard the English and American languages rather than the Helvetic German. Towards the close of each day, there was a general stampede along the roads, in order to be first at the hotel and get the best rooms. The telegraph, however, runs across the glaciers, and our prudent guide always had our quarters engaged two days in advance, to the astonishment of many tourists who took pains to rush past us. The expense is but a franc, and I would advise travellers to take advantage of this improvement during the fashionable season.

My intercourse with the travelling crowd was mostly confined to looking at them during dinner-time. The sum of my observations was, that it is best to travel alone, unless you know your companion nearly as well as yourself; and further, that it is advisable to make acquaintances among the natives of the country you visit, rather than among other travellers. Of the English one meets in Switzerland, one-tenth may prove agreeable acquaintances; of the Americans and French, one-fourth; and of the Germans, one-half. The principal topic of conversation was—not the scenery, but the merits of different hotels. I heard a ruddy Londoner gravely recommend a certain house because the tea-cups had handles to them, and another was delighted with Lucerne because he had found a good confectioner's shop there. The principal test of a hotel, however, as I learned from the confidential recommendations of several gentlemen, was one of so ludicrous a character, that I regret being unable to state it.

We fell in, nevertheless, with some very pleasant people, and I could not help noticing that the English are becoming more malleable and tractable of late years. Those who had cast their insular shell met us with Continental freedom and cordiality. One experiment which I made turned out unsuccessfully, to my regret. Going down the valley of the Aar, I saw approaching me a German gentleman and lady, followed at a little distance by an English party. I bowed to the former, and was repaid by a ready and gracious acknowledgment. I then repeated the process to the English ladies, who deliberately

> "Gorgonized me from head to foot
> With a stony British stare."

Many American ladies, let me confess, would have done

the same thing. I kept statistics of female politeness for some months in the Sixth-avenue cars, and found that not more than one lady in twenty thanked me for giving up my seat to her.

From Interlacken we went to Berne (where I was fortunate enough to make the acquaintance of Mr. Fay), Freyburg, and Vevay. At the latter place, as well as Geneva, all the hotels were filled to overflowing, and we had some difficulty in getting quarters. The cost of travel in Europe is much increased of late, partly by the increase of travellers, and partly by the rise in the price of provisions. I was glad to find, however, that there are fewer attempts at extortion than formerly; the hotel business is systematized and regulated, and the rates, though high, are tolerably uniform all over the Continent—so that, if a traveller suffers serious imposition, it is probably owing to his own carelessness or verdancy.

On entering the valley of Chamouni I recognised the rocks of the Grand Mulets, just under the eaves of the clouds which concealed the dome of Mont Blanc, from their resemblance to Albert Smith's panorama; but an English tourist, familiar with the valley, declared that I was mistaken. I appealed to a sun-burnt, grizzly-headed old fellow, who was walking beside us. "They are the Grand Mulets," said he, "and I ought to know, for I have been fourteen times on the top of Mont Blanc." He was the noticed guide Coutet. At the hotel, a limping waiter showed us to our rooms. "I have just come down from Mont Blanc," he said apologetically, "and am very tired and sore." He had employed the greater part of his

Summer's earnings in hiring two guides, with whom he had gone as far as the Rochers Rouges, only one hour's journey from the summit, when they were driven back by a furious storm. Nothing daunted, he had made up his mind to try again so soon as the weather should be favorable. Such is the fascination of the mighty Mountain.

We had bad weather, and only succeeded in crossing the *Mer de Glace*, from Chapeau to Montanvert, where we waited twenty-four hours, in a snow-storm, intending to push on to the *Jardin*, a spot of green in the midst of eternal ice, ten thousand feet above the sea; but we were compelled to give it up. Crossing the pass of the Tête Noire to Martigny, we took the diligence over the Simplon, and descended to Lago Maggiore on the second day. Except the gorge of Gondo, on the Italian side, which, for picturesque effect, is one of the finest things in the Alps, the Simplon road is less striking than that over the St. Gothard. In one respect, however, it should be preferred by those who cross the Alps for the first time—the transition from Swiss to Italian scenery is sudden and complete. A few miles of bare, rocky defile, and you exchange the fir for the chestnut, mulberry, and fig—the mountain châlet for the vine-covered verandas of the bright southern country houses.

My holiday time was getting short, and I could only indulge my companions with a flying trip through Italy. We spent a day in Milan, and then set out in a heavy rain for Venice. Radetzky, with his staff, left at the same time for Verona, and at Coccaglio, where we waited an hour for the train from Brescia, we came together. The old Marshal and his company took possession of the refreshment room, keeping the rest of us, who were very hungry, out of it until they had finished. Nothing could have been more politely done. The guards begged our pardon, asked us as a special favor not to go in, and admitted us even before Radetzky had retired. I looked at the old veteran with much interest. He was then upwards of ninety, yet still performed his duties as Military Governor of Austrian Italy. He had at length been obliged to give up his horse, and reviewed his troops in an open carriage. He was a short, thick-set man, walked rather slowly, but firmly, and had a face full of vitality. His short white hair, thick white mustache, heavy brows, prominent cheek-bones and square jaws, gave him the precise expression of an old bull-terrier. Such courage, resolution, and unyielding tenacity of purpose I never saw in an old man's face before. If he got his teeth set once you might be sure he would hold on. Such a man was Carvajal, Pizarro's magnificent old warrior.

In Venice we had four cloudless days, and four nights in a gondola, under the full moon. Such days and nights are dreams, and my return to Padua was the awaking upon a dull reality. The vineyards on the road to Bologna were purple with abundant grapes, for there was a vintage in Italy, for the first time in five years. The disease of the vine appears to be gradually disappearing, like that of the potato, and these two invaluable plants are now healthy, with few exceptions, throughout Europe. The failure of the vintage for so many years had greatly impoverished the Italian people. Wine had risen to full five times its former price, and was withal so bad that one could scarcely drink it. Montefiascone and Montepulciano wholly belied their old renown, and those who tasted the golden Orvieto could not understand why it should have been so praised.

We had a week in Florence. I saw much of my old friend Powers, who was dividing his time between Art and Invention. His statue, *La Penserosa*, which is now in the possession of Mr. James Lenox, was nearly finished. It is thoroughly Miltonic, and I don't know what more I could say. The face is uplifted, abstracted,

> "With looks commercing with the skies,
> The rapt soul sitting in her eyes;"

the figure large and majestic, with a sweeping train, partly held in one hand, as she moves slowly forward. In many respects it is Powers's best work, though it may not be so popular as his "California."

We hastened on to Rome, although it was rather early in the season. My companions, however, had little fear of either fever or robbers, and so, after ten years of absence, I acted as their cicerone through churches, palaces, and ruins. I saw little change in Rome since 1846, except along the Appian Way, where many new exhumations have been made, and a number of glaring tablets, headed with "Pius IX. Pont. Max.," inserted in the venerable fronts of Roman baths and amphitheatres. There was also a tablet in St. Peter's, on the left of the Apostle's Chair, commemorating the sublime absurdity of the Immaculate Conception. Oh, Pio Nono! you are as vain as you are weak, and we who once respected you can now only pity you. On the evening of our departure, the Pope drove past our hotel in his carriage. We leaned out of the dining-room windows, looked in, and received his benediction. He has a kind, amiable, grandmotherly old face, and his blessing could do no harm. Poor man! I think he means well, but he is in Antonelli's evil hands, and Rome, which had a transient sunrise during the first years of his Pontificate, is now sunk in as blind a night as ever.

My respect for the Roman people is increased, by comparing them with the Florentines, who are an impersonation of all that is mean and corrupt. There is honor and virtue to be found among the Tuscan peasants, I doubt not, but for the bourgeoisie of Florence one can have no feeling but that of utter loathing and contempt. No lady can walk alone in Florence without being grossly insulted, and even in a carriage, with a gentleman's protection, she must run the gauntlet of a thousand insolent starers. The faces of the youths express a precocious depravity, and the blear-eyed old men show in every wrinkle the records of a debauched and degraded life. There is no help for such a people; they are slaves, and deserve to be so.

But of all cheering signs of progress in Europe, there is none so truly encouraging as the present condition of Sardinia. I passed through the country first in August, 1845, and now, in October, 1856, I returned to witness what had been done in those eleven years. Then, Sardinia was scarcely in advance of Tuscany, and her material development seemed to be at a stand-still. Now, nearly 500 miles of railroad were in operation, her commerce had been doubled, her productive industry vastly increased, her agriculture fostered and improved, and—best of all—she has a liberal Constitution, an enlightened and energetic Government, and a happy and hopeful people. From Genoa to Turin, along the old road where I then walked in dust through sleepy villages, all is now activity and animation. New houses have been built, new fields ploughed, bare mountain-sides terraced and planted with vine, new mills bestride the idle streams, and a thrifty and industrious population are at work on all sides. Sardinia has set a noble example to the other Italian States, and her success is the surest basis for the future independence of Italy.

As King Victor Emmanuel was not at home, we were freely admitted into his palace at Turin, even the private apartments being thrown open to us. Turin is a stately and beautiful city, although it contains little to attract the traveller. We were obliged to wait two days before we could obtain places in the diligence for Chambery. The passage of Mont Cenis was made by night; we had a snow storm on the summit, where we found a diligence overturned and the passengers scattered about, but more frightened than hurt. Our diligence (the French) raced the whole day with one of the Sardinian line, so that we averaged nine or ten miles an hour, and thundered along the beautiful valleys of Savoy to Chambery, in much less than the usual time. The next day we returned to Geneva, via Aix and the Lake of Annecy (see Rousseau's "Confessions," and Lamartine's "Raphael"), through one of the loveliest regions in Europe.

I had an interesting interview on my return from Lausanne to Gotha. At Bâle the diligences from Neufchâtel and Berne came together at the railroad station, and their respective passengers were deposited in the cars for Heidelberg and Frankfort. We found ourselves in the company of three strangers, one of whom immediately attracted my notice. He was a slender man, about thirty-five years old, with black eyes and beard, and a pale yellow complexion. He spoke German with perfect correctness, but slowly, and addressed me in very tolerable English; yet I could not fix upon his nationality.

I happened casually to speak of Venice, when he stated that he had just come thence. He then mentioned Corfu, and we compared our impressions of that island; then of the Grecian isles, then of Lebanon, and the Syrian shores. "I know Syria very well," said I, "from Jerusalem to Aleppo." "So do I," said he. "I travelled from Aleppo through Asia Minor to Constantinople," I continued. "And I," he rejoined, "went from Aleppo to Nineveh, down the Tigris to Baghdad, and thence to Bombay." "I also visited Bombay," I said, "travelled inland to the Himalayas, and down the Ganges to Calcutta." "Just the route I followed," he again replied. "But," I remarked, "there are few Germans who travel so extensively as you." "It is true," said he, "that few German travellers visit India, but there are several German missionaries stationed there." "I have heard of one," I answered—"Dr. Sprenger, who has written a most admirable life of Mohammed." "Why!" he exclaimed, in mingled surprise and delight, "I am Dr. Sprenger!"

I regretted that I could spend but six hours in the society of so estimable a man, and so thorough a scholar. He was returning home from an absence of thirteen years in India, bringing with him a quantity of rare and valuable Arabic manuscripts. He had passed a year at Damascus, where he had many opportunities of making acquaintances among the desert Arabs, and I was gratified to find that we entirely agreed in our estimate of the character of that noble race of men. He was fortunate enough to get possession of a geographical work of the fourth or fifth century, a work of exceeding value and importance, which he intended to translate and publish.

On landing at Trieste, Dr. Sprenger was gravely informed by the authorities that his collection of Arabic MSS. must be submitted to the inspection of the Censor, before he could be permitted to retain possession of them. "Why?" he remonstrated, "they are Arabic." "So much the worse," said the officer; "it is the more probable that they are insidious and revolutionary." "But," he again urged, "the Censor cannot read them." "That is unfortunate for you," was the answer: "you will have to wait until we find a man who can, for there is no knowing what dangerous sentiments may be concealed under these hieroglyphics." And so the traveller was obliged to part with his treasures, until the sublimely stupid Austrian Government shall be convinced that there is no treason in the heroics of Antar or the word-jugglery of Hariri of Bosrah.

XXVI.

A GERMAN HOME.

Gotha is one of the quietest towns in Germany, but it would be difficult to find a pleasanter one. It is built on the undulating table land at the foot of the Thüringian hills, 1,000 feet above the sea, whence its climate is rather cold for Germany, but very bracing and healthy. A tourist is an unusual sight there, and therefore one finds the old heartiness and simplicity of German home-life in all its purity. As it is one of the court residences of the Duke of Saxe-Coburg-Gotha, there is a small but intelligent and refined circle, some of the members of which have a European reputation in their departments of science and art. Hansen, the astronomer, and Dr. Petermann, the geographer, both of whom reside here, are also well known in America. Here came Barth in the summer of 1856 to recruit from his African travels; and most of the explorers, of whose labors Perthes, the renowned map-publisher, makes such good use, may be seen here from time to time. Gerstäcker, Bodenstedt, the author of the "Thousand and One Days in the Orient," Gustav Freitag, Alexander Zeigler, and other German authors, hover about here through the summer, and in the neighboring village of Friedrichsroda the brothers Grimm sometimes make their abode.

The home which German friendship has provided for me here, is in entire harmony with the character of the place.

The little garden-house (inhabited only by Braisted and myself) fronts on the avenue of lindens leading into the town, while the rear overlooks a garden of three or four acres in extent. It was built by one of the Ministers of Duke Ernest II. in 1760, when the French style infected Germany, and the steep bulging roof and quaint windows of the upper half-story faintly remind one of the chateaux of the time of Louis XIV. The same taste characterizes the garden. The house stands on a gravelled terrace, bordered with flowers, whence a flight of stone steps, guarded by statues of laughing fauns, descends to a second and broader terrace, in the centre of which is a spacious basin and a fountain better than that in the New York Park, for it plays day and night. Beyond this, a sloping arcade of the dwarf beech, trained so as to form a roof of shade, impervious to the sun, leads down to the garden. Still beyond are flower-beds open to the Summer warmth, a pool edged with flags and lilies, and groups of trees studding the smooth sward on either side.

An arch of vines at the end of the garden-walk ushers you into the grove, where a Pomona on her pedestal offers samples of fruits which you need not expect to find; for I have none other than forest-trees here—fir, oak, ash, chestnut, and beech. You would not guess that the grove was so small. Its winding footpaths are led through the thickest shade, and the briery undergrowth shoots up to shut out the patches of garden which shimmer through the lowest boughs. In the centre, under venerable firs, stands a hermitage of bark, beside a fountain of delicious water, which is surmounted by a triangular block of sandstone, erected by an extinct mason who once possessed the property. This mason had more money than learning: he put up the stone as a monument to his ancestors, and inscribed thereon, as he supposed: "To my Venerable Forefathers," but, in fact, through his misspelling: "To my Venerable Trout." (*Forellen* instead of *Vorältern.*) Some one, however, has since then engraved on the three sides of the stone the following words of wisdom: "Forget not Yesterday"—"Enjoy To-day"—"Uncertain is To-morrow."

At the end of the grove, on the frontier of my domain, which is shut in by a hedge of fir-trees, is "The Duke's Tree," planted by the hand of Ernest II. Although nearly a hundred years old, the trunk is not more than a foot in diameter, but the tree is branching and shady, and throws its boughs over the rustic seat and stone table, whereupon my friend and I sometimes lie on our backs and smoke the pipe of meditation. My friend's garden adjoins mine, and there is no fence between us; so that I can walk from my hermitage directly into his stables and inspect his thirty stall-fed cows, and his pens of high-born English swine. Beyond our joint territory, a rich banker has his garden, and his fountain (which, by the force of money, spouts ten feet higher than mine) is a pretty sight enough over the hedge that divides us. His garden terminates in an artificial mound, covered with tall pines and firs, which also has its historic interest. Here the Court of Gotha, aping the grand sentimental silliness of that of France, played at pastoral life, and lords and ladies, with satin ribbons on their crooks and flowers in their hair, gave themselves such names as Corydon, and Doris, and Alexis, and Chloe, and tended sheep, and ate curds, and played flutes, and danced, and sang, and looked languishingly and amorously at each other; but always returned to beer and sausages, cards and scandal every evening. They even built a pastoral village of thirteen houses, which has long since disappeared, and instituted a Court of Love on the summit of the mound, where Phillis was tried for slighting the passion of Amyntor, or Florian for his faithlessness to Melissa. It is difficult, in our day, to imagine the possibility of such ineffable absurdities.

My own room, under the steep French roof of the garden-house, was once the studio of a sculptor, to whose hand, I believe, I am indebted for the six thinly-clad statues which stand in my garden. The laughing fauns are jolly and good-humored enough, as they stand listening to the plash of the fountain, but Venus Anadyomene, down in the grove, leaves one to infer that the artist did not mingle in the most reputable society. So oddly are things managed in this place that, although I live just between the palaces of the reigning Duke and the Dowager Duchess, both within a stone's throw, I hear the noises of the farm-yard every morning, and listen all day to the measured beat of the flails on a threshing-floor across the way. The diligence to Coburg rattles past every afternoon, and the postilion blows me a merry hunting-song on his horn; sometimes wagons come in from the fields laden with turnips or potatoes, but other noises I rarely hear, and from my windows I see little except trees and garden-walks. The Duke is at present chamois-hunting in the Tyrol, the theatre is not yet opened, and the only recent excitement has been the arrival of four hundred oysters from Ostend. They came one evening, and by noon the next day they were not.

The Castle of Friedenstein, on the summit of the hill on which the town leans, is the old residence of the Dukes of Gotha, before the union of this Duchy with that of Coburg. It is a massive, imposing pile, forming three sides of a quadrangle, open to the south, and looking across twelve miles of grain and turnip fields, to the waving blue line of the Thüringian Forest. A residence no more, it now contains a curious collection of pictures by the old German masters, a library of one hundred and eighty thousand volumes, an excellent museum of natural history, and one of the best collections of Chinese and Japanese articles out of Holland. The adjoining park is a noble piece of ground, just sufficiently neglected to make it delightful. A few footpaths meander through its groves of superb oak, fir, and beech trees, and long, lazy pools of dark green water furnish swimming room for some venerable swans. There is an island in the largest pool, in which lies the body of Ernest II. who, at his own request, was buried there, in the moist earth, without shroud, coffin, or headstone. The parks and gardens are open day and night to everybody, and I felt as much right of possession therein as the oldest inhabitant.

The *Jahrmarkt*, or Annual Fair, is held here in October, and draws together crowds of the peasantry from the surrounding villages. The Fair itself is insignificant, compared with what I have seen in the larger German cities, but I found it interesting to watch the jolly peasants who hovered around the booths, and bought glaring handkerchiefs, immense pipes, Winter caps, dream-books, and "Rinaldo Rinaldini," or "The four Sons of Haymon." They are a strong, sturdy, ruddy race—a little too purely animal, to be sure, but with a healthy stamina which is not often seen among our restless American people. The girls, in particular, are as fresh as wild roses, with teeth which can masticate tougher food than blancmange, and stomachs, I have no doubt, of equal digestive power. Their arms and ankles are too thick and strong, and their hands too red and hard for our ideas of beauty, but they are exempt from a multitude of female weaknesses, and the human race is not deteriorated in their children. They are an ignorant, honest, simple-hearted race, and, although so industrious and economical, are generous so far as their means allow them to be.

Lately, the field-laborers on my friend's property commemorated the close of the season by bringing him, according to custom, an *Erntekranz* (harvest-wreath) of ripe rye and barley-stalks, mixed with wild grasses, and adorned with fantastic strips of colored and gilded papers. This wreath was formally delivered to the landlord, who, also, according to custom, regaled the laborers with plum cakes and wine. They passed the afternoon and evening in one of the outer rooms, settling their accounts and partaking of the cheer, after which a gittern was brought forth and the room cleared for a dance. We had some of the old Thüringian songs, with a chorus more loud than musical, and two-step waltzes danced to the tinkling gittern. I was content to be a listener and looker-on, but was soon seized by the strong hands of a tall nut-brown maiden, and whirled into the ranks. Resistance was impossible, and at the end of five minutes I was glad to beat a giddy retreat.

I must not close this gossip from Gotha, without referring to the map-publishing establishment of Bernhard Perthes, whose productions, for thoroughness and correctness, are unsurpassed in the world. I relied upon them for my guidance through Ethiopia, Asia Minor, and India, and found them far more perfect than any others. In Africa, in fact, I boldly ventured to contradict my guides whenever their statements differed from my map, and the result always justified me. Mr. Perthes commenced last year the publication of a monthly periodical entitled: "*Mittheilungen über wichtige neue Erforschungen auf dem Gesammtgebiete der Geographie*" (Communications concerning New and Important Researches in the realm of Geography), the editor of which is Dr. A. Petermann, who, although a young man, ranks among the first living geographers. This periodical is admirably got up, and its contents are of the highest interest and importance. It has already attained a circulation of 4,000 copies, about one hundred of which go to the United States.

XXVII.

LIFE IN THE THÜRINGIAN FOREST.

[OCTOBER, 1856.]

THERE are some aspects of German life which wholly escape the notice of most travellers, and which can only be reached through an intimate familiarity with the domestic life of the country. The festivals, no less than the costume and manners of the Middle Ages, have already disappeared from many parts of Germany, but fragments of them still linger in the more secluded districts—in the little villages hidden in mountain valleys which no post-road traverses, and in all those nooks and corners of the land which are not yet represented in the guide-books. Here, one who speaks the language and understands the character of the people, and fraternizes with them as a traveller should, will find his life enriched with many a quaint and picturesque experience. The Thüringian Forest, well known to Germans, but rarely visited by foreigners, is one of those regions, and my visits to its valleys have furnished me with a few pictures of peasant-life, which I propose to sketch for American eyes.

My acquaintance with the Forest dates from four years back, when, in company with my friend, I spent eight or ten days in exploring it from end to end. On that occasion I first met the Forester. It was at twilight, high on the mountain, at a hunting-lodge in the woods, called the King's House. How we kindled a fire of fir-logs, how we sat till past midnight in the open air, telling stories and roasting potatoes in the ashes, and how we slept side by side on a bundle of straw, are things which we keep in choicest memory, and the reader need not expect me to reveal them. Suffice it to say, that night the Forester and I became friends, and when, the next morning, his gray mustache brushed my cheek at parting, I promised to return to the King's House after a few years, and spend another night with him by the camp-fire.

A fortnight ago, when the mornings were bright and frosty, and the days bracing and cloudless, we set out for the Forester's home in the little village of Thal. The old man was on the look-out for us, and long before we reached the patriarchal linden which stands at the entrance of the village, we saw his sunburnt face, his thick gray mustache, and his green hunting-coat on the way to meet us. "Ah!" he cried, as he welcomed us with a Teutonic embrace, "I have been on burning coals for the last two hours, for fear you would not come; the wood is all ready for our fire, up yonder. Schmidt has gone ahead with the beer and potatoes, and if you have brought your cigars, there is nothing more wanting." But first we must go into his house, distinguished above all others in the village by the head of an antlered buck nailed upon its front. The little room had an air of comfort and elegance: pots of flowers filled the windows, and a glossy ivy-plant was trained to run along the joists of the ceiling. A case with glass doors contained his armory, which was in thorough order; a chintz sofa, broad enough for a Turkish divan, occupied the other end of the room, and a stove, big as the tower of Babel, stood between. His daughter had coffee in readiness, and while we were enjoying it after our walk, the house-maid, Katarina, was dispatched into the forest, with the remainder of our provisions and equipments upon her sturdy back.

We shortly followed, up a little dell between the two hills which guard the village—the Schlossberg, with its rocky cavern, and the Scharfenberg, with the tower of Castle Scharfenstein on its summit. The meadows were still fresh as in Summer, the tall alders shading the brook were dark-green, but the woods of oak and beech on the hills wore the dark purple-brown hues of a German Autumn. Our path led upwards, through alternate forest and mountain meadow, for nearly three miles to the King's House, which we reached as the broad landscape, stretching away for forty or fifty miles to the northwards, began to grow dusky in the twilight. Schmidt had just kindled his fire under the lee of a high bank, and a great pile of split logs at his back gave cheering promise for the night. A huge jug of beer, with a turnip for a stopper, leaned against the house; a loaf of brown bread, a bag of potatoes, and a pot of butter, lay upon the rude table before the door, and the sight of these preparations gave an additional whet to our appetite, already sharpened by the keen mountain air. "God knows," said the Forester (than whom there is no man less profane), "this is what I have been wanting to see for the last four years. This is a night to be remembered!"

We piled on the logs until the flames rose high and red, and snapped in the frosty wind. Schmidt, at the Forester's order, went into the wood for green fir-boughs, which crackled resinously, and sent up clouds of brilliant sparks. But it was long dark before our potatoes were boiled and the sausages done sputtering upon the gridiron. We ate in the open air, with the thermometer below the freezing point. The meal was royal; but how long it lasted is a secret not to be revealed, except among the freemasonry of hunters and trappers. "Now," said my friend, as the last potato disappeared, "let us turn to nobler indulgences." Four faded, antique chairs were brought from the lodge, the Forester, my friend, sailor and self took our seats around the fire, and Schmidt, with the pipe hanging from his teeth, picked up a burning stick and pointed out the way that we should go. The wind had fallen, and the roaring logs diffused a warm atmosphere around the house; beams of light streamed between the tree-trunks, and turned the yellow leaves to ruddy gold; the stars looked down as their turns came, and twinkled with good-humor. In short, peace was upon the earth, and (so far as we were concerned) good-will towards men.

The Forester, chuckling now and then with inward satisfaction, went back through his record of sixty-two years, and took out whatever chapters he thought would interest us—his boyhood in the stormy Napoleonic times, his youth and manhood in the forest, stalking alone for game, fighting with poachers and outlaws, or accompanying princely amateurs on their frigid hunting excursions. I asked him whether he had ever seen Napoleon. "Yes," said he, "twice during the Congress of Erfurt. The first time, I was going home from school with a big slate under my arm, when I saw an immense crowd of men in front of the Castle. A carriage was standing in the midst, and I heard the people say: 'It is the Emperor.' For a hundred feet around they were packed as close as they could squeeze, but I thought to myself, 'Karl, thou must see the Emperor, if thou get'st a broken rib for it.' So I stooped down, shot between the leg of the first and pushed towards the carriage. When the crowd became so thick that I could get no further, I punched first one and then the other with the sharp corner of my slate, and did not spare the blows, until they made a way for me. After this subterranean passage, I found myself, with very little breath left, just behind Duke August, who was talking with the Emperor. I looked over the Duke's shoulder, directly into Napoleon's face."

"What did you think of him?" I asked. "Why," said he, "the portraits you see represent the man very well. He had the same square, solid head, but his skin was yellow, and looked unclean and unhealthy. His eyes, though—*Donnerwetter!* such eyes! They bored into you like a couple of augers. Some time after that he was driving around Erfurt in his carriage, and I ran for a quarter of an hour along the top of a high bank beside the road, keeping up with the horses and looking at him. He had a table in the carriage with him, covered with letters and papers; and as long as I ran he never once looked up, but read, and wrote, and arranged. At that time the Germans used to say that his death would be the salvation of the country, and the thought came into my head, 'Now, if thou hadst but a pistol, thou mightst easily shoot him dead before he knew anything about it.' "

As the night wore on, stories gave place to songs, and the Forester, insisting on a chorus, gave bout for bout with my friend, and revived many of the popular ballads of those times. There was a droll catch, ridiculing the Tyrolese, of which I only remember the following:

"What's the drink of the Tyrolese?
What's their drink?
Nothing but water and sour wine,
Which they swill like thirsty swine.

"Say, what smoke the Tyrolese?
What do they smoke?
Fine tobacco they smoke, to be sure:
It smells no better than stable manure.

"Where are the beds of the Tyrolese?
Where are their beds?
Beautiful beds have man and spouse,
Among the calves and among the cows," &c.

About midnight our supply of logs, large as it was, began

to fail. We had been too prodigal in our holocaust, and the Forester recommended a retreat into the lodge, the floor of which was covered with straw, while the backs of the old chairs, turned bottom upwards, supplied the place of pillows. I will not say that we slept particularly well, but we rose all the earlier for that. The meadows were snow-white with frost, and the autumnal woods shone brilliant in the rising sun. Opposite us was the Hörselberg, where the Frau Venus (so called by the German peasantry) continued to haunt the earth as late as the twelfth century. Many a knight went into the cavern on the northern side of the mountain, to seek her, but none ever returned. The faithful Eckart, the squire of the last adventurer, still sits at the entrance and waits for his master.

We walked over the mountain to the village of Ruhla, celebrated for its length, its wealth, and its pretty girls. "Ah," said the Forester, as we came out of the woods, and looked over the wide sweep of sun-illumined hills, "such days as this are a blessing of Heaven. I remember the time when just a sunny morning made me so happy that I did not know what to do with myself. One day in Spring, as I went through the woods and saw the shadows of the young leaves upon the moss and smelt the buds of the firs and larches, and thought to myself, 'All thy life is to be spent in the splendid forest,' I actually threw myself down and rolled in the grass like a dog, over and over, crazy with joy. I have longed to have the same feeling once more in life, but it never comes back again." "Oh," said I, "a man who has such lively blood in his veins, does not get old so soon." "I am growing old, nevertheless," he answered; "my sight is not so keen as it was, and lately I was obliged to feel ashamed before my dog. I shot at a partridge and missed; the beast turned around and looked me full in the face, but I couldn't meet his look—I turned my head away and blushed. I have no doubt the poor dog tries to account for my failure to this day, but he can't make it out."

We came home again the same night, after promising to return to Thal the following week, when the *Kirmse* would be celebrated. This is an annual festival of the peasantry, of very remote origin. It generally takes place in the Fall, during the interval between Summer and Winter work, and lasts from two to three days. Formerly the *Kirmse* was ushered in with many ceremonies which are now almost entirely obsolete. The young men and girls, in holiday dress, formed in procession, and after a cock had been killed by the leader, marched to the church, where an appropriate service was performed. A sheep was then slaughtered and roasted, and the *Kirmse* was thoroughly inaugurated by the repast which followed.

The church service is still retained, and in this respect the festival bears some resemblance to our Thanksgiving. The preparations are made by a committee of the young peasants, who are called Kirmse-boys, and elect a leader whose command is law. Each boy chooses a maiden as his partner, and the latter is bound to purchase him a gay silk cravat (which he pins upon his right shoulder while dancing), as well as to furnish him with food and drink during the three days. This costs the girls from two to three thalers ($2) apiece, a considerable sum in these parts, but they manage to curtail their expenses by hiring a common eating-room, and levying contributions of meal, potatoes, sausages, and beer, upon all the families in the neighborhood. The boys furnish the music, the dancing-hall, and the *schnaps*, which they pay for from the fees exacted from those who do not belong to the committee. The *Kirmse* is, in fact, a sort of carnival for the German peasantry, and they allow themselves all sorts of liberties while it lasts. In the ducal meadows near Coburg, for instance, the Duke and Duchess attend, and any Kirmse-boy is privileged to call out the latter, while the Duke, in his turn, waltzes with the prettiest peasant girls.

We went again to Thal on the last day of the Kirmse. The fine weather was past, the air threatened snow, and the revellers were beginning to show signs of fatigue; but the Forester comforted us with the assurance that in the evening all would be merry enough. Soon after our arrival the village band appeared and performed a melancholy serenade under the window. It was followed by an awkward and riotous company, who proved to be masqueraders—the boys being girls in male attire, and vice versâ. Having paid our initiation fees to these visitors, they withdrew, and we took advantage of the temporary quiet to climb to the ruin of the Scharfenstein. We found nothing left except the tower, whose walls were of remarkable thickness and solidity, and a fragment of a wall and gateway, over which was sculptured a coat of arms, with the inscription, "House and Hearth of the Lord of Scharfenberg, A.D. 1442." The snow was blowing fast down the valley, and by the time we reached the Forester's house his daughter announced that dinner was ready.

We did full justice to the roasted hare and roe's liver, and did not slight the slim-necked urns filled by the Rhenish naiads. Towards the close of the repast, the Forester insisted on opening a stout old bottle, in order, as he said, to see what was inside of it. An oily, dark-golden fluid slid into his glass from its open mouth. "*Allewetternochhinein!*" he exclaimed, on tasting it; "that is something! That is the bottle I have had in my cellar nine years, and kept for a great occasion—and there never was a better time to open it!" We followed his example: it was genuine Constantia, full of African sun and fire, and from twenty to thirty years old. "*Allewetter!*" he again cried, "I had forgotten which was the true bottle, and to think that it should turn up to-day! The Herr Inspector X—— gave it to me for my birthday; but I thought to myself, 'Thou dost not need any such good wine for thy birthday—keep it for something better!' and as long as I live I shall be glad that I did so."

By this time the band had made its appearance under the mighty linden in front of the parson's house, and waltzing couples began to wheel around under the boughs, notwithstanding the snow and the raw wind. Presently a deputation, consisting of the Kirmse-leader, his adjutant, and two stout maidens, came into the room and gave us a ceremonious invitation to join the dance. The leader was a rosy, bright-eyed fellow of twenty-two, and his partner a tall maiden of great strength, who stood firm upon her feet. "Directly," said the Forester, in answer;

"but we must first have our pipes. If every one of you," he added, turning to me, "were lying dead in this room, I should sit down and howl like a dog, but in fifteen minutes I should get up and light my pipe."

As our pipes burned slowly, the deputation came a second time and carried us off to the linden-tree. The strong maiden, Elisabetha by name, was transferred to me, and we were soon whirling around inside the ring of admiring spectators. Elisabetha was light on her feet, but very firm; she needed no support; she moved like a revolving pillar, around which I revolved in turn, striving to keep pace and to moderate her speed, but I might as well have attempted to regulate the earth's motion on its axis. The Forester, meanwhile, brought out the parson's daughter, and his gray moustache occasionally whizzed past me. I would have transferred the strong Elisabetha to him, but it was too late: round and round we went, and the boughs of the linden seemed to grow broader and to stretch over vast spaces. Finally, there were lindens on every side, and we were obliged to circle all of them; but at last a voice roared in our ears, "You are out of time!" and the strong maiden stopped. The dances under the linden terminated soon afterwards, and the peasants went off to prepare for the night.

We first visited the Heiligenstein, across the valley—once a monastery, now a tavern; but as the maidens of Ruhla, with their picturesque dress and their fair complexions, did not arrive according to expectation, we returned to Thal, where the Kirmse-boys had already collected in the dancing-hall. It was a low room, opposite the village tavern, with the orchestra on a platform at one end. The floor was crowded with peasants, leaving only a ring-shaped space vacant for the dancers. On our appearance there, about nine o'clock, I was immediately accosted by the Kirmse-leader, who conducted to me the strong Elisabetha. It was impossible to decline, for she was his chosen sweetheart, and one of the first maidens, in point of her worldly prospects, in the valley. I resolved, however, to let her dance for both of us, and confine my exertions merely to holding on. My companion was furnished with a rather pretty partner, named Barbara Hornshoe, and the manner in which her feet pattered upon the floor did justice to her name.

The Kirmse-leader seemed to consider us the guests of the village. We were consulted with regard to the dances, and exempted from all obedience to his rule. When he touched the other dancers with his wooden baton, as a sign for them to cease, he passed us over, greatly to the delight of our powerful partners, whom nothing could tire. One of the dances was a *Polonaise*, and consisted in the whole company following the leader, who was Schmidt's son. He danced us down stairs into the street, across the brook and up again, winding up with a rapid *galop*. After awhile the leader came up with a glass of some dark beverage, which he insisted on our drinking. I tasted it: it was *schnaps*, the most villanous kind of brandy, and as strong as it was bad. One taste was sufficient, but it was no sooner offered to the strong Elisabetha than she emptied the glass without changing a muscle of her countenance. The quantity of this vile drink consumed by the peasant girls, without any apparent effect, surprised me. It was a stronger proof than I had yet had of the vigor of their constitutions.

Before leaving the dancing-hall I gave the leader what we should consider a very trifling fee, but it was so large in his eyes, that the munificence of the American guest was talked of all over the village. We were serenaded again the next day, and through the harmless fraternization of the *Kirmse*, received the most friendly and familiar greetings on all sides. As for the Forester, who accompanied us a mile or two of our way, we parted from him as from an old friend, and the days we spent under his roof and beside his camp-fire will not live longer in his memory than in ours.

XXVIII.

INTERVIEWS WITH GERMAN AUTHORS.

WHILE at Coburg in the beginning of October, 1852, I paid a visit to Rückert, the poet, who has a small estate in the adjoining village of Neusass. He has the reputation of being a cold, ascetic man, and never mingles in society. Very few of the Coburgers know him, and many have never once seen him. I fell in with a student of the Oriental languages who had some acquaintance with him, and accompanied me to his house. As we were passing through the garden we came upon him suddenly, standing in the midst of a great bed of rose-bushes and gathering the seeds of flowers. In this occupation I recognised the author of "Oriental Roses," but scarcely the poet of Love, the ardent disciple of Hafiz, in the tall, stern, gray-haired man who stood before me. His manner at first was rather cold and constrained, but it was the constraint of a scholar, unaccustomed to strange faces, and therefore ill at ease.

He invited us into the house, and commenced the conversation awkwardly, by asking me: "Where have you been?" "In the Orient," I answered. This was enough. A sudden enthusiasm shot into his face, his keen, deep-set eyes kindled, and his whole bearing changed. For two or three hours the conversation flowed on without a break—on his part a full stream of the richest knowledge, sparkling all over with gleams of poetry. His manner towards me was earnest, kind, and cordial, and charmed me all the more, because I had decided before seeing him, that he was unappreciated and misjudged by his neighbors.

I was surprised to find that Rückert, who is probably the finest Oriental scholar in Europe (witness his remarkable translation of the *Mâkamât el-Hariri*), was unacquainted with the true Arabic pronunciation. This, it appears, is not taught in the German universities, probably on account of the difficulty of giving the correct guttural sounds. Nevertheless, he is the only one who has ever reproduced, in another language, the laborious and elaborate Arabic and Persian metres. His knowledge of all European languages is even more profound, and although he does not speak English, he seems to comprehend its genius as thoroughly as that of his native tongue.

Just four years afterwards, I revisited Coburg, principally for the sake of seeing again the noble old poet, who, having heard that I was in Gotha, kindly asked me to call upon him before leaving Germany. I found him living the same studious, secluded life in the little village of Neusass, buried in his Oriental manuscripts and rarely seen by men. His wife (the Luise of his earlier poems) welcomed me with cordiality, and two blooming daughters kept up a lively conversation until the poet appeared. How well I remembered that frame, tall and slender as Schiller's, but erect as an Arab chieftain's; that stately head, with the gray hair parted in front and falling in silver masses on the shoulders; the strongly modelled brow, under which looked out eyes full of a soft, lambent fire, like those of a seer; the straight, strong nose, firm, stern lips, and projecting chin, a milder counterpart of Andrew Jackson—the head of a thinker and a poet!

Rückert must be nearly, if not quite, seventy years of age. He is still (I venture to say) as productive as ever, although he has published little for some years past. His habits of study have made him shy and abstracted, but the same habits give to his conversation a vigor of thought, a richness of illustration, and a glow of fancy, which I think could scarcely have been surpassed by the monologues of Coleridge. With his soft, bright eyes directed steadily before him, as if he saw the horizon of the desert, he talked of the Arabs who lived before Mohammed with the same familiar intelligence as he would speak of his contemporaries. The lifting of his glance, as he turned towards me now and then, in the earnestness of his discourse, was like an Eastern sunrise. The East lives in his soul, and warms his old age with its eternal summer.

Uhland only disputes with Rückert the title of being the first of living German poets. He is more simple and pathetic, and his verses appeal more directly to the German heart. Rückert, on the other hand, is half an Asiatic, and in the splendor of his imagination, as well as his wonderful command of the dexterities of his native language, is scarcely surpassed by El Hariri himself. There can be no comparison between the two; they stand on different pedestals. Personally, also, the men have no resemblance. I was in Tübingen in 1852—the home of Uhland—and could not find it in my heart to leave without speaking to the man whose "Minstrel's Curse" and "Little Roland" had been haunting my brain for so many years. I wrote a note stating my desire, and immediately received an invitation to call upon him. I found him in a house overlooking the valley of the Neckar, in a little, dark, barely furnished library. He came forward to meet me—a small, wrinkled, dry old man of at least seventy, with a bald head and curious puckers in the corners of his mouth and eyes. But the eyes themselves were as soft, blue, and clear as a child's, and there was a winning, child-like simplicity in his manner, despite a certain awkwardness and frigidity which at first showed itself.

We sat down together on the little leather-covered sofa behind his desk, and he talked very pleasantly for an hour. I asked whether he had written anything recently, or whether he had, perhaps, grown weary of that

> "Pleasure in poetic pains,
> Which only poets know."

"I should not like to swear," he said in answer, "that I shall write no more songs. I have as much pleasure in what I have done, as ever; but there is no longer the same necessity for expression, and I never write without a strong necessity. I hear the same music in my brain, but am content to hear it without singing it." Just the answer I should have expected from a true poet.

At the table of a friend in Coburg I met with Frederick Gerstäcker, the distinguished traveller and author. I had spent an afternoon with him in the Rosenthal, near Leipsic, eleven years before; but he had compassed the earth since then—had ridden across the Pampas, washed gold in California, played the guitar in Tahiti, tramped through Australia, and listened to the songs of Malay girls in Java. He was but little changed, except in wearing a thick brown beard, which mitigated the somewhat harsh projection of his under jaw. There was the same lithe, wiry frame, unworn by much endurance, the sloping brow, expanding to a wedge-like shape at the temples, and the quick, keen, vivacious gray eye, as I remembered them in 1845. Gerstäcker has one of those faces which are never forgotten. His individuality is strongly marked; he takes and gives impressions with equal force, and thus adventures and picturesque experiences come to him unsought, which is the greatest fortune a traveller can have. His works have been very successful, and yield him (what few German authors can boast of) a handsome income.

Duke Ernest of Saxe-Coburg Gotha, who is distinguished among German princes by an intelligent taste for literature and art, has made choice of Gerstäcker as his special friend and companion. The latter, who is an enthusiastic hunter, accompanies him every fall to the Tyrol, where they spend weeks on the mountain-tops, sleeping in chalets, and creeping all day among the rocks to waylay the chamois. They had just returned from such an excursion, during which Gerstäcker, in spite of a bullet-wound in his left hand, succeeded in shooting nine. He was then engaged in writing romances, the material for which was in most part derived from his experiences of travel. I do not believe, however, that his daring, adventurous spirit will be long satisfied with the quiet of his home at Rossenau. He will soon crave a fresh stock of those vital experiences, which in their present enjoyment far surpass all anticipation and all memory.

At Dresden I was welcomed by my friend Alexander Ziegler, who had just returned from a visit to the midnight sun at Hammerfest. His face had waxed round and ruddy in the breezes of the North, and from the interest with which he spoke of his journey I at once anticipated a new volume from his pen. Ziegler is known in Germany as the author of Travels in America, Spain, and the Orient. His works are distinguished by a clear, practical, serious habit of observation, a scrupulous attention to details, combined with considerable power of generalization, and a cheerful, genial tone, which never rises into the realms of the imagination, but often sparkles with touches of graphic humor. He is enough of the cosmopolite to enjoy the most widely-separated spheres of travel, and it is scarcely likely that he will remain very long at home while his nature retains its present buoyancy and restless activity of life.

Dresden is at present the literary capital of Germany, although the King of Bavaria, by drawing around him such men as Bodenstedt and Geibel, seeks to secure that distinction for Munich. Freytag, the author of that admirable novel, "*Soll und Haben*," resides in Leipsic, and

Mügge, whose "Afraja" has charmed American readers, in Berlin ; but in Dresden are grouped Auerbach, Gutskow, Dr. Andree, Wolfssohn, Julius Hammer, and Otto Roquette, besides Professor Reichenbach, Steinle, the engraver Dahl, the old Norwegian painter, and a host of other artists. I was fortunate enough to find the pass-word to this charmed circle. Authors and artists have the same masonic signs all over the world, and the cloud of smoke which filled their private hall of meeting in the rear of the Café de l'Europe was the same familiar atmosphere which my fellow centurions are wont to inhale at home.

Auerbach, whose "*Dorfgeschichten*" (Village Stories) from the Black Forest have a European reputation, is a short, broad-shouldered, muscular, ruddy-faced man, about forty-six years of age. His eyes are large, wide apart, and brownish-gray, and the lower part of his face is comfortably enveloped in a short, thick brown beard. He is one of those hale, honest, clear-seeing natures, of which there are too few in the world—a mixture of keen intelligence and child-like simplicity and naïveté, such as we find in the dramatists of the Elizabethan age. He knows the woods and mountains too well to be fettered by the frigid conventionalities which rule the talk of society. He is too unconscious of them even to notice them with his scorn; but speaks straight from the heart, whatever comes first, and everything as it comes—fun, earnest, satire, enthusiasm. He says many good things, and even where he hits pretty sharply, is so genial and true-hearted thereby that no wound is left behind.

I was interested to find how immediately Auerbach and

my companion understood each other. Authors have perhaps the truest instincts of character in other men, but those who lead a free life in close communion with nature —hunters, sailors, and lumbermen, who can dare to act without subterfuge, compromise, or even the ordinary considerations of worldly prudence—are scarcely less correct in their sympathies. They may be unable to appreciate particular ranges of intellect, but they read character at a glance. The German author and the American sailor, in spite of their totally divergent lives and experiences of mankind, knew each other at first sight, with as just an estimation as the literary friends of the one or the fàithfulest shipmates of the other, after years of familiar intercourse.

Dr. Karl Andree, the distinguished geographer, was in one respect a wonder to me. There is not a man in Europe, I venture to say, and not a great many in the United States, who possess such an intimate knowledge of our country and its institutions, its geography, its statistics, and its social and political life. It was curious to sit in his library in Dresden, knowing that he had never crossed the Atlantic, and to hear him discuss the aberrations of American editors, and reveal the wire-working of our demagogues and political jugglers, even to the smallest. Andree is at the same time one of the hardest workers and best companions in the world—a mixture which I wish were more common in America. We have the workers in plenty, but work too often robs us of the social amenities of life.

In company with Ziegler I called upon Gutzkow, the dramatist, who unquestionably stands at the head of living German writers for the stage. His play of "*Zopf und*

Schwert" (Queue and Sword) has for many years kept a place on the boards of all the theatres between the Alps and the Baltic. He is a small man, forty years of age, with blonde hair and moustache, gray eyes, a forcible nose, and an expression in which keenness and clearness of mental insight is predominant. Judging by his face, I should say that he is patient, persevering, and conscientious in execution, sharp and rapid in his appreciation of what he needs and can use, but effective rather through his outside knowledge of men and of life, than from great power and warmth of passion in himself. His bearing was courteous and kind, but he impressed me like a clear winter morning after feeling the mellow summer glow of Auerbach.

Wolfssohn, whose recent success as a dramatist, in his play of "*Nur eine Seele*" (Only a Soul), has delighted his friends, and brought him what true success always brings—envy—is also distinguished for his translations from the Russian. He resided for some time in Moscow, and has made his knowledge of Russian life very effective in his plays, which are mostly Russian in subject. He is a quiet, genial, studious man, and I regretted that a temporary indisposition prevented me from seeing as much of him as I wished.

Julius Hammer is the author of a volume of poems entitled "*Schau in Dich und Schau um Dich*" (Look within Thee and around Thee). It is one of the most successful of recent books of German poems, having rapidly run through five editions. Its character is serious and reflective, rather than imaginative, but pervaded with warm human sympathies. In calling upon Hammer I met with one of those pleasant surprises which rarely come to those who send their children into the world, trusting their existence to their own powers of vitality. He was sitting at his desk, writing the last line of a translation of one of my own poems, which he immediately read to me in its new dress.

While in Berlin, the same year, I paid a visit to Dr. Karl Ritter, the distinguished geographer, to whom I had a letter of introduction from my friend Ziegler. I found him at his rooms, overlooking the Gendarm-markt, and, though I happened to call during his hours of study, was at once admitted. Through two rooms, crammed with books from floor to ceiling, I passed to his workshop, which was furnished in the same manner, and exhaled the same delightfully infectious odor of antique leather. He was sitting at his desk, in the midst of a chaos of books and papers, but rose and came forward as I entered. Here was again a massive Teutonic head, larger than Humboldt's, but not so symmetrically balanced, a broad, overhanging brow, shading large and friendly eyes, a strong nose, and one of those ample, irregular mouths, in which the expression of kindness and goodness atones for the absence of beauty. His hair was gray and thin, for he must have seen at least sixty-five summers, but his tall figure was still erect and full of strength. The dressing-gown he wore, with his unbuttoned collar and bare throat, gave a certain grace and dignity to his appearance, not unlike that which belongs to the picture of Goethe in his latter days.

Our conversation was mostly geographical, and though I remained but half an hour, through fear of interrupting his labors, it served to illustrate his immense knowledge. He touched upon the Japanese and the Chinese, the Tartars and Thibetans, the Lapps and Samoyeds, the Shillooks, the Dinkas, and the Bushmen; described the formation of their respective countries, the climate and productions, their habits, laws, and religions. My projected journey to Lapland appeared to interest him, and he advised me to notice the result of the Swedish missionary labors among that people, and to contrast it with the operation of similar labors in India and China. The interior of Swedish Lappmark was, he admitted, a comparatively unknown region, and he commended my design of visiting it in the winter, when the facilities of getting from point to point are much greater than in summer, and the Lapps are gathered together in their villages. He recommended the work of Leopold von Buch as the best description of Norway and Lapland. Ritter is now engaged in the publication of a Universal Geography, which, so far as it has appeared, far surpasses all previous works of the same character, in the richness and accuracy of its information. The Germans are undoubtedly at present the greatest geographers in the world, and the French, despite their claims, the worst.

I was fortunate in having a letter to Theodor Mügge, the author of "Afraja" and "Eric Randal." When I called at his residence, according to a previous appointment, a pretty little girl of seven or eight years opened the door. "Is Herr Dr. Mügge at home?" I asked. She went to an adjacent door and cried out, "Father, are you at home?" "*Ja wohl*," answered a sturdy voice; and presently a tall, broad-shouldered, and rather handsome man of over forty years made his appearance. He wore a thick, brown beard, spectacles, was a little bald about the temples, and spoke with a decided North-German accent. His manner at first was marked with more reserve than is common among Germans; but I had the pleasure of meeting him more than once, and found that the outer shell covered a kernel of good humor and good feeling.

Like many other authors, Mügge has received hardly as much honor in his own country as he deserves. His "Afraja," one of the most remarkable romances of this generation, is just beginning to be read and valued. He was entirely unacquainted with the fact that it had been translated in America, where five or six editions were sold in a very few months. I could give him no better evidence of its success than the experience of a friend of mine, who was carried thirteen miles past his home, on a New-Haven railroad train, while absorbed in its pages. He informed me that the idea of the story was suggested to him during his residence at Tromsöe, on the Norwegian coast, where, among some musty official records, he found the minutes of the last trial and execution of a Lapp for witchcraft, about a century ago. This Lapp, who was a sort of Chieftain in his clan, had been applied to by some Danish traders to furnish them with good wind during their voyage. He sold them breezes from the right quarter, but the vessel was wrecked and all hands drowned. When asked, during his trial, whether he had not furnished a bad instead of a good wind, he answered haughtily: "Yes, I sold them the bad wind, because I hated them, as I hate you, and all the brood of thieves who have robbed me and my people of our land." I referred to the character of Niels Helgestad, and spoke of his strong resemblance, in many respects, to one of our Yankee traders of the harder and coarser kind. Mügge assured me that I would find many of the same type still existing, when I should visit the Lofoden isles. He spent a Summer among the scenes described in "Afraja," and his descriptions are so remarkably faithful that Alexander Ziegler used the book as his best guide in going over the same ground.

XXIX.

ALEXANDER VON HUMBOLDT.

I CAME to Berlin for the first time, in November, 1856, not to visit its museums and galleries, its magnificent street of lindens, its operas and theatres, nor to mingle in the gay life of its streets and salons, but for the sake of seeing and speaking with the world's greatest living man—Alexander von Humboldt.

At that time, with his great age and his universal renown, regarded as a throned monarch in the world of science, his friends were obliged, perforce, to protect him from the exhaustive homage of his thousands of subjects, and, for his own sake, to make difficult the ways of access to him. The friend and familiar companion of the king, he might be said, equally, to hold his own court, with the privilege, however, of at any time breaking through the formalities which only self-defence had rendered necessary. Some of my works, I knew, had found their way into his hands: I was at the beginning of a journey which would probably lead me through regions which his feet had traversed and his genius illustrated, and it was not merely a natural curiosity which attracted me towards him. I followed the advice of some German friends, and made use of no mediatory influence, but simply dispatched a note to him, stating my name and object, and asking for an interview.

Three days afterwards I received through the city post a reply in his own hand, stating that, although he was suffering from a cold which had followed his removal from Potsdam to the capital, he would willingly receive me, and appointed one o'clock the next day for the visit. I was punctual to the minute, and reached his residence in the Oranienburger-strasse, as the clock struck. While in Berlin, he lived with his servant, Seifert, whose name only I found on the door. It was a plain two-story house, with a dull pink front, and inhabited, like most of the houses in German cities, by two or three families. The bell-wire over Seifert's name came from the second story. I pulled: the heavy *porte-cochère* opened of itself, and I mounted the steps until I reached a second bell-pull, over a plate inscribed "Alexander von Humboldt."

A stout, square-faced man of about fifty, whom I at once recognised as Seifert, opened the door for me. "Are you Herr Taylor?" he asked; and added, on receiving my reply: "His Excellency is ready to receive you." He ushered me into a room filled with stuffed birds and other objects of natural history; then into a large library, which apparently contained the gifts of authors, artists, and men of science. I walked between two long tables heaped with sumptuous folios, to the further door, which opened into the study. Those who have seen the admirable colored lithograph of Hildebrand's picture, know precisely how the room looks. There was the plain table, the writing-desk covered with letters and manuscripts, the little green sofa, and the same maps and pictures on the drab-colored walls. The picture had been so long hanging in my own room at home, that I at once recognised each particular object.

Seifert went to an inner door, announced my name, and Humboldt immediately appeared. He came up to me with a heartiness and cordiality which made me feel that I was in the presence of a friend, gave me his hand, and inquired whether we should converse in English or German. "Your letter," said he, "was that of a German, and you must certainly speak the language familiarly; but I am also in the constant habit of using English." He insisted on my taking one end of the green sofa, observing that he rarely sat upon it himself, then drew up a plain cane-bottomed chair and seated himself beside it, asking me to speak a little louder than usual, as his hearing was not so acute as formerly.

As I looked at the majestic old man, the line of Tennyson, describing Wellington, came into my mind: "Oh, good gray head, which all men knew." The first impression made by Humboldt's face was that of a broad and genial humanity. His massive brow, heavy with the gathered wisdom of nearly a century, bent forward and overhung his breast, like a ripe ear of corn, but as you looked below it, a pair of clear blue eyes, almost as bright and steady as a child's, met your own. In those eyes you read that trust in man, that immortal youth of the heart, which made the snows of eighty-seven Winters lie so lightly upon his head. You trusted him utterly at the first glance, and you felt that he would trust you, if you were worthy of it. I had approached him with a natural feeling of reverence, but in five minutes I found that I loved him, and could talk with him as freely as with a friend of my own age. His nose, mouth, and chin had the heavy Teutonic character, whose genuine type always expresses an honest simplicity and directness.

I was most surprised by the youthful character of his face. I knew that he had been frequently indisposed during the year, and had been told that he was beginning to show the marks of his extreme age, but I should not have suspected him of being over seventy-five. His wrinkles were few and small, and his skin had a smoothness and delicacy rarely seen in old men. His hair, although snow-white, was still abundant, his step slow but firm, and his manner active almost to restlessness. He slept but four hours out of the twenty-four, read and replied to his daily rain of letters, and suffered no single occurrence of the least interest in any part of the world to escape his attention. I could not perceive that his memory, the first mental faculty to show decay, was at all impaired. He talked rapidly, with the greatest apparent ease, never hesitating for a word, whether in English or German, and, in fact, seemed to be unconscious which language he was using, as he changed five or six times in the course of the conversation. He did not remain in his chair more than ten minutes at a time, frequently getting up and walking about the room, now and then pointing to a picture or opening a book to illustrate some remark.

He began by referring to my winter journey into Lapland. "Why do you choose the winter?" he asked: "Your experiences will be very interesting, it is true, but will you not suffer from the severe cold?" "That remains to be seen," I answered. "I have tried all climates except the Arctic, without the least injury. The last two years of my travels were spent in tropical countries, and now I wish to have the strongest possible contrast." "That is quite natural," he remarked, "and I can understand how your object in travel must lead you to seek such contrasts; but you must possess a remarkably healthy organization." "You doubtless know, from your own experience," I said, "that nothing preserves a man's vitality like travel." "Very true," he answered, "if it does not kill at the outset. For my part, I keep my health everywhere, like yourself. During five years in South America and the West Indies, I passed through the midst of black vomit and yellow fever untouched."

I spoke of my projected visit to Russia, and my desire to traverse the Russian-Tartar provinces of Central Asia. The Kirghiz steppes, he said, were very monotonous; fifty miles gave you the picture of a thousand; but the people were exceedingly interesting. If I desired to go there, I would have no difficulty in passing through them to the Chinese frontier; but the southern provinces of Siberia, he thought, would best repay me. The scenery among the Altai Mountains was very grand. From his window in one of the Siberian towns, he had counted eleven peaks covered with eternal snow. The Kirghizes, he added, were among the few races whose habits had remained unchanged for thousands of years, and they had the remarkable peculiarity of combining a monastic with a nomadic life. They were partly Buddhist and partly Mussulman, and their monkish sects followed the different clans in their wanderings, carrying on their devotions in the encampments, inside of a sacred circle marked out by spears. He had seen their ceremonies, and was struck with their resemblance to those of the Catholic church.

Humboldt's recollections of the Altai Mountains naturally led him to speak of the Andes. "You have travelled in Mexico," said he: "do you not agree with me in the opinion that the finest mountains in the world are those single cones of perpetual snow rising out of the splendid vegetation of the tropics? The Himalayas, although loftier, can scarcely make an equal impression; they lie further to the north, without the belt of tropical growths, and their sides are dreary and sterile in comparison. You remember Orizaba," continued he; "here is an engraving from a rough sketch of mine. I hope you will find it correct." He rose and took down the illustrated folio which accompanied the last edition of his "Minor Writings," turned over the leaves and recalled, at each plate, some reminiscence of his American travel. "I still think," he remarked as he closed the book, "that Chimborazo is the grandest mountain in the world."

Among the objects in his study was a living chameleon, in a box with a glass lid. The animal, which was about six inches long, was lazily dozing on a bed of sand, with a big blue-fly (the unconscious provision for his dinner) perched upon his back. "He has just been sent to me from Smyrna," said Humboldt; "he is very listless and unconcerned in his manner." Just then the chameleon opened one of his long, tubular eyes, and looked up at us. "A peculiarity of this animal," he continued, "is its power of looking in different directions at the same time. He can turn one eye towards heaven, while with the other he inspects the earth. There are many clergymen who have the same power."

After showing me some of Hildebrand's water-color drawings, he returned to his seat and began to converse about American affairs, with which he seemed to be entirely familiar. He spoke with great admiration of Colonel Fremont, whose defeat he profoundly regretted. "But it is at least a most cheering sign," he said, "and an omen of good for your country, that more than a million of men supported by their votes a man of Fremont's character and achievements." With regard to Buchanan, he said: "I had occasion to speak of his Ostend Manifesto not long since, in a letter which has been published, and I could not characterize its spirit by any milder term than *savage*." He also spoke of our authors, and inquired particularly after Washington Irving, whom he had once seen. I told him I had the fortune to know Mr. Irving, and had seen him not long before leaving New York. "He must be at least fifty years old," said Humboldt. "He is seventy," I answered, "but as young as ever." "Ah!" said he, "I have lived so long that I have almost lost the consciousness of time. I belong to the age of Jefferson and Gallatin, and I heard of Washington's death while travelling in South America."

I have repeated but the smallest portion of his conversation, which flowed on in an uninterrupted stream of the richest knowledge. On recalling it to my mind, after leaving, I was surprised to find how great a number of subjects he had touched upon, and how much he had said, or seemed to have said—for he had the rare faculty of placing a subject in the clearest and most vivid light by a few luminous words—concerning each. He thought, as he talked, without effort. I should compare his brain to the fountain of Vaucluse—a still, deep, and tranquil pool, without a ripple on its surface, but creating a river by its overflow. He asked me many questions, but did not always wait for an answer, the question itself suggesting some reminiscence, or some thought which he had evident pleasure in expressing. I sat or walked, following his movements, an eager listener, and speaking in alternate English and German, until the time which he had granted to me had expired. Seifert at length reappeared and said to him, in a manner at once respectful and familiar, "It is time," and I took my leave.

"You have travelled much, and seen many ruins," said Humboldt, as he gave me his hand again; "now you have seen one more." "Not a ruin," I could not help replying, "but a pyramid." For I pressed the hand which had touched those of Frederick the Great, of Forster, the companion of Capt. Cook, of Klopstock and Schiller, of Pitt, Napoleon, Josephine, the Marshals of the Empire, Jefferson, Hamilton, Wieland, Herder, Goethe, Cuvier, La

Place, Gay-Lussac, Beethoven, Walter Scott—in short, of every great man whom Europe has produced for three-quarters of a century. I looked into the eyes which had not only seen this living history of the world pass by, scene after scene, till the actors retired one by one, to return no more, but had beheld the cataract of Atures and the forests of the Cassiquiare, Chimborazo, the Amazon, and Popocatepetl, the Altaian Alps of Siberia, the Tartar steppes, and the Caspian Sea. Such a splendid circle of experience well befitted a life of such generous devotion to science. I have never seen so sublime an example of old age—crowned with imperishable success, full of the ripest wisdom, cheered and sweetened by the noblest attributes of the heart. A ruin, indeed! No: a human temple, perfect as the Parthenon.

As I was passing out through the cabinet of Natural History, Seifert's voice arrested me. "I beg your pardon, Sir," said he, "but do you know what this is?" pointing to the antlers of a Rocky-Mountain elk. "Of course I do," said I, "I have helped to eat many of them." He then pointed out the other specimens, and took me into the library to show me some drawings by his son-in-law, Möllhausen, who had accompanied Lieut. Whipple in his expedition to the Rocky Mountains. He also showed me a very elaborate specimen of bead-work, in a gilt frame. "This," he said, "is the work of a Kirghiz princess, who presented it to His Excellency when we were on our journey to Siberia." "You accompanied His Excellency then?" I asked. "Yes," said he; "*we* were there in '29." Seifert is justly proud of having shared for thirty or forty years the fortunes of his master. There was a ring, and a servant came in to announce a visitor. "Ah, the Prince Ypsilanti," said he: "don't let him in; don't let a single soul in; I must go and dress His Excellency. Sir, excuse me—yours, most respectfully," and therewith he bowed himself out. As I descended to the street, I passed Prince Ypsilanti on the stairs.

In October, 1857, I was once more in Berlin, on my return from the North of Europe. As I had some business to transact, which would detain me three or four days, I sent a note to Humboldt, asking permission to call upon him again, in case his time permitted the visit. The next day's express from Potsdam brought me a most kind and friendly reply, welcoming me back to the "Baltic sand-sea," as he called the Brandenburg plain, and stating that, although the Emperor Alexander and his suite were to arrive that evening, he would nevertheless take an hour or two from the excitement of the Court to talk to me about the North. He was residing in the Palace at Potsdam, where he directed me to call at noon on Monday.

The train by which I left Berlin was filled with officers and diplomatic officials in full uniform, going down to do homage to the Czar. In the carriage in which I sat, were two old gentlemen who presently commenced conversing in French. After a time, their talk wandered to the Orient, and they spoke of Diebitsch and his campaigns, and the treaty of Unkiar-Iskelessi. Suddenly, one of them asked in Arabic, "Do you speak Arabic?" The other answered in Turkish, "No, but I speak Turkish." The first replied in the same language, which, after a time, the two exchanged for Modern Greek, and finally subsided into Russian. I made out that one was a Wallachian, but could discover nothing more, notwithstanding there was an air of a secret mission about them, which greatly piqued my curiosity.

Potsdam was all alive with the Imperial arrival. The King of Saxony was also coming to dinner; and, that the three monarchs might be pleasantly diverted in the evening, the sparkling Marie Taglioni, who had arrived with us, tripped out of the cars and off to the Royal Theatre. The park at Sans Souci was in brilliant holiday trim, the walks newly swept, and the fountains jetting their tallest and brightest streams. The streets of the dull little court-town glittered with resplendent uniforms, among which the driver of my carriage pointed out Carl, Albert, and various other princes of the House of Prussia. As we were crossing an open space near the palace, a mounted guard, followed by an open carriage, drawn by a span of superb black horses, suddenly appeared. I at once recognised the punchy figure in a green military coat, buttoned up to the chin, who sat on the right hand, although I had never before seen his Majesty. My driver reined up on one side and took off his hat. I lifted mine as the King passed, looked at him, and he replied with a military salute. His face was slightly flushed and his eyes bright, and I remember thinking that the heavy and rather stupid air which he wears in his portraits did him injustice. But he was even then laboring under that congestion which struck him down the same night, and from the effects of which he will never recover.

I was glad when the clock struck twelve at last, and I could leave the rattling streets for that quiet corner of the palace in which Humboldt lives. The door was opened, as before, by Seifert, who recognised me at once. "Welcome back!" he cried; "we know where you have been—we have read all your letters! His Excellency has been quite sick, and you will not find him so strong as he was last year, but he is in tolerable health again, thank God! Come in, come in; he is waiting." Opening the door as he spoke, he ushered me into a little library, on the threshold of which Humboldt, who had risen, received me. He was slightly paler than before, a little thinner, perhaps, and I could see that his step was not so firm; but the pale-blue eye beamed as clear an intelligence as ever, and the voice had as steady and cheery a tone. He shook hands with the cordiality of a friend, and, after the first greetings were over, questioned me minutely concerning my travels in the North.

But one topic soon suggests a hundred others, and he was ere long roaming at large over the whole field of geography and climatology, touching the farthest and darkest regions of the earth with the light of his stupendous knowledge. The sheets of the new volume of Cosmos lay upon the table. "Here is what I have been doing, since you were here before," said he, taking it up, "the work will be published in two or three weeks." "You find yourself, then, still capable of such labor?" I ventured to ask. "Work is now a part of my life," said he; "I sleep so little, and much rest would be irksome. Day before yesterday, I worked for sixteen hours, reviewing these sheets." "Are you not greatly fatigued," I asked, "after such an exertion?" "On the contrary," he replied, "I feel refreshed, but the performance of it depends greatly on my state of bodily health. I am unconscious of any mental fatigue." As I saw in the face, and heard in the voice of the splendid old man, all the signs of a sound, unfailing intellect, I could well believe it. I had prided myself a little on having worked with the brain fifteen hours a day for six months, yet here was Humboldt, in his eighty-ninth year, capable of an equal exertion.

The manner in which he spoke of his bodily health was exceedingly interesting to me. His mind, full of vigor and overflowing with active life, seemed to consider the body as something independent of itself, and to watch, with a curious eye, its gradual decay, as he might have watched that of a tree in his younger days. "I have been unwell through the Summer," said he, "but you must not believe all you may have seen in the newspapers concerning my illness. They stated that I was attacked with apoplexy, but it was only a vertigo, which soon left me, and has not been followed by any of the usual effects of apoplexy. One result, however, shows that my body is beginning to give way. I have not the same power of controlling my limbs as formerly; the will does not seem to act upon the muscles; there is a link broken somewhere, which it is probably too late to restore. For instance, very often, when I attempt to walk straight forward, I do not feel certain that my legs will carry me in a straight line; they may go either to one side or the other, and, though I cannot notice any ieal want of strength, I feel uncertain and mistrustful. For this reason, I must have assistance when I go up or down stairs. After all, it is not singular that some parts of the machinery should get rusty at my age." Soon afterwards, while speaking of Thibet, he referred to a very fine copper-plate map, and I noticed that he saw the most minute names distinctly, without the aid of spectacles. But then he had the eyes of a youth of twenty years. Age might palsy his limbs, but it never looked out of those windows.

After I had been sitting an hour, Seifert came to the door and said: "The two gentlemen have come—shall I admit them?" I rose to leave, but Humboldt said: "No, no—remain. They are from Hong-Kong: perhaps you know them." I looked at the cards, and recognised an acquaintance in the name of the editor of a Hong-Kong paper. The other was a Government official. After they entered, the conversation took a more general tone, but I was not sorry for this afterwards, as it gave Humboldt occasion to recall some scenes of his early life. One of the visitors spoke of Frederick the Great. "I remember him well," said Humboldt, "I was sixteen years old when he died, and I can see his face still as plainly as I can see yours. I was but eighteen when I visited England for the first time. It was during the trial of Warren Hastings, which I frequently attended. I remember that I heard Edmund Burke, Pitt, and Sheridan all speak on the same night."

After the visitors left, I remained with him until it was time for him to prepare for the dinner given to Alexander

II., to which he was bidden. "You will pass through Berlin on your way to Moscow?" said he. "Yes." "Well—I must be polite enough to live until then. You must bring your wife with you. Oh, I know all about it, and you must not think, because I have never been married myself, that I do not congratulate you." After these cordial words, and a clasp of the hand, in which there was nothing weak or tremulous, I parted from the immortal old man.

XXX.

SUMMER GOSSIP FROM ENGLAND.

[1857.]

As it was necessary that I should visit London on matters of business, before proceeding to Norway, I took the opportunity of accompanying my brother and sisters as far as Southampton, on their voyage home. Leaving Gotha on the 9th of June, we went by rail to Bremen, by way of Cassel and Hanover. The only thing in the former city which we had time to visit was the celebrated *Rathskeller*, or crypt of the old Hall of Council. This is renowned through all Germany for its tuns of Rhenish wine, of the most undoubted antiquity. They are kept in great vaults, distinguished by different titles. That of the "Twelve Apostles" has been immortalized by Hauff and Heine, but the apostolical wines are not so fine as those authors would have us believe. Each cask bears the name of one of the Apostles; they contain wine of the vintage of 1718, which has now, I was informed, a pungent acid flavor. That of Judas, alone, retains a pleasant aroma, and the sinner, therefore, is in greater demand than all the saints together. In the "Rose Cellar" are enormous casks, yet filled with Hockheimer (Hock) of the vintage of 1624. For a couple of centuries it was carefully treasured, but the City Fathers of Bremen finally discovered that the longer it was kept the worse it grew, and now sell it to visitors, in small bottles, at a moderate price.

We sat down in one of the stalls in the outer cellar, and had a bottle uncorked. Think of drinking wine which grew when the Plymouth Colony was but four years old—of the same vintage which Ariosto might have drunk, and Milton, and Cromwell, and Wallenstein, and Gustavus Adolphus! Shakespeare had been dead but eight years when the grapes were trodden in the vats; and Ben Jonson may have sung his "Drink to me only with thine eyes" over a goblet of the golden juice. We filled the glasses with great solemnity as these thoughts passed through our minds—admired its dark, smoky color, sniffed up reverently its musky, mummy-like odor, and then tasted. Fancy a mixture of oil and vinegar, flavored with a small drop of kreosote! This, as I afterwards recognised, was the impression made upon the palate, though my imagination was too busy at the time to be aware of it. We all said, "It is not so bad as I expected," and, by keeping the fact of its age constantly before our eyes, succeeded in emptying the bottle. So pungent, however, was the smoky, oily, acidulous flavor, that it affected my palate for full twenty-four hours afterwards, and everything I ate or drank in that time seemed to be of the vintage of 1624.

I reached London in season to hear the last of Handel's oratorios—*Israel in Egypt*—in the Palace at Sydenham. I doubt whether any composer, dead or alive, has ever had such an ovation. Two thousand singers and nearly three hundred instrumental performers interpreted his choruses to an audience of more than seventeen thousand persons. The *coup d'œil* alone was sublimer than any picture. The vast amphitheatre of singers, filling up the whole breadth of the western transept, stretched off into space, and the simultaneous turning of the leaves of their music books was like the appearance of "an army with banners," or the rustling of the wind in a mountain forest. We were so late that we could only cling to the outskirts of the multitude below, and I was fearful that we should not be able to hear distinctly—but I might as well have feared not hearing the thunder in a cloud over my head. Not only was the quarter of a mile of palace completely filled with the waves of the chorus, in every part, but they spread beyond it, and flowed audibly over the hills for a mile around. I kept my eye on the leader, Da Costa, whose single arm controlled the whirlwind. He lifted it, like Moses, and the plagues fell upon Egypt; he waved it, and the hailstones smote, crashing upon the highways and the temple-roofs; he stretched it forth, and the Red Sea waves parted, and closed again on the chariots of Pharaoh. He was lord of the tuneful hosts that day, and Handel himself, as he wrote the scores of the immortal work, could not have more perfectly incarnated its harmonies. Following him, I trod in the thunder-marches of the two-fold chorus, and stood in the central calm of the stormy whirls of sound.

There is no doubt that, with the masses of the English people, Handel is the most popular composer. The opera is still an exotic, not yet naturalized to their tastes; but Handel, with his seriousness, his cheerfulness, his earnestness, his serene self-reliance, and undaunted daring, speaks directly to the English heart. His very graces have the simple quaintness of the songs of Shakespeare, or those touches of tender fancy which glimmer like spots of sunshine through the cathedral gloom of Milton. The effect of the grand performance, however, was frequently marred by the sharp, dry sound of senseless clappings, demanding an encore, which Da Costa sensibly refused whenever it was possible. We who stood in the edges of the crowd were also greatly annoyed by the creaking boots of snobs who went idly walking up and down the aisles, and the chatter of the feminine fools, who came only to be heard and seen. In New York one might have the same annoyance, but by no possibility could it happen in Germany.

Don Giovanni was having a great run in both Italian Operas, Grisi and Piccolomini being rivals in the part of *Donna Anna*. I heard the former, and wondered at the consummate skill with which she managed a failing voice. Bosio was the *Zerlina*, but, though sweet and graceful as ever, she seemed to have lost something since she was in New York, five or six years before. Herr Formes, as *Leporello*, was admirable, and Cerito appeared in the ballet scene with all her former grace and beauty; but the Italian

Opera in London is not now what it was in Lumley's palmy days. Entertainments by individuals—single-string performers playing on "a harp of a thousand strings"—are now very popular. The success of Albert Smith and Gordon Cumming has led the way to a number of solo performances, nearly all of which are very well attended. Mr. Drayton (an American, I believe) gives what he calls "Illustrated Proverbs;" Miss P. Horton exhibits something of the same kind; Mr. Woodin pours forth an "Olio of Oddities;" Mr. and Mrs. Wilton announce their "Evenings with the American Poets," etc. All the world crowds on a Sunday to hear the Rev. Mr. Spurgeon, who preaches in the Surrey Musical Hall. He is, in manner, of the Beecher school, but with less ability, and impresses principally by his earnestness and the direct, practical nature of his sermons. People seem to be agreed that he is a sincere man, though his face, as it appears in the shop-windows, is anything but an agreeable one to look upon—being round and full, with round eyes, flat, flabby cheeks, a pug nose, and short lips, gaping apart to exhibit some very prominent front teeth.

At a dinner-party one day I met with Layard, and Kinglake, the author of "Eothen." The latter is a small, pale man, with blond hair and moustache, and bluish-gray eyes. His manner is quiet and subdued, and only a few would guess his concealed capacity for enthusiastic feeling and courageous action. He had just entered Parliament, and broke down shortly afterwards, in his first speech—but it was a failure which only stimulated his friends to believe the more firmly in his future success. He is now writing a

History of the Crimean War, all of which he saw, sharing its dangers with the same steady nerve which he opposed to the infection of the plague in Cairo. Layard is a man of forty, with a frank, open, energetic face, clear gray eyes, and hair prematurely gray about the temples. He had just astonished the artistic world by some very remarkable researches which he had been making in Italy during the past two years. Taking Vasari as his guide, he set off upon the hunt of the lost frescoes of Giotto and other painters of the Pre-Raphaelite period, and brought back *seven hundred* tracings of works, the existence of which had been hitherto unknown.

I heard Dickens read his "Christmas Carol" in St. Martin's Hall, to an audience so crowded and enthusiastic as to surprise the London reporters, though its equal in both these respects is a very common sight in America. His reading of the dialogue was wonderfully fine, although in the narrative parts it had a smack of the stage, and a tendency to shrillness at the end of every phrase, which had a curious effect. Dickens is now in his forty-fifth year, and Time is beginning to tell upon his exuberant locks, but his eye has all its old keenness and sparkle. "Little Dorrit," though acknowledged on all sides to be a great falling off from his previous stories, has had a more extensive sale than anything he has written—which proves the truth of a saying of old Sam. Rogers—that there is only one thing harder for a man to do than to write himself down, and that is, to write himself *up*.

Thackeray, the noblest Roman of them all, was falsifying the charges of the rampantly loyal Canadian papers, by giving his lectures on the Four Georges in all parts of the United Kingdom, and with the most gratifying success. It is cheering to see a man of his independence and honesty rewarded by such a sound and steady increase of popular respect and appreciation.

I spent two fortunate days at Freshwater, on the Isle of Wight, the residence of Tennyson. In the scenery round about the poet's residence, I recognised many lines of "Maud." He lives in a charming spot, looking out on one side over the edges of the chalk cliffs, to

> "the liquid azure bloom of a crescent of sea,
> The silent sapphire-spangled marriage-ring of the land,"

and on the other, across the blue channel of the Solent, to the far-off wavy line of the New Forest, on the northern horizon. Never shall I forget those golden hours spent with the noble poet and noble man, on the rolling windy downs above the sea, and under the shade of his own ilex and elm!

Buchanan Read, who had just come from Rome to fulfil some painter's engagements, took me one evening to visit Leigh Hunt—the sole surviving star of that constellation which dawned upon the literature of England with the present century. The old poet lives in a neat little cottage in Hammersmith, quite alone, since the recent death of his wife. That dainty grace, which is the chief charm of his poetry, yet lives in his person and manners. He is seventy-three years old, but the effects of age are only physical; they have not touched that buoyant, joyous nature, which survives in spite of sorrow and misfortune. His deep-set eyes still beam with a soft, cheerful, earnest light; his voice is gentle and musical, and his hair, although almost silver-white, falls in fine, silky locks on both sides of his face. It was grateful to me to press the same palm which Keats and Shelley had so often clasped in friendly warmth, and to hear him, who knew them so well, speak of them as long-lost companions. He has a curious collection of locks of the hair of poets, from Milton to Browning. That thin tuft of brown, silky fibres, could it really have been shorn from Milton's head? I asked myself. "Touch it," said Leigh Hunt, "and then you will have touched Milton's self." "There is a love in hair, though it be dead," said I, as I did so, repeating a line from Hunt's own sonnet on this lock. Shelley's hair was golden and very soft; Keats's a bright brown, curling in large Bacchic rings; Dr. Johnson's gray, with a harsh and wiry feel; Dean Swift's both brown and gray, but finer, denoting a more sensitive organization; and Charles Lamb's reddish brown, short and strong. I was delighted to hear Hunt speak of poems which he still designed to write, as if the age of verse should never cease with one in whom the faculty is born.

XXXI.

THE CASTLES OF THE GLEICHEN.

[SEPTEMBER, 1858.]

No part of Germany is so rich, either in romantic legends or in picturesque historical associations, as that portion of ancient Thüringia which is now parcelled into the Duchies of Saxe-Coburg-Gotha, Saxe-Weimar, and Meiningen. The range of mountains, called the Thüringerwald (Thüringian Forest), the Wartburg with its memories of Luther and the Minnesingers, and the beautiful valleys of the Saale and the Ilm, have become not only storied, but classic ground; yet, I venture to say, not more than one out of every hundred of the American travellers who visit Germany ever see more of this region than may be caught from the window of a railway carriage, bound from Frankfurt to Leipzig. To me, many of those spots are almost as familiar as the place of my nativity; and for that very reason, perhaps,

I have passed them by unnoticed in former narratives of travel.

Eastward from Gotha, and about one-third of the distance between that city and Erfurt, three isolated peaks rise from the plain at the northern foot of the Thüringian Mountains. Each is crowned with a castle of the Middle Ages; and the three, collectively, are known far and wide as *die drei Gleichen* (The Three Similars), on account of the resemblance in their position and general appearance. I had seen these peaks almost daily during several months of residence in Gotha, at different intervals—from the breezy top of the Seeberg, from the balcony over the beer-flowing streams of the Walkmühle, and from every swell in the undulating landscape stretching away to the mountains. Sometimes the gray wall of the most northern of the three castles, rising over a conical pile of foliage, gleamed like gold in the setting sun, seeming to advance nearer and nearer as the day declined; and again, in the blue vapors of an autumn noon, it would recede far into the distance, as if passing into the sphere of another landscape beyond. So picturesque and suggestive were these objects, that I was satisfied to view them thus afar off, and felt even reluctant to destroy the fascinating uncertainty in which they lay by a nearer approach.

One day in September, however, the charm was broken —or, as it proved in the end, intensified. The sunny sweetness and repose of early autumn proved too tempting. We felt an intense desire to explore some unknown region; and as every other point within the range of our vision was exhausted, nothing was left but the Gleichen. Our party consisted of four—Russian, German, and American—mutually resolved to devote the day to pleasure, or to that something still better, which is partly expressed by the Italian, *dolce far niente*, and wholly by the Arabic *keyf*, but for which our impetuous Anglo-Saxon blood has neither name nor idea. I had learned the thing itself in the Orient, and my companions were all apt apprentices, at least. The day was just fitted for such an indulgence (very few days in our climate will answer), and under the seats in our easy open calêche were stowed a variety of necessary appliances—black bread, ham, herrings, Rhenish wine, pipes, and the like. Only in such style can you truly taste the flavor of the Past.

Leaving the Seeberg on our left, we dipped down into a warm, rich hollow in the plain, in which stands the flourishing village of Wechmar. It had been devastated by fire a few days before, but the grape-vines still hugged the blackened fronts of the cottages, with their leaves scorched to ashes and their blue clusters dried into raisins. An hour's drive over the plain beyond brought us to two of the Gleichen, which take their names from the villages of Wandersleben and Mühlberg, nestled at their respective bases. The peaks, which rise to the height of five or six hundred feet, are planted at the entrance of a valley about half a mile broad, through which wanders a bright little stream. To the south-east, three or four miles distant, rises the third, or Wachsenburg Gleichen, on a loftier, but less abrupt and picturesque eminence.

Leaving our carriage at the foot of the Wandersleben Gleichen, we ascended by a spiral road, shaded with thickets of hazel and wild plum. The top of the hill is encircled by a moat, beyond which rise the old walls of inclosure. A massive portal on the northern side conducts to a spacious courtyard, now overgrown with turf, and shaded by the ruins of three different ages. The silence was undisturbed, save by the chirping of a few autumnal birds, and the rustle of a fox, which darted among the stones of a fallen wall, as we appeared. We chose the grassy foundation of an old bastion, on the sunny side of the hill, and inhaled the beauty of the landscape while Sebastian tottered up the winding path, with our baskets on his arms. The dismantled towers of the Mühlberg Castle smiled grimly across the valley, saying to Wandersleben: "We are old, and ruined, and neglected, brother, but we still stand." Wachsenburg seemed to float in the thin vapors of the morning—the whole line of the Thüringian Mountains filled the southern horizon, and the spires of Gotha in the west, and Erfurt in the east, marked the boundaries of the view. The indolent enjoyment of an hour's lounge on such a spot and at such a time, belongs exclusively to a land where indolence is permitted. The peasants, looking up at us from their turnip-fields, did not say or think: "What worthless loafers!" as many an American farmer would have done, but rather: "How pleasant it must be up there, this morning! How fortunate they are!"

Full before us, basking warm in the sunshine, was the estate of Field-Marshal von Müffling, the old campaigner of 1813 and 1815. "There," said one of my friends, "I spent three years of my life, in charge of the old general's estate; and many an hour have I stolen away to climb this hill and sit where we sit now. The western front of the castle was then almost in a habitable condition; the roof was still standing, and the floors resting on heavy beams of wood, were entire. But, as the place was not visited for weeks together, so many beams were sawed out and carried off by night, that the roof finally fell in, and the general was obliged to sell the remainder of the timber, in order to prevent it from being plundered. Superb timber it was, after a seasoning of two hundred years! Yonder, where the old chambers were, I experienced, one night, the greatest terror I ever felt in my life."

"Oh, a ghost story!" we exclaimed, and our hair rose in delightful anticipation. For my part, knowing my friend to be as courageous as a grizzly bear, I was curious to hear by what means he could have been made to feel fear. "It was when I was living with the general," said he. "The jail at Gotha was broken one winter, and four or five prisoners made their escape. The whole country was aroused, of course; they were sharply followed, and finally all were caught with the exception of one, the most desperate felon of them all. For weeks nothing was heard of him: but at last, through a Jew in Erfurt, it was discovered that he was hiding among these ruins. The general was apprised of the fact by the officers who came to take him, and who called to obtain aid. One of the shepherds attached to the estate, and myself, were detailed on this duty—not a pleasant one, I confess. The officers, however, determined to wait until late at night, when they would be more sure to find the fox in his hole.

"It was near midnight when we started. I was armed

with a sword—and the shepherd, who carried the lantern, with an old musket. On reaching the base of the hill the two officers posted their men so as to form a cordon around it, and we four then ascended to the castle. It was very dark, and the wind howled through the broken arches and windows. We first entered the vaults, groping cautiously around, and throwing the light of the lantern as far ahead as possible. Finding nothing, after a cautious search, we explored the upper chambers, one after another, and finally came to the western wing, where we were sure the robber must be hidden. The officers posted themselves at the two doors, while I entered, followed by the shepherd, whose terror increased with every minute. After examining the first floor, nothing was left for us but a large room above. The staircase had been pulled down, but a rough ladder supplied its place. Here the shepherd stopped, overcome with fear. Taking his lantern in one hand and my sword in the other, I directed him to wait at the foot of the ladder, and commenced mounting the rounds. I own I was excited and nervous, imagining that the felon might be standing over the opening, with a club raised to crack my skull the moment it should be within his reach.

"Full of this idea, I raised my head to take a cautious survey. Suddenly there was a quick, rustling sound—a loud, shrill cry, and the lantern was instantly dashed from my hand, and shattered upon the floor below. I followed it at a single leap, still holding my sword. The scream was echoed by one of terror from the shepherd, who, in his excitement, pulled the trigger of his musket, firing he knew not where. The officers stumbled in at opposite doors, in the dark. 'Where, where is he?' they cried. 'Light! light!' I demanded, and 'there! there!' yelled the shepherd, startled by a thumping sound at one of the windows. Bang went another gun, and the flash showed us a large bird of prey, flapping against the bars in his endeavor to escape. We were sufficiently vexed and mortified, but our courage was completely restored. Our search, however, was all in vain, and we would willingly have avoided our outposts, who, hearing the shots, rushed up the hill to help us secure the captive."

"And was the man ever caught?" I asked.

"Yes, two months afterwards. And what think you? The rascal was all the time hidden in the main vault, but so skilfully crammed into a hollow below two large stones, that we had actually walked over and around him a dozen times. Of course, he was remanded for several additional years—but the fellow had his revenge. He made a confidential declaration to the court, that there was a chest full of ancient armor and other curious articles in that very vault, and asked to be paid something for the discovery. The story soon got abroad, and thereupon arose a pretty dispute for the possession of the chest, between the Prussian Government, the Duchy, and the old Field-Marshal. Heaven knows how long the difficulty would have continued, had not the general taken advantage of his right of possession to search for the chest. But he didn't find it! There never had been any chest there; and the whole thing was a cunning lie, which kept the scamp supplied with his own private fun, for a year at least."

In wandering through the tumbling halls, that rare story

of love and liberality, of which they were once the scene, was constantly before my mind. Most of my readers have doubtless heard it—heard and disbelieved, yet it is historically true; and here, on the Wandersleben Gleichen, its beautiful conclusion occurred. Let me tell it, as it actually took place.

Among the princes who followed Louis IX. of France on his disastrous crusade in the Orient, was Ludwig, Landgrave of Thüringia, at the head of a small but zealous band of noblemen and their retainers. Prominent in his company was Otto, Count of Gleichen, who left a young and lovely wife, to say prayers for him during his absence. Whether he locked her up in one of those guarded chambers, wherewith the knights of that day imprisoned their "Palestine widows," is not recorded. Let us hope not. Ludwig died somewhere on the shores of the Adriatic, but a few of his followers, among whom was the Count of Gleichen, pushed on, joined St. Louis, and in the course of time crossed lances with the Saracens at Rosetta.

The Count was a passionate hunter, and it happened one day that, as he was chasing gazelles, attended only by his faithful servant, Kurt, he was suddenly surrounded by a band of Saracens and made prisoner. The two were carried off to Cairo, where the Count was thrown into a dungeon, while Kurt was employed as a slave in the Governor's gardens. The latter, who seems to have been a keen-witted knave, soon acquired the Arabic language, and so ingratiated himself into the favor of the head-gardener, that he persuaded him to apply for the services of the Count, whose skill in gardening he extolled greatly. Being thus freed from his dungeon, Count Otto found his captivity much more endurable; and, with Kurt's assistance, managed to keep up his reputation as a gardener, though he probably knew nothing more about it than to distinguish between roses and cabbages. Thus years passed away, and the chances of their release from this bondage seemed more hopeless than ever, when a wonderful providence at last opened a way for them.

By this time the governor's daughter had reached the age of womanhood. Fond of flowers, as all the Orientals are, she was naturally interested in the curiosities of gardening (very remarkable they were, no doubt!) produced by the combined art of the count and Kurt. Finally, she became interested, also, in the gardener. To make a long story short, she pitied first, then loved him; while he, in return, loved her for her pity. She proposed that he should become a Mussulman; but this he steadfastly refused. After all other plans seemed vain, she finally proved the sincerity of her love by professing her willingness to escape with him and become a Christian. The Count (an honorable man, be it acknowledged) then explained that he was already married. But this was no impediment in the eyes of the fair Melek-e'-Saleh; and at length, overcome by his desire for freedom, he accepted her proposal. The three escaped by night into the house of a Jewish physician, in the cellar of which they lay concealed for two or three months. When the terrible commotion consequent on their flight had subsided, they were each packed into the middle of a bale of dried herbs, and sent as freight to Alexandria. What will not love endure? Embalmed for a week in catnip and wormwood, it comes out breathing as deeply of roses as before!

The Jewish physician and the Venetian merchants at Alexandria were rewarded with some of Melek-e'-Saleh's diamonds, and proved faithful. The bales were immediately shipped for Venice, and the odoriferous captives liberated at sea. Fortune favored them, and the voyage to Venice was accomplished without accident. But what of the Countess Gertrudis? She, with a faith and patience unequalled since, save by Lady Franklin, waited for the return of her lost lord. When the few survivors of the Crusade made their way back, bringing no tidings of him, she nevertheless was not discouraged. When the messenger whom she had sent to the Mediterranean returned with a rumor of the count's death, she asked, "Did you see his dead body?" "No." "Did you see any one who had seen it?" "No." "Then go back again!" Finally, the messenger hired permanent lodgings in Venice, not daring to return until something positive should turn up. He waited several years in vain. But one fine morning his persistence was rewarded: the Count, with Kurt and the soldan's daughter, walked up the steps of the quay.

Good Catholic as he was, the Count proceeded first to Rome, in order that Melek-e'-Saleh might be received into the Christian Church. The wonderful story created a great sensation in the holy city, where the pope (one of the Gregories) baptized the fair Saracen under the name of Angelica. The Count then applied for a special dispensation to marry her, on account of the sacrifices she had made for his sake. The matter was considered so important, that a council of cardinals was called together; but the stony-hearted celibates, whose ventricles pumped sand instead of blood, refused the prayer. Thereupon Angelica threw herself at the pope's feet, and so warmed them with her tears and the sunshine of her beauty, that one drop of thawed blood finally crept up to his heart, and he declared that the Count of Gleichen, alone, of all Catholic Christians, then, and for ever afterwards to be born, should be allowed two wives. The espousals were celebrated at once, and the happy pair set out for the Castle of Gleichen.

But one chapter of the story remains. The Countess Gertrudis had received regular dispatches from her agent, informing her of all that had taken place. What tears and struggles the news cost her, that noble woman never told. She took counsel of her heart, and, having once chosen her course, kept it unflinchingly. At last, on such an autumn day as we enjoyed, the Count approached his castle. He was full of doubt and trouble, for he knew not that his wife had heard from him. Leaving Angelica and all his cortège in the valley beyond the Mühlberg hill, he rode on alone towards Wandersleben. What was his surprise when, on turning the corner of the Mühlberg, and seeing the towers of his home rise before him, his banner was unfurled from the highest turret, and joyous peals of horns and trumpets rang across the valley! Down the hill rode Gertrudis, on her white palfrey, clad in her bravest apparel, and the glittering ranks of his retainers followed behind. Let me not violate the sanctity of that meeting by attempting to describe it. An hour afterwards Gertrudis and Angelica met, at the eastern base of the hill—a spot which is called *Freudenthal* (the Joy-Valley) to this day. The Saxon lady's crown of golden-blonde pressed the night-black locks of the Saracen girl, as she said to her (with holy tears, we are sure), "Welcome, Angelica! you shall be to me a sister, as you are a wife to him."

The chronicle assures us that the trio passed their lives together in unalloyed peace and happiness. One account says that Angelica was childless, while Gertrudis bore five sons to the Count, while another—which we would gladly believe if it could be relied upon—declared that two babes were added to his household every year. Angelica died first, about eight years after their marriage; Gertrudis in two years afterwards: and the Count Otto outlived them many years, to lament his double widowhood. They were buried in the St. Peter's Church, in Erfurt, where you may still see their marble effigies, lying side by side on the tomb, and their mingled skeletons within. The Saracenic character of Angelica's skull has been recognised by modern craniologists. At Schwarzburg on the Saale, I am told, is yet preserved the nuptial bed, of remarkable breadth. It has been somewhat damaged by the peasants, who retain the belief that a splinter of it, kept in a house, is a charm against all domestic discord, besides being a certain cure for toothache, if held in the mouth.

Fate, that seems to delight in absurd contrasts, reserved for the squire a very different experience from that of the knight. Kurt was a native of Ohrdruff, a considerable town at the foot of the Thüringian mountains, where he had left his wife Gretel. The latter, however, had neither the love nor the patience of the Lady Gertrudis. At the end of three years, she married again; and at the time of Otto's return was the mother of several bouncing boys. Poor Kurt, however, knew nothing of this, but hastened back to Ohrdruff, eager to embrace his Gretel. Finding her place of abode with some difficulty, he entered the house, and, recognising Gretel in a strong, raw-boned woman, surprised her by a vigorous salute. Gretel screamed, and the new husband appeared. Kurt was recognised; but that did not mend matters. Both wife and husband fell upon him, beat him without mercy, and threw him out of the house. Kurt never returned to claim Gretel.

Of the ruins of the castle we could only feel certain that the vaults and two upper chambers belonged to the age of Count Otto. There was one window, looking eastward, where I am sure Angelica must have sat, remembering the palms of Cairo, or pining over the reproach of her sterility.

We drove past the Mühlberg castle without climbing the hill. Only the outer walls remain, worn and broken into fantastic shapes; and it has no history which can interest us after that of its fellow. Wachsenburg is in better repair. A portion of it is reserved as a prison for political offenders, and the remainder, including the former state apartments, is at the service of pleasure-seekers like ourselves. In the grand hall hang some hideous old portraits, among which is one of Angelica of Gleichen, painted at least three hundred years after her death, and, of course, merely imaginary. A short history of the castles, which I purchased of the guardian, states that in the year fourteen hundred and something, all three were struck by lightning on the same night.

XXXII.

WEIMAR, AND ITS DEAD.

IF the traveller, on his way from Frankfurt to Berlin, will look out of the right-hand window of his railway carriage, about three-quarters of an hour after passing Erfurt, he will see a small town, with three tall spires, seated in the bottom of a broad, natural basin, or hollow, the sides of which are formed by gradual sweeps of hill-side finally merged into an undulating upland. Around the edges of the town the houses become more scattering, diminishing as the gardens increase, so that the place seems to be an architectual deposit, which has been washed down from the circling hills, and has settled itself, like an alluvial layer, deepest where the depression of soil is greatest. This is Weimar, the Mecca of German literature.

I have seen the place many times in passing, and have thrice made, pilgrim-like, the round of its shrines. Though dull and quiet now, as if no grand creative life ever fermented within its limits—though no oracle is heard within its Dodonian groves—it possesses, nevertheless, the charm of stately repose, in addition to that of immortal associations. He who seeks in it quaint and picturesque effects, as well as natural beauties, will not be disappointed; but he who expects to find a single breath of that atmosphere of Art and Taste which surrounded it fifty years ago, will go home wiser and much sadder than he came. It seems to be the rule, in all lines of hereditary rulers, that the son is the reverse of the father. A despotic king is sure to have a liberal son, and *vice versâ*. Karl August, of Weimar, whose name will be for ever luminous in the reflected lustre of his great friends, was succeeded by a son who was little better than a fool. After the death of Goethe, who was the last of the Men of Weimar, the Muses spread their wings and flew. "Pan is dead!" was the cry, and the temples fell, and no other gods arose. Weimar is now the least literary, the least artistic, the most stupidly proud and aristocratic, the dullest and most ignorant town in Germany.

A single anecdote will illustrate the character of Karl August's successor, and explain how rapidly the tropical growths of genius, which shot so high under the genial reign of his father, must have withered and fallen to the earth under his. It was one of his delusions that he was very witty and brilliant in conversation. Two original ideas, in particular, delighted him so much, that for years he repeated them to every new acquaintance. He would first ask his unlucky guest: "What would you do if you were a dentist?" The latter, being taken aback by the question, would probably answer: "Pardon me, your Highness, I have never thought of such a thing." "Ha!" was the duke's triumphant declaration: "I'll tell you what *I* would do—I'd draw out the tooth of Time! But what would you do, if you were a diver?" To this there would be, of course, the same uncertain reply. "If *I* were a diver," the duke would then say: "I'd sink the tooth of Time in the sea of Eternity!" But the present demented King of Prussia, who at one time was really very brilliant and witty, quite spoiled the effect of those questions. He had heard of them in advance, and when he visited Weimar, was fully prepared to have them propounded to him. When the duke, therefore, asked as usual: "What would you do if you were a dentist?" the king instantly replied: "I'd draw out the tooth of Time and sink it in the sea of Eternity!" The present duke, however, though a man of ordinary abilities, does not inherit his father's stupidity, while he possesses a little of his grandfather's taste for Art. The only celebrity of whom Weimar can now boast is Franz Liszt, the pianist and composer.

The central part of the town is old and quaint, yet clean, and with an air of respectability, if not of pretension. The beautiful river Ilm touches the eastern side, threading the noble park, for the charming arrangement of which we are mainly indebted to Goethe. On this side are the palace, library, ministerium, and the residences of the principal families, in which class the authors may be included. Weimar has no antiquities of more than local interest, no fine specimens of architecture, and few pictures to exhibit —all the better for the reverent visitor, whose mind is not disturbed by various classes of associations, and who quietly tracks out the immortal footsteps of the poets.

You go first to Goethe's town-house, which is a plain, yellow, two-story building, on a small triangular square. (This bull cannot well be avoided in English.) I have never been able to visit the private apartments, which are only exhibited on certain days, but on one occasion was admitted into the garden in the rear. The back wall of the house is overgrown with ivy, and has a quaint, home-like, yet neglected air. The arrangement of the garden has evidently been changed, so that there are but two arbors which we could with certainty ascribe to the time of Goethe. Still, it was a pleasure to walk in those alleys, where the old man was wont to pace, in his dressing-grown, with hands clasped behind his back, repeating, perhaps, his own couplet, as his thoughts wandered over the wrecks, the passions, and the triumphs of the Past:

"What I possess, I see far distant lying,
And what is lost, is real and undying!"

There has been a great deal of absurd talk about Goethe, as there has been about Byron, Shelley, Tegner, and every other author, who happens to violate, now and then, the sacred decencies of Society. The offence consists, not so much in what they may do, as in the contemptuous candor with which they avow it. A little dissimulation would have made them very proper men. They would have received a sort of canonization from public opinion, and the world would have been none the wiser. Schiller, with a narrower grasp of intellect, a more undemonstrative, if not a colder nature, is mounted on an immaculate moral pedestal, while Goethe (to those who are incapable of appreciating him) is smutched with the rankest faults and heresies. Yet on the monument just erected in their honor, they stand side by side, and the hand of each rests on the same crown of laurel. Who shall say which was best, purest, and most consistent? Not the generation, nor even the century, in which a man lives, can judge him impartially.

Schiller's house is an old, quaint, yet comfortable building, on one of the broadest streets. It has been purchased by a general subscription, for the purpose of being preserved, and now contains a collection of relics associated with the poet's residence there. The halls and staircases are dark and narrow, the rooms cramped and low, and the furniture —judging from the specimens remaining—was of the plainest kind; yet everything suggests quiet, contentment, and unpretending simplicity. The upper (third) story belonged especially to Schiller. From the top of the staircase you step into a plain drawing-room, beyond which is his study, with the pictures, writing-desk, and piano, just as he left them. The writing-desk is of plain, unpainted wood, with drawers for MSS. on each side, and a recess for the feet in the centre. Here the poet was accustomed to sit for the greater part of the night, with a bottle of champagne or Rhenish wine before him, and his feet in a tub of cold water. With such a double stimulus acting on the brain, it is not so surprising that he should have written "Wallenstein" or "Wilhelm Tell," as that he should have lived to the age of forty-five.

The personal impression made by Schiller was that of a colder and more taciturn man than his poems would lead us to imagine. Except in the company of his few intimate friends, he was reserved and melancholy. This, no doubt, was the result of ill-health, and the cares which oppressed him during the best years of his life. The overplus of enthusiasm which inspired his "Hymn to Joy," in youth, was speedily chilled, and the sweetest, tenderest tone of sadness pervades his later poems. In his address "To the Ideal," he relinquishes every golden dream, and finds but two sources of strength and consolation—Friendship and Occupation—amid the trials of the actual life which surrounds him. He does not accept Life as it is, with its stern truths and relentless disenchantments; but pines for that impossible existence which once seemed so near. Yet this sadness, which would otherwise be a weakness, is redeemed by his unshaken faith in the good—his incessant aspirations for the elevation, the happiness, and the freedom of his fellow-men. Thus, with less knowledge of human nature than Goethe, he had a profounder sympathy with the race, and will for ever retain a warmer place in the German heart.

The pictures in Schiller's study are rude, colored prints of Italian scenery, whose only attraction for him could have been the subjects. The piano is a queer little cracked affair, and the chairs are of the plainest and stiffest pattern. The original cast of characters for the first performance of "Wilhelm Tell," in his own hand, hangs near the desk. His coffee-cup and saucer, penknife, pencil, and various other small articles, lie upon a table. A portrait of his wife, Charlotte von Lengefeld, in pencil, represents her as a large, aquiline, determined woman—the proper stamp to advise and assist, as well as passively appreciate. On a table in the drawing-room lies the Schiller Album, consisting of autographic contributions from nearly all the authors and artists of Germany. Behind the house is a little, narrow garden-plot, with an arbor of American ivy (*ampelopsis*)—called "wild wine" by the Germans—which was the poet's favorite resort on summer evenings.

One interesting relic of Schiller—his court sword—is now in my possession. It fell into the hands of Mr. Thackeray, during his residence at Weimar, in 1830, at which time there was no difficulty in establishing its authenticity. After having had it in his possession twenty-eight years, Mr. Thackeray presented it to me, enriched by the double association, as he had himself frequently worn it at the court of Weimar.

The houses of Herder and Wieland are not, I believe, open to public inspection, and I was obliged to be content with an outside view of them. Both these authors have also been honored with bronze statues. The park, however, which has, ordinarily, all the seclusion of a private pleasure-ground, interested me more than the vacant tenements of the dead poets. It takes in the deep, winding valley of the Ilm, and its undulating southern bank, for a distance of nearly two miles, the trees being left, as much as possible, in their natural disposition. Two or three artificial fancies only, deform the else unstudied scenery—the *ars celare artem* of landscape gardening. There is an ivied ruin, on the summit of a knoll—very well done, indeed, but it can deceive no one for a hundred years to come. A rocky grotto near the river bank is better, for Nature has lent it one of her clearest and coldest fountains. The bed of the valley is level, with a scattering growth of majestic elms and lindens, dappling the flowery turf with cold, blue shadows. There are no extensive views, nothing grand and imposing; but all is peaceful, idyllic, Arcadian.

This park is full of memories of the classic age. In one of the walks, Herder and Jean Paul met for the first time, embracing each other at sight, with unhesitating love and confidence. In a secluded nook there is a summer-house of rough wood and bark, which, it is whispered, witnessed many a secret midnight revel of the duke and the poets; and where the Ilm rests his waters in a deep, quiet dam, the young Goethe delighted, on moonlight nights, to dive from the shaded bank and reappear suddenly, with wild shrieks, in the centre of the pool, to the awful terror of peasants passing over the bridge above. Here walked Schiller, tall, stoop-shouldered, and grave; here the short, slender, compact brothers Von Humboldt, overflowing with boundless energy and ambition; Madame de Stael, stout, brilliant, and belligerent; Wieland, with his puckered face, and Herder, portly and prosperous; Bettine, the smart, sentimental, and affected little imp, performing her monkey-like antics around the knees of Goethe; the Schlegels, whose genius only saved them from being snobs; Novalis, the pure and beautiful soul, and Theodor Körner, who struck a more heroic harp than Tyrtæus—all of these, and scores of others, whose places in the German Pantheon are a little lower, knew these cool, embowered walks and grassy glades.

On the other side of the Ilm, facing the meadow, is the "Garden House" of Goethe, where his summers were spent, and many of his finest works written. It is a plain, old-fashioned residence, hardly better than the *amtmann* of any country village inhabits—shaded by a steep, wooded hill from the morning sun, yet open to the soft afternoon light and the flush of sunset. A friend of mine, a distinguished German gentleman, described to me his interview with Goethe in this house, in the year 1819. My friend is an enthusiastic geologist, and in the autumn of that year was fortunate enough to procure a portion of an aerolite, which fell in the valley of the Saale. On his return home, he determined to profit by the opportunity, and exhibit his treasure to Goethe, who was then prosecuting his geological studies. "It was just after the assassination of Kotzebue by Sand," said he, "and the excitement throughout Germany was very great. There were rumors that Goethe, also, who was obnoxious to the patriotic party, feared a similar fate. On my way to his residence, I reflected that the aerolite was in my breast-pocket, and the inserting of my hand in order to present it, would have just the appearance of drawing a concealed dagger. In order, therefore, to avoid a possible embarrassment, I put the stone into my hat.

"After waiting in the ante-room a few minutes, the door opened, and Goethe appeared in his dressing-gown, tall, massive, and majestic. My first thought was the exclamation of Lear: 'Ay, every inch a king!' He had the grandest presence of any man I had ever seen. I advanced, hat in hand, and taking out the aerolite, made it at once an apology and an introduction. He was both pleased and interested, and after a long interview, during which he exhibited to me his entire mineralogical cabinet, we parted, with a cordial invitation on his part to visit him again. I tried in vain to get his opinion with regard to the formation of aerolites, and came to the conclusion that he knew no more about it than I did myself. His manner was stately, yet not cold; and his voice, though not entirely reminding you of 'deep-toned thunder mixed with whispering rain-drops,' as Jean Paul said, was certainly very rich, full, and in unison with his whole appearance."

Yet this philosopher-poet, who wrote not only "Faust," but the "Theory of Colors," and the "Metamorphoses of Plants," could touch a string as delicate and tender as that of Ariel—could sing the songs of the zephyr and the brook, as well as the chorus of the archangels.

"Under the tree-tops is silent now!
In all the woodlands hearest thou
Not a sound:
The little birds are asleep in the trees;
Wait, beloved! and soon like these
Sleepest thou!"

—is the serenade which he whispers at dusk. And this song—which, dissatisfied with the way in which Aytoun and others have turned it into English—I have translated for myself: is it not the voice of a summer afternoon?

Up yonder on the mountain
A thousand times I stand,
Leant on my crook, and gazing
Down on the valley land.

I follow the flock to the pasture;
The little dog follows them still:
I have come below, but I know not
How I descended the hill.

The beautiful meadow is covered
With blossoms of every hue;
I pluck them, alas! without knowing
Whom I shall give them to.

I find, in the rain and the tempest,
A refuge under the tree—
But yonder the doors are fastened,
And all is a dream to me.

Right over the roof of the dwelling
I see a rainbow stand;
But *she* has departed for ever,
And gone far out in the land!

Far out in the land, and farther—
Perhaps to an alien shore:
Go forward, ye sheep, go forward!
The heart of the shepherd is sore.

Leave the park on your left, and follow its western boundary until you pass the suburbs of Weimar. Here, on a gentle slope, is the City of the Dead, in the midst whereof rises the mausoleum of the reigning family. The lodge-keeper will unlock the ponderous doors for you, and permit you to descend to a grating, through which you look into the dim vault. There, side by side, are the sarcophagi which contain the ashes of Goethe and Schiller.

Karl August, their princely friend, lies near—not *between* them, as he desired—for Weimar is intensely aristocratic and proper. But it is better so. The true noblemen sleep together, separated from the crowd of nominal and accidental ones.

XXXIII.

A GERMAN IDYL.

[SEPTEMBER, 1858.]

A SHORT time before leaving my Gothaic or Gothic home (the tradition is, that Gotha was founded by the Goths, whence its name), a marriage took place. My friend, Eckart, the announcement of whose betrothal with Emilie was proclaimed on the very day of another bridal, some ten months previous, finished the momentous business in the church of St. Margaret, with the assistance of the Rev. Mr. Beercup. But a wedding in the old central, Saxon portion of Germany, is by no means the stiff and stately affair that it is in Anglo-Saxon countries. As all possible publicity is given to a betrothal—which with us is often kept a profound secret—so marriages are always solemnized in the church, and give occasion to open and unrestrained expressions of joy and good-will on the part of the relatives and friends.

In England and the United States, a man shrinks from any observed demonstration of love, as if it were a weakness to be concealed: in Germany, the bridegroom desires that all the world should witness his bride and happiness. To be sure, tears are always shed (no wedding seems to be complete without them), but the newly-married are always sure of the heartiest sympathy and respect. The Court Chapel in Gotha has a weeping sexton, whose tears fall heavy or light, in proportion to the amount of his fee.

The evening before the happy day has a peculiar celebration of its own. It is called the *Polter-Abend*, or "Crock Evening," from an ancient custom, which still prevails to some extent, of smashing an old crock on the door-sill of the bride's residence for good luck. This performance, however, is only part of a very extensive scheme of merry-making, in which all the friends of the parties are free to indulge, no invitation being necessary. The bride and the bridegroom, enthroned upon a dais, receive the visits of all who choose to come in fancy costume, assuming some appropriate character. Of course, there is great room for the display of fun as well as good-will, and the parties are very often good-humoredly teased for their real or supposed shortcomings. Formerly, the *polter*, or crock, was smashed at the feet of the couple, previous to the masquerade of characters. Now, it is broken at the door during the evening, and sometimes omitted altogether. The programme is always kept a secret from the betrothed, and, as far as possible, from the rest of the company, so that the performance is all the more entertaining from its unexpected features.

Eckart's polter-evening was very diverting. After he and Emilie had been seated in their places of honor on one side of the frescoed saloon, and all the friends who came simply as mere spectators were in attendance, a darkhaired gipsy, picturesque in crimson and black, made her appearance, and in some neat rhymes pronounced her prognostications of the future happiness of the pair. Then came the two bridesmaids, in white, carrying the bridal wreath of myrtle, which it is their special duty to furnish. As it is woven by virgin hands, it can only be worn by a virgin bride. A widow who marries again has no right to the myrtle, but may wear a wreath of other flowers. The wreath is always presented with an appropriate poem, and this is one of the pleasantest features of the evening.

The Master of Ceremonies now announced an arrival from China. A Celestial lady with oblique eyebrows (painted for the occasion), hair of the latest Pekin *frisure*, and wide gown of rich figured silk, rushed into the saloon, and fiercely upbraided Eckart for his infidelity to her. She was, however, consoled by a little mandarin, in a poetical dialogue, and the twain finally presented the bride with a bird's nest for her wedding-soup, and danced a funny Confucian jig. Next appeared a Patagonian giantess, over six feet high, and attired in skins. She created much amusement by her assumed maiden modesty, and her languishing appeals to the single gentlemen present. There was also an Ethiopian, with an attempt at a break-down—a thing in which no German could possibly succeed; a handsome Greek boy, bearing a mystic communication from the oracle of Delphi; and finally, a whale, extended on a bench, brandishing a forked tail of black chintz, and spouting water through his nostrils upon the company, with a garden syringe!

The prettiest apparition, however, was the Fairy of the Thüringian Forest, whose golden hair and floating white dress were decorated with sprays of fir, beech, and oak. In a charming poetical address, she presented the bridal pair with branches of the same trees, typical of beauty, strength, and fidelity. O blue-eyed maid of Holstein! may thy beech find an oak to shelter it, and the steadfast fir never be absent from the garden of thy life! When the procession of characters was completed, we had liberal refreshments, consisting of varieties of sandwiches, *bratwurst* (another feature of the polter-evening), and cups of punch. A good performer took his place at the piano, and the saloon was cleared for dancing. The company dispersed before midnight, in order that the family might rest themselves for the morrow.

I pass over the wedding, which was like all other weddings in church, except that the Lutheran marriage service is simpler, and, to my thinking, more appropriate and agreeable than that of the English Church. Half an hour sufficed to give love the supremest sanction, and to impose upon the parties the solemn duties and obligations of the marriage state. Then we sat down to a sumptuous dinner, which was prolonged by a multitude of courses through the whole afternoon. There was carp from the ponds of Ohrdruff; reindeer steaks from Norway; capercailzie and venison from the forests; wine from Rhenish, Franconian, and Burgundian hills, and a bewildering variety of those artistic salad-mosaics, in which the German culinary mind delights.

The foresters in their green uniforms, the rotund editor, the country pastor, and the benign grandmother, seated together, blended into a social salad of equally heterogeneous elements; and I was not surprised when the evening music struck up, that their individualities should have become slightly confounded—that the pastor waltzed merrily with the bridesmaid, the editor gossiped quietly with the grandmother, and the foresters talked politics.

You are shocked at this, O my evangelical reader! But do not be too hasty. Remember that in the German theology asceticism has no place—that the clergymen, even those of the most orthodox stamp, are faithful disciples of Luther, whose great warm, mellow, merry heart it was, rather than his inkstand, which put the Devil to flight. Their position does not debar them from the enjoyment of any innocent and cheering amusement. If my friend, the pastor, had danced in the sight of all his congregation, they would have listened to him on the next Sabbath with no less dutiful reverence. The milestones along a German's life are his domestic and social festivals. On this track his religion walks hand-in-hand with him, not frowning, with averted head, on a distant path, where no roses spring from the flinty soil.

But the short September dusk deepened into night, and the grandmother's cart was at the door; so the new husband and wife took their seats with her, and the three set out for the castle of Friedrichswerth, of which the old lady was sole castellan. It is seven or eight miles distant from Gotha, in a secluded valley, behind the barren Hörselberg. I had often intended to visit the old ducal castle, but probably should never have carried out my design, had not Eckart and his wife gone to spend the first week of their honeymoon there. Two days afterwards, on one of the loveliest and sunniest days that ever blessed the world, I set off alone, in a light open carriage.

What is sweeter than a golden autumnal day in Mid-Germany? The first yellow leaves are falling from the linden colonnades on either side of the road; the fields, uninterrupted by hedge or fence, spread their mosaic of green, brown, and tawny squares over the wide, undulating hills, until, in bluer waves, they meet the indistinct horizon; nestled in every hollow, the red roofs of the villages are softened to pink or purple by the gauzy air; and beyond all, the mountain-ranges, dark with firs, are basking softly in a noonday dream. The knobs of scarlet berries gleam on the wild-boar ash; the meadows are sprinkled with the lilac blossoms of the colchicum, and the winding belts of tall alders which mark the course of the streams will defy the frosts for a month to come. There is no jubilant vintage, with its bonfires and rockets, as on the Rhine, but the villages are jolly with the *Kirmse*, and the blonde youths you meet have gay rosettes on their caps. From the beer-gardens you hear the clink of the heavy glasses, or a genial chorus, or that sweet song which everybody knows:

"Down in a cool, green valley
There goes a mill-wheel round;
But my sweetheart she has vanished—
The sweetheart there I found."

In the placid enjoyment of such sights and sounds, I was carried on towards Friedrichswerth, and the blue, ringleted breath of my contentment floated behind me on the autumn air. Gotha, despite its lofty perch, disappeared behind the wooded ridge of the Krahnberg, and a new valley opened before me—a broad basin, sweeping away to the northern base of the Hörselberg, and bounded on the west by gently-rounded hills, to the green declivities of which villages were clinging. In the centre of the landscape was Friedrichswerth, the square gray front of its castle rising above the rounded, billowy green of the pleasure-garden belonging to it. The naked heights of the Hörsel, usually so brown and forbidding, were now muffled in a violet film, as fair as the veil of the enchantress, Frau Holle, who still sits within their caverns, to lure a new Tannhäuser to her fatal arms. It must have been on such a day that the dry staff of the despairing pilgrim burst into miraculous bloom, the sign of pardon and of rest. Gazing on the haunted hills, I found my mind involuntarily following the thread of that legend, and it occurred to me that nine men out of every ten would have done just as Tannhäuser did.

Leaving my carriage at the village inn, I crossed the bridge over the empty moat, and entered the castle. It is a plain, massive building, occupying three sides of a parallelogram, and built in the style of the sixteenth century. Entering a door at a venture, I found myself in a spacious, arched kitchen, large enough to furnish a meal for five hundred men. At the sound of my footsteps, the door opened, and the grandmother appeared. She at once conducted me to an inner chamber, likewise vaulted, where I found Eckart and his wife. I had not taken my seat before I was presented with a large mug of foaming beer—the beginning of a series of hospitalities from which there was no escape, save in flight.

The whole castle—which is uninhabited, except by the good old commandress—was put at our disposal. A hundred years ago it was the favorite summer residence of the Dukes of Saxe-Gotha-Altenburg; but since the extinction of the old house, and the union with Coburg, it has been emptied of everything but a few bad pictures, and entirely neglected. It was built, I believe, about 1670, by Duke Frederick II., and further adorned and beautified by his successors. The princely builder seems to have been annoyed by strictures upon his architectural taste, for he placed at the bottom of the staircase, in the main hall, a large carved figure of a fool, grinning maliciously, and pointing with his right hand to an unfolded scroll in his left, on which was written—as nearly as I can recollect the words—"Ha! ha! here is the Fool, you say. The castle has been built solidly and in good style, by the Prince Friederich II. for his pleasure and satisfaction. Now it is finished, and if you don't like it, take care; for perhaps the style of it may be better than your own, and then *you* are the Fool, after all!"

The state chambers were in a ruinous condition, from sheer neglect. The heavy gilded cornices were tarnished, the frescoes faded and chipped off in spots, the plaster reliefs broken, and the carved wainscots riddled with rat-holes. Only the chapel, with its silent organ, and its altar, piously kept clear of dust, retains a little of the olden state.

Around the choir is an elaborate frieze of wood-carving, representing a multitude of cherub choristers and musicians, of the size of life. Many of the baby figures are charming —lightsome and graceful, in spite of the giant mushrooms (meant for *clouds*) in the midst of which they are singing. A few paintings of court beauties, of a century ago, have been left; but the most of them are damaged and faded.

Another bridge crosses the moat to the garden, which is a specimen of horticultural pomp relapsing into barbarism, and more beautiful, perhaps, in its unpruned and neglected state, than it ever was when its rectangular walks and pyramidal trees mimicked Versailles. In a dark, circular grove of lindens are the old grottoes and fountains; but the grotesque rock-work has tumbled down, the fountains are dry, and the marble nymphs have veiled their nudity in a thick garb of yellow mould. Only a little dark water at the bottom of this basin glimmers through the funereal shade. On either hand, hedges of yew and holly, which once presented smooth-clipped walls to the walk, have shot out lawless boughs in all directions—taking forms all the wilder for their previous restraint. A few statues are still standing at the turns of the walks; and there are some tables and benches under the lindens, where you can drink your tea—or beer.

At the northern end of the garden, a broad flight of steps leads to a large artificial terrace, surrounded by a massive stone balustrade, now falling to pieces, and half concealed in the wildest tangle of vines—ivy, roses, nightshade, grapes, honeysuckles, and blackberries, matted together in a wrestle for the lordship of the place. In the centre of the terrace is another cirque of Druid lindens, protecting a mutilated statue of Diana. The high garden walls are hidden on the north side with close hedges of yew, and on the south are covered with bounteous grape-vines. Around the whole tract, which comprises from fifteen to twenty acres, runs a broad, deep moat, outside of which stood, prior to 1848, a noble avenue of lindens, inclosing the whole. During the revolutionary excitement, however, the people cut them down.

As we sat on the terrace, under the lindens, while the blue summit of the Hörsel darkened against the sinking sun, the old grandmother told us of the traditionary splendors of the court; how the dukes came hither for summer gaiety, and were visited here by all the neighboring princes, and by noblemen from Paris and Berlin; how they hunted over the northern hills, and danced at evening in the great hall; how the moat was then full of water, and splendid barges rowed around castle and garden by torchlight, to the sound of music; what glittering coats the gentlemen wore, what diamonds the ladies; how rich and grand they were—yet, for all that, no better than they should be; in short (although she did not say that), what a selfish, affected, vain, licentious, stupid crew once housed in this paradise. How sweet the present seclusion and neglect, contrasted with those glittering orgies!

I have rarely seen a place which fascinated me so entirely. Its aspect was not sad, but soothing and happy, as if every tree said to itself: "Now they have let me alone, I can grow as I please, and take some comfort in living." The silent garden, clasped in the centre of the broad, tranquil landscape, was a happy valley, away from the restless world. The whistle of the locomotive does not pierce the rocky Hörsel, on the other side of which the railroad runs. The peasants who inhabit the valley rarely leave their homes; neither foreign nor native tourist ever comes thither; perhaps a few papers are taken, but they don't often contain any news: and so the valley lives on, in a lazy, undisturbed life of its own. If I ever should become thoroughly exhausted in body and brain, tired of work, sick of excitement, and surfeited with the restraints of society, I shall take two chambers in the old castle (the grandmother promised to let me have them), and bury myself in Friedrichswerth, until its repose ceases to be a balm, and labor is welcome again.

I did not return to Gotha at sunset, as I had designed. First, I must have coffee in the duke's cup; then a table had been set in one of the vaulted chambers—the parson was there, and the roast would soon be ready. "Go now? No, indeed. You don't stir until after supper!" said the commandress. The roast was done to a turn, the salad succulent, and the wine (out of princely vaults, if of plebeian quality) genial and cheering. Extra candles were lighted, and the eyes of the bold beauties on the walls brightened as they beheld the unusual festival. The hour was late when at last my carriage was allowed to start; and the clocks of Gotha struck midnight before I reached the city. But I carried with me a new picture; and if you could see it as I now do, you would not exchange it for a genuine Claude Lorraine.

18

XXXIV.

THE THREE HUNDREDTH ANNIVERSARY OF THE UNIVERSITY OF JENA.

[AUGUST, 1858.]

IN Europe the year 1858 was distinguished principally for the number of civic and military festivals of a national character, which were celebrated in various countries. Greece had her royal jubilee; Russia, the dedication of her greatest church; Sweden and Norway, their camp at Axevalla; Spain, her water celebration at Madrid; and France, her pompous show at Cherbourg. In Germany, the great event of the year was the celebration of the three-hundredth anniversary of the University of Jena—a festival which possesses more than local importance, through the peculiar history of this University, and the part which its students have taken in the political movements of the last half century. To no institution of the kind in all Germany belongs such a multitude of interesting associations, and probably no other circumstance could have called together so remarkable an assemblage of persons as were collected in the valley of the Saale in August 1858.

Among the German youth Jena has been for a long time the favorite University; and if not at present so largely attended as those of Heidelberg, Leipzig, or Berlin, it has lost none of its ancient popularity. It is the seat of liberal principles, in religion as well as in politics, has been often assailed as revolutionary and heterodox, yet has always steadily maintained its character. In song, in the traditions of the *Burschenschaft*, and in German history, it holds a proud pre-eminence; and this magnetism continues to draw into its folds, as heretofore, the best minds, the most active, free, and daring characters of each generation.

Before I describe the festival, a part of which I saw and was, let me devote a little space to an account of the foundation of the University, and to some of the most interesting points in its history. These are not only worthy of note in themselves, but are necessary to an understanding of all that took place during the celebration, which was especially of a character to recall and reanimate the past.

John Frederick the Magnanimous, Elector of Saxony, the friend of Luther and Melancthon, was the most faithful and zealous of all the Protestant princes. When, after Luther's death in 1546, Charles V. determined to crush the Reformation by force of arms, he at once put himself at the head of the Protestants. Deserted by his treacher ous cousin, Duke Maurice of Saxony, and overcome by a superior force, he was taken prisoner, the greater part of his principality given to the duke, and himself condemned to death. The Emperor, however, did not dare to carry this sentence into execution, but kept him for five years a prisoner in Austria, allowing his sons to retain a number of Thüringian towns. The territory ceded to Maurice, to whom the title of Elector was transferred, comprised Wittenberg, whose university, founded by Frederick the Wise, was the very hot-bed of the Reformation.

The first thought of John Frederick was to replace this loss by the establishment of a new university in the Thüringian domain spared to his sons. Though a prisoner, and so impoverished that he had difficulty in supporting a small retinue of faithful followers—though discouraged even by Melancthon—he resolved to found a Protestant school. Passing through Jena in 1547, as a captive in the Emperor's train, he had an interview with his sons in the crypt of the castle (still existing), and secured their co-operation. The Dominican convent in Jena was selected for the purpose; and Melancthon, who was then living in Weimar, was appointed Professor of Theology and Philosophy. He resigned, however, before the school opened; but two of his pupils—one of them, Johann Stigel, a noted poet and scholar of that time—took his place. The new academy was solemnly inaugurated in March, 1548, in the presence of the three young Dukes, while their father, the noble old Elector, was still a captive in Austria. Students from all quarters soon flocked to Jena; and when, after the Treaty of Passau, John Frederick, the Magnanimous, was restored to liberty and to his dignity as reigning prince, the great desire of his heart was already accomplished. The chronicles of those days describe his triumphant return, in September, 1552; how he stopped for some days to hunt in the forests of Saal-valley; how he dined at the Prince's Spring, so called to this day; how he entered Jena in the afternoon, received by the authorities, burghers on horse and afoot, ringing of bells, and bonfires in the evening; and finally, how, on reviewing the long ranks of students, he turned to his friend Lucas Cranach, the celebrated painter, who sat in the carriage at his side, and exclaimed, with a laugh of delight: "See, there is *Brother Studium!*" The epithet was taken up and remembered, and "Brother Studium" is yet a household word in Jena.

The new school, however, had not yet attained to the dignity and the privileges of a university. It was simply an academy of the higher class—a decree of the German emperor being necessary to invest it with the former character. John Frederick died in 1554, but in his last will, he solemnly commended his sons to continue the work, and to spare no expense in making it successful "for the glory of God and the advancement of the truth." After Ferdinand I. had succeeded to the crown of Charles V., the young duke John William made personal application to him, and obtained a conditional promise of his consent. Johann Schröter, of Vienna, who had been called to Jena as Professor of Medicine, was sent to continue the negotiations; and finally, on the 15th of August, 1557, an imperial decree was signed, granting to the Academy of Jena the same rights, powers, and privileges as were then enjoyed by the universities of Padua, Pavia, Paris, Leipsic, etc., with the remarkable clause, that the preservation and propagation of the Lutheran doctrine was fully and freely permitted. The university was thus founded on a principle of tolerance unusual in those days, and has never yet forfeited its character.

On his return from Vienna with the imperial charter, Schröter was received with the honors due to a conqueror. The students and burghers of the town, with the young dukes at their head, went out three miles to meet him, and escorted him in triumph within the gates. On the 2d of February, 1558, the university was inaugurated with all possible pomp and solemnity—the nobility of Thüringia taking part in the procession. There is still extant a description of the scene, from which we learn that twelve mounted trumpeters led the way, blowing joyous melodies; that many suits of gilded armor and mantles of velvet were to be seen; that the students, three abreast, reached from St. John's Gate to the market-place, that the solemnities commenced with singing the hymn: "Come, holy Spirit," and terminated with a princely joust in the market-place, which had been covered with sand—with many other less important particulars. The 2d of February, 1858, was therefore in reality the three-hundredth anniversary; but the celebration was postponed to the 15th of August (the date of the charter), on account of the more favorable season, and of the latter date being vacation time throughout Germany.

The history of the past and present student life in Jena,

as given in the recently published work of the Drs. Keil, is exceedingly curious and amusing. A correct account of almost any single class of individuals, continued through three centuries, illustrates the relative character and spirit of the time, and no class more so than the students. We are therefore not much surprised to learn that, previous to the Thirty Years' War, the sons of the Muses at Jena were a most savage and ungovernable set, who fought, plundered vineyards, stole chickens, damaged houses, and violated every one of the Commandments. In short, they did everything but study. The "evangelical Lutheran doctrine" was propagated but indifferently by these roystering youths, whose great delight, next to drinking, was to array themselves in the enormous hose of the time (we have an account of sixty-six yards of silk being frequently used for a single pair), velvet jacket and cap, and sword, and thus, with throat bare and hair floating over the shoulders, to sally out to the neighboring villages, beat the young men, and seduce the girls.

Wolfgang Heider, who was professor in Jena at the end of the sixteenth century, gives a wrathful picture of the student at that time. The irate old fellow cannot find words violent enough to express his dislike of the class. He says: "He either visits the public exercises not at all, or quite too seldom; he attends no lectures. Sometimes he listens before the door, in nowise that he may learn something advantageous, but so that he may pick up a few phrases, and retail them afterwards among his brother carousers, imitating the voice, manner, and gestures of the professors, and creating laughter. In the morning, the lovely and tender youth sleeps until nine; and thereafter, where there remaineth any time before dinner, he employs it in combing his hair, curling, adorning, rubbing, hunting vermin, and dressing the rum-blossoms on his face. When he has seated himself at the table the beast devours but little (for the violent drunkenness of yesterday will not permit it, and because all senses are stupified, Nature will not suffer it), and he also converses but little (for what kind of civility can dwell in such a hoggish body and soul?). In the meantime, however, he shakes from himself a full burthen of nonsensical stupidities and disgusting nastinesses—and truly in such wise, that as soon as he opens his vile snout, all boys and maidens run away, lest they may be infected by the breath of the pestilential plague." Enough of the old professor, who quite unconsciously paints his own character at the same time, and does not damage his subject quite so much as he supposes. The students were bad enough in those days, as the records of Jena testify, but somewhat is due to the character of the times. Study and seclusion were still considered monkish; and there was altogether too much restless blood in the veins of the race for that system of "oxing" (a slang word for "drudgery") which the German students practise nowadays.

The Thirty Years' War, it appears, exercised a most demoralizing influence upon all the German Universities. During that long and bloody struggle, all classes of society became more or less brutalized. Every city had its garrison; the halls of learning became barracks for the soldiery, and the students adopted the lawlessness of the latter without their discipline. An old writer, Philander of Sittenwald, thus paints the character of the academic youths at Jena: "They consider it as boorish as a bear's-hide to be diligent; but a sign of nobility to be foolish, fantastic, asinine, loaferish, and rowdy." Even in those days, Jena distinguished itself above all other universities for the number of duels daily perpetrated there—a distinction which it still enjoys. A rhymed by-word, which originated then, is even yet in circulation:

> "Who comes from Leipzig without a wife,
> And from Halle, in body sound,
> And from Jena without a wound—
> He may boast of a lucky life!"

During the seventeenth century, a practice called "Pennalism," very similar to the English custom of fagging, prevailed. The younger students were obliged to serve the older for the term of one year, six months, six weeks, six days, six hours, and six minutes. The system was finally broken up, no doubt to the great improvement of the manners of the students. The "pennals" were treated in the most abominable manner; obliged to give up their new garments to their masters and go about in rags; to render them all sorts of menial service, and be beaten in acknowledgment of it. They were sometimes forced to eat a mess composed of sausage, bread, chopped nettles, pounded bricks, ink, mustard, butter, nut-shells, salt, and clay! The students finally carried their lawlessness so far as to give out that one of their number was dead, and got up a grand funeral, at which the clergy and faculty officiated; but on opening the coffin at the grave, as was then customary, it was found to contain—a pickled herring! On another occasion, they surrounded the carriage of a neighboring princess, seized her horses and guards, deliberately turned her Highness's bonnet wrong side foremost, and then liberated her.

These wild proceedings were, of course, met by attempts, on the part of the faculty, to establish a rigid and despotic discipline, and the collision between the two extremes was all the greater. Early in the last century, however, a better spirit began to appear. As the proportion of educated men increased, the desire for knowledge and the ability to study inrceased also. As the students became more diligent, their manners and morals improved, and the scandalous excesses of the former century gradually disappeared. The influence of the French Revolution, and the wars which followed, was precisely the opposite of the Thirty Years' War. The thousand students of Jena displayed a degree of frank, manly character, a conscientious adherence to their studies, an elegance of manner, and a refinement of dress and language, which presented a most remarkable contrast to their predecessors of fifty years before. In their enthusiasm for the Rights of Man, caught from the millennial dreams of the early French Republicans, the brutal element melted away. The birth and rapid growth of a grand national literature also exercised a powerful effect upon them. Lessing, Herder, and Klopstock had written: Goethe and Schiller were in the prime of youth. From this period on, the German students have exhibited a steady enthusiasm for whatever is best and noblest in the national character. They have kept alive that spirit of enlightened progress, which has already broken many a rusty shackle of the Past.

I have not space to follow, in detail, the later history of the University. There was the famous "March to Nohra," in 1792, when they left in a body, because the government endeavored to enforce an obnoxious order by the power of the soldiery; the fiery times of 1813, when, singing the songs of Körner, they marched to battle for the common Fatherland; the establishment of the *Burschenschaft*, as a means of creating and preserving a truly national spirit throughout Germany; the mass convention on the Wartburg, in 1817, which made the treacherous princes tremble in their shoes; and the waves of sudden excitement which followed the Revolutions of 1830 and 1848. All these associations are the inheritance of every student who enters Jena. The ground he treads is not simply a quiet sanctuary of learning; it is hallowed in his eyes by events which are part of the political history of Germany, and not without some reason does he call the place "Athens," as he remembers the eloquent voices that have spoken for German freedom there.

One of the features of the Three-hundredth Anniversary was the inauguration of a bronze statue of John Frederick the Magnanimous, by Drake, of Berlin. The stout old duke stands in the centre of the market square, with an open Bible in one hand, and a drawn sword in the other. His face is square and heavy, neck thick, and shoulders broad, but there is a great deal of energy in his firm-set jaws and bold brow. An interesting feature of the inauguration was the singing, by a full choir, of the famous "Hymn of Consolation," composed by John Frederick himself, when a captive in Austria. As a specimen of the sturdy, downright language of the times—of the dialect whose words were more potent than cannon-balls, in the mouth of Luther, I translate a few stanzas of it:

As't pleases God, so it pleases me:
Nor am I led astray,
Though biting smoke confound mine eyes,
And though along my way
All is obscure,
Yet I am sure
That God doth clearly see it:
As He may send,
So must it end:
If't must be, then, so be it:

As't pleases God, I am content,
I care not for the rest;
What's not to be, why, let it go—
The obedient heart is blest.
Although my mind
Be scarce resigned,
His grace will grant assistance:
I firmly trust—
What must be, must;
'Gainst God there's no resistance.

As't pleases God, so let it pass:
The birds may take my sorrow:
If fortune shuns my house to-day,
I'll wait until to-morrow.
The goods I have
I still shall save,

Or, if some part forsake me,
Thank God, who's just,
What must be, must;
Good luck may still o'ertake me.

As't pleases God, so I accept,
For patience only pray;
'Tis He alone, whose arm can help—
Can reach me, though I lay
In anguish sore,
At Death's dark door:
There's rescue for the sinner!
I am but dust:
What must be, must;
So be it—still I'm winner!

The 15th of August, 1858, fell upon Sunday, on which day it was not possible for me to be present; but as the celebration lasted three days, I had the pleasure of witnessing what, to me, were its most interesting features. Leaving Gotha early on Monday morning, I quitted the railroad at Apolda, a large manufacturing town on the Saale, nine miles from Jena. It was well, perhaps, that I had not arrived on the preceding day. The influx of eight thousand visitors into the little town had quite exhausted the means of transportation and the sleeping accommodations. Every vehicle in the country, from the baronial calèche to the peasant's dung-cart, was in requisition; and in all the villages, for miles around, every bed and hayloft had been bespoken weeks before.

By good luck we obtained seats in a sort of extemporaneous omnibus, and were among the first departures. The long street of Apolda, down which we drove, wore the gayest festival dress. From every house floated long streamers, bearing the colors of the German States and of the students' societies—conspicuous among them the red, black, and gold of the old German Empire, the blue and white of Saxony, and the blue, yellow, and white of Saxe-Weimar. The beer-houses, freshly sanded and decked with green boughs, were wide open to the day, and a vision of brown mugs crowned with foam continually flitted past the windows. Emerging from the town, we slowly climbed to the high, undulating upland, where, fifty-one years before, the power of Prussia was crushed at a single blow. Far as we could see, the harvest-fields were deserted; the golden wheat waved idly in the hot wind; over leagues of landscape labor had ceased. It was a universal holiday.

Our progress, slow enough at best, from the load we carried, was rendered still more so by our impatience; but the upland was crossed at last, and we rapidly descended into the valley of the Saale. On our left rose a huge wooden cross, on the summit of a precipitous rock, whence Luther, it is said, once preached to the multitude. Pleasant cottages began to appear, then scattering beer-gardens, and finally, a triumphal arch of fir and oak welcomed us to the rejoicing Jena. The town lies in a deep basin, at the intersection of three valleys, surrounded on all sides by high, dry, bare-washed hills, which produce an excellent red wine. The Jenavese boast of the resemblance of the landscape to that which surrounds Athens; but I could not flatter them by finding it out. In front of us, it is true, there was a single conical peak which might answer for Mount Lycabettus; but where was the Acropolis?—where Pentelicus?—where the Ægean and its isles?

"Ah!" exclaimed a dignified old gentleman in black, who sat beside me, "there is the Hausberg! there is the Fox-tower! Yonder is Ziegenhain, under the woods—do you see? And there goes the path to Lichtenhain! I wonder if the beer is still as good as ever!" Behind us somebody sang the old song, familiar to all Jena students:

"On the mountains the castles,
In the valley the Saale,
In the city tho maidens,
The same as before:
Ye dear old companions,
Where wait ye my coming?
Alas! ye are scattered
The wide world all o'er!"

I looked around on the wonderfully picturesque forms of the mountains, which inframe the valley-basin. The Fox-tower stood against the sky, on its lofty ridge; the Kunitzburg rose blue in the distance, and many a fair village lay nestled in the heart of the green dells. Bright and beautiful as they appeared to me, basking in sunshine, gay with banners, and ringing with jubilant music, there was a tone of sadness in the landscape for the gray-heads around me, and their eyes grew suddenly dim.

I felt that I had no right to witness their emotion, and turned my eyes upon the city. There was a flapping of flags in the wind: a bee-like hum of music gradually filled the air, and the quaint old gabled dwellings, buried up to their roof-tiles in garlands, seemed to sway hither and thither as their drapery was moved. Thick wreaths of oak leaves, studded with the scarlet berries of the mountain ash, hung from window to window; young firs, dug up bodily, were planted at the doors, and long streamers of gay colors floated from the eaves. In all Jena, there was not a house or building of any description without its decoration of flags and garlands. The windows were open and full of bright faces, the streets crowded with student-caps of every hue, even the old graduates wearing the colors of their youth, and our progress was continually impeded by rollicking companies, singing "*gaudeamus igitur*" or some other classic melody.

But most impressive of all was the sight of the recognitions of old friends. The gray-heads in the omnibus were continually shouting: "Karl, is it thou?" "God bless me, there is Hardenberg!" "Ah! brother Fritz, art thou here, too?"—while, more than once, as we passed onwards, I saw men stop, stare doubtfully at each other, and then open their arms for a glad embrace. "Ah!" thought I, "it will be the merest chance if I find any one of my friends in this crowd." But as we drove into the market-square, where John Frederick the Magnanimous stood resplendent in new bronze, my name was suddenly shouted, and a powerful but friendly arm pulled me down from the omnibus. "Andree!" I exclaimed, for it was really that distinguished geographer. "To-day's procession is over," said he, "but come into 'The Sun' and drink a *seidl* of beer, and then we will go to dinner in the *Deutschen Hof*, where there are many people whom you will like to know."

So said, so done: but the way into "The Sun" was blocked by a crowd of young students, gathered about an aged man, cheering, shaking his hand, and talking all together with a singular enthusiasm. "Who is it?" we asked. "Have you not seen him before?" answered a young fellow: "it is ——, from Holstein. Look at his hat—*class of* 1789! He heard Schiller's introductory as Professor of History, and took part in the March to Nohra! His son and grandson are both graduates of Jena, and are here with him!" What an unwonted light there was in the old man's eyes! How he joined, with cracked voice, as, forming a circle around him, they sang the stirring "Schleswig-Holstein, sea-surrounded," the Marseillaise of the Baltic shore!

One could not be ten minutes in such an atmosphere, without feeling its contagion. The pulse beats quicker, the blood runs warmer, the eyes brighten, and the frame seems to dilate, as if you felt

—— "the thews of Anakim,
The pulses of a Titan's heart."

Soon your lungs become accustomed to the oxygen of the popular excitement, and you live a faster, freer, more exalted life. It is an intoxication which no earthly vintage can produce; and the man who can or would desire to withstand it, deserves that his name should never make a single human heart throb the faster.

On the way to dinner we passed the University Buildings, including the old Dominican Convent wherein the institution was first founded. As we were looking at the window of the *Carcer*, where refractory students are imprisoned, an old man, who was surveying the ground, shook his head, saying: "Ah! there are great changes here. Everything is ruined—ruined. Once there was a deep moat under the carcer window. We could hide there at night, and when our friends above let down strings, we sent them up *seidls* of beer and pipes of tobacco. It is filled up—you couldn't do it now. This they call Progress —Civilization!" he added scornfully, turning away from us. In the dining-hall I found many characters renowned in the annals of the Burschenschaft. There was Karl Horn, of Mecklenberg, the founder of the Society, who, on the 19th of January, 1816, when the students solemnly celebrated the Peace of Paris and the Liberation of Germany, planted an oak tree in the square where the French had encamped ten years before—a tree dedicated to German Freedom and German Unity, which is still flourishing, and held as sacred as was ever any oak of the Druid groves. There was Hase, Member of the French Academy, who had come from Paris to attend the celebration, Brockhaus of Leipzig, and many other men of note.

A rosy-cheeked, white-headed old gentleman sat opposite to me at the table. I discovered, ere long, that he was Dr. Vogel, father of the lost African traveller. The latter, it will be remembered, reached Wara, the capital of Waday, in 1856, whence came, shortly afterwards, a report that he had been beheaded by order of the Sultan. Since then, nothing further has been heard from him, and it seems now but too certain that his name must be added to the list of those heroes who have fallen on the great geographical battlefield of Africa. His father, however, assured me that he still has hope that his son is only kept a close prisoner in Waday, and that, if he lives, he may yet find means of escape. I could not give him any encouragement for this belief, although Dr. Barth had favored it.

In the afternoon the visitors betook themselves to the summer resorts of their favorite societies, in the villages round about. The Thüringians marched out to Lichtenhain, where my friend Ziegler reigned as Thus XLVII., clad in coronet and ducal robes, with his ministers, minstrels, and jesters. The Franconians went off up the valley of the Saale, the Germanians and members of the old Burschenschaft to Ziegenhain; while others, deterred by the heat, remained in the city to drink the cool brewage of the "Burgkeller" and the "Rose." We fell in, by chance, with the Franconians, among whom we found two acquaintances, but as their rendezvous did not promise much amusement, we set off over the mountain to Ziegenhain. It was a terrible job to climb the height, with the afternoon sun beating upon our backs, but we were well repaid by the superb view from the summit. Jena lay at our feet, wrapped in wreaths and banners, and the sound of her rejoicing came up to us in a faint, melodious murmur. In a deep dell on the right was Ziegenhain, with the lofty gray square of the Fox-tower crowning the height beyond it.

The houses of the village were deserted, and we were at a loss which way to turn, when a prolonged shout rose from among the trees below. Here some hundreds were assembled, in a close beer-garden, shaded with vines, and half-a-dozen barrels on tap outside. Politics was the order of the day, and opinions were uttered with an eloquence and a boldness which astonished me. The old blood of 1817 awoke again in the sluggish veins of the gray-headed *Burschen*, and the sentiment "One Parliament for Germany, and *above* the German Princes!" was received with a storm of cheers. When the sun set, they began to return. I fell into the long procession beside a clergyman from Holstein, and thus, singing the *gaudeamus*, we marched back the three miles, and disbanded before the statue of John Frederick.

In the evening there was a grand *kneipe* in the Prince's Cellar. The halls were crowded to suffocation, as the men of 1813 and 1817 were to be present. The songs, by five hundred voices, were grand and stirring beyond all description. Horn, after a speech wherein he described the planting of the sacred Oak, called for a song of Ernst Moritz Arndt, which was sung on the Wartburg, soon after the Burschenschaft was founded:

"In happy hour have we united,
A mighty and a German band,
Our souls, to truth and honor plighted,
From earnest lips a prayer command;
For solemn duties we assemble,
In high and holy feeling bound,
So let our breasts responsive tremble
Our harps give out their fullest sound!"

On these occasions the affectionate and confidential *Du* (thou) was altogether in use. Stately diplomatists and reverend doctors of divinity hailed as brothers the wild, young generation of students, who, with long hair, bared throats, and ribbons of black, red, and gold, darted hither and thither. "Brother," said one of these fellows to me, as I leaned against the wall, "canst thou find no place? where is thy beer? Ha! take this *seidl.* Strike—hurrah for Jena!"

Towards midnight it suddenly occurred to us, that we had made no provision whatever for our lodgings. The night was warm and balmy, but our aching bones coveted an easier bed than the paving-stones. Hurrying back to "The Sun," we succeeded with great difficulty in catching a waiter and holding him fast. "Can you give us beds?" The question, coming at such a time, struck him dumb. "Beds! there is no bed to be had in Jena." "Is there a hay-loft?" "Yes." "Then," said I, "reserve twenty-four square feet, and send me the groom immediately!" The man departed: presently I saw him in communication with the head-waiter, and my surprise may be guessed when the latter came up and said: "If the gentlemen will not object to sleeping in a room through which two other guests must pass, I can furnish them with beds." I took out my purse and offered to pay for them in advance, saying: "We have no baggage, as you see, and could therefore easily slip off in the morning." His eyes opened wide. "What an idea!" he exclaimed; "I never heard of such a thing!" The next morning, two of my friends inquired for "the Americans." "They are no Americans," said he; "I've been in America myself, and can tell one when I see him. Don't let these people deceive you, if they say they came from there!"

At ten o'clock in the forenoon, the grand commemorative procession was repeated for the third and last time, in the same order as on the previous days. Two features in it particularly interested me—the student-marshals, in their picturesque costume of the Middle Ages (slashed black velvet doublet, hose, hat, plume, and sword), and the Faculty of the University, in their heavy gowns of blue, green and purple velvet, and plain, round caps of the same material. Some of the latter wore gold chains, and other ancient badges of their office. Conspicuous in the procession were the various deputations of students from other Universities, distinguished by the different colors of their scarfs, and the feathers in their mediæval caps. The Prime Ministers of the Duchies of Saxe-Weimar, Saxe-Coburg-Gotha, Saxe-Altenburg, and Meiningen—which lands are the joint protectors (*nutritores*) of the University—had also their place, and glittered gorgeously in their State uniforms. On this day the honorary degrees were conferred, in Latin speeches of astounding and insupportable length. This is the great fault, on all occasions of the kind, in Germany. Whatever speaking there is, is sure to run into the abstract and prolix. Nothing is short, clear, practical, to the purpose: every fact stated represents a long chain of ideas and principles, which must be elucidated; and so true eloquence is the rarest of treats.

I had not the patience to sit in the church and hear the classical pumping, but prepared myself for the afternoon's work by a swim in the cold waters of Saale. This, being the last of the three days, was to be closed by a *Commers* (which is a beer-and-tobacco festival, mass meeting, student-initiation, and much more, all in one), on the grandest scale, at the expense of the city. A large space in the beautiful public meadow adjoining the town, called "The Paradise," was inclosed by a lofty hedge of woven fir boughs, in the centre of which stood a hall 300 feet long by 150 broad, with a roof of fir-thatch, resting on pillars muffled in oak leaves. There were seats at the narrow tables in this hall, and in the space around it, for nearly four thousand persons. The meadow was shaded by magnificent elm and linden trees, through the trunks of which gleamed the blue waters of the river.

At three o'clock a steady stream poured into the inclosure. A grand orchestra occupied a lofty balcony in the centre of the hall, opposite to which was a tribune for speakers. In less than an hour nearly every seat was filled, while a great number of curious "outsiders," ladies principally, moved up and down the avenues between. After the commencement of the ceremonies, they were necessarily excluded, but gradually gathered on the outside of the fir barricade, over the dark-green wall of which they formed a second hedge of beauty and of brilliant color. I had seated myself in a quiet spot, contented to remain a looker-on, but was suddenly seized upon by the daughter of Germany's greatest living poet, who begged my escort through the multitude. By this chance I was thrown into the company of several Thüringian friends, and agreeably installed at one of the tables of the Saxons, outside of the hall.

Presently shouts and music announced the arrival of the Grand Duke, Karl August II., whose duty it was, as *Rector magnificentissimus* of the University, to open the *Commers*. Accompanied by the hereditary prince, he mounted the tribune, made a few appropriate remarks, and drank prosperity to the institution in a huge glass of beer. A trumpet then gave the signal, and the first song, pealing simultaneously from three thousand voices, buried us in its magnificent surges. Enormous casks of beer—the gift of the city —rolled one after another into the inclosure, stopping at the headquarters of the various societies, where they were instantly placed upon tap. Pipes and cigars were lighted, and the *Commers* was soon in full blast.

At the head of each table sat a President, in the old German costume, with crossed swords before him. As the festival became more unrestrained and jolly, the strict arrangement of the societies was broken up; old friends sought each other, and groups were formed by mutual attraction. I found myself near the traveller, Zeigler, and opposite the younger Brockhaus; on one side of me was a Thüringian editor, on the other Dr. Alfred Brehm, whose ornithological studies had carried him to Abyssinia and the White Nile. To us came afterwards Fritz Reuter, a noted Low-German humorous poet, whose heavy round face and Saxon beard suggested Hans Sachs. A stream from the Thüringian cask flowed upon our board, and the fresh acquaintances, dipped into the brown flood, were as thoroughly seasoned in ten minutes as in months of ordinary intercourse. Flood after flood of the mighty sea of song overwhelmed us, but in the intervals we wandered over the world, and through the realms of Literature and Art. We clashed glasses with the publisher, and with some venerable professors who flanked him; Fritz Reuter plied us from the inexhaustible resources of his fun; and finally Brehm and I, exchanging recollections of Soudan, fell into Arabic, to the great edification of the others. I had not spoken the language for five years, and at first my tongue moved but awkwardly: then, as if the juice of German barley were an "open sesame!" to the oriental gutturals, the words came fast and free. The green turf under our feet became burning desert sand, and the lindens of the Saale were changed into tufted palms.

The sun sank, but it was not missed. A mellow glow of inner sunshine overspread the festival—the hearty, genuine merriment of four thousand hearts. And still the beer flowed, and still the glasses clashed like the meeting sabres of hostile armies, and the hedge of beautiful faces looked over the fir wall. As the stars began to twinkle, the white and red glare of pyrotechnic fires streamed over us; rockets burst into meteoric rain far above, and bonfires were lighted on all the hills. Then came the *Landsfather*, or "Consecration Song," with its solemn ceremonial of pierced hats, clashing swords, and vows of honor and fidelity. On account of the immense number present, it lasted nearly an hour, though the orchestra so timed the performance that at every one of the hundreds of tables the same stage of the consecration might be witnessed. A more impressive scene could scarcely be imagined.

Finally, the discharge of a cannon and the flight of a storm of rockets announced the termination of the jubilee, although the *Commers* was prolonged until after midnight. For two or three days afterwards, however, there were festivals of the societies in all the neighboring villages, and the three or four thousand guests who departed on the 18th were scarcely missed, so great was the crowd that remained. Before leaving, I again made the round of the city, in order to view the residences of the distinguished men who have, at different times, made their homes there. Every house where a great man had resided bore a shield, inscribed with his name and the date of his visit. The popularity of the University may be judged from the fact that there were nearly three hundred of these shields. I will give some of the most notable:

Arndt, 1794.	Melancthon, 1527–1535.
Blumenbach, 1770.	Musæus, 1754.
Eichhorn, 1775–1788.	Oken, 1805–1819.
Fichte, 1794–1799.	Puffendorf, 1656.
Charles Follen, 1818–1819.	Ruckert, 1811.
Goethe.	Schelling, 1798.
Hegel, 1801–1807.	Schiller, 1789-1799.
Wilhelm von Humboldt, 1797.	Schlegel, 1798-1802.
Alexander von Humboldt, 1797.	Schubert, 1801.
Klopstock, 1745.	Tieck, 1799.
Kotzebue, 1779–1781.	Voss, 1802-1805.
Leibnitz, 1662.	De Wette, 1805.
Martin Luther, 1522.	Winkelmann, 1741.

Count Zinzendorf, 1728.

On the following afternoon we bade adieu to Jena, footing it back over the uplands to Apolda. The garlands of oak leaves were a little withered, but the scarlet ash-berries still gleamed splendidly on the panels of the triumphal arches, and the multitude of banners waved as gaily as ever in the wind. The faces of the townspeople were bright and joyous, with no signs of lassitude and exhaustion; and we left them, not glad that the festival was over (as one usually is, after such an excitement), but regretting that we could not participate in it until the last song should be sung. From beginning to end, I did not hear one unfriendly word spoken, nor did I see one man completely intoxicated, although, of course, there were many who were flushed and gaily excited. It was, in the best sense of the word, a *jubilee*, and as such, the only one I ever beheld.

XXXV.

SOME ENGLISH CELEBRITIES.

During a visit to London in September, 1851, I spent ten days in the same house with Robert Owen, the great Socialist, whose recent death has recalled public attention to his life and labors. He was then nearly eighty years old, but as bright, gay, cheerful, and hopeful as a young man. Even then, after so many failures and disappointments, his confidence in the speedy success of his plans was unbounded. In fact, when you looked upon the mild, benevolent brow, the clear bluish-gray eye, and the persuasive mouth of the old man, it was difficult to call him away from his sunny theories to the hard, conflicting facts which arose in your mind. But he would not be called away: his hope overflowed everything, and your arguments lay buried a thousand fathoms deep under his gorgeous promises for the future. In this respect, he was almost a phenomenon.

"Why," he would exclaim, "you have only to let mankind know what the right plan of Government, the true organization of Society, is, and they cannot reject it. Let me have the control of the newspapers of Europe, for two years only, and all the despotisms will be peacefully overthrown, war will be made impossible, labor will be properly rewarded, and the suffering nations will be happy!" As I was connected with a newspaper, he at once commenced the great work, by sending me a large package of his pamphlets the next morning. It was rather embarrassing to me, thenceforth, to be asked every day at dinner: "Well, are you not now convinced? Is it not as clear as the sun?" when I had found no time to read the bulky documents.

Mr. Owen believed that he had made a great impression on Prince Metternich, from the extreme politeness with which that most courteous of statesmen had received him. I could easily fancy the cold, elegant, silver-voiced Prince saying: "Quite true: your arguments are indeed unanswerable," at every pause in his visitor's enthusiastic statement. The latter described to me his final interview. "I proposed," said he, "to establish the reign of Love, and Justice, and Humanity, and demonstrated how immensely every country must prosper under such a rule. 'At present,' said I, 'every Government in Europe is supported by two powers—Force and Fraud!' The Secretaries who were present at the interview turned suddenly from their desks and stared at me, astonished at what they considered my audacity. The Prince noticed this, and very quietly said: 'Do not be surprised, gentlemen: what Mr. Owen has stated is perfectly true.' Ah, what might he not have done, if he had acted according to his knowledge of the truth!"

A year later I was in London again, preparing for the overland journey to India. In the dull, drizzly October weather, the great capital was awaiting the funeral of Wellington, and my recollections of my visit are brightened only by three interesting interviews. The first of these was with Kossuth, who was living in a very quiet and unostentatious way in Kensington. I had been absent from America during his triumphal visit, from the fatigues of which he had not entirely recovered. His air was serious, if not sad, though he still spoke of Hungary with a desperate hope.

Mazzini, who, though proscribed and exiled, was the terror of Italian despots, was then residing in Chelsea, not far from Kossuth's residence. My friend, James Russell Lowell, had occasion to call upon him on some business of a purely literary nature, and I accompanied him. Entering the dark little brick house to which we had been directed, we were ushered into a narrow sitting-room, where we were presently visited by an Italian secretary. We were questioned rather closely as to our object, for it was known that there were secret spies, both of Naples and Austria, in London, and Mazzini's friends took all possible precautions to guard him against surprise. After waiting some time, we were visited by a second Italian, whose inspection was apparently satisfactory, for he informed us that Mazzini would receive us.

Finally, at the end of an hour the great Revolutionist—the ex-Triumvir of the last Roman republic—appeared. He was of medium height, slender, and about forty-five years of age. The character of his head presents a striking contrast to that of Kossuth. It is smaller, but the forehead is high, symmetrical, and nobly arched at the temples. His large black eyes burn with the light of an inextinguishable enthusiasm, and when he speaks, the rapid play of the muscles of his mouth expresses the intensity of his nature. His complexion is a pale olive, almost sallow, his hair black, thin, inclining to baldness, and his short beard and moustache slightly sprinkled with gray. He had a worn appearance, as if exhausted by incessant labor, yet spoke of the future of Italy with an enthusiasm and a faith which nothing could dampen. Though so far off, Rome, Naples, and Milan were then ripening for revolution, under the potency of his ardent brain. I could easily understand the magnetism by which he has drawn all the hopes of Italy to himself—it is this intense faith in his object.

If there ever should come a time when the true biography of Mazzini may be safely written and published, it will be one of the most wonderful books of the age. His adventures during the last ten years (judging simply by what little is hinted, not told), surpass those of Baron Trenck, La Tour, and the Chevalier d'Eon. There is scarcely a parallel to the splendid audacity with which he has visited Italy, again and again, with the whole detective force of Austria, both open and secret, lying in wait for him. It is sad that a life of such self-devotion should be slowly wasted away in disappointments.

I shall never forget the dark, rainy day, when I took the train to Reading on my way to visit Mary Russell Mitford.

More than one friendly message had the kind old lady sent to me on my wanderings; but, although we had thus exchanged greetings for years, I had never seen her. Now, however, on the eve of a long journey to China and Japan, knowing that she was feeble and not likely to live long, I could not leave without confirming my pleasant knowledge of her by a personal interview. She was then living in her cottage at Swallowfield, a little village six miles from Reading. In answer to my note of inquiry, she wrote: "I do not apologize for asking you, who have lodged in the huts and tents of all the tribes of the earth, to visit an invalid, in her simple hermitage. I shall look for you, and there will be another plate at my little table."

On reaching the red, stiff, stately town of Reading—which Miss Mitford describes, under the name of "Belford Regis," in "Our Village,"—the rain descended in torrents. There was one forlorn hack at the railway station, and the driver hesitated a little when I mentioned Swallowfield. He looked at me a moment, and named a plumping fare. As I did not flinch, but placed my hand on the cab-door, he shook his capes, jammed his hat down on his brows, mounted the box, and off we went. Through the floods which streamed down the panes, I obtained but a blurred and unsatisfactory view of the scenery. There were thorn hedges, still green, on either side of the road; the yellow leaves of the elms and the dead foliage of oaks fell in blinding showers, and gray hills rose or sank against the blank gray sky.

In an hour I saw that we had entered a little village, the houses standing apart from each other, and well embowered in trees. Presently the cab stopped at a triangular garden-plot, in front of a tall old two-story house of brick. Before I had alighted, a serious old man-servant appeared, coming down the gravel walk with an umbrella. I sent my conveyance to the village inn, and under the guidance of "Sam," Miss Mitford's faithful servitor, was soon ushered into her comfortable parlor-library. Almost at the same moment, she entered through another door, stretching out one hand in welcome, while the other held a cane which supported her slow and tottering steps.

I think I should have recognised her anywhere. The short, plump body, the round, cheerful old face, with cheeks still as rosy as a girl's, the kindly blue eyes, the broad, placid brow, and bands of silver hair peeping from beneath the quaint frilled cap, seemed to be all features of the picture which I had previously drawn in my mind. But for a gay touch in the ribbons, and the absence of the book-muslin handkerchief over the bosom, she might have been taken for one of those dear old Quaker ladies, whose presence, in its cheerful serenity, is an atmosphere of contentment and peace. Her voice was sweet, round, and racy, with a delicious archness at times. Sitting in deep arm-chairs, on opposite sides of the warm grate, while the rain lashed the panes and the autumn leaves drifted outside, we passed the afternoon in genial talk. Charles Kingsley had left but half an hour before my arrival. He had brought with him some pages of his poem of "Andromeda," the character of which Miss Mitford described to me, although she could not repeat the lines.

Her talk was rich with reminiscences of the great authors

of the past generation. Walter Scott, Hannah More, the Porters, Miss Edgeworth, Charles Lamb, Hazlitt, and Coleridge she had known; but her literary sympathies were of the most catholic kind, and she spoke with a glowing appreciation of the younger race of authors. For Mrs. Browning, especially, she entertained a warm personal as well as intellectual attachment. Towards evening, Sam announced dinner, and we sat down to the neat little table, on which stood a venison pie that needed no apology. While we were thus engaged, the Dowager Lady Russell, Miss Mitford's neighbor and friend, arrived, accompanied by her younger son. It was pleasant to see the cordial affection with which they regarded her. Presently arose a lively debate concerning Louis Napoleon, whom Miss Mitford admired, while young Mr. Russell (like most Englishmen at that time) disliked and distrusted him. The latter told a bit of gossip, however, at which his good-tempered opponent was obliged to laugh heartily. "Have you not heard," said he, "what Mrs. ——, who knew Louis Napoleon well, as a refugee in England, said to him in Paris the other day? She was at the ball at the Hotel de Ville, and, desiring to renew her acquaintance, placed herself several times in his way. Noticing that he saw, but avoided her, she at last took a position where he would be obliged to recognise her. 'Ah, Madame ——,' said he, suddenly, '*depuis quand êtes-vous à Paris?*' '*Depuis quinze jours*,' she quietly answered,—'*et vous?*'"

But the twilight now began to fall, and it was necessary that I should hasten back to Reading, in order to catch the evening train. Sam ordered the cab from the village tavern, I took once more the old lady's hand, and bade her an eternal farewell. She lived three years more, and we still corresponded, even when voice and motion failed, and she lay for months propped in an easy chair, with life only in her brain and heart, power only in eyes and hands. Thus was her last letter to me written, but a few days before her death—a letter sublime in the spirit of peace, and tenderness, and resignation, with which she takes leave of the world.

I had twice called upon Barry Cornwall with letters of introduction, and as often been disappointed, owing to his absence from London, in former years. In July, 1856, however, I was agreeably surprised by a cordial note from him, inviting me to breakfast on the following day. The poet is a small man, with a slight, yet well-proportioned frame, and a head, which at first sight reminds one of the portraits of Sir Walter Scott, although you afterwards see that it is much more softly and delicately modelled. His hair is gray (he must be at least sixty-five years old, having been a schoolfellow of Byron and Sir Robert Peel, at Harrow), and his face rather pale from illness, but his cheeks are smooth and unwrinkled, his eyes are clear, soft gray, and his mouth and dimpled chin expressive of great sweetness and gentleness. Honeyed rhymes, you could well believe, would drop naturally from those lips. With him I found his wife, a daughter of Basil Montague, and their three daughters, of whom Adelaide, the eldest, has since proved her claim to inherit her father's mantle by a volume of lyrics. To them entered (as the play-books say) Robert Browning, and the breakfast party was complete.

I had met both Browning and his wife five years before, in the company of John Kenyon ("Kenyon the Magnificent," Browning called him), when they first returned to England after four years in Italy. The hearty, genial, impulsive, un-English character of the poet (much like what we fancy Shelley to have been) made a strong impression upon me. He overruns with a boyish life and vivacity, darting out continual flashes of wit and imagination, like the pranks of heat lightning in a summer cloud; while his wife, with her thin, pale face, half hidden by heavy brown ringlets, shines between, with the mildness and steadiness of moonlight. They form almost the only instance I know of poets happily mated—both great, yet each respecting the other's individuality, each proud of the other's fame.

On this occasion Browning was in a very lively mood. He entertained us at breakfast with quotations from a dream the previous night, in which he had rewritten Richard the Third. The tent-scene, in particular, was one of the maddest mixtures of Shaksperean poetry and modern slang that could be imagined. Mrs. Proctor is a brilliant talker, and Barry Cornwall, though exceedingly quiet and unobtrusive in his manner, now and then dropped a remark, the quaint humor of which reminded me of Charles Lamb. After breakfast I spent a delightful hour in his library. From a drawer under his writing-desk he produced two or three small books, bound in leather, which contained the original drafts of most of his songs. Among others he showed me "The Sea," "The Stormy Petrel," and "Touch us gently, Time." I was interested to hear that many of his finest lyrics and songs were composed mentally, while riding daily to the City in an omnibus.

I had so long known the greatest of living English poets —Alfred Tennyson—not only through his works but from the talk of mutual friends, that I gladly embraced an opportunity to know him personally, which happened to me in June, 1857. He was then living at his home—the estate of Farringford, near Freshwater, on the Isle of Wight. I should have hesitated to intrude upon his retirement, had I not been kindly assured beforehand that my visit would not be unwelcome. The drive across the heart of the island, from Newport to Freshwater, was alone worth the journey from London. The softly undulating hills, the deep green valleys, the blue waters of the Solent, and the purple glimpses of the New Forest beyond, formed a fit vestibule of landscape through which to approach a poet's home.

As we drew near Freshwater, my coachman pointed out Farringford—a cheerful gray country mansion, with a small, thick-grassed park before it, a grove behind, and beyond all, the steep shoulder of the chalk downs, a gap in which, at Freshwater, showed the dark-blue horizon of the Channel. Leaving my luggage at one of the two little inns, I walked to the house, with lines from Maud chiming in my mind. The "dry-tongued laurel" shone glossily in the sun; the cedar "sighed for Lebanon" on the lawn, and the "liquid azure bloom of a crescent of sea" glimmered afar. I had not been two minutes in the drawing-room before Tennyson walked in. So unlike are the published portraits of him that I was almost in doubt as to his identity. The engraved head suggests a moderate stature, but he is tall and broad-shouldered as a son of Anak, with hair, beard, and eyes, of southern darkness. Something in the lofty brow and aquiline nose suggests Dante, but such a deep, mellow chest-voice never could have come from Italian lungs.

He proposed a walk, as the day was wonderfully clear and beautiful. We climbed the steep comb of the chalk cliff, and slowly wandered westward until we reached the Needles, at the extremity of the island, and some three or four miles distant from his residence. During the conversation with which we beguiled the way, I was struck with the variety of his knowledge. Not a little flower on the downs, which the sheep had spared, escaped his notice, and the geology of the coast, both terrestrial and submarine, was perfectly familiar to him. I thought of a remark which I had once heard from the lips of a distinguished English author, that Tennyson was the wisest man he ever knew, and could well believe that he was sincere in making it.

I shall respect the sanctity of the delightful family circle, to which I was admitted, and from which I parted, the next afternoon, with true regret. Suffice it to say, that the poet is not only fortunate and happy in his family relations, but that, with his large and liberal nature, his sympathies for what is true and noble in humanity, and his depth and tenderness of feeling, he deserves to be so.

XXXVI.

SCENES AT A TARGET-SHOOTING.

[AUGUST, 1858.]

NEXT to the *Kirmse*, or autumnal festival of the German peasants, which I have described elsewhere, comes the annual shooting-match. This is called the *Vogelschiessen*, or bird-shooting, because the target is always the crowned, double-headed eagle of the German Empire. The festival, which usually lasts a week, is commonly held in August. In the Saxon principalities of Middle Germany it has almost an official and national character, the rulers, ministers, and nobility participating in it as well as the burghers and peasantry. In the court towns, where it lasts an entire week, it is accompanied by circuses and shows of every kind, and therefore furnishes an excellent picture of the popular amusements of the country.

At Gotha there is a special target-ground, kept for the occasion, on the flat summit of a hill which touches the town on the northwestern side. Here there is a spacious dancing-hall, and a large shooting-house, the front part of which is fitted up as a restaurant, while the rear contains a gallery with open boxes for the marksmen. Back of this extends an alley, about eighty yards in length, at the extremity of which is planted a mast, fifty feet high, bearing the double-headed eagle upon its top. The bird is cut out of a thin plank of tough wood, and measures four or five feet from tip to tip. The various parts of the figure have different values, according to which the merits of the marksmen are determined. Thus, he who shoots away a crown takes the first prize; the shield on the breast ranks next, and the feet and wings last. A Kentucky rifleman would be far from considering this a just standard. The shooting is governed by a long list of rules and regulations, any violation of which expels the competitor.

I did not attend the festival until the second day, when all the shows were in full operation, and the crowd of visitors greatest. The large open space in front of the dancing-hall was covered with regular streets of booths, as at a fair, and it was no easy matter to force a way through the crowd of citizens and peasants in holiday dress, who had flocked in from all parts of the country, far and near. On the right stood the tent of a circus company; on the left a *carrousel*, or race-course of hobby horses. Then followed exhibitions of strange animals, human monstrosities, panoramic views, and marionettes, with a pleasant alternation of beer-booths, shops for the sale of poppy-seed and onion cakes, roasted sausages, pretzels, punch, and ices.

Beyond the dancing-hall rose a crescent-shaped terrace, shaded with tall linden trees, and literally covered with tables and benches, at which hundreds were enjoying their coffee and ices, while a band played waltzes and overtures from the balcony of the shooting-house. Scattered about through the crowd, each surrounded by a ring of admiring children and amused peasants, were ballad-singers, dancing monkeys, fortune-tellers, and venders of "Tragic Occurrences." The combination of gay colors, odd costumes, and picturesque forms, surging through broad belts of light and shade, in a sea of noisy merriment, made a picture that would have delighted Wilkie or Ostade.

In the shooting-house, there was not much going on. There were but few competitors present, and they fired with a lazy, nonchalant air, discussing gunnery and beer between the shots. The bird was pretty well riddled, but had lost neither crown nor shield, although the feet and a part of one wing were gone. On the following afternoon, however, the crown was shot away by the president of a target society from one of the neighboring towns. The lucky marksman not only received the first prize of a silver cup, but was immediately saluted as King of the Festival, adorned with the ancient golden collar always used on the occasion, and led in triumphant procession around the grounds. He was a stout, phlegmatic man of middle age, and blushed up to the roots of his blond hair, as he passed through the shouting crowd, followed by the other competitors, walking two and two. The distinction brings with it also the obligations of making a speech, and of presiding at the banquet which followed, so that the embarrassment is fully equal to the honor. Two years before, the Duke himself bore away the first prize.

The ball in the evening was made select by a charge of one thaler (71 cents) for admission, and the prescription of a black dress, with white kid gloves. Therefore it was like any starched and respectable ball anywhere else in the world, and I had no curiosity to witness it. All such rigid recreation is an inevitable bore, except to very pretty young ladies, whose means allow them to dress handsomely, and to shallow-headed young gentlemen, expert at the polka and in the parting of their back-hair. A military drill, or a dance of naked savages by torchlight, is a much more diverting spectacle. If my reader prefers, with me, the grotesque, the curious, and the comic, to the stupid and the proper, we will leave the genteel society to simper and dance in the banquet-hall, and accompany the peasants to their penny-shows.

As we pass around the corner of the building, we are attracted by a series of remarkable paintings hung against the wall. They are illustrations of terrible murders and robberies, the full narratives of which you may buy for a cent apiece. Let us look at the titles, which sufficiently illustrate the character of these fictions—for fictitious they assuredly are. Here is a "Terrific and Fearful Occurrence, which took place at Cologne in the year 1856, and the Culprit was Executed on the 6th of August, 1857." Lest, however, you should sup exclusively on horrors, here is a more cheerful, though still fascinating title: "The Miraculous Rescue of a Child, and Description of a Terrible Band of Robbers in the Mountains of Naples," followed by

"Maria Carleton, the French Princess, spouse of six Husbands, and leader of Banditti, executed in London, in 1851." Also, "Freja, the Orphan of Silistria, who was Killed in Battle and Promoted to the rank of Captain, including Who her Parents Were." The style of these productions, it is scarcely necessary to say, is very childish and silly. After a murder, generally follow the exclamations: "Oh, what a horrid deed!" "Alas, alas! how terrible!" and to the end of each narrative is attached a poem, describing the tragedy and embodying its moral lesson, so that the reader, who has made himself familiar with the circumstances, may adapt the verses to some favorite melody, and sing them for the edification of his friends.

The Censorship of the Press, which at one time was very rigid in Germany, never prohibited these blood-streaming publications, the Government, no doubt, recognising the fact that men would much sooner give up the discussion of abstract principles of Right and Wrong, than the privilege of feasting their curiosity on the records of crime. This desire seems to be a normal trait of human nature. Among our weaknesses is a craving for the sensation of horror, while our self-love is flattered by the comparison which we naturally institute between the criminal and ourselves. Conscience, which at best has a long account scored against us, suggests that there are still worse men than we are in the world: our own vices diminish in importance as we compare them with some colossal crime. Nobody would take a newspaper, if it did not contain the police reports. We cannot, therefore, wonder at the uncultivated taste which creates a demand for such disgusting trash—for, if the style were classic and the story well told, we should purchase a copy ourselves. The yellow-covered literature of the United States is one step above these rough penny pamphlets, because the mental calibre of the class who read them is somewhat greater than that of the same class in Germany. After much observation and reflection, I am inclined to doubt whether any serious harm can be ascribed to such productions. The mere habit of reading imperceptibly improves the taste of the reader, and a man who can swallow the blood-and-thunder of George Lippard to-day, will relish Dickens ten years hence.

Leaving the literary department behind us, we pass on to the booths. Presently we are attracted by a flaming sign: "Here is to be seen the wild African Man of the Forests, the Only Specimen in Existence." The entrance fee amounts to ten cents, and the unusual expense makes us hesitate; but we have five eager boys in our charge, and their longing glances soon decide us. Entering a tent, every avenue into which is carefully screened from the multitude, we behold a small black chimpanzee, seated upon a table, while his proprietor is thus expatiating to a small but select audience: "A most extraordinary animal, your lordships! I bought him from the captain of a vessel, direct from Africa. The English government offered £200 for him afterwards. You see, he is exactly like a human being; the only difference in fact is his language. These animals live in the unknown regions in the centre of Africa. They build themselves houses and live in villages, just like men. The negro tribes catch and make slaves of them, employing them to cultivate their rice-fields. It is necessary, however, to have an overseer, as they will not work if left alone. They cannot live in Europe, on account of the severity of the climate, but as this one is very young, I have succeeded, with great difficulty, in preserving his life."

It was a poor old beast, less than three feet high, and with a beard gray with age. He surveyed us with an unhappy look, peeling and sucking an orange meanwhile. "You are mistaken," said I to the keeper, "in supposing that this animal comes from Africa." "Pardon me, sir," said he, "this is the genuine African man of the forests." "But I have travelled in the interior of Africa," I answered; "you only find this variety in Java and Sumatra, where I have seen them." I thereupon overwhelmed him with information (most unwelcome) concerning the animal. The next day, when I came again with a fresh company of children, he was in the middle of his accustomed speech; but seeing me, stopped very abruptly, while he threw towards me a helpless, imploring glance, as much as to say, "Please don't stay long—your presence is very embarrassing."

Near this tent stood another, with the sign—"The Great Sea-Lion of the Polar Regions." The price of admission was three cents, and the animal, as I supposed, was an ordinary seal, named "Jacob," which looked at us appealingly out of its beautiful human eyes. It was not a very profitable monster, requiring a tank of water, and refusing to appear when called for. The Giant and the Dwarf, who had a booth in common, did a much better business. The former was stupid, as all giants are, and the latter malicious, as are most dwarfs. It was pleasant, however, to see the latter standing with both feet in the empty shoe of the former.

The fortune-tellers were not very well patronized, probably because the printed oracular slips, which they furnished for two cents, were already familiar to most of the crowd. To me, however, they were new. By two judicious investments I ascertained not only my own character, but that of my destined wife. I learned, to my surprise, that I had a secret enemy, who was working hard for my ruin, but was cheered to find that I should in the end triumph over him. I had also many friends, but I must not trust everybody. I should have bad luck a while, then good, then bad again, and in the end all would be fortunate. The latter part of my life—which, if it did not terminate sooner, would extend to a great age—would be illuminated by all kinds of gorgeous pyrotechnics. Having learned thus much, I must needs behold the face of the partner of my destiny. The oracle looked at me—noticed probably that hair and eyes were dark—turned a wheel, and directed me to place my eye to a large lens in the side of a box. I beheld a blue-eyed and blond-haired lady, properly flounced and crinolined, with a bonnet like an oyster-shell behind her ears. She resembled one of the fashion-figures in Godey's Lady's Book, and of course I was happy. My companion, whose complexion was very light, was introduced to a lady with dark eyes and hair.

The sound of a shrill voice singing, "Oh, but I am weary; oh, but I am fatigued!" attracted our attention.

A large raw-boned woman, accompanied by her son, were the minstrels. They stood in the midst of a group of peasants, some of whom had purchased slips containing the words of the song, and were attentively following the melody in order to catch and sing it themselves afterwards. This is their usual method of learning new songs and ballads, and where these are of a popular character, the wandering music-teachers are rewarded with a good stock of *groschen.* Here, however, the difference in taste between the uncultivated classes of Germany and America is much to the credit of the former. Their songs were, for the most part, of a more refined and sentimental order than those which adorn the Park railing in New York. The fun is never so coarse as in "Bobbing Around" or "Villikins and his Dinah," nor the sentiment quite so silly as in "Marble Halls" and "Barbara Allen." Here is one which, from the crowd of lusty young peasants who followed the raw-bcned minstrel, to catch the air, must have been a great favorite:

Thou hast diamonds, and pearls, and jewels,
  Hast all the heart wishes, in store;
And ah, thou hast eyes so lovely—
  My darling, what wouldst thou have more?

And upon thine eyes so lovely,
  That pierce my heart to its core,
Uncounted songs have I written—
  My darling, what wouldst thou have more?

Alas, with thine eyes so lovely,
  Thou hast tortured and wounded me sore;
Thine eyes have compassed my ruin—
  My darling, what wouldst thou have more?

And, because of thine eyes so tender,
Have I ventured more and more,
And so much, ah, so much have I suffered—
My darling, what wouldst thou have more?

There are also booths containing panoramic and stereoscopic views, which I noticed were visited by great numbers of the poorer people. The marionette theatres and the perambulating Punch-and-Judy shows were remarkably popular, and the swings and flying horses never ceased their rounds. *Bauer* from the northern country, with their short-waisted coats, long jackets, and knee-breeches, crowded around the stalls where onion-cakes, hissing hot from the pan, were displayed on the greasy board, and then moved off beerward, to give room to the women, in their high fantastic caps, glittering with golden pins and brooches, and with manifold streamers of silk dangling from the summit. In envious contrast to these were the maidens from some western villages, with hair combed *à la Chinoise* to the top of the head, where it was covered by a small, cup-shaped piece of embroidered cloth. The petticoats of these damsels reached barely to the knee, but they made up in diameter what they lacked in length. They were hardy, healthy creatures, with arms like a butcher's, calves like a mountaineer's, nut-brown cheeks, and teeth which could bite off a tenpenny nail.

At night, when the laborers took their holiday, the multitude presented a still more picturesque appearance, in the flaring light of lamps and torches. Then the music was redoubled; the great hall shook under the measured stroke of the dancers' feet, and little circles of waltzers were formed on level spaces under the trees. The fountains of beer flowed from exhaustless reservoirs; the onion-cakes steamed with more enticing fragrance; the new songs spread from mouth to mouth among the young people, while the cackle of gossip ran around the circle of the aged. Until ten o'clock, it was a picture of the merriest, loudest life; then the circles began to break up, and the throng slowly drifted back to town. The *Vogelschiessen* is the delight of the peasant who is so fortunate as to have his week of holiday, and ten thalers in his pocket. When the festival is over his thalers are gone and his stomach is deranged; but he has had a jolly good time of it, and his sour season of labor is sweetened by the recollection of the sights he has seen, the beer he has drunk, the music he has heard, the dances he has danced, and (why not?) the kisses he has stolen from his sweetheart.

XXXVII.

ASPECTS OF GERMAN SOCIETY.

FROM a cursory view, there would appear to be little difference in the outward form and mould of Society, in all civilized countries, at the present time. So great is the amount of intercourse between the different nationalities, that a uniform set of conventional observances now passes current everywhere. The same ordinary forms of courtesy flourish in the latitude of New York and St. Petersburg, Stockholm and Madrid.

It is, therefore, only in the more intimate circles of private and domestic life, that we still find the peculiar traits existing, which distinguish one people from another—traits which will no doubt be gradually effaced under that tremendous levelling system, which has already swept away the distinctions of costume and of address. These characteristic aspects of Society are most interesting among the German and Scandinavian races, on account of their marked domesticity, and the affectionate pertinacity with which they cling to customs and observances which have been hallowed by Time. Their languages possess the word "Home"—a word unknown to the Frenchman and the Italian.

Perhaps the first peculiarity which strikes the traveller on entering Germany—and which, unless he be a fool, impresses him most agreeably—is the frank and unrestrained character of public intercourse. It would be impossible to leave four Germans, strangers to each other, alone for half an hour, without their becoming tolerably well acquainted. The Englishman, when abroad, avoids his kind, unless, indeed, he be a nobleman of good sense, who runs no risk of compromising his social position; the German seeks his countryman, by natural affinity. In this respect, the American is a cross between the two. Yet it is as rare a thing to make a new acquaintance in a railroad car, here, as it is common in any of the German States. Then the new arrival courteously salutes the other passengers on entering; the departing traveller does the same thing. Time is considered lost if devoted to silence, when it might be agreeably spent in conversation, and all who have purchased tickets of the same class consider each other as equals for the time being. Almost the only examples of reserve which you meet with are the military gentlemen, whose assumed importance is the more insufferable, because it is generally based neither upon wealth, character, nor intellect.

This pleasant trait is not confined to the masculine sex. Ladies, also, enter into conversation with a cheerfulness and cordiality which illustrates alike their good sense and their inherent courtesy. I travelled two days in a diligence in company with an Austrian Baroness and her daughters, and on parting received a most friendly invitation to visit the family. On another occasion, I met with a very intelligent lady in the depot at Munich, and on reaching Augsburg, where she resided, was introduced by her to her husband—a physician of repute—and cordially invited by both to spend a day with them. In these cases, the ladies knew nothing about me except what they had learned during our brief intercourse. Even in England, I think, such a thing would sooner be possible than with us.

Gallantry towards ladies is a fine manly characteristic, and we Americans have none too much of it. But have we not a right to ask of our ladies *courtesy towards gentlemen?* There is no man worthy of the name but would feel that there was a delicate flattery in the fact of a lady addressing herself to him for information, during a journey in which they were chance neighbors; and there is no man but would be conscious of a sense of insult if his respectful attempt to while away the tedium of travel by conversation, were repulsed. It is the risk of such repulse, not only between travellers of different sexes, but even those of the same sex, which makes our railroad society so grim and depressing. When a lady has not sufficient consideration to thank you for a seat, you may be sure she has no desire to converse with you. If she happens to know who you are, and is sure of your respectability, you may be successful; otherwise, there is something in her mannner, which says: "Bless me! what does he mean! an entire stranger —I never heard of such a thing! what would people say?"

Here, again, is another difference. When strangers meet,

enjoying the hospitality of a mutual acquaintance, there is a tacit social recognition, which dispenses with the formality of an introduction. Any hesitation is justly con sidered as an offence against the host, implying that he would ask persons to meet you whom it was not proper that you should know. The same custom prevails in England, and is there carried to such an extent that you are frequently embarrassed by receiving invitations from persons whom you may know by sight, but not by name. But the absence of all reserve in such cases—the frank freedom of social intercourse—is a mark of true refinement. All politeness which is not founded on common sense has but fictitious value.

There is, however, one element of courtesy in which the Germans are deficient. Being a people of abstract ideas, and much given to that species of theorizing which breeds intellectual egotism, they lack a proper consideration for the ideas and opinions of others. Hence, a mixed conversation very often assumes the character of an argumentative combat. I have frequently heard facts denied, because they conflicted with some pet theory. As an American and a republican, I was constantly liable to be assailed by those who advocated the monarchical system—not in the way of courteous inquiry, but direct attack. In Art, Literature, and Science, it is the same thing. The Germans have adopted the idea that the great characteristic of the American people is *Materialism*—because this forms a convenient antithesis to the German trait of Idealism—and all the facts one may adduce to prove its falsity go for nothing. So with their ideas concerning European politics. They are based upon abstract doctrines—theories of race, of "national elements"—which every year sees scattered to the winds, but, nevertheless, they put the fragments together again, and look upon the structure with the same unshaken complacency as before. This intellectual egotism is at first offensive to a stranger, and one never becomes entirely reconciled to it. The same characteristic may be observed among the various classes of ultra-reformers in the United States.

The Teutonic heart cannot beat without expression. The emotions are never subjected to that self-restraint which our Anglo-Saxon pride forces upon us. Tears are shed, and lips kissed, and sacred words spoken, if not in public, at least not in secret. No man is ashamed to let the world see that he loves or grieves. We shrink from such an exhibition because the sanctity of passion is profaned by the presence of curious eyes and unfeeling hearts, but among a people whose sympathies are sensitive there is no restraint. Even in the advertising columns of the newspapers, side by side with announcements of groceries and dry goods, you may read the words of hope, and joy, and lamentation. Let me give a few illustrations. The first act in the universal drama of human life is thus exhibited:

"Our betrothal, which took place yesterday, we hereby joyfully make known to all relatives and friends.

"KARL SCHUMANN,
"ANNA STIEFEL."

A year afterwards, if the course of true love runs

smooth—which, I must admit, it seems to do more frequently than among us—you may read the following:

"Our conjugal union, which was yesterday consummated, we hereby announce to all relatives and friends.

"KARL SCHUMANN,
"ANNA SCHUMANN,
née Stiefel."

During the three or four following days, the emotional column of advertisements is filled with congratulations, a few only of which need be given. There is usually a great similarity of style, although sometimes congratulatory poems appear. Here are two specimens:

"We hereby offer our heartiest good wishes to our relative, Karl Schumann, on the occasion of his recent marriage. May he and his beloved wife live long and happily together!

"THE GLANZLEDER FAMILY."

"The marriage of our friends, Karl Schumann and Anna Stiefel, on Wednesday, was joyfully celebrated here the same evening, when our glasses were emptied to the prosperity of the dear couple. All united in a loud and glad hurrah! (*hoch!*)"

In another year (be the same more or less), the second act is chronicled in like manner. What would those exquisitely prudish persons, who object to the publication of births, say to this:

"The fortunate delivery of my beloved wife, Anna Schumann, *née* Stiefel, of a sound and healthy boy, yesterday evening, at fifteen minutes before six, I hereby joyfully announce to all relatives and friends.

"KARL SCHUMANN."

More congratulations follow the happy event. The christening, however, which usually takes place in six weeks, is only announced in the official register. Most children receive from three to six names, only one of which is used, except in signing legal documents. Supposing the Schumanns to be prolific and long-lived, we must wait fifty years for the final advertisement, which then appears in the following form:

"The gentle departure, after long and patiently endured sufferings, of our beloved husband, father, grandfather, brother, father-in-law, cousin, and brother-in-law, Karl Schumann, yesterday afternoon at 3 o'clock, at the age of seventy-five years, two months, and nine days, we hereby sorrowfully announce to all relatives and friends, and beg for their silent sympathy with us.

"The Mourners, who are left Behind."

One good result of this publicity, at least, is the absence of gossip. Nevertheless, it is repulsive to us, who have been educated in different ideas. I confess, I read such advertisements habitually for the purpose of amusement, rather than "silent sympathy." An undemonstrative Englishman is sure to be considered phlegmatic, if not cold-hearted, in Germany. Whatever feeling is not expressed is not supposed to exist. *We* err in the opposite extreme, of concealing much honest and noble affection. How often have I heard sincere manly friendship made a taunt, and suspected love a subject for unmerciful badinage!

But Society in Germany has also its tyrannical aspects. The intercourse between the unmarried is most rigidly restricted; the interchange of visits is as punctiliously regulated as in any other part of the world; and the distinction between the various social degrees is still shown in many ways. Customs and forms of address which ought to be classed among the obsolete absurdities of the Past, keep their place. The stranger, in a new neighborhood, is obliged to make the first calls—a custom which seems the reverse of hospitable, although they excuse it by saying that they wish to leave the new-comer free to select his society.

The betrothed must make a formal round of visits to all their relatives; the newly-married ditto; the mother, after confinement, must make her first public appearance in church, and the corpses are followed to the grave only by males. In Weimar, Altenburg, and other remote parts of the country, the superanuated laws of this sort are numberless. Nowhere can a young lady walk with a gentleman, unless she is betrothed to him, but after that event all restrictions are removed. She is called a "bride," her lover a "bridegroom," and each is at once considered as a member of the other's family.

The forms of address are exceedingly awkward and inconvenient. Every person who has any official position, must be addressed by a corresponding title, and (good news to the strong-minded!) his wife takes the same, with a feminine termination. Thus, if Herr Schmidt happens to be a Counsellor of the Superior Court of Appeals, it is a violation of etiquette to call him Herr Schmidt. You must say: "Herr Counsellor of the Superior Court of Appeals, how is the Frau Counselloress of the Superior Court of Appeals?" Even the Master-Shoemaker, Herr Duntz, is addressed in the same way, and his wife would be mortified if you did not greet her as "Mrs. Master-Shoemakeress Duntz." Could anything be more comical than to hear: "Mrs. Inspectoress of Penitentiaries, let me introduce you to Miss Fire-Insurance Company's Presidentess?"—and yet this may happen any day in Germany. As the husband climbs upwards on the official ladder, his wife climbs with him. She shares his ambition and his triumphs, and rejoices to be called "Madame Field-Marshaless" or "Madame Prime Ministress;" almost as much as if herself had won the star or baton.

A most delightful feature of German life is the conscientiousness with which domestic anniversaries are observed and celebrated. No birth-day passes by unremembered: gifts, even if trifling, flowers, and the favorite dishes at dinner remind each one, in his turn, that his place in the world is still warm. The married celebrate their wedding-day, and Christmas and Pentecost come to all. I am glad that we are gradually naturalizing the former festival, and would willingly see all the others transplanted into our soil, although, when such customs become universal and inevitable, they lose something of that spontaneity which is their greatest charm. *Our* life, on the other hand, is too barren; we press continually forward, on a hard, hot, stony road, neglecting every tree that invites us to rest awhile by the wayside. The Germans are much better economists than we. Recreation and domestic enjoyment are always included in the estimate of expenses, and the business of the household is managed in so careful and systematic a manner, that a family with one thousand dollars a year manages to extract much more enjoyment from existence, than most American families whose incomes are triple that sum.

I have heard travellers speak of the bad manners of the Germans; of their heterogeneous meals; of their heaviness and awkwardness; and of their uncomfortable mode of life. Such persons generally belong to that class whose standard of judgment is: "*I* don't do so and so: therefore, the people are wrong." One of them, whom I pressed closely to give me some instances of bad manners, finally stated that he had seen Germans eating fish with knives and drinking Champagne out of Madeira glasses! The little details of the table vary in different countries, and in different generations. Sir Philip Sydney drank beer for his breakfast, and Queen Elizabeth picked her teeth with her fork. Refinement (by which I mean what is snobbishly termed "gentility") does not consist in such small matters. He was a gentleman who died at Zutphen, even though he had never used a pocket-handkerchief. An American woman, travelling in Germany, *minus* the language, has recently published a volume entitled "Peasant Life in Germany," which is filled with the grossest blunders. She measures everything she sees by an American standard, as if that were the only admitted test of excellence.

There is this lesson to be derived from an intimate acquaintance with other lands and other races—that *no country possesses the best.* The advantages and disadvantages of life are distributed more impartially than one would suppose. It would be very difficult for an American to endure the annoyances of living under European laws, but he could scarcely fail to enjoy the order and security prevailing under a long-established Government, and the freedom of a matured and settled Society. With complete political independence, we must still endure a *social* tyranny. The opinion of the community in which we live, with regard to our own opinions, actions, and habits of life, is the Autocrat that rules us. Where this public opinion is enlightened, liberal, and generous, very well; no home in the world can be more fortunate. But where it is narrow and uncharitable, resist it and you will become a social martyr.

XXXVIII.

A TRUE STORY.

On the 15th of October, 1856, a celebration of a peculiar character was held in a small village near Jena. It was an occasion of an entirely local nature, and might have passed over unobserved, and unknown to all, except the immediate vicinity, but for its connexion with the battle which, fifty years and one day before, annihilated the power of Prussia. An account of it, however, was published in most of the German newspapers, and through this circumstance the sequel of the story which I am about to relate, was brought on. At the time the celebration took place, I was residing in Gotha, not more than fifty miles from the spot, and received the story almost in the very words of the chief actor in it. I am sorry that his name, and that of the village, have escaped my memory. All other particulars made too deep an impression upon my mind to be easily forgotten.

We must first go back to the 14th of October, 1806. On that day the windy uplands north-east of Jena witnessed the brief but terrible combat, which resulted in the triumphant entry of the French army into Berlin, eleven days afterwards, during which time Prussia had lost 60,000 men, 65 standards, and 600 cannon. A portion of the French army was encamped on the battlefield, or quartered in the villages around. The poor inhabitants, overwhelmed by this sudden avalanche of war upon their quiet fields, where, for a hundred years or more, they had reaped their harvests in peace, submitted in helpless apathy while their houses and barns were plundered by the lawless soldiery. The battle was over, but there was no lull in the blast of ruin. Through the clouds of cannon-smoke which settled into the bosoms of the deep valleys, as the raw October evening came on, were heard in all directions shrieks of fear, yells of rage or triumph, and cries of pain or lamentation.

Davoust, the "Butcher of Hamburg" (as the Germans call him), took up his quarters for the night in one of the most convenient and comfortable houses which could be found in the neighborhood of the scene of slaughter. Here he rapidly issued orders for the disposition of the forces under his command, gave directions for the morrow, and received reports from his adjutants. He had taken his cloak, and was about retiring to an inner chamber for repose, when an officer entered. "Pardon me, General," he said, "but here is a case which requires attention. This German *canaille* must be taught to respect us. Ten soldiers of Company ———, of the Fourth Infantry, who quartered themselves in the village of Waldorf [let us say] have been driven away by the people, and two or three of them are severely injured."

Davoust's cold eye glittered, and his moustache curled like the lip of a mastiff, as he turned, halting a moment at the door of the bed-room. "Send a lieutenant and twenty men to the village, pick out any ten of the vagabonds and shoot them down!" was his brief order. "Where is Waldorf?" he added, turning towards one of those useful creatures who are always willing to act as guides and interpreters for the enemy in their own land.

"There is a village called Upper Waldorf, which lies near the head of a small valley, to the left. Middle Waldorf is on the other side of the hill, and Lower Waldorf about half an hour's distance beyond."

The Marshal, not caring to annoy himself by more minute inquiries, went to bed. If ten men were shot, that was sufficient.

The next morning at sunrise, Lieutenant Lamotte, with twenty men, marched over the trampled hills to seek Waldorf. It was a disagreeable business, and the sooner it was over the better. On reaching a ridge which overlooked the intersection of two or three valleys, more than one village was visible through the cold fog, now beginning to rise. "*Où est Waldorf?*" inquired the officer, of a peasant whom he had impressed by the way. "*Das*," answered the man, "*ist Ober-Waldorf*," pointing to a village on the left. "*En avant!*" and in fifteen minutes more the Frenchmen marched into the little hamlet.

Halting in an open space between the church and the

two principal beer-houses, the officer summoned the inhabitants together. The whole village was already awake, for few had slept during the night. Their ears were still stunned by the thunders of yesterday, and visions of burning and pillage still danced before their eyes. At the command of the Lieutenant, the soldiers seized all the male inhabitants, and forcibly placed them in line before him. The women and children waited near, in terrible anxiety, for no one understood the words which were spoken, and these ominous preparations led them to imagine the worst.

At this juncture the son of the village pastor appeared upon the scene. He was a young man of twenty, who was studying theology, in order to become his father's successor, and fortunately had some knowledge of French. The appearance of things, without the cries and entreaties of the terrified people, told him that his help was wanted; he immediately addressed himself to Lieut. Lamotte, and begged for an explanation of the proceedings.

"I am ordered to punish this village," answered the latter, "for your treatment of some of our soldiers last night. The Marshal orders that ten of you must be shot. The only thing I can do is, to allow you to draw lots among yourselves, or to point out those concerned in the outrage."

"But," exclaimed the young man, "your General has been misinformed. No French soldiers have visited our village before you. We have truly been in great fear and anxiety the whole night, but the valley is deep, and the village is partly concealed from view by the wood on this side. There are also the villages of Middle and Lower Waldorf, which lie further down in the open valley. You can soon satisfy yourself, sir, that this village is entirely innocent, and I entreat you not to shed the blood of our harmless people." "There is no time for investigation," said the officer; "I was ordered to proceed to Waldorf, and I am guided hither. I will wait until you make your choice of ten to be sacrificed, but have no authority to do more."

By this time the people had learned the fate in store for them. The women, with tears and appealing gestures, crowded around the officer, begging him to spare their sons and husbands; the men stood silent, with bloodless faces and dumb imploring eyes. The scene was evidently painful, both to the officer and the soldiers, accustomed as they were to the unmerciful code of war. They were anxious to put an end to it, and leave; but the clergyman's son, inspired with the belief that the fate of ten men rested upon his efforts, continued to urge his plea with a zeal and eloquence that would not be set aside. Lieut. Lamotte struggled awhile between his sense of duty and his natural humanity, while the young advocate appealed to his conscience and to the obedience which he owed to a higher Commander than Davoust. Finally, he consented to wait while a sergeant was dispatched to headquarters, accompanied by a peasant, to show him the nearest way. A few lines, hastily pencilled, stated the facts in the case, and asked for further instructions.

Meanwhile the inhabitants waited in a state of suspense scarcely to be endured. Lieut. Lamotte, who, as a thorough Frenchman, soon wearied of a painful emotion, and shook it off at the risk of appearing heartless, said:—

"The morning is keen, and a walk before sunrise does not diminish the appetite; can you give us some refreshment from your hidden supplies?" At a word from the young man many of the women brought together coffee, which they had prepared for their own breakfasts, with black bread, mugs of beer, and a small cheese or two, sufficient for a rough meal, of which the soldiers partook, with the usual laughing comments on "*la cuisine Allemande.*" The company of victims looked on in silence, and more than one muttered gloomily, "We are feeding our executioners."

"Even if that should be true," said the young man, "it is but doing as Christ has taught us. Whether or not we obtain Christian charity from these men, let us at least show them that *we* are Christians."

This solemn rebuke had its effect. A few of the men assisted in entertaining the soldiers, and the latter, with their facility of fraternization, soon made themselves at home. As the stomach fills the heart also enlarges, and the men began to say among themselves: "It is a pity these good fellows should be shot by mistake."

It was not long before the sergeant and his guide arrived. The former handed the Lieutenant a note, which he hastily tore open and read:—"Waste no more time in parley. It is indifferent which village is punished; an example must be made. Do your duty, and return instantly." So ran the pitiless answer.

"Choose your men," said the Lieutenant, rising to his feet, and grinding his teeth to keep down his faltering heart. But now the lamentations broke out afresh. The women clung around the men who were dear to them, and many of the latter, overcome by the general distress, uttered loud cries and prayers for mercy. The young man knelt down in front of them, saying to the officer: "I do not kneel to you, but I will pray to God that He may remove the sin of this slaughter from your soul."

As the officer met his earnest eyes, full of a sublime calmness and courage, his own suddenly filled with tears. He turned to his men, who stood drawn up in line behind him. They looked at him, but no word was spoken. Their hands were in the proper place, according to drill regulations, and there were drops on many cheeks which they could not wipe away. There was a silent question in the officer's eyes, a silent answer in theirs. The former turned again hurriedly, beckoned the young man to him, and whispered in an agitated voice:—

"My friend, I will save you by a stratagem. Choose ten of your most courageous men, place them in line before me, and I will order my soldiers to shoot them through the head. At the instant I give the order to fire they must fall flat upon the ground. My soldiers will aim high, and no one will be injured. As soon as the volley is fired I will give the order to march, but no one must stir from his place until we are out of sight."

These words were instantly translated to the people, but so great was their panic that no one offered to move. The pastor's son then took his place, alone, in the vacant space before the line of soldiers. "I offer myself," said he, "as one, trusting in God that we shall all be saved, and I call upon those of you who have the hearts of men in your bodies, to stand beside me." Young Conrad, a sturdy farmer, and but newly a bridegroom, joined him, casting, as he did so, a single encouraging look upon his future wife, who turned deadly pale, but spoke not a word. One by one, as men who have resolved to face death—for the most of them had but a trembling half-confidence in their escape, eight others walked out and took their places in line. The women shuddered and hid their eyes; the men looked steadily on in the fascination of terror, and the little children in awed but ignorant curiosity. The place was as silent as if devoid of life.

Again the Lieutenant surveyed his men. "Take aim!" he commanded—"aim at their heads, that your work may be well done!" But though his voice was clear and strong, and the tenor of his words not to be mistaken, a clairvoyant flash of hidden meaning ran down the line, and the men understood him. Then came the last command, "*Fire!*" but in the second which intervened between the word and the ringing volley, the ten men were already falling. The crack of the muskets and the sound of their bodies as they struck the earth, were simultaneous. Without pausing an instant, the Lieutenant cried "Right about, wheel!" "*Forward!*" and the measured tramp of the soldiers rang down the narrow village street.

The women uncovered their eyes and gazed. There lay the ten men, motionless and apparently lifeless. With wild cries they gathered around them, but ere their exclamations of despair were turned into those of joy, the last of the soldiers had disappeared in the near wood. Then followed weeping embraces, as all arose from the ground, laughter, and sobs of hysterical joy. The pastor's son, uncovering his head, knelt down, and, while all reverently followed his example, uttered an eloquent prayer of thanksgiving for their merciful deliverance.

What this young man had done was not suffered to go unrewarded. A blessing rested upon his labors and his life. In the course of time he became a clergyman, filling for awhile his father's place for the people he had saved, but was afterwards led to seek a wider and more ambitious sphere. He was called to Leipzig, received the degree of Doctor of Divinity, and finally became known throughout Germany as the founder of the *Gustav Adolf-Verein* (Gustavus Adolphus Union), which has for its object the dissemination of Protestant principles by means of voluntary contributions. In some respects it resembles the Home Missions of our own country. Many churches built by the association are now scattered through the German States, many poor clergymen are assisted and other religious works advanced. It has become a permanent and successful society.

The inhabitants of Waldorf never forgot their pastor, nor he them. He came back from time to time to spend a few days in the quiet little village where much of his youth, and the most eventful crisis of his life was passed. In 1856, three out of the ten pseudo-victims of Davoust were still living in their old homes, and the people bethought them that the semi-centennial anniversary of such an event deserved a special celebration. Dr. ——— of Leipzig (formerly the pastor's son) was invited to be with them. He came—he would have come from the ends of the earth—and after a solemn and religious service in the church proceeded to the very spot on which he had stood and faced the French muskets, and there related to the children and grand-children of those he had saved, the narrative which I have here given in less moving and eloquent words. Those who were present describe the scene as having been singularly impressive and affecting. The three old men sat near him as he spoke, and the emotions of that hour of trial were so vividly reproduced in their minds, that at the close they laughed and wept as they had done on the same day fifty years before.

In conclusion the speaker referred to the officer whose humane stratagem had preserved their lives. "Since that day," said he, "I have never heard of him. I did not even learn his name, but he is ever remembered in my thoughts and prayers. Most probably he died a soldier's death on one of the many fields of slaughter which intervened between Jena and Waterloo; but if he should still be living it would cheer my last days on earth if I could reach him with a single word of gratitude."

In the same year there lived—and no doubt still is living—in Lyons, an invalided and pensioned Captain of the Napoleonic wars. After a life of vicissitudes he found himself, in his old age, alone, forgotten, and poor. Men no braver and better than he had achieved distinction by some lucky chance; fortune had come to others, and others had begotten children to cheer and vitalize their declining days.

Him the world had passed by, and for years he had been living a quiet, silent, pinched life, by the aid of his scanty pension. His daily resort was a cafè, where he could see and read the principal European journals, and perhaps measure the changed politics of the present time by the experiences of his past life.

One day in November, 1856, he entered the cafè as usual, took his accustomed seat, and picked up the nearest paper. It happened to be the Augsburg *Allgemeine Zeitung;* but he had spent some years in Germany, and understood the language tolerably. His attention was attracted by a letter dated Jena. "Jena?" he thinks—"I was there too. What is going on there now?" He reads a little further—"Celebration at Waldorf? Waldorf? The name is familiar: where have I heard it?" As he continues his perusal, the old captain's excitement, so unusual a circumstance, attracts the attention of the other habitués of the cafè. "*Grand Dieu!* Davoust—Waldorf—the ten men—the pastor's son! Did I dream such a thing, or is it the same?" Forgotten for years and years—effaced by a hundred other military adventures—overlaid and lost in the crowded stores of a soldier's memory, the scene came to light again. The pastor's son still lived, still remembered and thanked the preserver of his native village! Many a long year had passed since such a glow warmed the chambers of the old man's heart.

That evening he wrote to Dr. ——, in Leipzig.

The latter was ill, and but a few months from his last hour, but the soldier's letter seemed like a providential answer to his prayers, and brightened the flickering close of his life. A manly and affectionate correspondence was carried on between the two while the latter lived. The circumstance became public, and the deed was officially recognised in a way most flattering to the pride of Capt. Lamotte. The Grand Duke of Saxe-Weimar and the King of Saxony conferred upon him the orders of their respective houses, which were followed soon afterwards by the Cross of the Legion of Honor from Louis Napoleon, and an increase of his pension which assured him ease and comfort for the remainder of his life. A translation of the Dr.'s narrative, published in the French papers, drew attention to him, and he was no longer a neglected frequenter of the café. He was known and honored, even without his orders.

"Cast thy bread upon the waters, and thou shalt find it again, after many days."

XXXIX.

THE LANDSCAPES OF THE WORLD.

THE doctrine of "Correspondences"—a system of parallels between the material and spiritual world—which forms so prominent an element in Swedenborgian Faith, asserts its truth in one respect, to the mind of every man who has travelled much. Landscapes exhibit almost as great a variety of expression as the human face—they embrace all moods and all characters in their infinite scale. Nature is both refined and savage, poetic and vulgar, friendly and cruel, beautiful and repulsive. Who has not felt, a thousand times, the sentiment of Leigh Hunt's lines:

> "And all the landscape—earth, and sea, and sky,
> Breathed like a bright-eyed face, that laughs out openly."

Some regions of the earth are as tame and barren as the minds of certain communities; others bask in superb opulence, and squander their boundless stores of beauty; and others again, rise in their unexpected sublimity and power, as far above the average character of scenery, as genius rises above the ordinary level of the human mind.

Nature has her masterpieces in every department of her realm. There is, if we knew it, somewhere upon the earth *one* river which transcends all other streams—*one* mountain whose majesty stands unapproached—*one* coast which makes the voyager forget all other shores—and one valley where the bee finds his sweetest honey and the winds their most delicious balm. I might demonstrate this, with all the ease of a proposition in Euclid, without being able to name any one of those favored spots—for who has ever beheld, or ever shall behold, all the landscapes of the world?

We must not be too hasty in trusting to the individual likings of travellers. Many persons are thrown into raptures by a beautiful view, the expression of which touches some taste or passion of their own. Scotland is more enjoyed, by most Americans, than Switzerland, and Rome makes a profounder impression than Athens: yet in the Gallery of Nature, the order of excellence is reversed. Every country has its chosen landscapes, which you must see, or you have missed "the finest sight in the world." The Neapolitan says: "See Naples and then die;" "Who has not in Granada been, verily, he has nothing seen," is the Spanish proverb; "I will not look upon Damascus, lest I should cease to desire Paradise," was the exclamation of Mohammed. The central point of beauty and of grandeur, in Humboldt's memories of scenery, was Chimborazo.

Do not ask me now "which is the finest landscape in the

world?" because it would be as difficult as to decide which was the best man you ever knew. But with regard to separate features there is less embarrassment. The grandest river in Europe is the Danube: but for his long intervals of monotonous plain, he would be the grandest in the world. The Rhine has his phases of extreme beauty—likewise the Rhone, the Elbe, the Connecticut, and the Ohio. None of the great main arteries of Continents—the Mississippi, the Amazon, the Nile, the Volga, and the Yang-tse-Kiang—exhibit a beauty of landscape proportioned to their length and volume. The main characteristic of their scenery—however exquisite it may be in detail—is monotony. But there is one river which, from its source to the ocean, unrolls a long chain of landscapes wherein there is no tame feature, but each successive view presents new combinations of beauty and majesty—which other rivers may surpass in sections, but none rival as a whole—and its name is, The Hudson.

As for cataracts, Niagara, in tremendous volume, drowns all others. The foamy whispers of Alpine streamlets are unheard beside it. But water is Protean in its forms and movements, and there are miracles of beauty which you cannot find clinging to the mighty emerald planes of our great fall. The Rhine at Schaffhausen winnows a stormy chaff of diamonds: the Throllhätta, in Sweden, tosses up globes of pink-tinted spray; the Aar descends like an avalanche of silver cauliflowers, and the Riukan, in Norway, flutters into scarfs of the richest lace. Each of these has its individual charm and fascination, but Niagara is the Titan in whose presence you stand dumb.

An Englishman will probably tell you that the Isle of Wight is the most beautiful island in the world. A New Yorker will mention Staten Island; an Italian point to the rocky lion of Capri, and an East-Indian think of Ceylon. Having never seen Madeira, or Oahu, or palmy Nukaheva, or Upolo, in the Samoan group, I am not capable of deciding; but of all the islands upon which I ever set foot, Penang is far the loveliest. Not more than ten miles in length, it rises on one side into a group of mountains, 2500 feet high, while on the other it spreads out its level orchards of nutmeg and cinnamon trees to the sun. Eastward, across emerald water and snowy reefs of coral, you see the shores of Malacca, and westward, beyond the purple sea, the volcanic peaks of Sumatra. Cold is unknown, but the tropical heats are never oppressive. The air bewilders you with its fragrance, the trees and flowers charm you with their beauty. The island is a miniature Eden,

> "Where falls not rain, or hail, or any snow,
> Nor ever wind blows loudly; but it lies
> Deep-meadowed, happy, fair with orchard-lawns
> And bowery hollows crowned with summer sea."

With the exception of the Altai and the Andes of South America, I have seen the principal mountain chains of the world, besides the most renowned isolated groups and separate peaks. Here, again, there are differences of glory. The Alps boast the contrast of pastoral loveliness with the icy desolation of the glaciers; the Taurus has its tremendous defiles and gorges, and the Himalayas their snowy wedges of supernatural height and brilliancy. But there is one mountain, which, having once seen, you acknowledge ever afterwards as monarch. This is the Peak of Orizaba, in Mexico. The Andes of Ecuador rise from a table-land 9,000 feet above the sea; the loftiest summits of the Himalayas lie behind two lower chains, the High Alps are buttressed on all sides—but Orizaba ascends in one splendid sweep from the level of a tropical sea to the height of 18,000 feet!

Standing on the mountain-terrace of Jalapa, which is between four and five thousand feet above the Gulf of Mexico, you see the entire mountain, like a colossal picture painted on the blue background of the air. Leagues upon leagues of palm forests cover the level, sandy plain made by the retrocession of the sea which once washed his feet. Then there are plantations of orange and coffee trees; higher up, woods of chestnut and oak; higher still, a broad, dark belt of pine, then, naked rock, and finally commencing four thousand feet below the summit, the region of eternal snow! The mountain is a steep and perfect cone, leaning, on its western side, against the table-land of Mexico. In certain conditions of the atmosphere, it is visible at a distance of two hundred miles, consequently the rays of the morning sun do not reach its base until nearly fifteen minutes after they have gilded its summit, and the immaculate peak shines like a blazing star in the sky, when the rapid twilight of the Tropics has already darkened Jalapa.

All these, however, are but single features of a landscape, and the crowning triumph of Nature is the grouping of them together in an order which shall heighten the effect of each, thereby producing a picture perfect an l sublime. If, as Mr. Tupper modestly desires, we had the Andes rising on either side of Niagara, the Cataract would gain nothing in effect thereby. On the other hand Mountains and the Sea are foils to each other; so are grim precipices and flowery meadows, white, glittering cities, and ranges of bare blue hills. Nature, at some times a bungler, is at other times a divine artist. Give her a broad canvas, rich colors, and the forms in which she most delights, and she occasionally produces pictures which seem to belong to some happy planet nearer the sun, rather than to this imperfect Earth of ours.

The Orientals have their four famous Gardens of Asia, the charms of which have been celebrated in their poetry for many a hundred years. They are: Damascus, Shiraz, Samarcand, and Cashmere. To these Broussa was added by the Ottomans, while Granada was assigned a still higher place by the poets of Saracenic Spain. But the beauty of a landscape, to the Oriental eye, consists in its abundance of verdure, traversed by running streams—a combination of shade, coolness, and grateful color, which only those can properly appreciate to whom yellow sand, and scorched red hills, quivering in heat, are the habitual features of the Earth. Enclose such a picture in a frame of mountains, some of which rise to the region of snow, and they can imagine nothing more beautiful.

They are so far right, that the masterpieces of landscape must be sought either within the Tropics, or upon their borders. A view which at times is dark and lifeless, or colorless with snow, gives no complete satisfaction to the mind. Edinburgh, from Arthur's Seat, and Florence from Fiesole, are superb in summer, and imposing at all times; but we cannot award them the first place. No city in the world presents such a wonderful picture as Constantinople, as seen from the entrance of the Bosphorus; Naples and Rio Janeiro are scarcely inferior, but in them that dazzling, fairy architecture, which seems to belong to the realm of dreams, is wanting.

Of the many thousands of landscapes which have delighted my eyes, there are four which remain indelibly impressed upon my memory, as supreme in all the elements of beauty and majesty—four pictures, each of which, in my gallery, occupies a hall of its own, wherein no inferior work shall ever be placed. They are: the Vega of Granada, Damascus, Broussa, and the Valley of Mexico. In attempting to paint them, with paper for canvas, and words for colors, I feel more sensibly than ever the imperfection of all human speech. Even could I select the special capacities of all cultivated languages, and use them as so many pure pigments—could I describe the forests in German, the sea in Swedish, the mountains in English, the running streams in Italian, and the cities in Spanish—I should still achieve but a partial success. For words lack perspective: they cannot truly represent the successive planes of distance; the crystal sea, which, invisible in itself, yet tints the mountains, near and far, with an enchanting scale of color, nor those subtle phases of expression which seem to be independent of the forms of Nature.

Let us first look upon Granada—a landscape more limited in extent than either of the others, yet lacking no important feature. Climbing the long street of the Darro, we enter the Albaycin, an ancient Moorish suburb, from the crumbling parapets of which the eye takes in at one glance, the city, the Alhambra, the Vega, and its ring of encircling mountains. Across the deep gorge through which the Darro issues from the hills, rises the headland crowned by the palace of the Moorish Kings, the huge red towers of which stand out in massive relief against the dark purple background of the Sierra Nevada. The summit of this single group of mountains rises nearly to the height of the Jungfrau, and their sides of dark-red rocks are streaked with fields of eternal snow. To the right, beyond the gay, glittering city, stretches for twenty-five miles the blooming Vega—a huge parterre of gardens, olive groves, fields, and forests, dotted with white towers and palace-fronts, and lighted by shining glimpses of the winding Xenil. Across the glorious plain towers the huge mountain of Parapanda, while a chain of lesser heights incloses it on all sides. Beautiful as the details of the landscape are, its breadth, and grandeur, and splendor of coloring are the charms which hold you captive.

The view of Damascus, from the Salahiyeh—the last slope of the Anti-Lebanon—is less perfectly proportioned, but more dazzling. It is transfigured by the magic of the Orient. From the mountain-chain whose ridges heave behind you, until, in the south, they terminate in the snowy head of Mount Hermon, the great Syrian plain stretches away to the Euphrates, broken, at distances of ten and fifteen miles, by two detached groups of mountains. The far horizon of sand quivers in a flush of roseate heat. In a terrible gorge at your side, the river Barrada (the ancient Pharpar) forces its way to the plain, and its waters, divided into twelve different channels, make all between you and those blue island-hills of the desert one great garden, the boundaries of which your vision can barely distinguish. Its longest diameter cannot be less than twenty miles. You look down upon an immense lake of foliage, and fruit, and blossoms, the hue of which, by contrast with the barren mountains and the red rim of the desert, seems brighter than all other gardens in the world. Through its centre, following the course of the river, lies Damascus—a line of white walls, domes, towers, and sparkling minarets, winding away for seven miles through the green sea! To this magnificent picture you have the contrasts of fire and snow—of eternal desolation and eternal bloom.

The finest view of Broussa is from the east, on the road into the interior of Asia Minor. Thence you overlook the entire valley, which, thirty miles long by five in breadth, stretches away to the westward, between the mighty mass of the Mysian Olympus on the one side, and a range of lofty mountains on the other. The base of Olympus is a vast sloping terrace, leagues in length, resembling the flights of steps by which the ancient temples were approached. From this foundation rise four great pyramids two thousand feet in height, and completely mantled with forests. Piled upon these are four lesser ones, above whose green pinnacles appear still other and higher, bare and bleak, and clustering thickly together, to uphold the central dome of snow. The sides of the lower ranges, on either hand, present a charming mixture of forest and cultivated land. Far in advance, under the last headland which Olympus throws out towards the Sea of Marmora, the hundred minarets of Broussa stretch in a white and glittering line, like the masts of a navy, whose hulls are buried in the leafy sea. No words can describe the beauty of the valley, the blending of the richest cultivation with the wildest natural luxuriance. Here are gardens and orchards; there, groves of superb chestnut-trees in blossom; here, fields of golden grain or green pasture-land; there, Arcadian thickets, overgrown with clematis and wild roses; here, lofty poplars beside the streams; there, spiry cypresses looking down from the slopes—and all blended in one whole, so rich, so grand, so gorgeous, that you scarcely breathe when it first bursts upon you. The only feature which you miss is the gleam of water.

In the valley of Mexico, however—the grandest of these four landscapes—this want is supplied. Whether you behold it from the rock of Chepultepec, or from under the pines of Iztaccihuatl, the great lakes of Chalco and Tezcuco form crystal mirrors for the mighty peaks which look down upon the valley. The landscape has a diameter of a hundred miles, and the average height of the mountains which enframe it cannot be less than twelve thousand feet. Above this majestic wall shoot the broken, snowy summits of Iztaccihuatl and the Nevada of Toluca, and the solitary cone of Popocatapetl. The view seems to embrace a world at a glance. In the centre lies the city with its white palaces and towers, like silver in the sun; all around it are gardens, fields of aloes, embowered villages and convents, cypress forests and orange groves; then, the flashing of the great lakes, dim fields, and faint villages in the distances; and lastly, the embaying curves of the mountains, now projected near in rugged and barren grandeur, now receding into purple distance, or seeming to overhang their bases, in the delusive nearness of their dazzling snows. When a few scattering clouds are in the sky, and moving belts of golden light and violet shadow lend their alternate magic to these grand and wonderful features, you can only say, again and again, "This is the one great landscape of the world!"

XL.

PREFERENCES, AFTER SEEING THE WORLD.

THE traveller, one would suppose, must necessarily become an optimist, an eclectic, since he has an opportunity of learning what is best in the varied life of the world. Yet, my friend, a little reflection will show you that a considerable amount of philosophy is necessary, to enable him to go through with such a range of experience, and therefore, that even after he has learned all that is best of its kind, he is scarcely the man to complain that he cannot enjoy the same in his own person. In fact, he must possess many standards of comparison—wide ranges of observation—before he is capable of deciding what *is* best, and long before that period arrives, there will be little of the Epicurean element left in his nature.

To begin with a paradox: he is best adapted for a traveller who is capable of the strongest local attachments. Without this characteristic, he will never thoroughly appreciate the sentiment of scenery, the significance of popular customs, or the thousand varying traits of domestic life, in other countries. At the splendid court of Kubla Khan, the Polos never forgot Venice; Ibn Batuta, after twenty-five years of wandering, returned to die at the foot of his native Atlas, and the last pages from Park, on the Niger, contained a remembrance of Scotland. It was once my good fortune to have in my hands, for a month, the Russian and Siberian journals of John Ledyard, together with a number of his letters to his relatives in America; and what most struck me in the perusal of the faded lines, was the warmth and tenderness of his attachment to early associations. But the co-existence of a travelled brain and an *untravelled heart*, is what few people can understand.

A thousand times a year (at a moderate estimate), I hear the question: "Now, you have seen all parts of the world, which do you prefer?" Of course but one answer can be given, and the question is no doubt sometimes asked for the gratification of hearing it. An American thinks: "We are the grandest nation in all creation; we have the best form of government, the finest scenery, the richest soil, and the most moral and intelligent population." When he asks "Where would you rather live?" and you answer, "Where I was born," it is a pleasant confirmation of this opinion—yet the reply by no means includes so much. No country has, or ever can have, all that is best. The magic that lies in the word "Home" reconciles us to many disadvantages, which may not exist elsewhere—yea, even petty inconveniences become attractive, when connected with the associations of youth. I find much in other lands to make life brighter and richer than it is here, at present, yet no temptation could induce me to give up my birthright and adopt a foreign home.

If the best government is that which governs least, then ours is certainly the best in the world. However dishonest our professed politicians may be, however grievous the errors which have crept into our administration of the laws, we nevertheless enjoy, as individual citizens, a degree of independence which makes all other systems unendurable to us. We do not feel the hard hand of Government pressing upon our heads, controlling our movements, repressing our free development. We buy and sell, build and pull down, learn trades, study professions, engage in business, without the permission or license of any one. Our local and municipal governments, it is true, are less carefully administered than in some parts of Europe; we do many things in a bungling manner; but all these minor evils cannot outweigh the one great fact of individual freedom. The law interferes as little as possible with our pursuits, our business transactions, and our habits of life. We may live for years, without being aware, through our own personal experience, that there is any Government at all.

With regard to Society, however, we are still in a transition state. Except in the four large cities of the Atlantic Coast, we find local conventionalities, but not that ease and repose which spring from the adoption of a few broad and general observances. There is no liberal recognition of a man's *social value*, without regard to his religious or political opinions. The main cause of this is, sufficient attention is not paid to the social amenities of life. In all country communities, work is the prescribed regimen, and a man who chooses to live without it exposes himself to censure and impertinent gossip. In the city of Cincinnati, with 250,000 inhabitants, there is but one man of leisure. (So I was informed by the individual himself, who had vainly sought a companion.)

Too often the prominent religious sect in a town determines the character of its society. Between those of widely diverging creeds there is rarely any familiar intercourse. I can conceive of nothing more unnatural and unchristian than what is called "close communion," which is still a characteristic of two or three Protestant sects, especially in the United States. The true basis of Society (by which I mean Social Intercourse) is Character and Cultivation, not a certain class of opinions. Hence, the introduction of a religious test, which prevails to a greater extent in the United States than in any other country in the world, defeats its object and narrows its character.

There is another feature of small communities, which springs from the nature of our political system. Democracy, which we have thoroughly incorporated into our Government, has two opposite modes of operation in our *Society*. It levels *down* as well as up. The practical effect is, not that the uncultivated many shall imitate the cultivated few, but that the latter shall be dragged down to the lower platform on which the former stand. This, however, is an evil which will remedy itself in the course of time. The progress in the right direction, which has been made within the last twenty years, is amazing.

Nevertheless, one who is thoroughly familiar with Society in the two hemispheres cannot but admit that in Europe it stands on a broader, firmer, and altogether more liberal and catholic basis than in this country.

In one respect we might profitably imitate the Germans. Our sorest need, as a people, is recreation—relaxation of the everlasting tension of our laborious lives. Among our Teutonic cousins, a certain amount of recreation, public as well as domestic, is a part of the plan of every man's life. The poorest laborer has his share—*must* have it—and the treadmill round of his years is brightened and sweetened by it. Our seasons of recreation, being so rare, too frequently take the character of excess. They are characterized by the same hurry and fury with which we prosecute our business. If we shall ever intercalate regular periods of genial relaxation into our working calendar, we shall be a healthier and happier people than we are now.

For *comfort* in domestic life we must look to England for an example. True, we have inherited much from our Anglo-Saxon ancestry, but in later times there has been engrafted thereon a French love of show, as well as a barbaric fondness for glaring colors, which I cannot but consider as a retrograde movement. "Look at the Hotel of St. Dives!" cries an enthusiastic patriot; "nowhere will you find such immense mirrors, such carpets, such curtains, and such magnificent furniture!" Perhaps so: but when I enter the hotel, and (after my eyes have recovered from the dazzle of the gilding) look upon the curtains of orange damask, the carpet of crimson and white, sprinkled with monstrous flowers of blue, purple, and yellow, and the chairs of rosewood and scarlet silk, I remember, in grateful contrast, the home-like parlor in the London hotel, with its quiet green carpet, its easy chairs of green leather, its scrupulous neatness, and its air of comfort, taste, and repose. So it is in our private residences—stiff splendor is preferred to comfort, everywhere. Clean bed linen, an unlimited supply of water and towels, and a neat table, though there is nothing but bacon and potatoes upon it, are the characteristics of the country inns of England. Are they of ours?

In regard to climate, we are met by this difficulty, that that which is most enjoyable is not best adapted to the development of the human race. Here, also, much depends upon the peculiar temperament of the individual. To me our American climate, even with its caprices and extremes, is more agreeable than that of Europe, north of the Alps. Our atmosphere has a dry, fresh, brilliant, vital character, which is there wanting. Nevertheless, our winters are too severe, and our springs too uncertain, so that, although the growths of our summer are those of Italy and Spain, we live practically, for five months, in the latitude of Copenhagen. A hundred miles inland from the Atlantic seaboard, the average duration of life is probably as great as in any country of the world, and the race, in spite of certain ethnologists, does not deteriorate from physical causes.

The most agreeable zone of climate is that where the olive, fig, and orange will grow in the open air. Here the springs are delicious, the summers long and with less extremes of heat than ours, the autumns mild and balmy, and the winters barely cold enough to brace and stimulate the system. To this zone belong Spain, Italy, Greece, Palestine, California, and Texas. I have visited all except the latter, and unhesitatingly give the preference to California. If a more equable, genial, and healthy climate exists, I know not where it is to be found. Here the air, even in summer, has a dryness and purity which take away all tropical languor from its truly tropical heats; the winters are green and mild, and the springs a foretaste of Paradise. The interior of Texas is said to be similarly favored with regard to climate.

Nothing can be more delicious than some portions of the Tropics, where there is no day of a man's life when he may not sit in the open air—no day without the falling of ripe fruit and the opening of new blossoms. There the climate is an opiate, and life an indolent, sensuous semi-sleep. But how delicious such repose!

> "Oh sweet it was, in Aves, to feel the landward breeze,
> A-swing with good tobacco, in a net between the trees,
> With a negro lass to fan you, while you listened to the roar
> Of the breakers on the reef outside, that never touched the shore!"

One, therefore, who wishes to taste the very cream of this terrestrial existence, must do his work in America, enjoy his recreation in Europe, and go to Java for his days of indolence.

The zone of action and achievement lies between lat. 35° and 55° North. On either side of this belt we have a superabundance of the benumbing or relaxing element.

Our country, stretching from 25° to 49°, enjoys a most fortunate range of climate. Extension southwards would be followed by a slow but certain deterioration in the stamina of the race—unless, perhaps, upon the high table-lands of Mexico, where the annual mean of temperature is not much greater than in Texas or Tennessee. We have, therefore, every reason to be satisfied with our lot in this particular. At least he who desires a change, may find whatever climate he prefers, without going beyond the limits of the United States.

Every country has its peculiar habits of life, and it is always most convenient to conform to them. Whether this or that is best, is a thing for each man to decide according to his circumstances, and his bodily temperament. The English dine at the close of the day, after the day's work is done, sit long at table, and do nothing to interfere with the subsequent process of digestion. The Germans dine at one o'clock, and make supper (which is always very substantial) a deliberate and social meal. The Americans eat all meals fast, and work both before and afterwards. Naturally, we have four dyspeptics where there is one in Europe.

Altogether, the most rational and convenient habit of life for a man who does just as much work as he *ought* to do, and no more, is that which prevails in Spain, Mexico, and parts of France. Immediately on awakening in the morning, you are furnished with a cup of coffee or chocolate, a biscuit, and a glass of water. You are then ready for your labors; your stomach is warmed, your head clear, and your brain nimble. After three or four hours—from ten to eleven o'clock, generally—you have breakfast, consisting of substantial dishes of meat and vegetables, with light wine and water, and a cup of coffee at the close. Five to six hours more available time are now before you, during which you accomplish your allotted day's work. At 5 P. M. dinner is served—a generous meal, followed by coffee. The evening is devoted to society or recreation of some kind. At nine o'clock you take a cup of tea, or an ice, but nothing more, and your sleep is untroubled by nightmares. I have never found myself in better health or more admirable working trim, than when following this programme of daily life.

However, each man is but a unit in Society, and must sacrifice many of his individual tastes and likings for those around him. One might as well cry for the moon, like an infant, as attempt to transplant all the pleasant features of life in other climates and among other races into a soil foreign to them. I am well satisfied with the land where my lot is cast, without feeling myself bound to say that nothing is better elsewhere. As I look up from this page, and see, through the open window, *my own trees* tossing the silver lining of their leaves to the summer wind, and the peaceful beauty of the vales and blue hills stretching beyond, I know that no tropic island, no palace on a Mediterranean shore, no advantage of wealth and position in the great capitals of Europe, could ever tempt me to give up the name, the rights, and the immunities of an American Citizen.

THE END.

www.ingramcontent.com/pod-product-compliance
Lightning Source LLC
LaVergne TN
LVHW021318110826
845150LV00003B/608

* 9 7 8 1 4 2 5 5 5 6 8 9 1 *